THE OTHER ROME
Building the Modern Metropolis 1870–1960

Dedicated to Léon Krier

THE OTHER ROME
Building the Modern Metropolis 1870–1960
Jean-François Lejeune (ed.)

Contributions by

Daniel Solomon
Lucio Valerio Barbera
Anna Irene Del Monaco
Jean-François Lejeune
Salvatore Santuccio

Photography by

Jean-François Lejeune

Birkhäuser
Basel

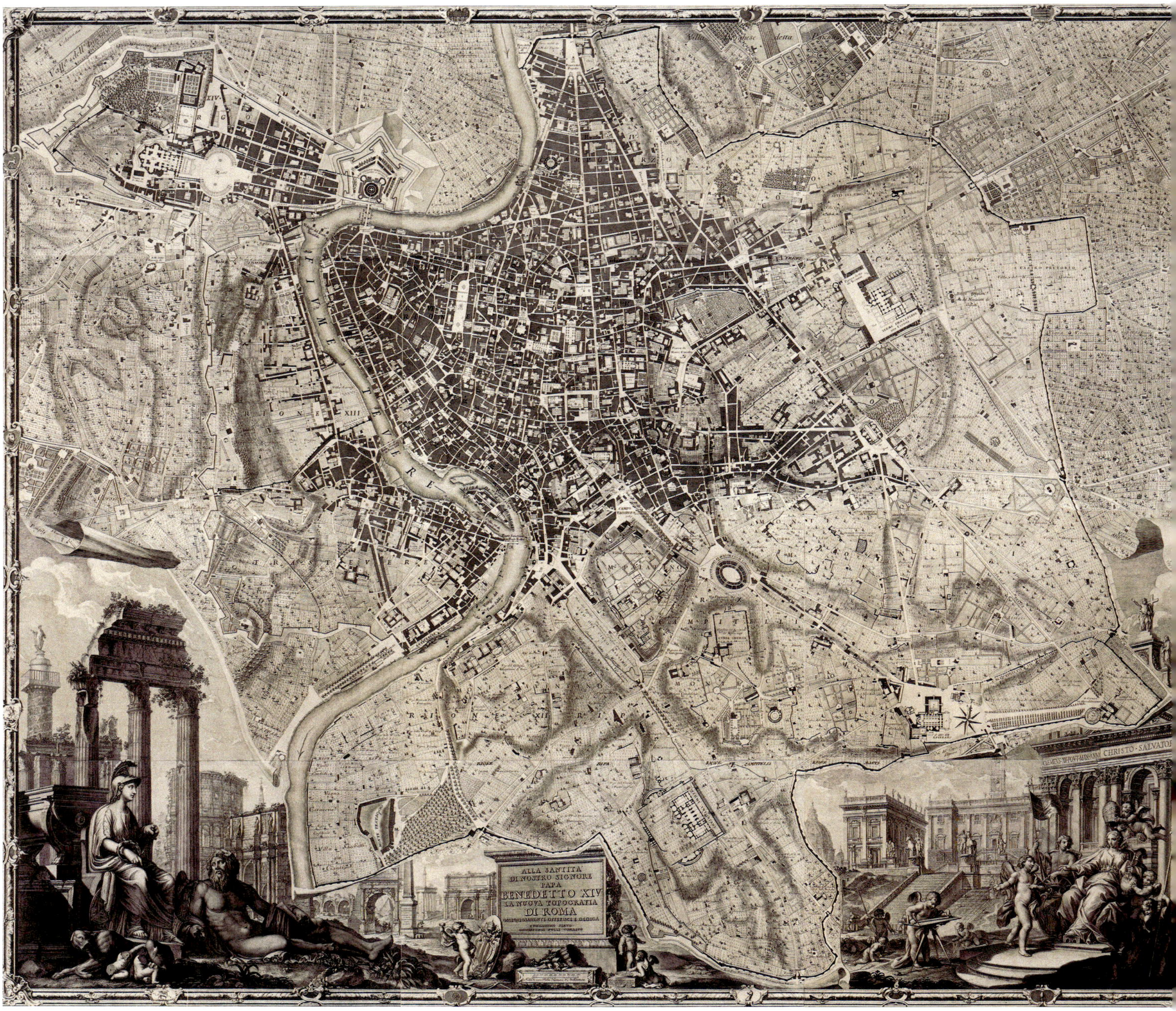

● Giambattista Nolli, *La Pianta Grande: La Nuova Topografia di Roma*, 1748. The Nolli plan gives a detailed image of the city in the middle of the 18th century, with topogra precision, complete with the incorporation of the antique ruins, the interior plans of all the churches and other public structures, as well as all the squares and public space Note that important courtyards and church interiors are shown as open and public.

Roma non Interrotta

Jean-François Lejeune

Mario Sironi, *The Architect*, 1922. The painting celebrates the importance and the status of the architect right before the rise of Fascism and the beginning of an important creative period of architecture and urban design. It marks the beginning of the *Novecento* aesthetic in arts and architecture in Milan and Rome.

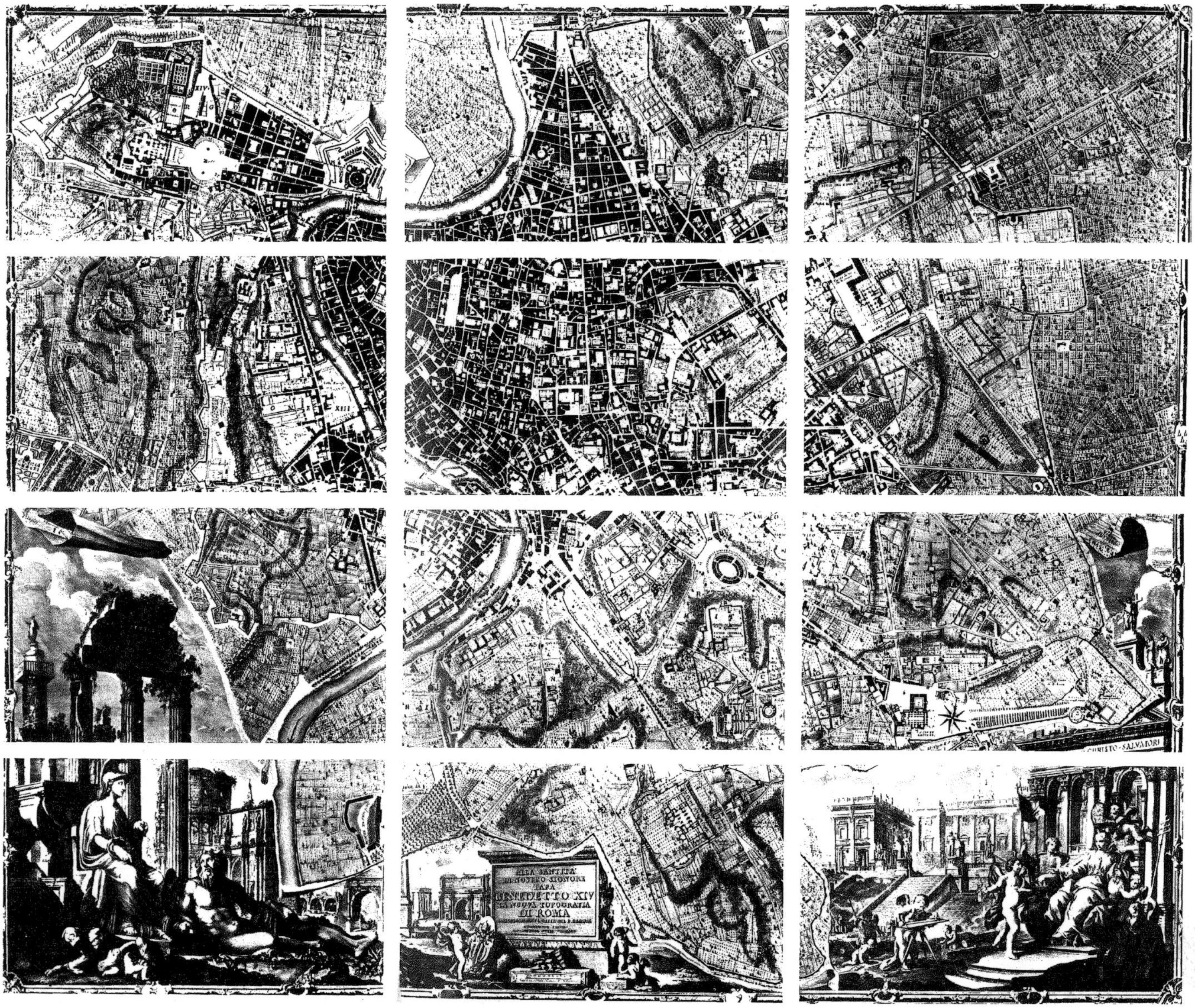

● *Roma Interrotta*, the twelve sections of Nolli's *La Pianta Grande: La Nuova Topografia di Roma*, 1978. Rome.

"Tens of books may be read with profit on the rise of Fascism and its subsequent career, some of the best among these written by non-Italians. But there is hardly anything in English or German or French, good or bad, to be read about the extraordinary physical transformation of Rome during this same century. Non-Italian scholars who have made exemplary contributions to the study of Roman art history and archaeology have failed to inspire research in the last phase of the fateful city—have failed or chosen not to. Their story ends with Piranesi and Valadier."[1]

Spiro Kostof

"It will be argued that the self-evident yet momentous fact that Rome became a capital of an altogether different kind than classical or Papal Rome in the period between 1748 and 1978 is almost entirely neglected. This elision reveals the views held amongst architects and architectural historians of Roma Capitale, but also the limits of *Roma Interrotta* and the kind of architectural practice it sought to promote."[2]

Maarten Delbeke

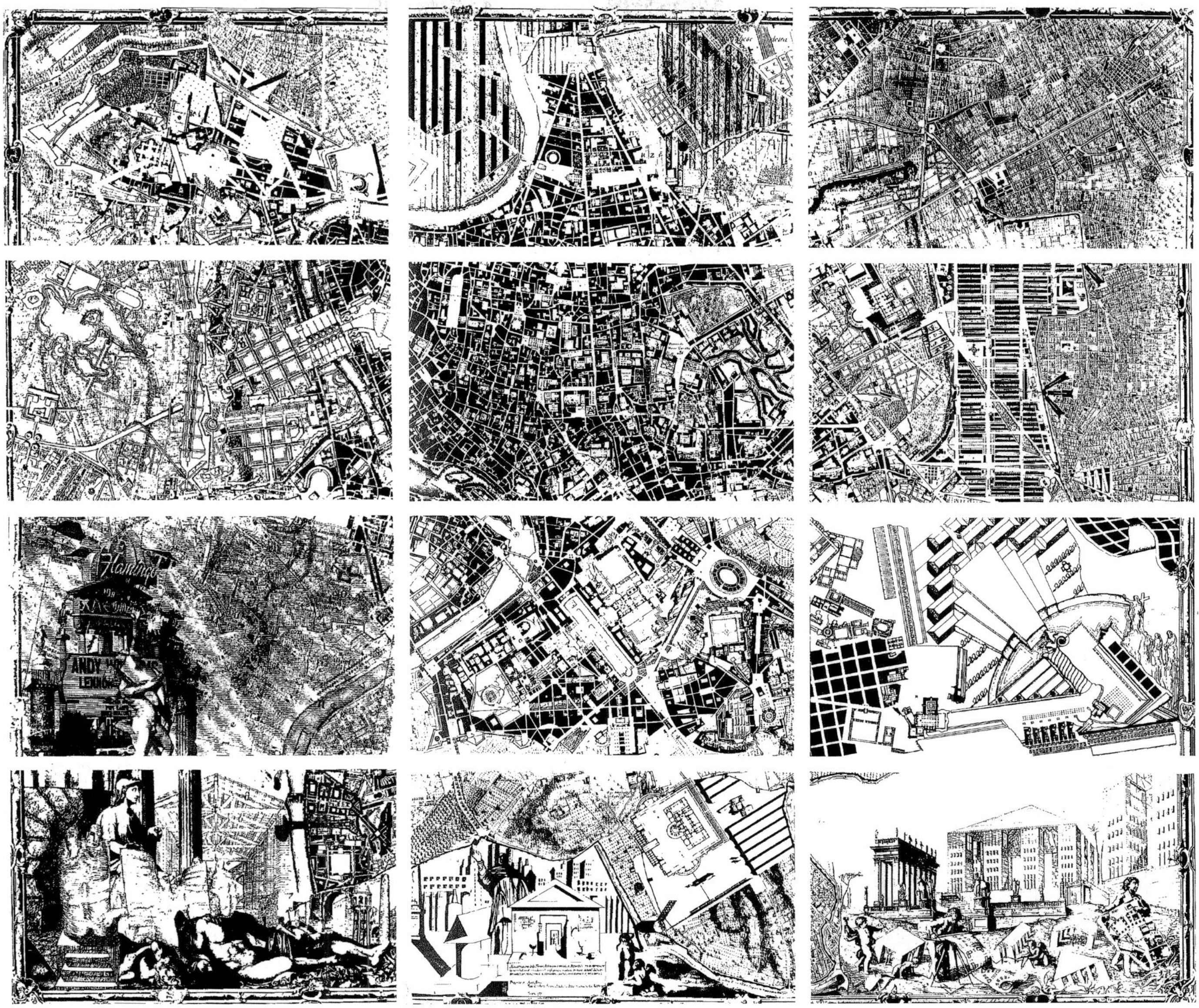

● The 1978 *Roma Interrotta* project initiated by Piero Sartogo. The twelve sections from the 1748 Nolli plan were reimagined by twelve architects. First row: Sartogo, Dardi, Grumbach; second row: Stirling, Portoghesi, Giurgola; third row: Venturi, Rowe, Graves; fourth row: R. Krier, Rossi, L. Krier

Why has Rome's modern history and more generally the formation and growth of the modern metropolis been obscured, neglected, and undervalued for so long? To be sure, Rome is an exceptional urban architectural container, identified with the very foundations of western civilization, modeled by the mix of Mediterranean cultures across centuries, and the capital of Christianity. From 18th-century travelers to 21st-century students and doctoral candidates, no other city has been the focus of such scrutiny and scholarship. There are more drawings, more maps, more photographs of Rome than of any other place on earth, and generation after generation of historians, architects, and students strive to discover it. Yet, most of that interest and scholarship has been lavished on the *centro storico* identified with the Nolli plan of 1748 and its minimal development during the last century of papal control. In 1871, Rome became the capital of Italy and from then onward grew quickly and—often too—organically to retake the metropolitan status that it had reached around the 4th century after Christ. Comparatively, few scholars and historians have paid much attention to the construction of this Third Rome—coming after the First Rome (Antiquity) and the Second Rome (that of the popes until 1870)—and the last 150 years of this large, problematic yet also exceptional, living metropolis: how it is organized, how it was built, how its architecture and urbanism reflected the evolving identity of a new nation, and why despite the long list of urban problems (such as public transportation, the maintenance of streets and parks, social inequalities, and the explosion of low-quality mass tourism) it has remained a good place to live. More importantly, in Italy, like in other European nations which had to suffer the consequences of 20th-century dictatorships, architectural historians either ignored, or gave an often contestable and reductionist interpretation of the urban and architectural works of Mussolini's dictatorship (1922–1943). For more than 60 years, and until recently, it has been inadmissible to say that anything positive in the realm of urban policy was accomplished at the foundation of the Italian State in 1870 and primarily during the Fascist years which established the concept of *La Terza Roma*. In addition, after the Second World War, the political divide between left and right impacted the profession of architecture and urbanism in ways unknown in most European countries, with as a result, a pattern of contempt and devaluation of the ordinary built environment and the speculative actions and projects of the private sector.

The October 1973 issue of the *Journal of the Society of Architectural Historians* was a seminal moment in the historiography of Rome. Historian Spiro Kostof's review titled "The Third Rome—The Polemics of Architectural History" summarized the question of scholarship and interpretation of the history of the Third Rome with an emphasis on the publications that were issued in the late 1960s to the early 1970s for the 100th anniversary of the establishment of Italy.[3] Of the eleven books he reviewed thoroughly, Spiro Kostof's critique of Italo Insolera's *Roma moderna* was among the essay's harshest. He made it clear that Insolera's writings, mostly based on secondary sources, were undermined by his one-sidedness and insistence of conspiracy. In brief, his book was "in fact a relentlessly negative story, from beginning to end, one in which heroes are as rare as good intentions or honest mistakes."[4] The Italian historian's negative interpretation of Rome's history did not even rescue the works of the Istituto per le Case Popolari (ICP, Institute for Social Housing) that were built before, during, or after Mussolini. He only offered praise to some public projects developed in accordance with the law 167 of 1962, built in isolation far on the periphery, without any continuity with the city and fundamentally in opposition to the urban design principles that made the city over more than 2000 years.[5] Likewise, Kostof was highly critical of Leonardo Benevolo's *Roma da ieri a domani*, where the author proposed to erase all the buildings and districts that had risen since 1870, including Fascist interventions, and replace them with a huge green belt on the other side of which new modern towns would be built. Interestingly, it was also in 1973 that Kostof published his own approach to *The Third Rome, 1870–1950: Traffic and Glory*, a fundamental reference for the understanding of the city's growth and transformation despite its concentration on the *centro storico* and its relative neglect of the modern neighborhoods that surround it.[6]

Roma Interrotta

A couple of years later, in 1978, the Italian Piero Sartogo initiated a project with eleven other international architects to design a "New Rome," based upon a flashback to the year 1748, the publication date of the *Nuova pianta di Roma* by Giambattista Nolli. Each architect was assigned one of the twelve sheets or "sectors" laid out by Nolli with the challenge to develop an alternative urban design. The assumed opinion of the organizers, including former mayor Giulio Carlo Argan, was that nothing of interest had been built since 1748 and even more so since 1870, and that the construction of Rome had been "interrupted."[7] The results of the *Roma Interrotta* project ◀◀ pp. 8, 9 ▶▶ were exhibited at the Mercato di Traiano (Trajan's Market) and reassembled at MAXXI (Museo Nazionale delle Arti del XXI secolo) in 2014. It is not the place to make here a full-fledged critique of the projects presented by the twelve architects involved but it is enough to stress how destructive many of the proposals were both to Nolli's city and to its surrounding landscape. Although it was introduced by Argan as a series of "gymnastic exercises for the Imagination," *Roma Interrotta* cannot be analyzed today except as a reflection of the immense state of confusion in which late-modernist urban design was in the mid-1970s, as well as the intellectual abyss of the hypocrisy of many architects—in particular Italian ones—who relentlessly condemned the Fascist urban works but did not hesitate to follow in their footsteps to support their own design ego.[8] For many of the architects who participated, imagination meant to reject thoroughly the system of streets and squares, the principles of continuity that had made Rome and all Italian cities the ultimate reference in urban design. Among the most unsettling and preposterous ones, Piero Sartogo's proposal adjoining the Vatican would have lacerated the historic Borgo fabric and St. Peter's Square with a series of senseless diagonals and objects. Adjacent to Sartogo's, Costantino Dardi intended to cover a large area of Prati with a grid of long housing bars in the suburban manner of German *Siedlungen* and planned to destroy the design order of the Villa Borghese—a strategy without any quality that Romaldo Giurgola also applied to the entire Esquiline, equally dismantling the network of villas and gardens. Surprisingly, Michael Graves reduced the complex of San Giovanni to an urban miniature in an incomprehensible landscape of mega-objects. The British architect James Stirling reimagined—in a more damaging manner—Piacentini's proposal (masterplan of 1931) to create a link between Chiesa Nuova and the Gianicolo. Planning a huge bridge-like cover over the Tiber and destroying a large section of Via Giulia and the

● Léon Krier, new social center on the Corso, *Roma Interrotta*, 1978.

fabric between the river and the Chiesa Nuova, Stirling's vision would have dramatically increased the scope of the demolitions that the Fascist regime carried out between 1936 and 1939, but which were fortunately stopped in time. In contrast, the most critical proposals by Paolo Portoghesi, Colin Rowe, Antoine Grumbach, Aldo Rossi, and Rob Krier emphasized the historic and morphologic importance of the topographical landscape of the city—including that of the ruins in Colin Rowe's expansion of Nolli's plan.[9] With its sacrilegious approach to the city, Léon Krier anticipated the crisis of public space and mass tourism by proposing the insertion of his typological invention—the new "social centers" ◖top◗—within the fabric of the city, one on Piazza San Pietro, one at the heart of the Corso, and the other on Piazza Navona.[10]

Reaction

In the 1996 *Dictionnaire de l'architecture du vingtième siècle*, historian Jean-Louis Cohen asked the fundamental question, whether one can "continue to reserve the label of 'modern' to those architects who simultaneously worked on the renovation of forms, the transformation of uses and technological development, while embracing radical political points of view?"[11] The negative answer that is implied in Cohen's question clearly refers to the major changes that have occurred in the historiography of modern architecture—and undoubtedly the Italian one—within the last decades and have significantly rebalanced the orthodox and canonical explanation of modernism. The mythical—too often self-carried by the major actors of the period—vision of architectural avant-gardes without historic roots has largely been dismantled or contested while the importance of the classical and the vernacular in the making of the "other modern" architecture in Rome has been emphasized. Indeed, the reaction started in the 1980s, as a new generation of scholars and historians initiated a serious revision of earlier writings and publications in favor of a more balanced and less ideologically oriented interpretation of modern urbanism and architecture as professional disciplines. Most of the works built in the early decades of Roma Capitale and under Mussolini's regime have in fact survived intact and are now an integral part of the urban life of millions of citizens.

Among the researchers who have definitely underscored and studied the development of Modern Rome—the construction of its neighborhoods and their housing typologies and programs—in a more comprehensive and less ideological approach, it is critical to include Gianfranco Caniggia, Paolo Portoghesi, Giorgio Muratore,

Beata Di Gaddo, Irene De Guttry, Alessandra Muntoni, Francesca Romana Stabile, Francesco Garofalo, Giuseppe Strappa, Luigi Prisco, Ettore Mazzola, Vittorio Magnano Lampugnani, among others, and all the writers who have been making *archidiap.com* an important website. Likewise, American scholars such as Spiro Kostof, Richard A. Etlin, Thomas Schumacher, Michelangelo Sabatino as well as from Berlin, Harald Bodenschatz, and from Basel, Emanuel Christ and Christoph Gantenbein have been at the forefront of the international research and diffusion.[12] To be sure, this new recognition often remains ambiguous, as, for instance, in Ludovico Quaroni's introductory essay to the superb anthology which is *Case Romane—La periferia e le case popolari*, in which he argued that the quality of Roman housing has always been inferior to other European cities.[13] Yet, 50 years after Spiro Kostof's polemical essay in the *Journal of the Society of Architectural Historians*, even though the overall literature regarding the development of modern Rome since 1870 has grown in quantity and quality, there is still no full-fledged assessment of the construction of the modern metropolis in English. Italo Insolera's *Modern Rome: From Napoleon to the Twenty-First Century*—translation in 2018 of a revised version of his *Roma moderna* - is the only major book that covers the growth of the city from 1870, but this edition did not correct the entirely negative approach to private but public development discussed earlier.[14] Insolera was a prolific and important urban historian, but his writings were ultimately biased by his reluctance to accept the fact that cities have always been the joint product of the public and private sectors.

The Other Rome

The publication *The Other Rome: Building the Modern Metropolis, 1870–1960* examines the morphological and typological history of modern Rome, from its establishment as the new Italian capital to the Olympic Games of 1960 and the rise of its metropolitan condition. For the authors of the book, and many other scholars, this Third Rome is also The Other Rome, the one whose study has been, as discussed, long neglected. But also the one where most of the population lives, considering that the decline of the population of the *centro storico* has continued unabated since the 1980s under pressure from mass tourism and for multiple reasons linked to socioeconomic issues, including changing ways of life. First, it is critical to state that this book does not cover, with rare exceptions discussed by Lucio Barbera, the great institutional monuments of public architecture that were built between 1870 and 1914 to represent the new Italian State, and in particular the Vittoriano (Monument to Vittorio Emanuele I), the Palace of Justice, the Palazzo delle Esposizioni, or the Galleria Nazionale di Arte Moderna. Only the great architectural moments which responded directly to the housing and functional needs of the emerging metropolis and were built during the Fascist regime—such as Stazione Termini, the post offices of Testaccio and Piazza Bologna, the Città Universitaria, the sport installations of the Foro Italico—were given more attention. Likewise, the authors did not stress the radical and highly problematic operations of urban renewal—the opening of the Corso Vittorio Emanuele across the historic center, and more importantly the Fascist-era *sventramenti* (large-scale demolitions) around Piazza Venezia for the Via dei Fori Imperiali toward the Colosseum, the isolation of the Capitoline hill with Via del Mare and that of the Mausoleo di Augusto at the center of Piazza Imperatore, and the Via della Conciliazione to Piazza San Pietro inaugurated in 1950.[15]

As a result, the real focus of the book is the working thesis of a *Roma non Interrotta*, which in contrast with the premises of the 1978 exposition recognizes the international value of the process of typological and morphological continuity and invention that the city witnessed from the 1870s to the inauguration of the Olympic Village—here discussed as the first discontinuous moment in the history of the city and a valuable yet problematic precursor of things to come. The authors analyze Rome's evolution from the late papal city into a modern metropolis, whose architecture and representation embody a kind of "Splendid Ordinary." It emphasizes the role of architects like Gustavo Giovannoni, Innocenzo Sabbatini, Quadrio Pirani, Marcello Piacentini, Mario De Renzi, Luigi Moretti, Adalberto Libera, Ludovico Quaroni, Saverio Muratori, and others in the development of a modern architecture, often socially oriented, and contextually integrated within a continuous fabric of streets, squares, and blocks. It is the importance of those architects and their attempts at modernizing the traditions of the city that painter Mario Sironi (1885–1961) celebrated in one of his portraits of *The Architect* (1922).[16]

Through the selection and analysis of sixteen districts, *The Other Rome* accentuates the importance of the social housing institutes (ICP, INCIS) in the making of the modern city between the 1900s and 1950s, as well as the typological and architectural wealth of its various contributions. It elucidates how a succession of architects worked to expand the city in harmony with the existing city while modernizing tradition. Except for the Esquiline and Via Vittorio Veneto districts that were built from 1870 within the Aurelian walls, the studied districts form a sort of a "ring" around the historic center and include Testaccio, Prati, and Trionfale, Mazzini, Flaminio, San Saba, Aniene Montesacro, Piazza Bologna, Piazza Mincio, and Piazza Verbano, Monteverde Vecchio, Appio Latino, Parioli, Tiburtino, Tuscolana, and the Villaggio Olimpico.[17]

Daniel Solomon's essay "The Splendid Ordinary" develops the concept of the Continuous City in contrast to the Ruptured City of physically isolated and automobile-oriented areas, often socially segregated, whose ultimate and most extreme example is the 1-kilometer-long housing bar of Corviale on the southwestern edge of the metropolitan area and built under the direction of Marco Fiorentino (1973–1982). He does so by emphasizing three directions of interpretation: spatially continuous through its continuum of streets and public spaces; temporally continuous with the constant presence of the past; and socially continuous at least until 1960, with the generally successful attempt at integrating all the classes of the population. Virtually all the residential fabric built between 1870 and 1960 fits the description of the continuous city, whereas most of the large-scale housing built after 1962 has been spatially and socially discontinuous, as can be seen at Casilina 23 ◖p. 31◗, one of the best social housing "urban object" designed by Ludovico Quaroni yet, an example of the ruptured city without any relation to the urban traditions of the millenary city.

Spatially, Solomon emphasizes the importance of the writings of Camillo Sitte in the process of modernizing urban design tradition.[18] Following the rigid "grid-like" planning of the Esquiline and other areas within the Aurelian walls during the first post-1870 decades, Gustavo Giovannoni and the Associazione artistica tra I cultori di architettura (AACAR) brought the figure of Sitte to the forefront of the urban debate.[19] As Richard A. Etlin argued in *Modernism in Italian Architecture 1890–1940*, the "picturesque" theories of Sitte enabled architects and cultural groups to reconnect with the centuries-old artistic spirit of the city of Rome.[20] Once freed from the "hygienic grid" and placed within a more artistic context, the vistas, the special points of views, the articulation of public spaces clearly helped Roman architects to develop an architectural language that achieved its full impact through its insertion in the new approach to the city form—at Flaminio, Garbatella, Montesacro, and most other new quarters. In this contextual approach it was logical that the renewed values of the vernacular cultures were brought to the forefront of the search for modernity in Rome at two specific moments of the city's history: in the 1910s–1930s with the social works of the ICP and after the war with the INA-Casa, whose architects attempted—with considerable success—to modernize the morphology of the urban block while searching for a working-class architecture that would merge but also differentiate itself from the bourgeois[21] *Cinquecentismo* or neo-Renaissance.

Divided into three temporal sections (1870–1907; 1907–1943; 1945–1960), Lucio Valerio Barbera's essay looks at the history and the construction of the Third Rome with a point of view that is at once intensely subjective—for him, modern Rome is the lived experience of a lifetime—and objective, as the author describes without political or ideological biases the progressive construction of a metropolis. While the *centro storico* is in fact an architectural and urban palimpsest, modern Rome can be characterized as a collage, a patchwork of neighborhoods whose very form, in connection with historical streets, landmarks, landscapes and topography, can be instantly recognized. The boyhood bus ride, described in detail in the first part of his essay is the key to the structural armature of Barbera's narrative as he visits and revisits the same sites with the insights of an ever-broadening historical understanding of what shaped them and how they shaped him. Most unique is Barbera's description of his own feelings in front of the first decades of the Third Rome, how he learnt to see it and appreciate it, a process that most Roman residents, visitors, and scholars have been faced with at some point or another. Barbera parallels the evolution of the city with the development of the School of Architecture at La Sapienza and the central role it played from its establishment in 1918 under the direction of Gustavo Giovannoni. He does not conceal the hidden face of the city during the Fascist period but does so with no preconceived ideological vision. He explains the history, describes the city and its evolution across the four important masterplans that guided its construction—1873, 1883, 1909, and 1931—acknowledging that the city is there to stay beyond the political apparatus that constructed it. For Barbera, following on from Gianfranco Caniggia and other scholars like Giuseppe Strappa, the period from the unification of Italy to the early post-war era is critical to understand and evaluate, because it embodies the "real city" in which hundreds of thousands live.[22] Like all the authors of this book he decided, after much reflection, to stress the fact that the socio-political history of Rome and the new Italy created a physical city which has survived and gone through crises. Along the three sections of his essay, Barbera constructs and reconstructs the steps and fundamental decisions and debates that eventually rebuilt, by 1960 and more than seventeen centuries later, Rome as a modern metropolis.

● Still shot from the movie picture *L'eclisse* (The Eclipse), Michelangelo Antonioni, 1962. View of a residential section of EUR, where Antonioni emphasized the solitude of the modern districts.

The readers and scholars who are familiar with the architecture and urbanism of Fascism, the post-Second World War crises, the inequalities of the so-called Italian Miracle of the early 1950s to the early 1960s, and the incapacity of the successive city administrations to control speculation may feel perplexed in front of this book's resolutely positive and somewhat apolitical reading of the evolution of the Third Rome. To counteract that critique, Salvatore Santuccio, an architect and scholar of Italian cinema, explores the image of modern Rome through the lens of important filmmakers of the 20th century, including Vittorio De Sica, Roberto Rossellini, Pier Paolo Pasolini, Federico Fellini, Nanni Moretti, Michelangelo Antonioni, and others. Santuccio argues that cinema more than any other medium, such as literature or the visual arts allows us to understand the complex socio-economic and political conditions under which the modern metropolis of Rome was thought and built. At the same time, the films propound a vibrant understanding of the intense process of social and urban transformation that has impacted the metropolis over more than the last six decades.

The deserted streets and latent violence of the Testaccio quarter have changed dramatically since Pasolini filmed *Accattone* in 1961, as the strong popular district is increasingly threatened by tourist-based gentrification; the looming aqueduct at the end of a street perspective in *Mamma Roma* (Pasolini, 1962) now belongs to one of the most beautiful Roman parks; *Il Boom* documents the psychological and urban damage of rampant speculation; the contrast between the cupola of Basilica Don Bosco and the shacks of *Il Tetto* (Vittorio De Sica, 1956) could not be stronger but is now part of history. In her book *EUR è cinema*, Laura Delli Colli listed more than 150 films which were shot within the EUR district, most of them focusing on the "metaphysical" monumental center. In *L'Eclisse* (1962) ◖ top ◗, Michelangelo Antonioni does not show us the EUR of the 1930s and 1940s, the EUR of Fellini, of love stories, and other comedies. This monumental and metaphysical EUR of Piacentini, Libera, and other great Rationalist architects, often described as "the modern city that becomes silence," is therefore the great absentee from the film, an absence clearly desired by Antonioni who concentrates on the "other side," the side occupied by modern housing areas. Like so many other Italian filmmakers of the post-war period, it is above all the periphery—or the contrast between the old city and the new districts—that interest Antonioni. It is the EUR of the modern *palazzine* that announces the inexorable and alienating framework of the upcoming "eclipse of the architecture," under the impact of industrial capitalism, consumerism, and globalization.[23]

1
Spiro Kostof, "Review: The Third Rome–The Polemics of Architectural History," *Journal of the Society of Architectural Historians*, October 1973, vol. 32, no. 3, 239–250; 239.

2
Maarten Delbeke, "Roma Interrotta. Barok Rome als een (post-modernistisch) model," *Baroque*, OASE, no. 86, 2011.

3
Spiro Kostof, "Review: The Third Rome–The Polemics of Architectural History," op. cit. Important publications in this context include: Franco Borsi, *L'architettura dell'unità d'Italia* (Florence: Le Monnier, 1965); Paolo Portoghesi, *L'eclettismo a Roma, 1870–1922* (Rome: De Luca Editori d'Arte, 1968); Paolo Portoghesi, *Roma un'altra città* (Rome: Edizione del Tritone, 1968); Ludovico Quaroni, *Immagine di Roma* (Bari: Laterza, 1969); Aldo Ferrabino and Vincenzo Cappelletti (eds.), *Il Veltro, rivista della civiltà italiana* (founded in 1957, www.ilveltrorivista.eu); *Roma cento anni fa nelle fotografie del tempo* (Rome: Romagrafik, 1971); *Cento anni di architettura a Roma, 1870–1970*; Gianni Accasto, Vanna Fraticelli, and Renato Nicolini, *L'architettura di Roma capitale, 1870–1970* (Rome: Golem, 1971); Saverio De Paolis and Armando Ravaglioli, *La Terza Roma, lo sviluppo urbanistico, edilizio e tecnico di Roma Capitale* (Rome: Palombi Editori, 1971); Italo Insolera, *Roma moderna, un secolo di storia urbanistica* (Turin: Einaudi, 1962); Leonardo Benevolo, *Roma da ieri a domani* (Bari: Laterza, 1971).

4
Spiro Kostof, "Review: The Third Rome–The Polemics of Architectural History," op. cit., 246.

5
See Lucio Barbera, "From the Reconstruction to the Olympic Games: 1945–1960," 122–150, in this volume. The law was important for social housing but favored isolated car-oriented projects in rupture of continuity with the historical urban fabric.

6
Spiro Kostof, *The Third Rome, 1870–1950: Traffic and Glory* (Berkeley: University Art Museum, 1973).

7
Roma Interrotta (London: Architectural Design, 1979), 11–12; republished in *Roma Interrotta: Twelve Interventions on the Nolli's Plan of Rome* (Monza: Johan & Levi, 2014).

8
Giulio Carlo Argan, *Roma Interrotta* (London: Architectural Design, 1979), 11–12.

9
See the fundamental essay: Christian Norberg-Schulz, "Il genius loci di Roma," in *Roma interrotta* (Rome: Officina Edizioni, 1978), 13–27.

10
It is difficult to agree with the concept of Roma Interrotta as a demonstration of post-modernism in Léa-Catherine Szacka, "Roma Interrotta: Postmodern Rome as the Source of Fragmented Narratives," in Dom Holdaway and Filippo Trentin, eds. *Rome, Postmodern Narratives of a Cityscape* (London and Vermont: Pickering & Chatto Publishers, 2013), 155–169.

11
Jean-Louis Cohen, "Mouvement moderne," *Dictionnaire de l'architecture du XXième siècle* (Paris: Hazan/Institut français d'architecture, 1996), 630. Radical is here intended in the sense of "left-oriented" politics.

12
The literature includes: Thomas Schumacher, *The Terragni's Danteum: Architecture, Poetics, and Politics under Italian Fascism* (New York: Princeton Architectural Press, 1996); Luigi Prisco, *Architettura moderna a Roma e nel Lazio* (Rome: Edilstampa, 1996); Vittorio Magnago Lampugnani, *Diccionario Skira dell'architettura del Novecento* (Milan: Skira, 2000); Irene De Guttry, *Guida di Roma Moderna dal 1870 ad oggi* (Rome: De Luca Editori d'Arte, 2001); Beata Di Gaddo, *Gli anni trenta–Gli elementi dell'architettura* (Rome: Officina Edizioni, 2001); Ettore Maria Mazzola, *"A Counter History" of Modern Architecture: Rome 1900–1940* (Florence: Alinea, 2004); Gianfranco Caniggia, *Lettura dell'edilizia di base* (Florence: Alinea, 2008); Alessandra Muntoni, *Roma tra le due guerre, 1919–1944* (Rome: Edizioni Kappa, 2010); Michelangelo Sabatino, *Pride in Modesty* (Toronto: University of Toronto Press, 2010); Harald Bodenschatz, *Städtebau für Mussolini: Auf der Suche nach der neuen Stadt im faschistischen Italien* (Berlin: DOM Publishers, 2011); Francesca Romana Stabile, *La Garbatella a Roma: architettura e regionalismo* (Rome: Editrice Librerie Dedalo, 2012); Emanuel Christ and Christoph Gantenbein, "Typology Transfer–Towards an Urban Architecture," *Typology: Hong Kong–Rome–New York–Buenos Aires* (Zurich: Park Books, 2012); Giorgio Muratore, Oliva Muratore, Clementina Barucci, *Elogio della cornice–Giorgio Muratore. Un intellettuale dell' architettura italiana* (Rome: Campisano Editore, 2018). For archidiap, see *Roma 500 Architetture Cinquecento Opere da Roma Capitale ai nostril giorni*, Roma: La Sapienza, https://www.archidiap.com/doc/ROMA_500_ARCHITETTURE.pdf

13
Ludovico Quaroni, "Abitare a Roma," in Paolo Angeletti, Luca Ciancarelli, Marcello Ricci, Giuseppe Vallifuoco, *Case romane. La periferia e le case popolari*, third edition (Rome: Prospettive Edizioni, 2009), 8–12.

14
Italo Insolera, *Modern Rome: From Napoleon to the Twenty-First Century* (Cambridge: Cambridge Scholars Publishing, 2018).

15
Spiro Kostof, *The Third Rome*, op. cit.

16
Mario Sironi (1885–1961) was one of the most important artists of the interwar period, working as a painter but also sculptor, architect, stage designer, etc. The painting represents a moment of transition between his involvement in Futurism (as shown at the *Grande Esposizione Nazionale Futurista* of 1919) and the aesthetic current known as *Novecento*, which reveals the influence of Giorgio de Chirico and his metaphysical painting. It celebrates the importance and status of the architect right before the rise of Fascism and the start of an important and creative period of architecture and urban design.

17
On the selection of the studied districts, see Jean-François Lejeune, "Neighborhood Portraits: Reform Blocks, Palazzine, and Metropolitan Density," in this volume.

18
On Sitte, see George Collins and Christiane Crasemann Collins, *Camillo Sitte and the Birth of Modern City Planning* (New York: Rizzoli, 1986).

19
The Artistic Association of Architectural Connoisseurs was founded on 23 January 1890 by Giovanni Battista Giovenale (1848–1934), to welcome "remarkable men of different training, whether technical or artistic or literary, always qualified, graduates in most cases, with a common strong interest in architecture; with a special propensity for the history of this art and for the conservation of the environment and ancient centers" (Alessandro Del Bufalo, *Gustavo Giovannoni*, Rome 1982, 9). It was active until the end of the 1920s, when it was transformed into the Cultural Circle of the Fascist Union of Engineers and Architects. It was subsequently absorbed by the Study Center for the History of Architecture, founded by Gustavo Giovannoni in 1938. See Lucio Barbera's essay "From Reform to Fascism," pp. 76–115 in this volume, and Francesca Romana Stabile, "Shaping Early Twentieth-Century Rome: The AACAR and the Contributions of Filippo Galassi and Gustavo Giovannoni," *Planning Perspectives*, vol. 37, no.3 (2022), 551–581.

20
Richard A. Etlin, *Modernism in Italian Architecture, 1890–1940* (Cambridge, MA: The MIT Press, 1991), 101

21
ON INA-Casa, see Stephanie Zeier Pilat, *Reconstructing Italy: The INA-Casa Neighborhoods of the Postwar Era* (London: Routledge, 2014).

22
Gianfranco Caniggia, "Permanenze e mutazioni nel tipo edilizio e nei tessuti di Roma (1880–1930)," Giuseppe Strappa, ed., *Tradizione e innovazione nell'architettura di Roma Capitale 1870–1930* (Rome: Edizioni Kappa, 1989), 13–25.

23
Jean-François Lejeune, "La metafisica del quotidiano: l'EUR di Antonioni e l'Eclisse dell'architettura," in Laura Delli Colli, ed., *EUR è cinema* (Rome: Palombi Editori, 2008), 43–55.

The Splendid Ordinary

Daniel Solomon

nocenzo Sabbatini, public housing complex ICP Trionfale III and Cinema Andrea Doria, Via Andrea Doria, 1923–1926.

"The contrast between the 'history of contemporary architecture,' as it appears from texts that have now become official and, therefore, of undisputed authority, and the 'real city,' the one which was actually built and in which we live every day, has taken on paradoxical dimensions of radical opposition rather than of reasonable comparability."[1]

Gianfranco Caniggia

Two Dreams

It is not unprecedented, not even unusual, for cities to grow like pituitary freaks—to increase their population twenty-fold in a short time. If such a thing happened to beehives or anthills it might denote the appearance of some strange molecular mutation; but for human habitation it seems almost normal. Wars, great migrations, the twists of political fortune have made these kinds of changes happen many times. It happened to Chicago and to San Francisco in a very short slice of the late 19th century. Starting with the unification of Italy in 1870, it happened dramatically to Rome, with the conversion of a sleepy small town nestled in a fabulous collection of relics into a major European capital.

At times, these eras of explosive growth have produced places of enduring vitality; sometimes, the production has been places of squalor and environmental and human degradation. Historically, the squalor/degraded places have gotten most of the attention. The tubercular slums of the European, English, and American cities of the Iron Age produced, among other things, Marxism and the Modern Movement—big attention indeed. The massive decanting of American cities into suburban sprawl after the Second World War provided gainful employment for more than a generation of sociologists, planners, writers, and filmmakers lamenting its effects—measuring the dimensions of environmental catastrophe, cultural vapidity, and alienation. There is no comparable body of theory or big bibliography, however, about cities that grew rapidly and well, places that built intelligently to provide large numbers of ordinary people with healthy habitation and the sociability, grace, and multiple pleasures of urban life.

There are many good reasons to try to unlock the secrets of places that work, especially places that are not just serendipitous, but were planned and built under the constraints of time, limited resources, and within the era of industrial economies. But there is a new and truly terrifying reason that such study is urgent: climate change, which is likely to produce human migration on a scale the world has never seen. Where, for example, will the entire population of Florida go when insurance companies and the politicians they own decide not to fund the rebuilding of the state for a seventh time? Climate change will exacerbate a dire situation, with the world already attempting to find refuge for 65 million people displaced from their homelands, many in desperate circumstances. The worsening crises to come appear inevitable. It seems likely that at some point in the future, the universal urgency of housing needs, abetted by climate change, will spur a large response, and some societies will again devote serious resources to providing housing for more than just the affluent. When that great day comes, it will be crucial to focus clearly on what went right and what went horribly wrong in sporadic but earnest, and quite expensive, attempts over the last century to house everyone decently.

A powerful thread in the last century of urban history is the idea that the traditional city has been an impediment to a just, healthy, and egalitarian society. Much of the canon of modern architecture and urbanism evolved to dissociate a rational and scientific new order from the insalubrious disorder of the urban legacy. Almost a century of building worldwide has been directly shaped or profoundly influenced by this idea. However, the utopian future that once shined so brightly has now become a deeply flawed, sometimes even tragic past. The 20th-century story of modernist urbanism fueling the latent divisions of society and creating communities of fury and despair has chapters from Los Angeles to Naples and Paris, and in many other places, including my city, San Francisco. Architecture and urbanism cannot be neutral in these matters. For good or for ill, by intent or by happenstance, the architect is a social actor and has been for long time. However, the hegemony of modernist urbanism is a project that was never quite completed. Here and there, for different reasons and at different times, the pre-modern city reshaped and reasserted itself robustly in thoroughly modern circumstances. These phenomena are not revivalist movements; they are adaptations of the built legacy of previous generations to radically new conditions. San Francisco is such a place and the city's reclamation of its own *genius loci* has been the context of much of my life as an architect.

The queen of cities that has become a modern capital while resisting as much as possible the fracturing force of orthodox modernist urbanism is Rome, perhaps the world's capital of modernity without modernism. The common bond among the authors of this volume is love of Rome. We all cherish the place and either live there or have managed to spend parts of our lives there. We share a profound belief that much of Rome has life-sustaining qualities that are fundamental to human existence, and that these qualities are poorly understood and assimilated into the practice and teaching of city building. If better understood, the joyous vitality of Rome's best districts may be replicable, at least partially so, and might become a more normative human condition. We are convinced that would be a blessing. It is why we have written this book. We are also convinced that the joyous sense of community that one can find in many parts of Rome has partly grown from the unique circumstances by which Rome avoided the destructive brunt of orthodox modernist urbanism that did so much damage around the world.

The principal creation myth of modernism in all its forms and incarnations is revolution. For a century, the most powerful convention in many realms of endeavor has been the shattering of convention. Across a broad range of disciplines, upheaval is routine, expected, and demanded; acceptability is unacceptable; heterodoxy is orthodoxy. There is nothing wrong with a state of perpetual revolution in the arts. It may be unfortunate that old skills and sensibilities atrophy as new ones evolve, but it is impossible to argue that the inventive, the critical, or the restlessly probing are linked to bad music, bad fiction, or bad painting. Perpetual revolution in these arts is healthy—as wit sharpening, as the builder of consciousness, as a political and social gyroscopic. Constant discontinuities between the present and the most recent past can serve cognitive growth. The best artists teach us new realities all the time and make us smarter; that is what they are for.

Modern urbanism and architecture also share the creation myth of perpetual iconoclasm, *The Lure of Heresy*—in Martin Gay's memorable title.[2] But urbanism and urban architecture reside in an entirely different category of endeavor from the other arts. Urbanism and urban architecture, like the utensils of daily life, have no proscenium, no frame, and no decontextualizing white gallery wall. They are frameless, unbounded. They are not commentary on the life of the world; they are the life of the world. This absence of frame or proscenium is a crucial difference, a difference that has frequently turned the iconoclasm of modernism from healthy cognitive renewal into a toxic, self-devouring malignancy. Discontinuity between present and past frequently serves the arts well and the city badly. Relying on the theory of one to produce the reality of the other is a malign confusion. Many places have tales about architecture, urbanism, and the ruptures in society—architecture and urbanism as an ameliorating force, or architecture and urbanism as a hot wedge driven into a wound.

The larger context of the story told here is the collision between two recurrent and mutually antagonistic dreams about cities, dreams that architects and their political sponsors have cherished and realized. Both dreams have recurred in many countries over a period of at least ninety years. Both appeared before the emergence of Fascism in Italy, persisted through it, and have carried on long after. There has been a constant ebb and flow between both dreams, each shaping parts of Paris, Rome, Amsterdam, Stockholm, San Francisco, and New York. A big part of each of these dreams has to do with how cities house or want to house their working people, their poor, and their newcomers. Social tensions always exist. For instance, the faring of the Muslim community in France and how it has been housed has frequently made headline news during the last two decades. For earlier generations, the pressure to decant Italy's impoverished rural hinterlands into cities of modern industry and into the administrative heart of a new nation caused similar tensions. The high drama of Paris' and Rome's sharply different confrontations between history and modernity is a textbook for these matters. It is a textbook for what should be a required course for city builders as peoples from the Middle East, Africa, and South Asia scratch at the doors of the West. Who has a plan?

The Ruptured City and the Continuous City

These two dreams encompass quite opposite concepts of urbanity, concepts that can be roughly equated with Love and with Hope, two highly touted human emotions, which as every adult knows, have many foolish manifestations. The clouded judgments that emanate from Love and from Hope constitute much of the world's literature, but writers on city building don't normally confront these subjects. We will associate the city based on love with the term "The Continuous City". Let us then call the city founded on hope "The Ruptured City". Hope takes many forms and has many nuances of meaning. I must ask you, my readers, for the time you spend with this text, to accept use of the word for just those forms of hope that contain within them optimism—naive optimism—and a belief that by acting in a certain way we can ensure conditions in the future will be fundamentally better than the present or the past, neither of which have been very good.[3]

The differences between the Continuous City and the Ruptured City are fundamental and easy to see. Simply put, love of the city and its layered history underpins The Continuous City, hence the City of Love is continuous in three ways, all intertwined. First, it is spatially continuous, or mostly so. Buildings join with one another to form a great continuum of built fabric—defining the essence of the urban grammar, the streets, lanes, squares, and courtyards. Importantly, it is not full of holes and gaps, and free-standing buildings asserting their autonomous thinghood with space all around them are a rarity. Second, the Continuous City is temporally continuous. Past and present blend together, and the past is present in daily life, giving it depth and dimension like underpainting on canvas. In Aldo Rossi's beautiful words, (continuous) "cities, even if they last for centuries, are in reality great encampments of the living and the dead."[4]

Finally, and importantly, the Continuous City is continuous socially. Everybody or almost everybody lives there; practically no one is excluded. It is the best place, really the only place, to experience the full range of human possibility close-up. If a Wall Street Master of the Universe who lives uptown doesn't want to get stuck in traffic on the way to the office, he can hop on the Lexington Avenue Express. For some time, he can't help looking into the eyes of a thugish sixteen-year-old and a Puerto Rican mom with two kids. He learns something about people whose life experience he cannot imagine.

The Ruptured City has many sources, but first among them is the belief that we can produce a city that is healthier, more rational, and more humane, especially for disadvantaged people, than the accreted layers that urban history bequeathed. This City of Hope contains both hubris and contempt, and it claims previously unattained wisdom for those who possess it. Proponents of the architecture of rupture have believed so deeply in their mission that they have been willing, even eager, destroyers of the traditional urbanity they have seen as impediments to their vision. Think of places like the bland suburban development known as Tyson's Corner outside of Washington D.C. or virtually all of Orange County, California; of much of Atlanta, Houston, and Phoenix;[5] of many Parisian suburbs on the other side of the ring road known as Périphérique; and, of course, of so many post-1970 social districts on the other side of the GRA (Grande Raccordo Anulare), the freeway ring that wraps around Rome. In these places, buildings, and streets each march to their own drummer (the architect and the traffic engineer respectively) and they scarcely greet each other in passing. The result is a proliferation of holes and gaps, left-over fragments and parking lots—a fractured townscape where it is unpleasant or pointless to walk anywhere. For most Americans living in places built in the last half-century, this is just the way things are.

The Ruptured City also tends to be perpetually new. Almost nothing is built to last very long, and it doesn't. There is no patina of time and no presence of ancestors, no deep roots for anyone. Yet, undoubtedly, the darkest side of the Ruptured City is the segregation it tends to impose by race and class, and the way in which many people's common life experiences are restricted to their own kind. An urban traveler with an eye for such things will discover that Love (The Continuous City) has a far better track record when it comes to city building than Hope (The Ruptured City), especially regarding housing the needy. Hope's record, in fact, is so negative in this regard that one would expect that what has passed for Hope for so long might be recast as hopeless. In fact, the City of Hope has two sides: a front and a back that almost always look very different from one another. We see the front of the City of Hope when it lies in the future, when its formulation is new and untested. We see the City of Hope from the back when it has been built for a while, when people have lived in it, and it has been through the hot crucible of reality. Architects, particularly those with ties to academia, frequently build their careers on their depiction of the front view of Hope. In many places, the protagonists of both the Continuous City and the Ruptured City have articulated their case, sometimes poetically, and they have built large sections of the modern city.

Architecture and urbanism have political dimensions, but it is astonishing how promiscuous the political embraces of both the Ruptured City and the Continuous City have been. The Ruptured City has at various times stood as an iconic symbol for the liberal social welfare state in the capitalist West, for Soviet Communism before and after Stalin, for the awakening of the capitalist spirit in communist China. The Continuous City has been the emblem for Social Democrats, for Euro-Communists, for Italian Fascists, for Nazis, and during the Stalinist era in the USSR. The 20th century's most influential architect, Le Corbusier, pedaled his own versions of rupture and continuity in the adversarial domains of the Soviet Union and Vichy France, and partially because he never consummated a deal in either place, he was welcomed as a player in post-war France, with the same goods for sale. The 20th- and 21st-century struggle between the radically new city and the tradition-based city are parallel to, but surprisingly independent of, the great historical struggles between left and right, and between the bright light of Enlightenment rationalism and darker cosmologies. While it is not possible to attribute tens of millions of deaths directly to the clash of ideas about urbanism, this clash—our clash—has been as bitter, as vicious, and as consequential as the ideological and economic collisions that have taken the world to its epic wars. The Ruptured City of Hope and the Continuous City of Love should not be judged for their political associations, which have proved to be contingent, temporary, and expedient, but only on the quality of life they sustain and their capacity to provide a home, a sense of belonging to a place, for the vast populations of the world's cities. Severing ideas about the city from their political sponsorship has been a hard leap for many, an acceptance of the unforgivable, but as we will see, there are urban treasures and deep lessons to be found in the darkest parts of the 20th century, especially in Rome.

Waltzing Modern Rome

This book is about Rome as the Continuous City par excellence, and about its thirteen-fold growth in the century after it was named capital of the newly unified Italy in 1871. We are introduced to modern Rome and the experience of the ancient and continuous city in the boyhood adventures of Lucio Barbera and his friends, first on a long bus ride of discovery, traversing the city north to south, and returning on foot. Barbera sees his lifelong quest to understand the layered stories of the city as his duty to his childhood bus companions, and a tribute to their shared memory. Barbera's magical bus ride of discovery has gone on all his life and for him the continuous city is the lived experience of his lifetime. He was a small boy in Rome in the late 1940s, at the time when Neorealist films, fiction, and poetry were populated by swarms of small boys, many of them scruffy urchins, living by their wits in the war-damaged anarchic city. In films, poetry, and in the novel *Ragazzi di vita* (1955) ◖ right ◗, Pier Paolo Pasolini made himself the spokesman and apologist for the lawless brats that he considered as escapees from the suffocating aspirations of the post-war bourgeoisie for whom a Fiat 1100 was their grandest dream.[6] One of the settings for *Ragazzi di vita* was a 1930s public housing project for poor people, known as Donna Olimpia, at the edge of the Monteverde Nuovo neighborhood.[7]

The physical and temporal dimensions of continuity in Rome are to some extent obvious, but the social dimension, the intimate exposure of different sorts of people to one another, has remained subtle and more elusive. On the surface, there was and still is, a high degree of social segregation in Rome, especially during the Fascist years of major building from 1922 to 1943. Under Mussolini, the poorest of the poor and those who, for many reasons, were labeled "undesirable" were banished to the *borgate*, self-contained suburban settlements on the far outskirts of the city, rarely visible from main roads. Within the city, huge programs of affordable housing served frequently homogenous populations—separate projects for the families of butchers, for bus drivers, for the legions of mid-level bureaucrats; separate, but often contiguous and connected to one another. Barbera's beautiful recounting of his boyhood vividly describes how the physical city taught him and his well-cared for bourgeois comrades, about the rough, footloose boys of Donna Olimpia and other such places. Barbera's home was on the opposite side of the city, in the respectable Mazzini district (*Bel Quartiere*) ◖ p. 211 ◗, an important 20th-century neighborhood that he discusses at length in the second part of his essay. The good boys of that district scrupulously respected the rough boys' claims to the turf nearby. From a short distance, the good boys saw the rough boys' confident manners, their enviable swagger, and listened to their strange dialects with a combination of fear, fascination, and admiration. Socializing between the groups occurred only on mutually accepted common ground, the beautiful Pincio Gardens above the city center, something of a sacred place for Barbera to this day.

As we visit the parts of this large and complex capital, largely built in the 20th century, we see in many modern neighborhoods a healthy urban life, vitality, sociability, sustainability, and sometimes beauty. The neighborhoods

● Cover of the first edition of Pier Paolo Pasolini's, *Ragazzi di vita*, Garzanti, 1955.

● Umbrella pines in the Parioli neighborhood.

built from 1870 to 1960 continue to deploy a rich sense of urbanity and community that has rarely been achieved elsewhere in the same span of years. Clearly, Roman planners, architects, citizens, builders, bureaucrats and political leaders did some things right and it is important that we learn their secrets as the pressures of urbanization are rampant everywhere in the world.

Romanità or Roman-ness

I must confess that my co-authors and I quietly share the quasi-mystical idea that cities have souls—at least some cities do—and Rome is laced through and through with its own soul. *Romanità* or Roman-ness asserts itself all over the city, a binding spirit one senses in the streets but cannot name. One sees it in the way Romans dress, especially men in winter: layer on layer—a couple of shirts, a sweater or two, a jacket, a parka, a skillfully tied scarf—all in the same muted palette of russets and earth tones, warm gray and black, bits of dun green—just like the layers of peeling patina of the buildings, just like the muted symphony of luminous color reflected all over the city in the magic hour each afternoon. *Romanità* is the motivating spirit that animates Roman *ragazzzi* and *ragazze* when they get dressed in the morning and it has permeated the hearts of the best architects working in the city for centuries.

Roman light is pervasive and special, an element of *romanità*, and its source is not such a mystery. Like other Italian cities, the clay soil on which much of the city is built is used to make cement plaster to render the surface of masonry buildings, and the most common color of Rome's clay is an intense iron-rich burnt orange. The city is literally of the earth on which it is built. Roman buildings on their colliding street grids are oriented in all directions. Therefore, Roman streets and the interiors of buildings either receive warm, direct sunlight, or an orange reflected sunlight off the rendered facades across the usually narrow streets. Indoors and out, one has a deep, subliminal sense of *romanità* from the color of the light, especially luminous at the magic hour late in the afternoon, when many Romans enjoy an aperitif. From many places in the city, one experiences another vivid element of *romanità* if one happens to be semi-conscious at the first gleam of dawn. Against the pale black of first light, one sees in impenetrable deep black the silhouette of the unmistakable umbrella pines ◖left◗, the Roman pines. Some just grow with long, bare trunks and a top-heavy splay of foliage; most are carefully pruned that way as adolescent trees. For Romans and visitors alike—and composer Ottorino Respighi—the umbrella pines of Rome moving softly in the wind are a part of the city mood that cannot be found anywhere else. Like artichokes *alla romana* that just taste good!

The premise behind this book is that *romanità* is a blessed state, a form of beatitude. Identification with the soul of a place, a deep sense of home, of belonging somewhere in the world is an emotion that all people aspire to and benefit from. This need has become ever more poignant as world events have deprived so many of this fundamental element of being alive. How fitting and perhaps simultaneously disturbing that one of the grandest Roman buildings of the 20th century is the Palazzo dell'Anagrafe ◖p. 23◗, the repository of Roman birth certificates, a monumental celebration of *romanità* built at the end of the Fascist period by the trio of architects, Ignazio Guidi, Cesare Valle, and Vincenzo Fasolo (1936–1939). Feeling located in the cosmos is an emotion and a need that Martin Heidegger understood. A Heideggerian "world" is the amniotic fluid of history, myth, and experience that we are formed within. Heidegger is a contextualist in a sense that is deeper and more evocative than the more literal way architects normally use the word. Layers of history are a predicating condition for existence. An erased world, a ruptured world, is an oxymoron; it is not a world at all. A city, therefore, is a Heideggerian world, not unlike the world of a Fellini film. For Fellini, Ravenna and Rome were the repositories of myth and memory, indelible and

● Ignazio Guidi, Cesare Valle, and Vincenzo Fasolo, Palazzo dell'Anagrafe, Via Luigi Petroselli, 1936–1939. The building is in the area of the antique Foro Boario and the later medieval district that was almost entirely destroyed in the 1930s to make way for a wide street for automobiles and various edifices for public administration.

irreducible. If that renders them enigmatic and incomprehensible, that is quite all right. Our texts and images seek to capture the elusive qualities that Rome managed to retain as it grew thirteen-fold and still gave millions of immigrants the immeasurable gift of being Romans. Our hope is to reawaken builders of cities (and cooks) to this profound obligation—making places that inspire the pride of belonging to a beloved place.

Colin Rowe and Rome

The great architectural theorist, historian, and teacher, Colin Rowe (1920–1999), selected Rome as the focus of his masterpiece, *Collage City*.[8] Rowe used the term collage to mean a palimpsest of overlapping and colliding ideas and fortuitous accidental relationships of sometimes incomplete parts. Rome for Rowe was the ultimate "Collage City". I have long thought that Colin Rowe's *Collage City* was the seminal text that shaped my identity and direction as an architect and as a teacher. It is a book I love and for years I assigned long passages of it to students, attempted to get them to read it, appreciate its importance, and also to be amused by its devastating wit.

Failure. Almost always failure. "Too hard" they said, almost all of them. Even the very smart ones found Rowe's cascade of learned allusions, his deep-sea dive into intellectual history, the mannered archaic elegance of his prose completely baffling and impenetrable. Finally, after years of pedagogical failure, I devised a strategy to get at least some students to understand what the book is about. Before reading, I told them ... "look at the pictures!" I asked them to look especially at the four pages of magnificent photographs of the model of Imperial Rome ◖ p. 24 ◗ located in the Museo della Civiltá Romana in Rome's EUR district. To look also at the final thirty pages of illustrations entitled "Excursus." Look at all those glorious urban images over and over as you read or try to read the text. Then you will understand what Rowe means by the term "Collage City" and why it is the glory of the world. In most books on architecture and urbanism the text elucidates the illustrations—it tells you what to look for. *Collage City* works the other way a round: the illustrations are the keys to enter the dense and difficult world of the text. Once inside, as I tried to convince students, one finds oneself at the most amusing and uproarious party for the mind. You will leave the dazzling conversation at the party with some understanding of the psychological importance of the physical substance of Collage City, why our lives are enriched by it.

● Model of Imperial Rome. The model reconstructs the city as it was in the 4th century AD and is based on the 1901 *Forma Urbis* by Rodolfo Lanciani. Researched and designed by the archaeologist Italo Gismondi, the first phase of the model was completed for the *Mostra Augustea della Romanità* organized in 1937 by the Mussolini regime for the 2000th anniversary of the birth of Augustus. The model was then expanded to include the entire urban area within the Aurelian walls and moved to its current location, a specially designed room within the Museum of Roman Civilization (EUR) in 1955. From bottom to top: the Aventine hill, the Circus Maximus, the Palatine hill, the Republican Forum, the Imperial Fora, and the Capitoline hill.

Two words or phrases that the argument in *Collage City* rests upon are "set-piece" and "collisive." A "set-piece" in Rowe's usage is an urban fragment that represents a complete, self-contained, iconic idea or pattern. Urban set-pieces are often incomplete, but the form of the completed whole is clearly implied by the realized fragment. Set-pieces are often left incomplete because of their collision with other set-pieces or topography, hence the "collusive" nature of Collage City. As one sees clearly in the photographs of the model of Imperial Rome: what is left between the colliding icons is what Rowe names "debris," an essential element of city-building. The presence or absence of a linking matrix of "debris" is what distinguishes Imperial Rome from an automobile-era collection of totally disjointed set-pieces like Atlanta or Las Vegas.

The four authors of this volume have different interests, personalities, and voices. We hope that the juxtaposition of our writings—history, mini-biographies of key players, descriptions of neighborhoods and individual buildings, as well as musings on the city—will turn out to be collisive in the best sense of the term. This strategy does raise the delicate question of the difference between a collage and a mishmash. I wonder how Kurt Schwitters, the acknowledged master of collage, would answer the question. Perhaps he had hundreds of failures he threw away on mishmash grounds. Colin Rowe surely saw Rome as a collage, not a mishmash—the difference being that in a collage, the disparate, sometimes accidental juxtaposition of elements adds up to a complex, sometimes astonishing unity—like Rome.

The Splendid Ordinary: Four Principles and Three Projects

While we think of *romanità* as a spiritual state, there are definite physical properties of building and city form that contribute to its existence. To explore some distinctly Roman principles of city building, let us begin with the neighborhood known as Quartiere Mazzini or Quartiere della Vittoria. This neighborhood was unique in the expansion of the city—not as an urban infill, but as a unified urban design planned on a large single parcel of vacant land in public ownership. It was the one opportunity for the principal planners Marcello Piacentini (1881–1960) and Gustavo Giovannoni (1873–1947) to embrace grandiose form-making like that with which Baron Georges-Eugène Haussmann and Napoleon III had transformed Paris.

Principle I: Big Buildings, Little Streets

At the heart of the Mazzini neighborhood is a Paris-like rond-point with tree-lined radial boulevards, the product of multiple urban iterations by Piacentini, Giovannoni, and their special guest, the German planner Josef Stübben (1845–1936) ◖p. 211◗. If we are looking at this district for its contribution to *romanità*, we can ignore the radial pattern of the masterplan, a landscape/urbanist idea that was generally executed and maintained much better in Paris, where trees are enlisted as obedient soldiers, impeccably uniform. Raffaele De Vico's (1881–1969) central garden at Piazza Mazzini is beautiful, but instead of the raggedy landscape that structures the neighborhood, it is best to study the continuously curving circumferential streets that begin a short block away from the piazza itself—where fake Paris ends, and real Rome begins.[9]

In the first decades after 1870, Roman architects had to grapple with the question of how to make neighborhoods for the substantial influx of functionaries of the new government and those who served it, and how to make these additions to the city, and the new residents themselves truly Roman. Leading architects turned to the history of their own city. Especially useful as a model for the new, post-1870 Rome, were the monumental residences of the great dynastic families often squeezed into the cramped medieval fabric and its narrow medieval streets: the Palazzo Farnese, Doria Pamphili, Braschi, Righetti, Massimo, and so many others beautifully documented in Paul Letarouilly's *Édifices de Rome moderne*.[10] The patronage of important architects by the grand families and powerful ecclesiastical orders to build urban palaces of unparalleled grandeur reached its peak in the 16th century. Grand *palazzi* on tiny streets are a unique Roman occurrence.

Today, it is normal to find oneself on a kerbless cobblestone lane in the historic center, 6-meters wide, amid swarms of alert pedestrians, poised to jump out of the way of cars moving in both directions at speeds that seem much too fast. The travel lane for cars is separated from pedestrian zones by universally ignored white lines painted on the cobbles. Cars and pedestrians both make full use of the street width, thus having to pay vigilant attention to each other. On both sides of many such lanes there are majestic large buildings, typically six-stories high, some short, some very long, often with monumental archways to grand internal courtyards. Because they originally accommodated horses and riders, ground floors are usually 4- to 6-meters high, with openings and details scaled accordingly. Window openings and their travertine surrounds are huge, with iron security grills, bronze bollards, and a multiplicity of big stone moldings

● Mazzini district showing the curvilinear design of Via Fulcieri Paulucci di Calboti between Viale Giuseppe Mazzini and Via Sabotino. In the background, the pedimented top of the ICP block designed by Innocenzo Sabbatini.

to match. Nowhere else are such enormous bits and pieces crammed into such a confined setting. The buildings, often have carefully considered facades, the overall composition of which cannot be seen from anywhere, but one has an overpowering sense of grandeur and great wealth.

There have been fine architects, sometimes great architects, in many eras, across a range of stylistic persuasions, who have given their works extraordinary shimmering presence using the subtle principle of over-scale—that is, deliberately making parts of their buildings surprisingly, a little larger than one expects them to be. The honor roll of architects who mastered and frequently employed this subtle technique include Baldassare Peruzzi and Palladio, no less. Nicholas Hawksmoor in London, Bernard Maybeck and Frank Furness in the United States, or Josef Plečnik in Ljubljana, also come to mind. Perhaps only in the historic center of Rome has the principle of over-scale been applied to a whole district by multiple architects over time. The result is a unique and memorable place of unequaled greatness. Hence, the lessons and the splendors of the historic center were not lost on the architects of the new capital. Over-scale dimensions in the narrow confines of Rome's medieval streets have a particularly dramatic effect. The circumferential blocks that surround Piazza Mazzini knowingly deploy similar lessons for public housing and subsidized worker housing. Housing blocks repeat the massing and proportions of Renaissance *palazzi*; vistas are closed by the narrow curving streets; there is a luminous Roman color palette and abundant over-scale detail. Welcome to Rome, you newcomers, *palazzi* for the working class. Roman grandeur as political art. The Splendid Ordinary.

Principle 2: Nolli Plans

Coherent and beautiful townscape is among architecture's highest and most complex achievements and ordinary people engaged in the minute-by-minute task of living are as deserving and appreciative of architectural grace in their surroundings as princes and priests in their palaces. Michael Dennis' seminal book of 1988, *Court and Garden: From the French Hôtel to the City of Modern Architecture*, builds upon Rowe's *Collage City* almost as a sequel.[11] It traces the architectural virtuosity that emerged over three centuries in Paris as the ever more complex internal needs of aristocratic dwellings required reconciliation with the streets and squares of one of humankind's most beautiful townscapes. Dennis chose the subject matter and method of illustration to address what he sees as the tragic deficiencies of modern architectural practice and pedagogy. Dennis drew upon the techniques and achievements of Colin Rowe's Cornell Urban Design Studio and his life-long friendship with his college roommate Fred Koetter, co-author of *Collage City*.[12] Rowe developed a method of urban analysis and design centered on gestalt psychology's drawing convention, figure and ground. In Cornell's use of figure/grounds, solid black ink represents the solid figure of buildings and the white of the page represents the unbuilt spaces between them. One learns to "read" figure/grounds as a kind of code that reveals complex truths about the spaces of the city and the spaces within buildings.

It was Giambattista Nolli (1701–1756) who, on his famous 1748 map of the city *La Pianta Grande: La Nuova Topografia di Roma* ◖pp. 4, 8, 27◗, first deployed the concept of the figure/ground representation with utmost precision. Moreover, in addition to the conventional figure/ground, where buildings are black and open spaces are white, Nolli included all public or communal spaces within buildings—mostly churches and *palazzi* courtyards—that are extensions of the public realm of streets and squares, thereby recording what has been a special richness of Roman urbanism since Antiquity. For more than 2000 years, visitors have experienced the magic of the city in the courtyards, passages, vestibules, colonnades, and grand civic rooms, i.e., all the linked sequences of spaces that he represented as the penetration of ground into figure. This was Nolli's contribution that his precursor Leonardo Bufalini never thought of for his 1551 map of Rome. The intrigue and beauty of Nolli's penetrations of figure by ground were not lost on the architects discussed in our volume *The Other Rome* as the photographs of lobbies, passages, and courtyards in post-1900 social housing in Mazzini, Prati, Garbatella, and Testaccio among others testify.[13]

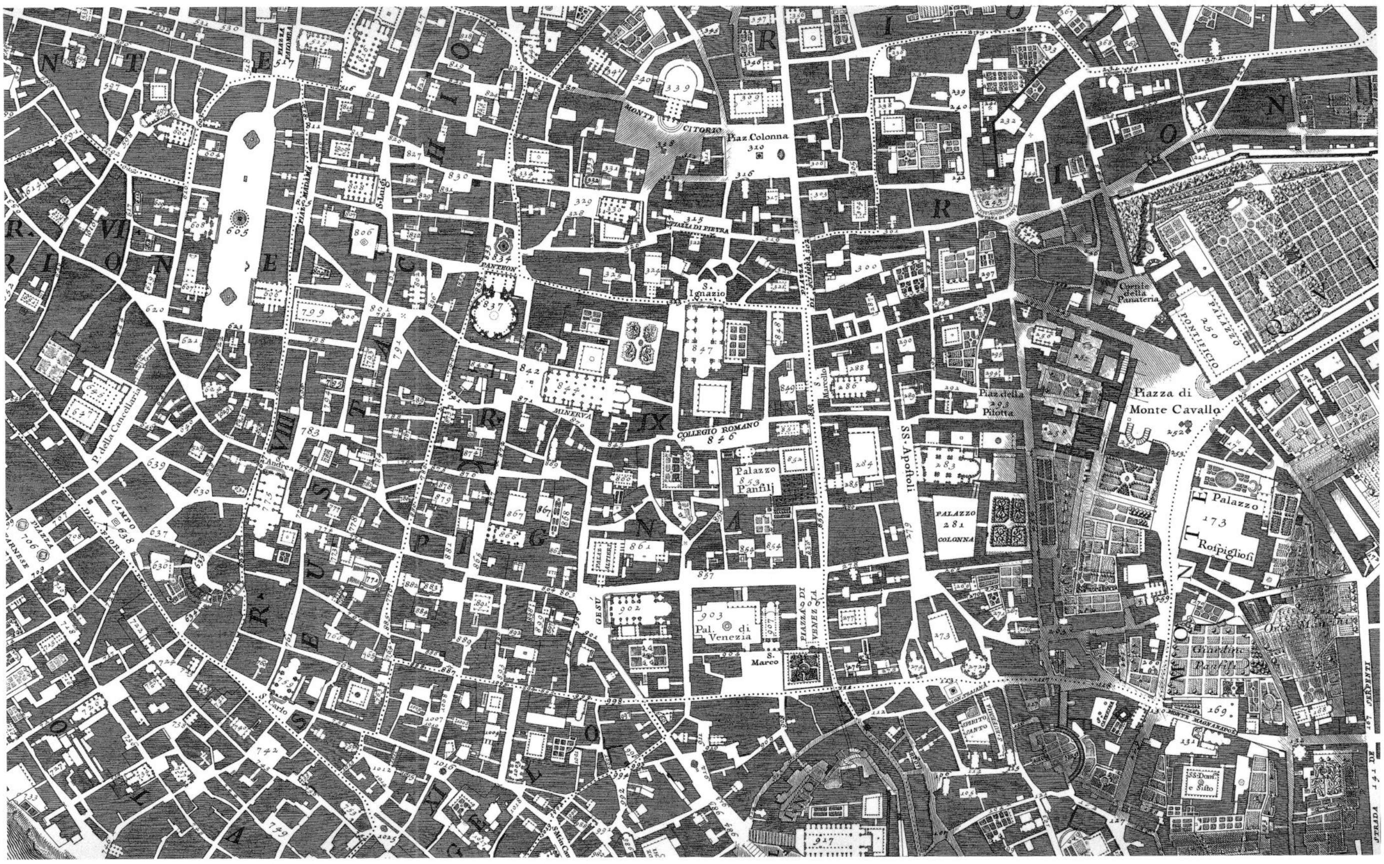

● Giambattista Nolli, detail of *La Pianta Grande: La Nuova Topografia di Roma*, from Piazza Navona (left) to the Piazza del Quirinale (right).

When *Court and Garden* was published, its brilliant figure/ground analysis of complex buildings and their relationship to the city confirmed and solidified my own ambitions as an architect, that is to devote my career to the quest to become a grand master at the great chess game of figure/grounds, making ordinary segments of city into beautiful sequences of streets, lanes, passages, courtyards, and rooms that grace the lives of ordinary people. Like chess, a beginner can play the game after learning a few simple rules, but a grand master can spend a lifetime learning its subtleties.

Principle 3: Fabric as Monument

When the movement known as New Urbanism burst on to the scene 40 years ago, a group of vivid drawings by Léon Krier, explaining fundamental principles of urbanism were in wide circulation.[14] The most influential of these drawings clearly depicted the widely held idea that proper city form consists of two types of buildings: monuments and fabric; that is, the normative matrix in which monuments reside. Many distinguished urbanists, including Aldo Rossi and Andrés Duany, subscribed to this idea and promoted it. According to this view, monuments have special symbolic importance, deserve honorific sites, and demand exceptional architecture to express the importance of the programs they house. Fabric buildings, by contrast, are the quotidian everything else, the background and frame for monuments. Fabric, so the theory goes, has a lesser need for architectural intelligence; it is the easy stuff. I have spent most of my 55-year career as an architect, teacher, and writer on a crusade against this simplistic idea.

One of the joys of being in Rome with my co-authors who know the city so intimately, was to be introduced to somewhat obscure fabric buildings that are architectural masterpieces. For millennia, the production of architectural masterpieces has been a staple of the Roman economy, and a highly competitive career path for architects. Nobody ever explained to the architects of hundreds of Roman churches and *palazzi* that they were not supposed to produce masterpieces because their commissions were embedded in city fabric. Try telling that to the ghost of Francesco Borromini. His oeuvre was mostly second-tier commissions, often small buildings on relatively undistinguished sites, but they produced some of the most complex and subtle works of the Western canon. Never have the ordinary and the extraordinary been reconciled with more sublime elegance than at Borromini's San Carlo

● Innocenzo Sabbatini, ICP housing complex at Villa Fiorelli, Via Crema, 1927–1929. Pedestrian passage and inner garden.

alle Quattro Fontane (1634–1667). Its interior is nothing less than a three-dimensional cosmological map, depicting in its intricate geometries and filtration of light the relationship of heaven and earth. But the sanctuary of San Carlo sits on a busy street corner at the intersection of Via delle Quattro Fontane and the consistent frontage of Via del Quirinale which frames the magnificence of Piazza del Quirinale, seat of the Italian presidency. Mediating between the glories of the San Carlo interior and the important but subservient role of the exterior is a subtly undulating thickened wall, true to the demands of both inside and out. In this most complex of mediations, Borromini left for Roman architects an enduring lesson in how to be both a humble city builder and an architect of thundering power. His legacy extended in time to many of those architects, like Innocenzo Sabbatini and Plinio Marconi, who in the 1920s–1930s deployed the wit and formal spirit of the *barochetto romano*, in multiple projects developed by the Istituto per le Case Popolari (ICP).[15] ◖ top ◗

Principle IV: Good in Every Style

In addition to the residential neighborhoods that constitute the Third Rome from 1870 to 1960, three major Roman projects should be added to our story. The lead designer for each of them was Ludovico Quaroni (1911–1987), mentor and friend to our co-author Lucio Barbera. Quaroni was an extraordinary character, whose works, career, and resilient thinking embodied some of the main tendencies that shaped the building of Rome through the most tumultuous parts of a tumultuous century. As a revered teacher and, for a time, Director of the Institute of Architectural Design at the Sapienza School of Architecture (University of Rome), his works and writings influenced more than a generation of Roman building. Of the leaders in the building of post-war Rome and of leading academicians, it was Quaroni more than others who carried on the spirit and eclectic skills of his mentor Marcello Piacentini.

His first project, designed in 1938 with Francesco Fariello and Saverio Muratori, was the competition-winning scheme (*ex-aequo* with that of Luigi Moretti) for the Piazza Imperiale ◖◖ right ◗◗, planned by Marcello Piacentini as the centerpiece of Mussolini's World's Exposition of 1942 (E42), later renamed EUR (Esposizione Universale Roma).[16] The Piazza Imperiale was the apotheosis of Fascist grandiosity, almost a satire of monumentality. What might be suspected today as a touch of irony was most definitely not seen that way by Quaroni, let alone Mussolini. The giant order of 15-meter monolithic stone columns springing atop a grand *piano nobile* all around the large forum-like square were a serious celebration of the Fascist spirit and urban program ◖ p. 30, top left ◗ ◖◖ p. 121 ◗◗. Behind the classical colonnades that made up the urban image of the Piazza, the four Palazzi dell'Arte—Museo dell'arte antica, Museo dell'arte moderna, Museo delle scienze, Museo etnografico—formed a barycentric ensemble whose plans and sections, particularly in the museums of antique and modern art (Francesco Fariello, Saverio Muratori, Ludovico Quaroni), revealed unexpected abstract strategies of composition. Completing the piazza was the spectacular three-dimensional structure of the cinema-theater, designed by Luigi Moretti. Its construction started before the war, but the project was not completed, and was eventually replaced in 1955–1958 by Saverio Muratori's headquarters ◖ p. 120 ◗ of the Democrazia Cristiana (DC, Christian Democracy Party).[17]

The second work by Ludovico Quaroni was the residential quarter of Tiburtino (1949–1954) ◖ p. 30 ◗ ◖◖ p. 127 ◗◗, a modest social housing district realized in collaboration with Mario Ridolfi, at the head of a group including Carlo Aymonino, Carlo Chiarini, Mario Fiorentino, Wolfgang Frankl, Federico Gorio, Maurizio Lanza, Sergio Lenci, Pier Maria Lugli, Carlo Melograni, Gian Carlo Menichetti, Giulio Rinaldi, and Michele Valori. Built under the

● Francesco Fariello, Saverio Muratori, Ludovico Quaroni, and Luigi Moretti. Perspective and model of the Piazza Imperiale, E42 (now EUR), 1938.

authority of the INA-Casa, the Quartiere Tiburtino rose as, in the words of Manfredo Tafuri, the "Manifesto del neorealismo architettonico," i.e., the small-town, quasi-rural antithesis of Fascist grandiosity.[18] Perhaps the most succinct way to convey the Neorealist spirit of these early years of post-war reconstruction is to quote from a savage skewering of the movement, written in 1948 by film director and critic Stefano Vanzani: "The inevitable Neo-Realist characters include: The overweight father searching the whorehouses of the town for his daughter who vanished during an air-raid. ... A priest bicycling toward the town of Comacchio. The village idiot (with a limp, lame, mute and stuttering at the same time) who has fallen in love with the provocative wife of the postman ... an accordion."[19] Post-war Neorealist film, literature, and the urbanism and architecture of Tiburtino were a celebration of the anti-heroic and the homely detail of the lives of common people in the shattered society of the war's aftermath. In the 1950s, Quaroni's students (including Lucio Barbera) expressed shock at the frankly scenographic folksiness of Tiburtino, calling it "a fake village, not a modern city." They asked incredulously, "How could you?" His laconic reply was, "I'm good in every style."[20] When I first read this quote in Barbera's tribute to Quaroni, I thought it was the flippant self-justification of a man without conviction; a man for whom Fascism and anti-Fascism, grandiosity, and ostentatious modesty were fashionable raiment to take on and off. In actuality, Quaroni was a subtle and serious character, not a flippant one.

"Good in every style" is a profound idea related to the complexity of Rome; its variations and nuances, its colliding set pieces, its linked agglomeration of precious micro-contexts, different every few meters. It was also Quaroni's humorous way of placing himself in the magnificent patrimony of 20th-century Roman architects who

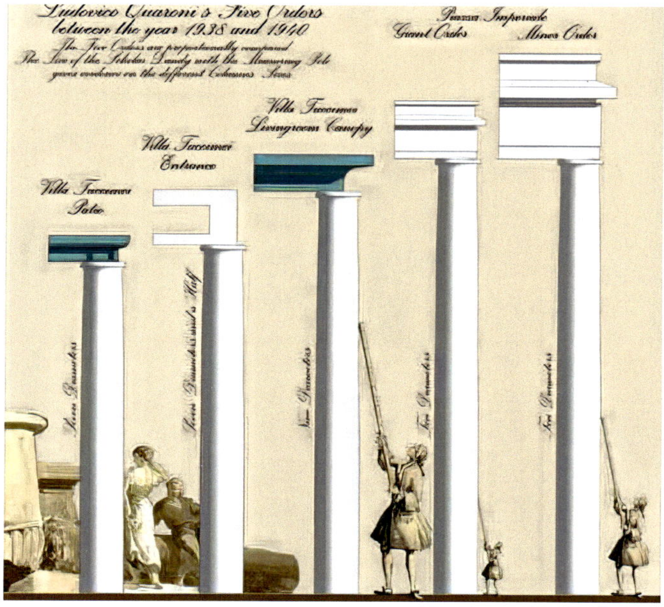

● Top: Lucio Barbera, *Ludovico Quaroni's Five Orders*. The Scholar Dandy with the Measuring Pole is taken from a 1607 engraving; the Arcadian scene in the background comes from a painting by Marco Ricci (1710). Bottom: Ludovico Quaroni, sketch drawn in the 1970s to remember one of his solutions for the Piazza Imperiale at EUR, "half draped in a Bernini-like curtain, carved in red marble and supported by Bronze cherubs" (from an interview with Ludovico Quaroni by Antonella Greco, 1985).

● Ludovico Quaroni, Mario Ridolfi with Carlo Aymonino, Carlo Chiarini, Mario Fiorentino, Wolfgang Frankl, Federico Gorio, Maurizio Lanza, Sergio Lenci, Pier Maria Lugli, Carlo Melograni, Gian Carlo Menichetti, Giulio Rinaldi, and Michele Valori. Townhouses in the social housing district of Tiburtino, 1949–1954.

● Innocenzo Sabbatini, southern entrance to La Garbatella at Largo Giovanni Ansaldo, 1930.

were the champions and preservers of *romanità*, most of them wildly eclectic and more than "good" in every style. Quadrio Pirani (1878–1970) was the first talented and unrestrained eclectic to provide joyous buildings for low-cost, subsidized housing in the new neighborhoods. Yet, the stylistically permissive and inventive tone for the city's expansion was established largely by Innocenzo Sabbatini (1891–1983), the architect of many housing blocks and all major public buildings in the extraordinarily charming and scenographic ICP neighborhood of La Garbatella.[21] Sabbatini's first intervention was the mixed-use Edificio di Maggior Mole (1921), a festive, jokey, mishmash of styles, which served as the first entrance to the district at Piazza Brin. He later brought the imperial Baths of Diocletian as a main reference for the multifunctional Bagni publici e residenze (public baths and residences, Garbatella, 1927–1929) and Borromini himself to the Cinema-teatro (cinema-theater, 1927–1931). Then, he joined Borromini to the Futurist spirit at the lavish, slightly madcap Alberghi suburbani (suburban hotels, 1927–1929), built for poor Romans displaced by Mussolini's demolitions of the Fori imperiali and other historic places.[22]

Quaroni's stylistic and ideological acrobatics continued between 1965 and 1974 with his design for the residential megastructure, Casilino 23 ◖ bottom ◗, to the very southeast of the metropolis. Bombastic megastructures were fashionable in those days, especially in schools of architecture where the celebration in the international architectural press of the graphic razzle-dazzle of Super-Studio, Archigram, and Archi-Zoom captured the minds and sensibilities of students in many places. Professor Quaroni, like architecture faculty everywhere, faced the desperate question of remaining erect in the crashing surf of the student revolutions of the 1960s, surf that had removed for good two of his most brilliant colleagues, Adalberto Libera and Saverio Muratori. He had to at least appear to take the mega-structure mania seriously. I arrived at Casilino 23 for my first visit, expecting (and hoping) to detest it, and thereby confirm the thesis of the relative merits of the Continuous City and the Ruptured City. From the drawings and photographs, this high modernist conceit, Casilino 23, seemed like Quaroni's final apostasy as the main legatee of Marcello Piacentini—anti-Fascism meets *Oedipus Rex*.

The approach to the site confirmed expectations. Though it stands out on the map of Rome as a set of giant housing bars radiating in a gigantic fan-shaped system, it is almost impossible to find. When one finally gets a glimpse, it is perched on a hill behind a mess of gas stations, auto-repair shops and the like, finally giving way to a forbidding twelve-meter-high retaining wall. So far, so good, if one is looking to discredit the Ruptured City. Then you climb a steep driveway to a non-descript parking lot, turn left, and there you finally confront Casilino 23. In disbelief, it is so superbly well-done it takes your breath away. Ghost of Ludovico Quaroni, I don't know what else to say to you. The housing bars recall the ubiquitous Roman apartment structure of post-1870, the *casa in linea*, this time much higher and raised up on pilotis in the manner of northern modernism. The difference between this housing ensemble and many similar ones across Europe is that Quaroni's is beautiful. On one side of each housing bar, there are heroic stair towers every other unit. On the other side is a syncopated rhythm of well-used balconies. The bars splay slightly and step from eight stories to four or five. Except for the concrete stair towers, the material throughout is a handsome Roman brick, impeccably detailed. At ground level between each line of apartments is a well-designed and perfectly maintained formal garden. Below the garden is a quite pleasant and efficient parking level with ample daylight.[23]

● Ludovico Quaroni, et al., masterplan for the public housing district Casilino 23, 1969–1974.

Yet, one can understand, but perhaps not excuse, lavishing such skill on an isolated and self-referential complex as a product of its time. Indeed, Casilino 23 was one of the earliest projects to respond to the "Legge 18 aprile 1962, no. 167," which is known as a "Legge 167" or Law 167. The law was a key element of Rome's *Piano regolatore* of 1962, an exact contemporary of "Title I Urban Renewal" that ripped apart many cities in the United States. Law 167 set out to counter land speculation by making expropriation for public utility possible to requisition land destined for public housing projects at a cost lower than the market value. This process allowed municipalities, the Istituto per le Case Popolari (ICP), and other public housing developers to acquire land at a relatively low price and to equip them with all the necessary residential and social services, which had to be foreseen in the same area plan. In brief, a well-intentioned program, whose practical result in terms of urban planning was to consolidate the Ruptured City as the most efficient way to respond economically to the critical housing needs of the post-war decades.

The Dominant Figure of Modern Rome

Marcello Piacentini (1881–1960) was the dominant figure in the building of modern Rome—an architect of protean talent; a modernist and a classicist, able to think boldly at the scale of the city and craft or direct the craft of individual buildings with exquisite skill. Perhaps the best decision Mussolini made during his tumultuous 22-year regime was to invest Piacentini with major architectural commissions and enormous power and responsibility for the expansion of Rome. It is important to note that he had secured its identities as planner and architect well before the Fascist ascendency. Its reputation grew from many accomplishments, including Piacentini's love and knowledge of Nordic classicism and its resonance with Roman history. For him, minimalist Nordic classicism contributed to a compelling "third path" between 19th-century revivalism and the modernist experiments in Germany, France, and the Netherlands—a way for Italy to be both modern and true to its history.[24]

Undoubtedly, the journalist and art critic Margherita Sarfatti (1880–1961), also Mussolini's Jewish mistress and hugely influential cultural advisor, played a great role in his ascendency. Sarfatti saw in Piacentini's talents Roman grandeur in modern dress: he made sure that she did. One cannot fail to be impressed at the shrewdness with which he and Sarfatti shaped their respective personas to align their mutual ambitions. Under their leadership, the most important architectural and urban design commissions were awarded to the finest architects and most intelligent academics. Mussolini can be credited with the very good sense to defer to them in these matters. Ultimately, Sarfatti and other Fascist intellectuals lost the battle to align Italy with the Allies—France, England, and the US—against Hitler. As a Jewess, Sarfatti was forced to flee, first to Paris, where she visited her friends Jean Cocteau and Coco Chanel, then to South America, where she survived the war in style and comfort, returning to Italy in 1947.[25]

Perhaps no one will ever unravel the paradox and the secrets of this crucial and powerful cultural alliance between a Jew and a raging anti-Semite. After the war, Piacentini was assigned to a special tier of the underworld reserved for leading Fascists, but his influence did not end. The *Piano regolatore* of 1931, of which he was the key designer, continued to provide an urban direction to the development of pre-war neighborhoods at Piazza Bologna, Parioli, or San Giovanni, and remained in place until the early 1960s. By various combinations of chicanery, penitence, hypocrisy, and irrepressible talent, many of the architects who flourished under Piacentini's and Mussolini's patronage, continued to work after the war, both in practice and some in the most prestigious and influential academic and bureaucratic appointments. Piacentini himself was strongly involved in the recovery and revitalization of the ruins of EUR, but his main and most contested realization was the completion of the Via della Conciliazione in the Vatican area in time for the Holy Year of 1950.[26]

For centuries, the Romans of Antiquity feared that the culture of Rome would be eradicated by barbarian hordes from the north. That ancient fear was somewhat like what many Americans of the 1950s felt toward Communists. In fact, the ancient Roman fears, like ours, never quite materialized. As Gibbon and many subsequent historians agree, Roman institutions and culture persevered well into the Christian era, and the changes from Antiquity to medieval Rome were gradual. Part of Rome's genius over centuries has been its ability to turn marauding invaders into Romans. Piacentini felt the same sort of apocalyptic fear of sudden cultural eradication when, in the 1920s–1930s he directed his attacks at what he called "trans-alpine rationalism." He could tolerate some Italian modernists and certainly had modernist tendencies in much of his own work, but for him, the Walter Gropius, Ernst May, Le Corbusier, Erich Mendelsohn crowd from across the Alps were potential barbarians who posed an existential threat to urban civilization. In particular, he feared that the Mediterranean sun would incinerate 2000 years of culture through the glass walls of northern modernism. His anxieties were undoubtedly intertwined with his fierce anti-Semitism that long pre-dated Fascism's embrace of Nazi racial policies in 1938.

For architects everywhere faced with the responsibility of preserving and perpetuating the soul of a city with a complex history of change and transformation, nothing is better training than studying the Roman masters of the 20th century: first Innocenzo Sabbatini and Quadrio Pirani, then Piacentini and his gifted crowd that included Mario De Renzi, Armando Foschini, Ignazio Guidi, and Vittorio Ballio Morpurgo, then Luigi Moretti, Ugo Lucchichenti, and of course Ludovico Quaroni. First, they created genuine modern buildings that are uniquely Roman and reside with appropriate gravitas and permanence amid the most precious and monumental antiquities. Their second achievement was to eradicate completely the distinction between fabric and monument, discussed above as Principle III. On the one hand, these great architects were masters of a contextual infill strategy, inserting and inserting big, practical, modern buildings into the complex, ever-changing, ever soulful fabric of Rome. They authored a great generation of public works still evident all over Italy: post and telegraph offices, state insurance offices, schools, stadia, residential districts, and superb housing blocks. Analyzed comprehensively, Italy's building program of the 1930s was programmatically and stylistically similar to, and contemporaneous with, the WPA (Works Progress Administration), America's finest hour of public building during the presidency of Franklin Roosevelt in the 1930s.On the other hand, one is forced to acknowledge that many of them uncritically embraced the imperial politics of Mussolini and participated in the destruction of major buildings and entire districts for the Via dei Fori Imperiali, the Via del Mare, and the Via della Conciliazione among other completed projects.

Gods and Goddesses

"Good in every style" is a short-hand statement of something essentially Roman. Pagan cosmology and images are never very far away in Rome. Here, at the center of Christendom, the gods and goddesses of the pagan cosmos are eternally gamboling, sometimes stark naked at the very center of things, sometimes in partial and temporary exile, modestly sheltered in frescoed clouds or behind fig leaves. For 2000 years the sumptuous marble flesh of two depictions of Venus in Museo Colonna has been burnished to a high luster by the surreptitious

● Annibale Carracci, *Giove e Giunone* (Jupiter and Juno), detail of fresco, Galleria Farnese, Palazzo Farnese, 1597.

nocturnal caresses of janitors and security guards. These divine effigies are where Bernini learned the tricks of making flesh from stone that find their orgiastic denouement in his *Ecstasy of Santa Teresa* in the church of Santa Maria della Vittoria. Pagan cosmology is the worship of the human, as the gods and goddesses in their fleshy eroticism, their divine variousness, promiscuity, violence, and soap-operatic mischief are the projection and personification of the human, everything human, all of it. Over the dome of the Pantheon is the hemisphere of the Roman sky, the great dome of the firmament where the Olympian gods live their lives parallel to the terrestrially bound mortals of the city—divine and profane locked in an eternal dance of mirror images. Olympus and the real city.

Up to a point, one can probably equate the everything-goes pluralism of the pagan firmament to the architectural and urbanistic complexity of terrestrial Rome, divine and profane as mirror images. The metaphor collapses though, when after 1960 a form of building appears in Rome that just doesn't fit the idea of the complex

● Pier Paolo Pasolini, scene from the film *Accattone*, 1961.

order of the mortal Collage City, mirroring pagan cosmology. Perhaps the only thing a writer can do once committed to such an over-stretched trope is to go all the way and assess whether the results are absurd or enlightening. 1960 was a moment of decisive cultural rupture in Rome. It was the year that Rome hosted the Olympic Games and the year Federico Fellini released *La Dolce Vita*. It was the year when Italy attempted to show the world that the gritty post-war Neorealism was over, replaced by the economic boom slickness of *La Dolce Vita*, but also *Il Boom* and so many other films discussed in this volume by Salvatore Santuccio.[27] The new goddess was the Swedish actress Anita Ekberg, but in reality, Rome's *lumpenproletariat* continued to inhabit the *baracche* at the fringes of the city—Accattone (Pasolini, 1961) ◖top◗ and the dark, hyper-earthy Anna Magnani was the other side of the Janus figure of Roman society, as Pasolini showed in *Mamma Roma* (1962). It was also the moment when the terrestrial city mirroring the pagan firmament metaphor fell to pieces with the building of Villaggio Olimpico, precursor to the *Piano regolatore* of 1962, its companion Law no. 167, and eventually the ruptured social housing districts such as at Casilino 23 and its followers.

At the very moment that the CIAM (*Congrès International d'Architecture Moderne*) imploded into warring factions, Rome embraced for the first time the placeless universalism of the movement's sacred text *The Athens Charter* of 1933. The Villaggio Olimpico ◖p. 332◗ was a late embrace of CIAM principles, a large superblock with no streets, bisected by an elevated motorway resting on columns sculpted by hero engineer Pier Luigi Nervi (1891–1979). Scattered around the superblock are bars of apartments hoisted up on pilotis with parking under neath them. Within the superblock there is nothing one could identify as a space, except for a feeble, half-hearted attempt at a piazza created by a little bend in two of the apartment blocks. There is none of the chummy sociability of all the Roman neighborhoods we study. Where, one wonders, does one walk or get a cappuccino?[28] The Olympic Village and the district Casilino 23 are the first Roman places where the principle of "good in every style" exceeded its urban limits, where an aphorism in support of Rome as queen of the continuous cities, became a weapon against the continuous city, and where Quaroni turned himself into an unwitting ally of his arch-antagonist Bruno Zevi (1918-2000). "Good in every style" does not mean that every style is good, at least when it comes down to *romanità*. Great skill at doing the wrong thing is no help to the city. The Olympic Village and Casilino were two of Rome's early experiments in international placelessness and both failed in all three measures of the continuous city—spatial continuity, temporal continuity, and social continuity. Both stand aloof from the city fabric around them; they are purposely untainted by it. Both make no attempt to place themselves in the story of the city, the passage of time. It is not so easy to divorce history in

● Aerial view of the Villaggio Olimpico in construction, c. 1959–1960.

Rome, but both manage the dubious feat of "pastlessness." Finally, both projects identify their tenants as "other." Who are the people who live in those strange places?[29]

If we cling to our tortured metaphor for a little while longer, we might say that the Olympic Village is where monotheism attempts to supplant pagan polytheism. One can look back at two important architectural voices in the early 1960s and find it hard to avoid the conclusion that modernism (as distinguished from modernity) had by that time achieved the status of religion, a rigid and monotheistic religion from which any deviation of belief or practice was punishable apostasy. The shrillest voices of biblical certainty were those of the acid-penned English writer and critic Reyner Banham and the then professor at the Sapienza (University of Rome) School of Architecture, Bruno Zevi. The English journal *Architectural Review* was Banham's international megaphone, while Zevi (1918–2000) published his own journal, *L'architettura. Cronache e Storia*. The bitter debates that would eventually shatter CIAM were conducted in the pages of Banham's and Zevi's journals and its antagonist publication *Casabella Continuitá*, the child of the Milanese architect Ernesto Nathan Rogers (1909–1969) who edited the periodical from 1953 to 1965.[30] For Banham and Zevi, the term *continuitá* embodied everything they found offensive, indeed sacrilegious, in the publication—the very idea that architecture and urbanism was graced by a living, continuing history, not an abrupt and final rupture with its past in

● Studio BBPR (Gian Luigi Banfi, Ludovico Barbiano di Belgiojoso, Enrico Peressutti, Ernesto Nathan Rogers). Torre Velasca seen from the roof of the Duomo in Milan, 1956–1958.

the 20th century.[31] The dispute reached the unbridgeable chasm of hysteria with Banham's vituperative attacks on two important buildings of the day, Eero Saarinen's scenographic Morse and Ezra Stiles' college dormitories (1961) at Yale University, and BBPR's splendid Torre Velasca ◖ right ◗ in Milan (1951–1958).[32] Both committed the crime of historic reference, to Banham a "betrayal of modernism," to which all architects apparently should owe a kind of religious fealty. At the same time, Zevi set out an anti-classical codebook that attempted to define modernity as a language of asymmetry and dissonance. He was the seminal theoretician of architecture as rupture and fragmentation, iconoclasm, and deconstruction.

It is understandable that a Roman Jew born in the late 1910s would carry the Shoah deep in his heart as an unhealable wound, even though he spent the war years in the safety and comfort of Harvard University. It is understandable that he would regard Marcello Piacentini, not just as a professional rival, but as an agent and perpetrator of everything diabolical and evil in the world—and not just in the living moment, but throughout history. The hysteria to cleanse the world of every trace of what he saw as classical/imperial/Fascist culture made organic sense in Zevi's biography, but how much sense did it make as an unformulated, unarticulated, but rigidly pervasive belief-system promoted half a century later in different circumstances altogether? Don't we look at the joys and follies of pagan Rome more charitably today, perhaps enviously? Wouldn't we enjoy a guilt-free Dionysian frolic now and then? But no. Without any ideological or moral basis whatsoever, the same apostolic proscriptions, the same aesthetic straightjackets survive today among the hordes of young architects cranking out mindless, placeless, watered-down modernism when they have no idea why. Legions of them swallow Zevi's dogma whole, even though they have never heard of him. Are they the legions of a new dark age of soulless mediocrity? It is worth looking at those crippling taboos, how they became taboos in response to just those formal conventions and skills that the Roman architects of the first sixty years of the 20th century put to work to build a more Roman Rome for its hundreds of thousands of new residents. Zevi as "the seminal theoretician" is the principal antagonist of Rome, the continuous city, at least co-responsible for the unspoken and phenomenally pervasive modernist taboos that have been binding the hands and minds of orthodox architects in drafting rooms to this day.

Partially because the union of past, present, and future and the reincarnation of the Roman Empire in modern dress were essential elements of Fascist mythology, Romans cultivated powerful skills at building the continuous city. Our needs for the continuous city are different, more psychological than political. Indeed, we need to help anchor people in time and space in times of cultural homogenization and disintegration, as we confront the desperate need for multitudes of displaced people to have a place to belong. It makes perfect sense for us to deconstruct the skills of the Romans and acquire them for our own purposes, unburdened by the stigma of Neofascism that Zevi and his like slathered so promiscuously on architecture or anything or anyone they didn't like. The neighborhoods documented in this book, from Testaccio to the Olympic Village, demonstrate that Roman skills at city building were not a tidy formula reducible to codes or pattern books or neatly defined methodologies. There are neighborhoods of different types, made in different ways, with radically different architecture and building typologies. The secrets of Rome reside in a big box stuffed with many sorts of complicated treasures. Rome may be the queen, and the great teacher, but she is not the only city with secrets and a soul, not the only city that built *The Splendid Ordinary*—great places where some of the placeless people of the 20th century found home and the divine gift of belonging to a beloved place.

● Innocenzo Sabbatini, ICP housing complex at Viale dei Quattro Venti, Monteverde Vecchio, 1929–1930. Detail of apartment house.

1
Gianfranco Caniggia, "Permanenze e mutazioni nel tipo edilizio e nei tessuti di Roma (1880–1930)," in Giuseppe Strappa, ed., *Tradizione e innovazione nell'architettura di Roma Capitale 1870–1930* (Rome: Edizioni Kappa, 1989), 13.

2
Martin Gay, *Modernism: The Lure of Heresy from Baudelaire to Beckett and Beyond* (New York: Random House, 2007).

3
For further development of those concepts, see Daniel Solomon, *Love versus Hope—Housing and the City* (Atglen, PA: Schiffer, 2018).

4
Aldo Rossi, *A Scientific Autobiography* (Cambridge, MA: The MIT Press, 1981), 20.

5
For an overview of the development of faceless and siteless architecture in the US, see Daniel Kaven, *Architecture of Normal: The Colonization of the American Landscape* (Basel: Birkhäuser, 2022).

6
Pier Paolo Pasolini, *Ragazzi di vita* (Milan: Garzanti, 1955). The literature on Pasolini and Rome is quite extensive. See for instance, Salvatore Santuccio's essay in this volume; Jacopo Benci, *"An Extraordinary Proliferation of Layers": Pasolini's Rome(s)* (London: Routledge, 2011).

7
On Donna Olimpia, see the essay "From Reform to Fascism: 1907–1943" by Lucio Barbera, pp. 76–115, and the section on Monteverde in this volume.

8
Colin Rowe and Fred Koetter, *Collage City* (Cambridge, MA: The MIT Press, 1979).

9
On Raffaele de Vico, see Alessandro Cremona, ed., *Raffaele de Vico, architetto e paesaggista: un "consulente artistico" per Roma* (Rome: Palombi Editori, 2020).

10
Paul Letarouilly, *Édifices de Rome moderne: ou recueil des palais, maisons, églises, couvents, et autres monuments publics et particuliers les plus remarquables de la ville de Rome* (Paris, 1840–1855); *Édifices de Rome moderne* [English edition] (New York: Princeton Architectural Press, 1997).

11
Michael Dennis, *Court and Garden: From the French Hôtel to the City of Modern Architecture* (Cambridge, MA: The MIT Press, 1988).

12
In 1963–1964, Rowe began to teach at Cornell University on the well-known program of Urban Design: a conceptual place that quickly became the reference of disciplinary exploration and intellectual springboard for the production of seminal works on the subject.

13
See Ian Verstegen and Allan Ceen, eds., *Giambattista Nolli and Rome: Mapping the City Before and After the Pianta Grande* (Rome: Studium Urbis, 2013).

14
See Tigran Haas, ed., *New Urbanism and Beyond: Designing Cities for the Future* (New York: Rizzoli, 2008).

15
The *barocchetto romano* is an architectural style that spread in Rome from the 1920s to the mid-1930s. The term was coined for the style used in the construction of the Garbatella by Gustavo Giovannoni. It is very present in other districts like Trionfale and Flaminio. The structural lines of the *barocchetto romano* recall both Baroque and medieval structures, marked by tall and narrow windows with round arches or broken timpani, turrets, curved balconies, and curved walls (often sections of ellipse or oval) that interrupt the flat surfaces and often emphasize the corners. See for instance, Francesca Romana Stabile, *La Garbatella a Roma: architettura e regionalismo* (Rome: Editrice Librerie Dedalo, 2012).

16
See for instance, Vieri Quilici, *EUR: una moderna città di fondazione* (Rome: De Luca Editori d'Arte, 2015).

17
See Antonino Terranova, *Ludovico Quaroni. Architetture per cinquant'anni* (Rome: Gangemi, 1985). Muratori's building still stands but Democrazia Cristiana became defunct in 1994.

18
Manfredo Tafuri, *Storia dell'architettura italiana 1944–1985* (Turin: Einaudi, 1989).

19
Steno (Stefano Vanzina), "The Inevitable Characters in a Neorealist Film" in *Star* (August 1948). Quoted by Bruno Reichlin, "Figures of Neorealism in Italian Architecture (Part I)," *Grey Room*, no. 5 (Autumn 2001), 83.

20
See Lucio Valerio Barbera, *La città radicale di Ludovico Quaroni* (Rome: Gangemi, 2019). Also see Ludovico Quaroni's self-criticism in Ludovico Quaroni, "Il paese dei barocchi," in *Casabella-continuità*, no. 215 (April 1957).

21
See Francesca Romana Stabile, *La Garbatella a Roma: architettura e regionalism* (Rome: Librerie Dedalo, 2012).

22
See Bruno Regni, *Innocenzo Sabbatini: architettura tra tradizione e rinnovamento* (Rome: Edizioni Kappa, 1982). Also see Barbera, pp. 38 ff and Lejeune, pp. 152 ff in this volume.

23
On Casilino 23, see Giuseppe Strappa, *Studi sulla periferia est di Roma* (Milan: Franco Angeli, 2012); Pippo Ciorra, *Ludovico Quaroni: 1911–1987. Opere e progetti* (Milan: Electa, 1989).

24
On Piacentini, see in particular Giorgio Ciucci, Simonette Lux, and Franco Purini, eds., *Marcello Piacentini, architetto 1881–1960* (Rome: Gangemi, 2010).

25
See Daniela Ferrari, Danka Giacon, and Anna Maria Montaldo, eds., *Margherita Sarfatti* (Milan: Electa, 2018).

26
Claudio Parini Presicce, ed., *La Spina: dall'Agro vaticano a via della Conciliazione* (Rome: Gangemi, 2016).

27
See Salvatore Santuccio's essay in this volume, 342–355.

28
For an extensive discussion of the Olympic Village, see the third part of Barbera's essay in this volume, 122–150.

29
The problem of design innovation's unwitting power to "other" has been a worldwide problem for decades. It is the focus of my book *Love versus Hope*, op. cit.

30
See Maurizio Sabini, *Ernesto Nathan Rogers: The Modern Architect as Public Intellectual* (London: Bloomsbury Publishing, 2021).

31
For a detailed study of the polemics, see also Matthew Critchley, "Continuity or Crisis? A Brief History between the Polemics of Aldo Rossi and Reyner Banham," n. d. https://www.academia.edu/11139308/Continuity_or_Crisis_A_brief_history_between_the_polemics_of_Aldo_Rossi_and_Reyner_Banham.

32
On BBPR and Torre Velasca, see Leonardo Fiori, Massimo Prizzon, eds., *La Torre Velasca: disegni e progetto della Torre Velasca* (Milan: Abitare Segesta, 1982).

Waltzing the Third Rome

Lucio Valerio Barbera

'opographical Map of the Suburban of Rome taken from the maps of the new census and trigonometrically outlined in the proportion of 1: 15,000, 1870. In the center is e at the height of the papal period, but the represented territory extends well beyond the boundary of the Aurelian walls. Toward the west from the right bank of the Tiber, ludes the range of hills that goes from the Bravetta estate to Monte Mario, and beyond to Ponte Milvio. Closer to the center is Monteverde, still green and devoid of any ement, and the Janiculum, included in the papal fortified walls. Toward the east from the left bank of the river, the map expands to include, beyond the large patrician villas the belt of gardens of the Roman suburbs, the large agricultural estates of Tor Sapienza, Quarticciolo, Quadraro, Centocelle, and Casal Rotondo.

● Aerial view of the *Bel Quartiere* or Mazzini district. In the center, the tree-lined Viale Giuseppe Mazzini; to the top left, the military barracks that mark the edge of the Prati district; to the bottom right, at the edge of the river, Piazza del Fante.

I. The Pirate Times: 1870–1900

● Piazza del Fante in the film *La Scommessa*, 1967. It is in this square that the timid Oberdan (interpreted by the famous comic actor Totò) gets lured by a group of girls.

At the beginning of the 1950s, Piazza del Fante—a small square along the Lungotevere delle Armi on the outermost edge of the Quartiere Mazzini—was an ideal place for us kids. The great star-like design of our neighborhood—imagined by Edmondo Sanjust di Teulada and Josef Stübben, and eventually designed by Gustavo Giovannoni and Marcello Piacentini—included a new bridge that would have connected Piazza Mazzini and our small square with the streets of the Flaminio district on the other side of the river. But the bridge had not been built and the gardens of the square, thick with evergreen holm oaks and public benches here and there, remained as a dowry to us. Our own private oasis of absolute tranquility, even for our parents. Those were the times in which boys and girls, even in a truly middle-class neighborhood like ours, finished their schoolwork and went down to the street to meet and be together. Mixed groups of peers were formed, boys and girls together, but separated by age; each age had a different group, a different style. The groups shared the space of the piazza and rubbed shoulders with each other, but each of us lived within our own group. Mine was that of the fifteen-year-old and even if it expanded elastically to newcomers or lost some members, the group identified us all as our own family.

We were free in those days. No fear of being on the street. We were born in the last years of Fascism, before the war. We had suffered the fear and restrictions of the fatal year of the Nazi occupation of Rome in 1943/1944. We had participated, with our parents, in the party that exploded when the Allied army arrived, demigods on huge Dodge and Chevrolet trucks. The first two years after the liberation had been our crash course in life. The war had continued for nearly another year in the north of the country and throughout Europe. Rome had become the rear of the front, an area of military camps, of war logistics, and civilian refugees. After a year the peace returned, yet the military atmosphere did not dissolve immediately. Our parents had to struggle for at least another year, inventing ancillary jobs to somehow support our families, which had fallen into poverty. The control over us little ones had loosened. And the city, almost devoid of any civil order, had been wide open since the end of the war, coarse and tempting as never again. My cousin and I were among the youngest on the street. We cautiously did not move away from the sight of our homes, always looking over our shoulders. But it was enough to walk down into the street or reach the lawn behind the building to find ourselves in the rapids of the social stream that had poured into Rome during those years of ruin. Hence, we learned to meet—trying not to get hurt—boys of unknown origins, uprooted, poorer than us, more daring perhaps: recent immigrants from the south, displaced from bombed towns and cities, escaped from the war front.

In addition to the Roman dialect, spoken in the street with an inadmissible vigor for us decent kids, we learned to recognize the cadence of their dialects. Dialects? Real languages unknown to us, children of a bourgeoisie defeated by the war, but still well educated. "They speak Calabrian"—the older children warned us about a band of southern peers that seemed to approach dangerously and we ran away. Closed in a small strip of our neighborhood, we began to discover the unsettled human variety of our country before knowing that of our city. Once, an unforgettable day in 1947, following three years of cautious street experience, we took advantage of the adventurous disorder that reigned in the city. Together with someone older, we finally organized a memorable raid far outside our neighborhood. With makeshift vehicles and on foot, we walked around the inhabited areas of the periphery until we reached the abandoned shores of the EUR district.[1] This journey marked both the triumph and the end of our freer childhood, the genuine graduation day of our crash course in life.

Everything changed quickly afterward. With the help of the Marshall Plan and the renewed desire that people had to do things, between 1948 and 1951, Rome reverted to the civil city that my parents remembered. To hear them, everything seemed to prepare Rome for an even better future. We had returned to our bourgeois world without jolts. The parents had taken up the reins, but they were holding them lightly, aware that we had learned early to manage on our own. Any dialectal inflection was once again forbidden, not only within the walls of the house. More than ever, Piazza del Fante, that secluded and civilized place, was our common arena. There we were among equals, speaking clean average Italian, with very slight hints of *romanesco*. Now we moved freely in our neighborhood, between our homes, our schools, and the two local cinemas. But above all, in our free time, the square was our home.

● Francesco Piranesi. View of the Villa Medici on the Pincio hill, 1838.

● Young men sitting on a bench at Villa Borghese, 1950.

Journey of the New Romans to Discover Old Rome: The Departure

A public bus stopped every half hour in Piazza del Fante, the number 90—*Piazza Zama—Piazza del Fante*. Piazza Zama was on the other side of the city, beyond Porta San Giovanni in a modern section of Rome to the south, almost contemporary with our neighborhood and yet quite different. "It looks like Piazza del Fante," someone told us, "but instead of the river there are the railroad tracks; and fewer trees." "Not poor, really, but more popular," so my father said when I told him about our project: the adventurous crossing of Rome that we had decided to undertake. On a sleepy and hot afternoon, having exhausted the chatter, the stories, and the short runs on the Lungotevere, the noise of the bus leaving for its odyssey woke us up and someone said: "Why don't we go by bus to Piazza Zama? And then walk back!" We all perked up, the skeptics and the adventurous. It was the girls, however, who gave the decisive push. From time to time, they accompanied mothers or older sisters to visit the shops in Via Condotti, Via Frattina, Via del Corso, in short, the center. And the best way to go was the number 90.

The route of bus 90 was linear. Once it reached Piazza Mazzini, the heart of our neighborhood, it headed directly to the Matteotti bridge and passed to the other bank, that of the historic center. In fact, from a geographical point of view, the Mazzini district, our *Bel Quartiere*, was designed as a new Trastevere. Very different from the original one, popular, and truly Roman, it was conceived to offer a truly bourgeois environment to the families of professionals, magistrates, teachers, and army officers, who came to Rome after 1871 from all over the country. Its urban form, eloquently stellar, had been chosen so that its social ambition and its urbanistic reference, the Paris of the Second Empire, were clear at first glance. Foreseen in the *Piano regolatore* of 1909, its general layout dates back to 1911, when the *Esposizione Universale Roma* (Universal Exposition of Rome) was opened on the right and left banks of the Tiber to honor the fiftieth anniversary of Rome as capital of the Kingdom of Italy.[2] The district was mostly built under Fascism, between the 1920s and 1930s, but its construction was interrupted by the advent of the war. The Mazzini quarter had and still has in common with the ancient Trastevere the convenience of being separated from the heart of the ancient city—thus enjoying a precious different identity—and of being directly connected to it. For this reason, as soon as we passed the Matteotti bridge, bus 90 began to totter around, screeching a little, on the route of the ancient Via Flaminia. In two minutes, it took us in front of Porta del Popolo through which it made us triumphantly enter the always stunning Piazza del Popolo.

The Ancient Garden Where the New City was Formed

As soon as we passed the gate of Porta del Popolo, we stopped playing fools and looked up at the terrace of the Pincio ◖left◗, the architectural triumph of Giuseppe Valadier (1762–1839). At that time, all the young people of the new neighborhoods built within and outside the Aurelian walls considered the grounds of Villa Borghese, and especially the Pincio, to be the main public garden in Rome. In this park we began to appreciate the dimensions of modern Rome and its division into neighborhoods, each with a strong identity. Boys and girls came, in small and large groups, from other parts of the city, and made friends. We learned the names of neighborhoods that spoke of other realities, of other streets or squares, and of other schools. Here, we encountered other lifestyles, a different repertoire of clichés, different collective movements, and even a different way of approaching girls. We even noticed that those who came from another neighborhood, even if they were born in Rome like us, all had a common dialectal inflection, the "tone of the neighborhood." It was sometimes a little more southern than ours, from the Abruzzi, Sicily, or even more northern, from Piedmont or Tuscany.

On the Pincio, we began to understand that the neighborhoods of modern Rome were populated not only by different social classes, but by migrants of different origins, who had come to Rome during the short modern history of the city. The first to immigrate were the Piedmont and Tuscan families, who settled in the Esquiline and Macao districts.[3] The families of the employees and managers of the ministries built along Via XX Settembre were quickly transferred, almost deported, first from Turin to Florence, and then from Florence to Rome in less than ten years, between 1861 and 1871. In the early 1870s as well, the employees and managers who had belonged to the Kingdom of Naples and Sicily moved to Rome. They came to live beyond the Tiber in the Janiculum neighborhoods overlooking the Trastevere district, around some ministry and public office that the Kingdom of Italy had built on that side of the city.

Other boys, among our friends at the Pincio, were significantly different from us. They had closer ties to each other and played rough and difficult collective games that seemed dangerous and that the municipal guards tried, almost always in vain, to interrupt. They came from more distant neighborhoods: Santa Croce in Jerusalem (which seemed like the battle cry of the Crusaders), San Saba (a vague early Christian memory), and La Garbatella, a name that meant "the little polite girl." The boys down there had something sweeter even in their usual rogue behavior. They came in groups of boys only, even though not far from them there were almost always a few girls who did not lose sight of their brothers, cousins, and other friends. They were sons and daughters of low-level municipal employees, of tram and taxi drivers, or mechanics on public transport lines. One of them was the son of an industrial blacksmith who brought with him extraordinary iron toys, complicated and ingenious, "made by my father," he told us proudly. And he sometimes gave them to us, scions of the *Bel Quartiere*, with a shy and generous gesture.

The representatives of an unknown lineage appeared from time to time on our Pincio. Males only, they wandered around with the cautious and contemptuous air of an exotic and ambiguous animal species. They seemed to have come out of hunger for adventure, or for mockery, or simply for having lost the ways of their territory. If you stopped and cautiously tried two words, they replied that they came from a *borgata* (a working-class suburban hamlet) with a fabulous and dark name—Donna Olimpia, Tiburtino Terzo, Trullo, Tufello— all names which in our minds sounded like a barbaric threat. Like so many of us, they were from Molise, Abruzzi, or Ciociara, but they were the sons of unskilled workers, maids, or horsemen. There were also children of truly Roman people, who were evicted and relocated in those *borgate* by the Fascist regime. Among them there were children of very poor and often unemployed people. One recognized in many of them the same fascinating and dark lineage that dwelled in small ghettos and self-contained villages, which were sometimes humanely designed by talented architects of our early modernity, on the edges, or even in the very heart of our bourgeois neighborhoods when they were built between the two wars. For this reason, we already knew their ways and languages, from which, in secret, we bourgeois kids gladly drew some movement, some forbidden expression, with the feeling of becoming bigger and transgressive.

Our bus left Piazza del Popolo to enter Via del Corso, but we were still looking toward the Pincio terrace. We began to think about and debate other possible detours to return home. Each of us proposed a place that he or she already knew or had heard about. Showing off their high school knowledge, the best among us suggested a magnificent return trip from south to north, up to Piazza del Popolo, without going through the streets traveled by the bus again. Many of the girls complained about not being able to take a look at the shops in Via del Corso, as they had hoped. Those who were already more interested in history reassured them: in Piazza del Popolo we will take the

90 again back in time to Piazza del Fante. The girls then asked to skip the terminus at Piazza Zama, to begin the return on foot sooner. Where to stop though? "At the Circus Maximus," I proposed, "we don't cross the modern districts and walk back through the most beautiful part of the city." Doubts, some nervousness, and then the agreement again. Our bus 90 made every stop along the Corso, slowly reached Piazza Venezia, then took a right, headlong down along the Ara Coeli and the Capitol, and then on the right the triple colonnade of the Theater of Marcellus. The large green basin of the Circus Maximus welcomed us immediately afterward. We got out. It was still early in the morning. The open air revived us all.

Journey of the New Romans to Discover the Old Rome

That long journey back remains in my memory as the first investigation conducted from life through the largest, most complete and precious architectural composition in Rome. That day in June, without any erudition, without studiousness, we spontaneously walked the entire edge of the hillside overlooking the narrow plain of the Campo Marzio, that a few years later, starting my education as an architecture student, I understood to be the great *Tema di Roma* (The great theme of Rome): the whole urban ensemble formed by the freely cadenced sequence, in time and space, of the extraordinary architectural arrangements invented to overcome the difference in altitude between the alluvial plain and the back of the hills on which the city had originated. In our jumbled return dance and with the great breath of early youth, our group managed to run up and down the Capitoline hill to the Trajan's Market, from the Piazza del Quirinale, to the Trinità dei Monti, the Villa Medici on the Pincio, and from which, finally, we went down the terrace to end up at Piazza del Popolo. Just in time to catch a bus 90 and get off at Piazza del Fante, very tired but triumphant. That lighthearted summer crossing of the ancient city remained in the memory of all of us; and still today, writing about it touches my soul.

For this reason, in the years of studies at the university, I went back many times to that great theme, analyzing it meticulously on the ancient Roman plans of Rodolfo Lanciani (*Forma Urbis Romae*, 1893–1901), on medieval prints, in Renaissance and Baroque views, on Giambattista Nolli's *Pianta di Roma* of 1748 ◖p. 55 top◗, in Piranesi's drawings, and in the weighty history books on Rome. I understood that from the edge of that antique hill and its natural balconies, the ancient Roman city of the seven hills surrounded by Republican walls overlooked the semi-marshy plain of Campo Marzio. And it is along that edge, in the most panoramic positions, that the most beautiful villas of ancient Rome were built. Later, it was precisely from those natural terraces that imperial Rome spilled down into the Campo Marzio, reclaiming it and filling it first with magnificent gardens, temples, monumental mausoleums, and thermal baths. Next, came the large residential *insulae* whose imposing remains support the medieval, Renaissance, and modern buildings between the Trevi fountain and Montecitorio. Then, the summit plateaus of the seven hills were abandoned in the Middle Ages by the surviving population. Without the water from the disused aqueducts, residents walked down from the hills, pulling behind what was left of urban life to stay closer to the water of the Tiber and the reassuring power of the pope. It took almost a millennium for the city of the popes, the Second Rome, to reach the fullness of the Renaissance, and to expand again on the hills where the most ancient Christian basilicas stood. The reconquest of the hills and their plateaus became, for centuries, the dominant theme of the architecture of the city. At the end of the reign of the popes, in 1870, the reconquest was complete. From north to south the jewels of the necklace of wonders stretched out in a light arch to adorn the face of the city of the popes: Piazza del Popolo, the Pincio, Villa Medici, Piazza di Spagna, the steps of Trinità dei Monti, the gardens, palace, and square of the Quirinale—further enriched with the monumental support of the papal stables (*Scuderie papali*)—almost a return to the Roman architecture of great wall structures, the Trajan's Market, and the sublime interplay of the double staircase of the medieval Ara Coeli and Michelangelo's Capitol square.

In the Footsteps of Papal Rome: How to Understand Modern Rome

At the university, I alternated the intuitive discovery of the city with the study of the texts, drawings, and scientific survey of the monuments, almost as if I had contracted a personal obligation with my old group of friends and had the task of continuing the sensual and naive discovery of the city. The first exercise was to try to recognize in the accumulated building fabric and palimpsest of the contemporary city, the shape, the breath, and the landscape of the papal city, which still lived, tampered with, but not entirely disfigured, in the heart of the Italian capital. My old friend Claudio Maroni—he too came from Piazza del Fante and we had enrolled together in the Faculty of Architecture—often joined me. To explore the "subconscious" of modern Rome, we carried with us two precious documents: first, a reproduction of the *Pianta di Roma del Censo papale* (Map of Rome of the Papal Census) ◖bottom◗, published in 1866 on which I hastened to highlight, with a purple pencil, the hilly edges of the "Theme of Rome."[4] The second one is a less famous but much larger map, printed in 1870: the *Carta topografica del Suburbano di Roma desunta dalle Mappe del nuovo censimento e trigonometricamente delineata nella proporzione di 1:15,000* (Topographical map of the suburban of Rome taken from the plans of the new census and trigonometrically outlined in the proportion of 1:15,000) ◖p. 39◗.

For young Romans, the names of agricultural estates visible on the 1870 map (like Tor Sapienza, Quadraro, Centocelle) no longer connoted the mysterious vastness of "the deserted countryside and immense solitude stretching for several leagues in the environs of Rome" as Stendhal wrote.[5] Now, they suggested the ring of estranged settlements, segregated beyond the confines of the city, from which came the boys whom we used to meet in the Pincio. Rigid and abstract, those settlements or *borgate* were designed in the interwar and early post-war periods to resolve the embarrassing presence of growing expanses of slum-like housing along the city edges. Designed by municipal architects and urbanists, they followed the "modern" principles of a suspicious and careful isolation of the poor and proletarian classes outside the bourgeois city. To us decent men of some social sensitivity, these foundations seemed—for what little we knew of them—quite inhospitable housing colonies, beds of culture of both despair and spirited courage.[6] The names of the ancient princely agricultural estates had become names of suburban fragments, which seemed to be kept away not only from the real city, but also from the luminous history of modernity. Who among us, kids of the second post-war period, does not have a vivid memory of

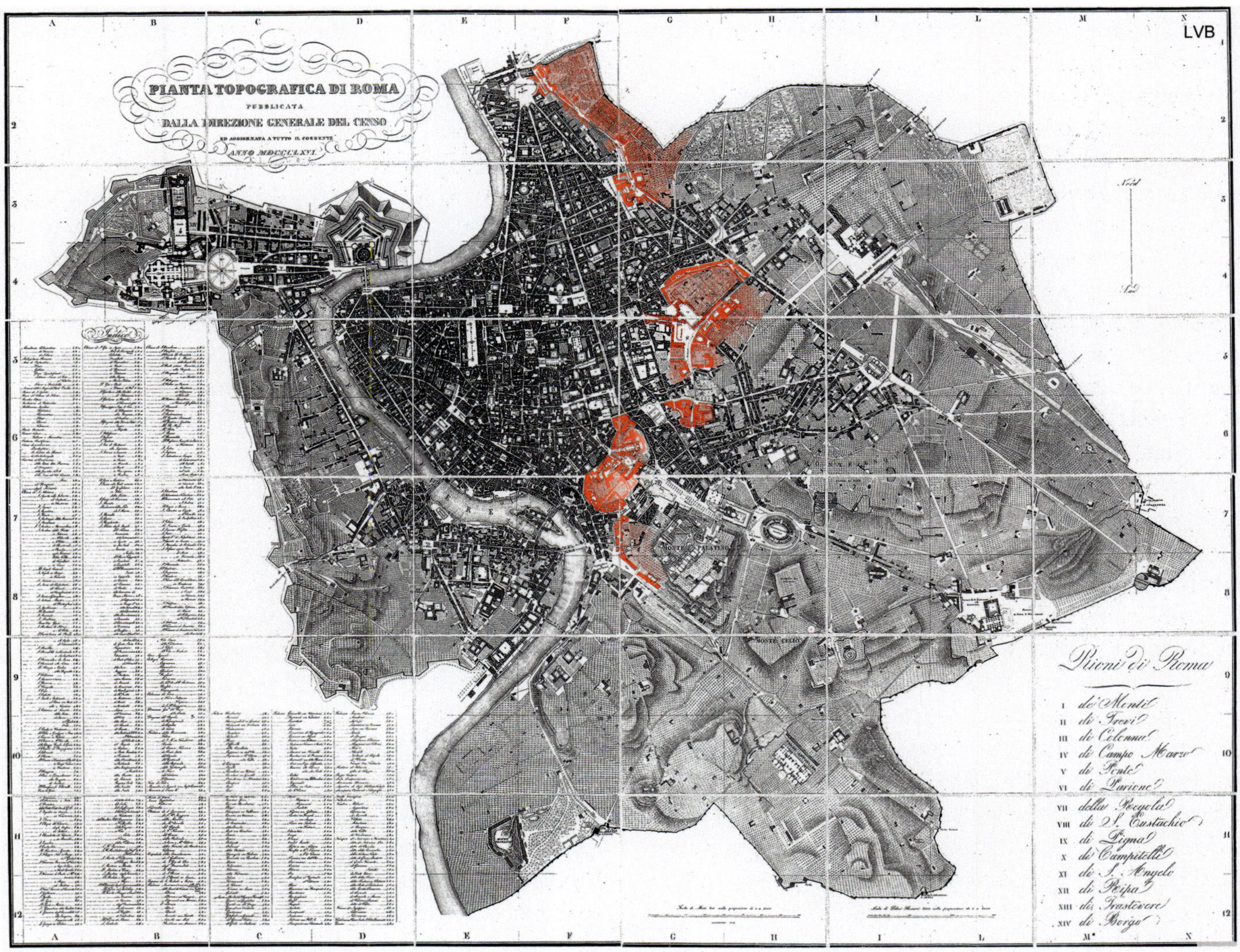

● Map of Rome of the Papal Census, 1866. In red, the hilly edges of the "Theme of Rome."

the gang of the Gobbo del Quarticciolo, one of the most important neighborhoods of that desperate constellation, which wrote its tragic epic in the years of the Nazi occupation and in the dark events of the immediate post-war period?[7] However, the proletarians and underclass who inhabited those neighborhoods from the beginning demonstrated over time that they were people proud of having maintained their dignity despite poverty, their hopes despite despair, and their poetry of living despite its crudeness. For these reasons, those neighborhoods and their residents were celebrated and represented in Pier Paolo Pasolini's books and films—a poet, author, and film maker who moved me and continues to do so.[8]

The Landscape Dear to the Gods: A Famous Painting and a Rare Photograph

Those were the years in which we read and discussed, in disorder but with passion, the memories of Rome contained in the diaries of the most famous travelers on the Grand Tour. Johann Wolfgang von Goethe (1749–1832) had the upper hand because of the great painting by Johann Heinrich Wilhelm Tischbein (1751–1829). *Goethe in der römischen Campagna* ◖p. 47◗ (1786–1787, now in the Städelsches Kunstinstitut in Frankfurt am Main. It depicts the great German poet, wrapped in a white wool cloak like an ancient *re pastore* (shepherd king), under a large-brimmed hat, sitting among ancient stones and broken bas-reliefs. In the background, only a few distant arches of ruined aqueducts and the solitary profile of the tomb of Cecilia Metella remind us of the decayed glories of imperial Rome, while the 8th-century BC landscape of "Rome before Rome" dominates the horizon with the profile of Monte Cavo, sacred to Jupiter and to Arcadia, of which the poet seems to show himself as the new ruler.

This Arcadian landscape seems to have been maintained for centuries, beyond the end of the ancient world, the privilege accorded to it by the official augurs of pagan Rome who forbade any construction that prevented its view from the Capitol. Even in the papal age, the slow and symbolic profile of the Alban hills culminating on Monte Cavo, was granted without obstacles to the spectator who would look for it from any elevated location in Renaissance and Baroque Rome, but also from the opposite end of the city, i.e., from the dome of St. Peter. But until when was that view possible in modern times? Visiting specialized libraries and old photographic archives I managed to purchase a black-and-white panoramic photo of Rome, taken in 1904 from the summit of Monte Mario, on the right bank of the Tiber not far from San Pietro. Measuring almost 4 meters and no more than 60 centimeters in height, it displays the complete panorama of Rome ◖p. 48◗, in the most intense years of its first transformation into a modern city. At the turn of the 20th century, the city is growing and changing rapidly. In the following decade, the municipal administration will finally prepare the design of a new *Piano regolatore* (1909) and in doing so will attempt to give modern Rome an urban identity that the new ruling class, in the fury of the first building transformations, tried in every way to sidestep. However, in that photo, the relationship between city and countryside has not fundamentally changed. Rome, which, at the time, had already doubled its inhabitants from just over 240,000 in 1870 was still mostly contained within the Aurelian walls. To be sure, many of the beautiful parks of the Renaissance and Baroque villas have already been engulfed by the real estate speculation and the genuine need for new housing. Yet, the agricultural space outside the imperial walls—Stendhal's deserted, solitary, and immense countryside—still surrounds Rome and acts as a backdrop to the city like in Tischbein's portrait of Goethe.[9]

In Search of the Architecture of the New Italy: Ancient Metrics, Modern Metrics

Along our walks and crossings of the city, Claudio and I attempted to imagine and reconstruct the great "silence" that stretched in the 1850s between the hilly frame that bounded the inhabited Campo Marzio and the Aurelian walls. Sometimes, we were so caught up in our intellectual game that it is from our deep memory and not from books that we literally extracted the surreal and melancholic images of the monumental ruins that once emerged from the fields, and the intense beauty of the immense villas and gardens that surrounded the city until the 1870s. Only one poet, Gabriele D'Annunzio (1863–1938), opposed and then mourned the destruction of these princely gardens, victims of the speculative fury that took over the new capital of Italy.[10] Later, I extracted and read his best writings and, among them, the poems he composed at the time he was collaborating on the *Cronaca Bizantina* (Byzantine Chronicle) ◖p. 49 right◗, the famous cultural periodical that accompanied, at the end of the 19th century, the debate on the architecture and the culture of modern Rome in construction.

Surprisingly, the first issue, dated 15 June 1881, opened with a brief "barbaric ode" by another poet, Giosuè

● Johann Heinrich Wilhelm Tischbein, *Goethe in der römischen Campagna*, 1787. Johann Wolfgang von Goethe is portrayed as the shepherd king of the "Campagna Romana". In the background, the Alban hills and the tomb of Cecilia Metella.

Carducci (1835–1907), who was regarded as the official national poet of late 19th-century Italy and an "adverse teacher" of D'Annunzio.[11] It was a programmatic and symbolic poem, written in an arduous and archaic language, entitled "Ragioni metriche" (Metrics Reasons).[12] After having deciphered it, not without effort, I understood it as an imperious plea to all artists, *therefore also to architects*, to abandon traditional stylistic metrics to seek the language of a modernity worthy of the new capital in the highest classical metric—the language of antique Rome. According to Carducci, the new Rome, represented in the poem by a young woman with the name of the mythical Roman heroine, Clelia, cannot be described or imagined—*thus designed*—, using the rhymes of the poetic tradition—*of the architectural tradition*—that came to us from the Middle Ages through the Renaissance, the Enlightenment, Romanticism, and the stylistic eclecticism of the 19th-century fin-de-siècle (the parts in italics are my adaptation of Carducci's poem in relation to architecture). In my reading of Carducci, it was thus necessary to turn to the skillful rhythmic discipline of antique times to sing—*to design*—modern Rome. The poem could be read as a sour and sensual metaphor, addressed to the greatest architects of the time: the architecture of modern Rome was to be sought in that of Antiquity. However, I was too young to know that after the First World War, the appeal of Carducci had been picked up by the artists, critics, and architects of the 1920s–1930s, gathered in cohort by Margherita Sarfatti (1880–1961) and then managed with authoritarian eloquence by architect Marcello Piacentini (1881–1960). And I still lacked the required sophistication to perceive the splendid complexity of classical metrics—which is not symmetry, and which lives architecturally in Giuseppe Terragni's masterpieces (1904–1943).[13]

● Panoramic photo of Rome from Monte Mario, 1904. On the left, the bend of the Tiber envelops the countryside where the Flaminio district will rise. The thin line of the ancient Via Flaminia clearly appears, with the small volume of the church of Sant'Andrea del Vignola leaning against the ancient path. Squeezed by the perspective, a little further on is the facade of the villa of Pope Julius III, Villa Giulia. At the opposite end of the photo, on the right, the dome of St. Peter stands out and the Leonine walls close the view. The star-shaped Quartiere Mazzini is not yet mapped out. In its area, only the hedges that divide the fields from the rustic yet monumental piers of the Casali of the Strozzi family emerge. Likewise, the Parioli hills, on the historic center side of the Tiber, are still free of any settlement except for some turreted villas on the highest places. Not far from San Pietro, almost in the foreground, the first buildings of the new Prati di Castello rise, and the regular grid street design is visible. Further south toward the horizon, one can glimpse the mass of new neighborhoods that have sprung up on the Esquiline. Finally, from the fabric of the city closest to the foreground, the construction sites of the two major modern monuments of the Italian capital emerge: the Palazzo di Giustizia and, further away, the Vittoriano (the monument to Vittorio Emanuele II), both of which will be inaugurated in 1911. In the very background, the tiny silhouette of Cecilia Metella's tomb stands out clearly in the space that still separates the city from the sacred Alban hills.

METRIC REASONS

Did you break the Tiber by swimming, Clelïa, as
Yours ancient, or to us new Rea Silva exited?

Scarce, O grandson of Rhea, the endecasyllable has the pace
To measure the cliffs of your beauties:

Only with the triumphal foot the heroic hexameter can
Scander the sacred way of the moonlit shoulders.

From the Capitoline arce of the soft Fidiac neck
The pentameter hangs, albanian garland, must.

It beats in the ray of the eyes, that fierce coruscates so as
Among the Prenestine hills behind the aurora the sun,

Beats the alcaic strophe trembling its wings, and warms itself
To the strong loves: back, thou vile septenary.

Giosuè Carducci

Anno I. Roma, 15 Giugno 1881. Num. 1.

CRONACA BIZANTINA

SI PUBBLICA DUE VOLTE AL MESE

RAGIONI METRICHE

Rompeste voi 'l Tevere a nuoto, Clelia, come
l'antica vostra, o a noi nuova Rea Silvia uscite?

Scarso, o nipote di Rea, l'endecasillabo ha il passo
a misurare i clivi de le bellezze vostre.

Solo co'l piè trionfale l'eroico esametro puote
scander la via sacra de le lunate spalle.

Da l'arce capitolina de'l bel fidiaco collo
pender, ghirlanda albana, il pentametro deve.

Batte nel raggio de gli occhi, che fiero corusca sì come
tra i colli prenestini fulvo l'occiduo sole,

batte l'alcaica strofe trepidando l'ali, e si scalda
a i forti amori: indietro, tu settenario vile.

Oh, su la chioma ondosa che pari a notte discende
pe'l crepuscolo pario de le doriche forme

(a le serve lasciate, o nipote di Rea, gli ottonari)
corona aurea di stelle splenda l'asclepiadea.

Giosuè Carducci.

● The title page of the first literary periodical issue *Byzantine Chronicle*. In the center is the poetry of Giosuè Carducci in Latin metrics, that invites the artists who deal with Rome not to use the tired styles of eclecticism, but to turn, instead, to the most heroic rhythms of antique Rome.

"What a Time That Was for Rome, for Italy, and for Architects!"

So did Carroll Meeks burst out on page 353 of his posthumous volume, *Italian Architecture 1750–1914*, after having described the chronicle of the first architecture competitions which aimed to make Rome the—symbolic—capital of the new Italian kingdom: among those, the Palazzo delle Esposizioni, the Palazzo di Giustizia, the Vittoriano (Monument to Vittorio Emanuele II).[14] Claudio and I had started studying the construction of the capital of Italy in the fourth year of our studies. We did not read books nor meet teachers who had Carrol Meeks' frankness, yet, from the available texts and voices of our professors we had understood—naturally with some feeling of envy—that the construction of the new Italian capital had been an exceptional laboratory of ideas and practices. However, within the general climate of conformism, even the best designers of *Roma Capitale* were asked to abide by a high level of stylistic conformity, especially for the realization of public works. At the most, they were allowed some eclectic experimentation accompanied by a not too ostentatious ability to use methods and materials that were up to date with the most advanced technological and architectural innovations in Europe. Yet, surprisingly, Carroll Meeks made clear to everyone, and with great sincerity, what an exceptional opportunity for field research and cultural affirmation those roaring Roman years were for the best architects.

My intuition was right. Giosuè Carducci had perfectly understood the uniqueness of the historic occasion constituted by the creation of the new Rome, spurring poets, artists, *and architects* toward strictly non-conformist research. He understood that the exhilarating challenge of building the Third Rome had the defect of being born in a climate of conformity and at the same time of "extravagant optimism," as Meeks argued, congenial to the spirit of superficial experimentation of the best architects of that era. He meant not only Roman architects, but also those who flocked to Rome from all over Italy to participate in the harvest that the new kingdom promised to the skilled in every profession, to the renowned, to the experts, and to the designers who had a sure practice of the stylistic burden of the history of Italian architecture. Apart from the effect that Meeks' words would have in instigating a slow revision of our ideas on the languages of modernity, his book revealed something unsuspected, i.e., the international recognition of the exceptional nature of building modern Rome. Accordingly, the neighborhoods of the late 19th century, that for a long time were seen as undeserving usurpers of the space and history of Rome, began to acquire value. To be sure, they were the result of a complex and pragmatic, fast and tumultuous, voracious and hasty history, but not without jolts of genius. They had to be looked at with new eyes, as a sequence of architectural and urbanistic events memorable for their grandeur and its singularity in the context of the modern European city.

Paraphrasing in his own way the French terms of a treatise on art written by Paul Claudel in 1913—*Art poétique: Traité de la co-naissance au monde et de soi-même*—one of our teachers, Claudio Tiberi explained to us that "connaissance" (knowledge) means "co-naissance" (being born with). In other words, getting to know a work of architecture or a city meant "being born with it, reliving its conception."[15] After all, did not we love our neighborhood because we were born with it and could "re-live" its conception from our parents' stories? But how and where could we begin to "be born together" with the 19th-century districts of Rome? In the mid-1960s we started to teach as young assistants on Ludovico Quaroni's (1911–1987) course of urban architecture. Rome, its neighborhoods, their past, and their future formed the framework of design and research. We had not only the time, but the duty to study modern Rome. For many years, until March 1968 when everything was swept up by the new generation, our journey through books and old documents to study the language of architecture of the Third Rome diligently took place around the events of the construction of the 19th-century districts of the capital.[16]

Rome's Secular Society in 1870

When the Italian army breached the Aurelian walls at Porta Pia in 1870 and the pope went into exile in the Vatican, the city could not be more unlike a modern European city. The "sleeping city" of Rome suddenly revealed that it was at once cautious, anxious, and rapacious. For a long time, the victors—the "Italians"—were even unsure of the duration of the conquest. The king of Italy, Vittorio Emanuele II, head of a fragile and uncertain nation since 1861, insistently requested to join an alliance with Germany—and even with Austria who had been the main opponent of the unification—to protect itself from the feared power of France which, since 1848, was the protector of the Holy See and had restored the pope to power following the short-lived Roman republic (30 April to 1 July, 1849). Hitherto dominated by a complex ecclesial society, rich in power and property, the secular society of 1870s

Rome presented itself to the conquerors in its rigid and ancient social scale.

At the top were the conservative *Patrizi* (patricians), divided internally into *Neri* (Blacks, aristocracy loyal to the pope), *Bianchi* (White, liberals in favor of the new kingdom), and *neutrali* (neutrals). A step below was the *Generone*, whose members were also called *Mercanti di campagna* (country merchants). They constituted a very privileged class of Papal Rome, made up of great merchants, tenants, and administrators of the patricians' and the Church's assets. A genuine Roman and modern bourgeois class would emerge from their families, economically strong, well prepared, politically and culturally conservative (sometimes narrow-minded but at times liberal), accustomed to paying homage to power, and certainly fearful of any radicalism. This wealthy class now looked to the Italian monarchy as the only lifeline against the most radical libertarian movements and the revolution. Further down, there was the *Generetto*, an almost caricatural name for a small bourgeoisie, clientele of the patricians and of the church, a petty bourgeois class that was equally divided between partisans of the kingdom and partisans of the Church, according to the orientation of its protectors. Finally, at the foot of the ladder stood the great mass of common people, artisans and families of different fortunes and uncertain economic means. In the days immediately following the "liberation" of Rome from the pope on 20 September 1870, they had filled the streets of the city with jubilation while the rooms of the Vatican resonated with bitterness and indignation. Cardinal Antonelli, the pope's Secretary of State, wanted to make it known abroad that "many people had offered their arm and life in defense of their sovereign [that is, the Pope]"[17] The American consul in Rome expressed himself much more realistically, noting that "not one of the people raised a hand for the defense of Papacy."[18]

At the heart of the city, the Jewish ghetto ◖bottom◗ was still standing even though its gates had been eliminated earlier. It was certainly the oldest Jewish community in Italy (from 1555), but also the most backward in its adherence to the pope's rigid discriminatory rules. At the same time, illiteracy was practically unknown, and many women worked in crafts, both conditions favorable to the future and rapid development of families of Jewish

● View of the Tiber river with the Tiberine island in the center. To the right, the recently cleared area of the former Jewish ghetto, c. 1890. The synagogue was not yet under construction.

culture. Yet, the 1868 census counted only nine engineers or doctors out of nearly 5000 members, and poverty was very widespread.[19] Two years later, as was to be expected, the entire ghetto community sided with the kingdom. In 1888, the old ghetto was destroyed, and in the following decade, an aseptic network of blocks and wide streets replaced the derelict but typologically rich former neighborhood. Following a competition, the architect Osvaldo Armanni (1855–1929) and engineer Vincenzo Costa designed the new synagogue ◖bottom◗ (1901–1904) in an eclectic style mixing Art Nouveau with Assyrian-Babylonian motifs. Erected on the edge of the river, its tall and metallic dome on a square plan rises tall and blends into the skyline of the city with elegance.

Alongside this rigidly stratified, and in many ways archaic Roman society, foreign communities of artists, intellectuals, diplomats, and art collectors were active. They had their favorite places, their mostly Protestant churches, their artists' studios, and their libraries. For that group, Rome in the first decades of its transformation into the capital of Italy was still the city of the Grand Tour, in which basically nothing of importance had happened after the end of the pope's secular power. The new neighborhoods under construction around the center were to be seen as mere utilitarian expansions, which added neither disturbance nor annoying modernity to the beloved city.

● Synagogue, 1901–1904, designed by Osvaldo Armanni and engineer Vincenzo Costa in an eclectic style.

First Phase: Via Nazionale, the First Street of Modern Rome

During the first three decades of Rome as the Italian capital, the government was in a constant hurry to respond to the challenge of moving the king and the administration of the State from Turin to Rome. There was no time to launch ambitious and memorable city regeneration projects. The hostility of the entire international Catholic world loomed over the destinies of the Roman enterprise and pushed the State's administration to consolidate its presence with undisguised anxiety, quickly relocating the court, all the ministries, and the large bureaucracy (still predominantly Piedmontese), as well as the military caste and soldiers with their families. The population grew rapidly, an imposing and "foreign" social body, which the Romans immediately called collectively with a dialectal and derogatory name, "the Buzzurri."[20] At the same time, by requisitioning large properties from the Church, many ministries were transferred to large convents in the center of the historic city, with the result that the rapid process of adaptation often entailed the disfiguration of the historical heritage. Furthermore, it was necessary to find housing areas for the families of bureaucrats and ministerial employees within the Aurelian walls, as these still constituted the only, albeit fragile, military defense. Within this climate of feverish tension, the patricians, the *Generone*, and the Church quickly grasped the opportunity for great financial gains. They stepped in by pushing forward their vast and historic properties, their creditworthiness, and their knowledge of the arcane complexity of the antique city. Perhaps Carroll Meeks should have added a few words to his famous exclamation, completing it like this: "What a time that was for Rome, for Italy, and for architects! And for landlords and for bankers …!"

On 22 September 1870, just two days after the conquest of Rome, General and Commander-in-Chief Raffaele Cadorna appointed the first *Giunta per la città di Roma* (Council for the City of Rome). It was the first of a series of ephemeral city councils that followed one another in a whirlwind sequence of partial and general elections for more than two decades. However, the interests at stake emerged immediately. Out of eighteen members of the *Giunta*, six were princes and dukes from the main Patrician families—from the Caetani, dukes of Sermoneta, to Pallavicini princes, from the Sforza Cesarini to the Ruspoli, from the Odescalchi to the Boncompagni, princes of Piombino—which represented a large part of the real estate interests in the city. Next to them stood three great families of *Mercanti di Campagna*, the De Angelis, the

Tittoni, and the Mazzoleni, representing the most conspicuous bourgeoisie of "financial service" and monetary liquidity, but also owners of large suburban and high-income agricultural areas.

Interestingly, the clerical society had anticipated this situation by some years. Well before the end of papal power, a prelate of Belgian origin, Archbishop Frédéric François Xavier de Mérode (Federico Francesco Saverio de Mérode, 1820–1874) had realistically foreseen the needs of the new Italian capital—its advent was now inevitable—and had purchased large areas of land in the healthiest area of Rome, that which slowly descends from the Baths of Diocletian toward the Renaissance city. Likewise, De Mérode played a critical role in the establishment of the first Termini train station (1863), the work of the papal architect Salvatore Bianchi (1821–1884), in front of the Baths of Diocletian on the Esquiline site of the Villa Montalto-Peretti—a decision that benefited the development of the new quarters toward the east. Accordingly, he began to plan the construction of the first and large district representative of the new Italian capital, a neighborhood centered on the first modern street of the Third Rome, the Via Nazionale ◀◀ right ▶▶ opened in 1871. The first urbanized streets in this area were via Torino (an important axis linking Santa Maria della Vittoria to Santa Maria Maggiore), via Firenze, via Napoli and via Modena. For this area the new municipality of Rome adopted, already in March 1871, the building agreement already stipulated between the Papal State and De Mérode.

As soon as they took possession of their benches in the new municipal council, the great patrician families and the country merchants hastened to open their large suburban properties and historic villas to speculation. They followed the same thoughtless method as that of De Mérode but were even more voracious. The great archaeologist Rodolfo Lanciani (1845–1929) who, at a very young age, was appointed Head of Antiquities by the new administration wrote: "As soon as this degenerate race [the patricians] discovered the possibility of making some money with the magnificent villas that their ancestors had built and kept for the refreshment, health, and well-being of their fellow citizens, they did not hesitate to sell, meter by meter, the glory and pride of their families."[21] It occurred to no one that it was necessary to imagine projects of decent, if not ambitious, design which would attempt to mediate between the various private proposals, each stubbornly defended by its very strong promoters. The urban axes of ancient Rome and the famous perspective and processionary streets traced at the beginning of the Baroque era by Domenico Fontana on the orders of Pope Sixtus V (1585–1590) naturally lent

● Early view of the newly opened Via Nazionale on the Esquiline. In the background, the entrance wall of Santa Maria degli Angeli. The trees were later removed.

● Current view of Via Nazionale from the steps of the Basilica dei Santi Vitale e Compagni Martiri in Fovea.

themselves to providing the basic infrastructure, no matter if insufficient, for the vast and compact carpets of modern buildings that were being considered.[22] The motionless melancholy of the ancient countryside and the aristocratic beauty of the patrician gardens were by now defenseless in the face of the functional urgencies of the new state, the greed of large landowners, and the efficiency of a ruthless model of urban development that appeared almost miraculously in the hands of the new and old rulers of the city—a model that combined new grid-based neighborhoods and, in the Campo Marzio, the Haussmannian-type demolitions of the historic fabric to improve traffic and modernize the city.

Second Phase: Viviani's *Piano regolatore* of 1873–1883

The territory covered by the expansion projects was too vast and the interests too many and conflicting. It was crucial to find consensus on a design that had at least the value of a notarial map of the agreements reached. On the one hand, a commission was set up for the transfer of ministries to Rome, chaired by Giuseppe Gadda, Minister of Public Works; on the other hand, a commission was hastily created to prepare the first *Piano regolatore* (Masterplan of Rome Capital), at the instigation of another Piedmontese general, Adolfo La Marmora. The commission for the plan was entrusted to the guidance of an eminent architect of the papal ranks, Pietro Camporesi il Giovane (1792–1873), flanked by the municipal engineer, Alessandro Viviani (1825–1905). While the commission chaired by Minister Gadda was longing for a "city of ministries," the only political direction dictated by the new government was to build the new Rome far from the Vatican, on the opposite side of the river from St. Peter's.[23]

The patricians immediately entered the field: Prince Massimo felt disadvantaged by this univocal indication of urban policy and bizarrely claimed that the task of choosing the areas in which to build the new neighborhoods was not up to the *Piano regolatore*. He supported the city expansion in the vast area known as Prati di Castello ◖ right bottom ◗, that stretched next to the Vatican and Castel Sant'Angelo. His position was not due to urbanistic and ideological reasons. He had his own interests on that empty side of the river and represented, in the municipal council, a strong international group of bankers and financiers, made up of Neapolitan, Torinese, and Roman construction companies, as well as bankers from Amsterdam, Vienna, Trieste, and Frankfurt. The other contender, Prince Ruspoli, disagreed and defended the choices of the Camporesi commission. He represented the block of mainly national interests, closest to the new political regime, and supported by the powerful minister of finance, Quintino Sella and by De Mérode himself, whose new district on the Esquiline had already begun. For Ruspoli, only the new masterplan could establish the directions for the expansion of the city.

The battle was bitter. The first *Piano regolatore* of Rome, amid thrusts and counterthrusts, was nevertheless put on paper in 1873 and signed by Viviani, a mediocre designer made famous only by that plan. The presence at that moment of Luigi Pianciani as Mayor of the city—liberal and anti-clerical—was decisive. At the same time, he pleaded for a capital that would not only be bureaucratic, but also the center of new and modern industrial activities. The finance minister Quintino Sella strongly opposed Pianciani's strategy. As both a conservative and a scientist, he intended to make Rome a capital of science, and not a working-class city. In those years the municipal councils formed and dissolved in rapid succession, while the city council was marred by frequent resignations, and constantly repopulated through the organization of partial elections.[24]

The *Piano regolatore* of the new Rome was approved in 1873, but it did not become law. The almost heroic and progressive mayor Pianciani lost his position the same year. Likewise, his great rival, Sella, who nevertheless strongly supported a major urban plan, lost his political office in August 1873. Consequently, and for almost ten years, the 1873 *Piano regolatore* continued to represent the agreement reached by the major real estate players and contented both factions. It included the first design for a new district in Prati di Castello, the only one to be built outside the city walls on De Mérode's initiative, but given the strong anti-clerical resistance to the proximity to the Vatican, no work started until 1883.[25] All actors were in turn very satisfied to make the construction of modern Rome gallop on in the areas close to Termini station on the opposite side of the city. The plan incorporated the project of the prescient archbishop De Mérode along the new Via Nazionale. Also on the Esquiline, it included two large new neighborhoods adjacent to each other. The first district was organized according to a Turin-like urban layout, centered around a large green square surrounded by wide arcaded sidewalks, Piazza Vittorio Emanuele II. Built for low-level officials, the square was made of large four- and five-story residential blocks with private courtyards in the center.[26] The other district was in the Castro Pretorio area and known at the time as Macao. Intended for the highest-level officials, it formed a strict grid but

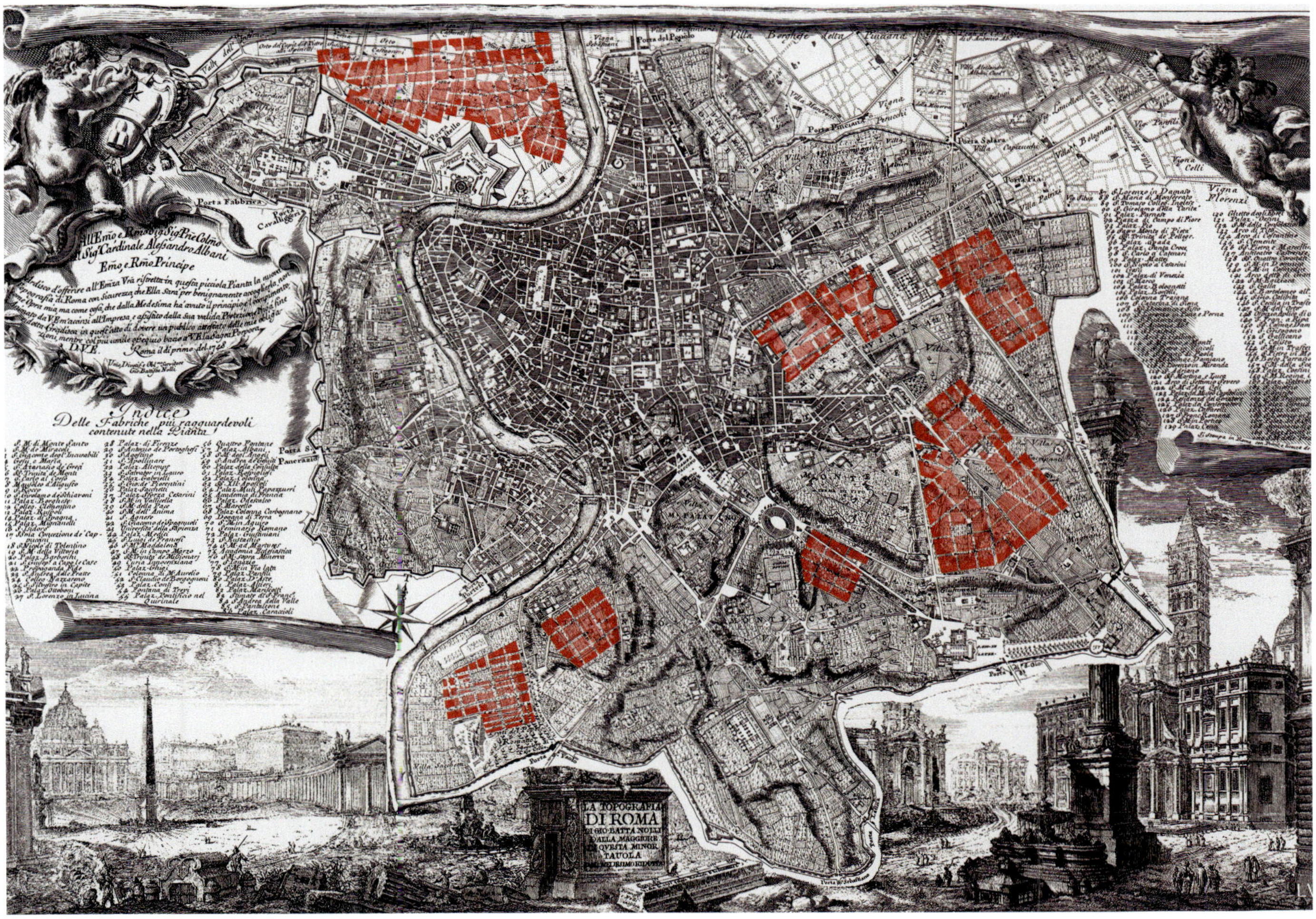

● Giambattista Nolli, *Pianta di Roma*, 1748 (the edition produced together with Piranesi). In red: the scattered new districts. Clockwise from the top: Prati, Castro Pretorio (Macao), Via Nazionale, Esquilino, Labicana/Celio, Aventino, Testaccio.

● Gaspar van Wittel, view of St. Peter's and the Vatican seen from Prati di Castello, oil on canvas, 1700.

was to be made up of villas with gardens. These new neighborhoods on the Esquiline hill leaned against the historic axis that the ancient Romans called Alta Semita and the popes, Via di Porta Pia. To remind all Italians of the conquest of Rome in 1870, it was renamed Via XX Settembre and many ministerial buildings would eventually be lined up along this modernized axis.

The 1873 plan did not stop there: the expansion to the east was completed to the north of Via XX Settembre by the proposed subdivision of Villa Ludovisi and to the south by the more impressive subdivision of Monte Celio, between the Basilica of San Giovanni and the Colosseum. On the other side of the Tiber—in the Trastevere, quite dormant in contrast with other areas—the last papal project for the expansion of the city was being completed. Built from 1859 on the initiative of Pio IX, the Quartiere Mastai was conceived as a small working-class enclave to house the workers of the Manifattura dei Tabacchi (tobacco manufacture). At its heart was the Piazza Mastai created by Andrea Busiri Vici (1818–1911) in front of the neo-classical factory (Antonio Sarti, 1860). A couple of years later, the Viale Trastevere was opened across the sparse fabric on the model of the French boulevard.

The new Rome really gave everyone his own—"*unicuique suum*"—as the ancient Latin saying goes. It appears as a motto in the headline of the Vatican newspaper, founded in 1861, *L'Osservatore Romano: Unicuique suum*—i.e., to the king his capital, to the patricians and to the merchants of the countryside their lavish financial advantage, to the Church a resounding respect. And to the people? Pianciani had promised a future for the working class: on the left bank of the Tiber, in the area called Testaccio where imperial Rome had built its great merchandise port, the progressive mayor advocated the design of the first Roman district mixing both industry and housing. It was included in the *Piano regolatore*, clearly separated from the rest of the city, but within the wide perimeter of the Aurelian walls. It was a bold promise, which was eventually largely implemented despite many delays, changes, and complex vicissitudes.[27] But the salacious people of Rome could console themselves: they had also been given many new and peppery occasions to mock their masters, old and new.

The Grid: A Life Raft Among the Rapids of Urban Growth

As Viviani prepared the 1873 plan, no time was wasted debating the question of what could be the most praiseworthy design for a new and modern European capital. In practice, the parks of the patrician villas and the large suburban vineyards could be easily subdivided into new building blocks. They only needed a very simple system of streets traced within the boundaries of the properties in question, and/or by following the design of some avenue or alleyway in the landscaped terrain of a villa, as happened in the case of Via Vittorio Veneto, drawn according to the design of the park of the Villa Ludovisi. In this climate of fury, fueled by the haste of the new government and the thrust of speculators, it seemed natural that the new neighborhoods provided in the masterplan were designed following a single, peremptory, and simple principle: that of the grid, adopted as a solid life raft to face the rapids of an unstoppable urban growth. The grid is a design solution genetically rooted in the ingenuity of *homo sapiens* as a default model, which was used from Antiquity to modern times to implant a villa, a village, or a city according to *ratio*. *Ratio* is a Latin word usually translated as "reason, thought, or intellect," but whose first and most profound meanings are "account, interest, advantage, and profit." Unsurprisingly, the grid, orthogonal or not, was adopted everywhere in that first phase of construction of the new capital. Sometimes it was organized around a rectangular square, sometimes along a dominant street axis. The new neighborhoods were born almost as autonomous parts of cities, as large islands of various orientations laid out where the interests of the landowners and the pressing needs of the bureaucratic structure of the new government dictated. In some areas, the grid was projected without considering the topography, and, in many cases, without considering the need to connect the other gridded "islands." Even De Mérode's great project, planned along the new Via Nazionale, was conceived and drawn without a real solution to connect it to Piazza Venezia and the ancient city. Despite its ambiguous non-legal status, the *Piano regolatore* gave a sort of public legitimacy to the building operations contemplated therein. It did not attribute to anyone the full responsibility of integrating them together. To some extent, it didn't matter and, as things progressed, the solutions and connections with the historic city and with the topography of the hills would eventually be found and resolved urbanistically.

The Tiber, the Forts, and the 1883 Masterplan

More than the planning of the new Rome, two very urgent issues beleaguered the new government: the recurring floods of the Tiber and the French military threat, which obsessively occupied the thoughts of those at the highest level of command. A few weeks after 1870—almost like divine punishment—the Tiber inundated the city in one of its most impressive historical floods. The flooding of the Tiber was part of the life of Rome. This is why the First Rome had built the city high up on the seven hills, and later developed advanced engineering solutions to better drain the center. Residents of all epochs dealt with it as they could. In the Villa Farnesina, built in 1508–1511 at the edge of the river, architect and painter Baldassare Peruzzi (1481–1536) had represented in the splendid Hall of Perspectives ◖top◗ the dramatic spectacle of an ideal Rome invaded by the waters of the Tiber. This was a spectacle that the new kingdom could no longer permit. The problem had to be resolved immediately and definitively. Therefore, while the fate of the *Piano regolatore* was left to a quarrelsome, opportunistic, and cynical city council, the government committed itself to the defense of the city from the wrath of the river. The comparison between the various technical proposals seemed to slow down the decisions, but in 1875, the law quickly attributed both competence and expense to the state. As a result, two years later, the construction of the *muraglioni* ◖bottom◗ (walls) commenced and eventually proceeded until 1926. It would forever sever the relationship between the houses and the river and erase a memorable image of the city dear to all residents and European travelers. Hundreds of buildings, including houses, palaces, churches, and theaters were destroyed along with many historic places and squares.[28]

However, the most serious obsession of the new state was of a military nature. Italy feared a replica of the French expedition which had seized Rome in 1849 to return it to the pope. The grand design for the new capital could wait, but not the realization of a modern military defense, as the capital was still defended only by the Aurelian walls. The military plan for the new defense of the city included fifteen Prussian-type forts and 4 minor batteries. Built in the countryside more than 4 kilometers from the ancient walls and a couple of kilometers from each other, the forts of Rome defined a circumference of about 45 kilometers around the Aurelian walls, thus establishing the widest territorial limit of the capital city. In 1877, after heated discussions between the

● This detail of architect and painter Baldassare Peruzzi's fresco in the *Sala delle Prospettive* in Villa Farnesina, c. 1510, shows the Tiber flooding the streets of the Campo Marzio.

● Construction of the new embankments along the Tiber river.

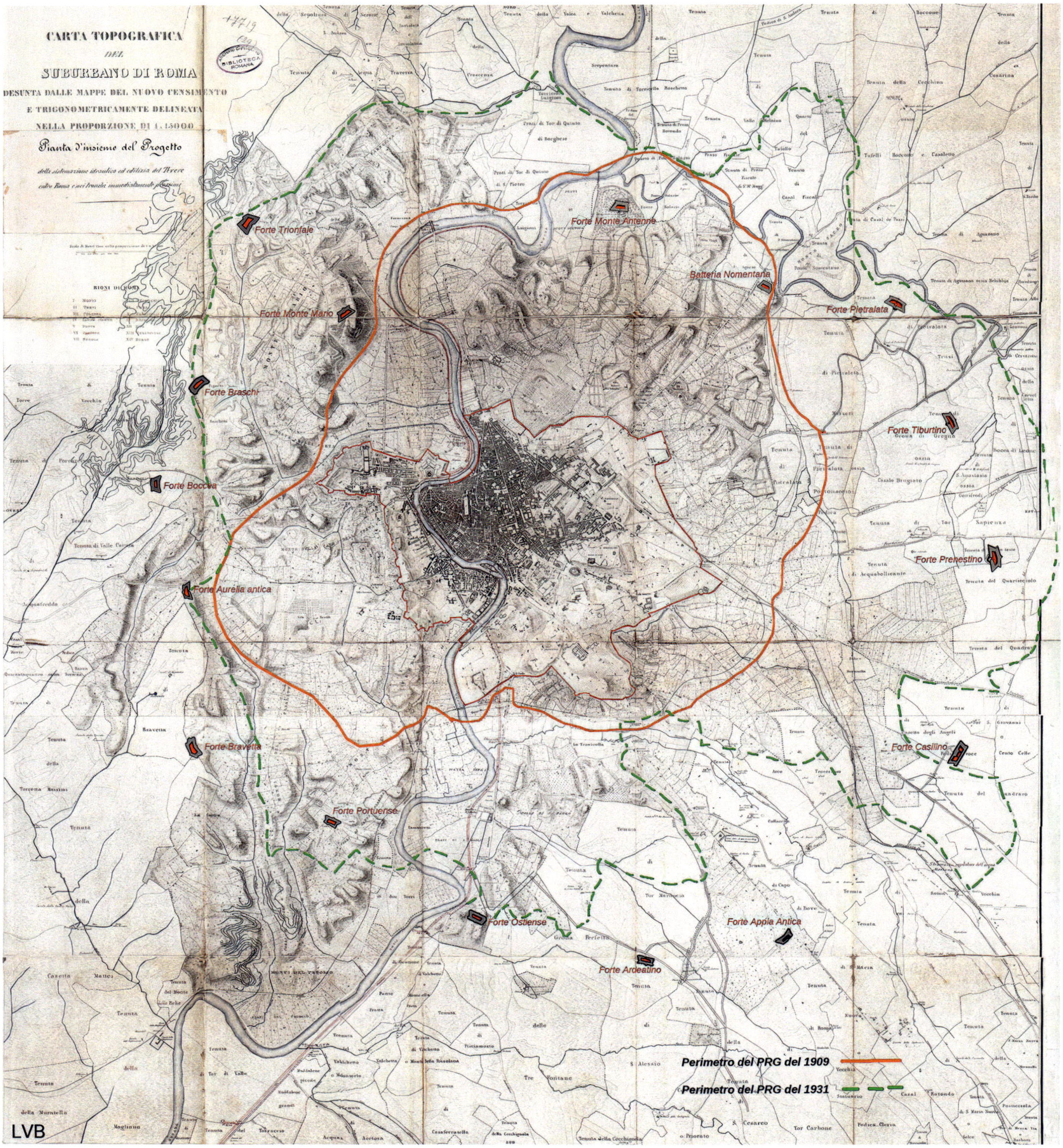

● The 1870 map of the suburbs of Rome with the location of the Prussian-type forts built in the 1870s and 1880s. The red line follows the Aurelian walls; the orange line marks the limits of the 1909 *Piano regolatore*; the green line forms the limit of the *Piano regolatore* of 1931.

ministries of war and finance, the construction of the first eight forts began. A few years later, the construction proceeded to its end (1882) under the umbrella of the new alliance with Germany and Austria.[29]

The government felt safer. In Rome, it was possible to resume the expansion and embellishment of the city in a more organic way. The following year, the first section of Corso Vittorio Emanuele II ◖p. 64 bottom◗ was contracted out. It was "excavated" from the urban fabric of the historic center, from Piazza Venezia to Largo Argentina and the Tiber, to enable city and military traffic to cross the center without the obstacle of its narrow streets and old fabric, as Baron Haussmann had suggested. But above all, a new *Piano regolatore* was finally approved in 1883, under the leadership of Pianciani, elected mayor again. The concept of the plan did not change fundamentally but it was now a legal instrument. Viviani's master plan of 1883 consolidated all the directions of its preceding version, while adding a series of new projects. Next to the Vatican and the Borgo, the *Piano regolatore* now integrated the final design of Prati del Castello, whose construction started in the 1880s from the nucleus of Piazza Cavour and the Palazzo di Giustizia designed by Guglielmo Calderini (1889–1911). On the other side of the river along Via Flaminia north of Piazza del Popolo, the masterplan included the first nucleus of what would eventually become the Quartiere Flaminio. A new district of villas was planned on the Aventino and the Testaccio neighborhood was extended to parallel the river. Finally, the 1883 plan included the first demolitions within the historic center and in particular the opening of Corso Vittorio Emanuele and its multiple connections to the new bridges across the river.

● Piazza Vittorio Emanuele II on the Esquiline, with the palazzo designed by Gaetano Koch in the foreground.

Searching for Order: Early Birth of the Imperial Style of Modern Rome

The order, or the "style," of the city does not necessarily derive from a unitary and hierarchically articulated thought throughout its territory. More often, in the history of the European city, as in Rome after 1870, it was a morphological order on the scale of the neighborhood—for example, the order of the orthogonal grid—as well as a typological and linguistic one on the scale of buildings or building complexes. As mentioned, the *Piano regolatore* of 1873 and its successor of 1883 exposed the use of a single system: the grid, mostly orthogonal, oriented according to the pre-existing infrastructures, or just deformed by the irregularities of the ground. It was interrupted only, when possible or necessary, by rectangular squares of various sizes, from which, on a couple of occasions, some diagonal streets depart as in Piazza Vittorio Emanuele II or Piazza Cavour.

As most historians have argued, it was the obvious result of the adoption of the cardo-decumanus system of the first capital, Turin. In the old capital of the House of Savoy, the lineage of the kings of Italy, the system invested the whole city according to a unitary design, while modern Rome was as a patchwork of independent parts. In so much urban conformism in Rome, only the square from which Via Nazionale opened by the will of Archbishop De Mérode stands out: Piazza della Repubblica ◖◖p. 60 top◗◗ (previously called Piazza dell'Esedra, 1888–1898) built by Gaetano Koch as the first "imperial" square of modern Rome in the shape of a large exedra, a semicircle traced on the layout of the underlying figure, and walls that were part of the enclosure of the Imperial Baths of Diocletian. In modern Rome, the footprint of the ancient and imperial city seems to have been the only presence, real and ideal, capable of giving the new city a magniloquent form and, at the same time, modern and worthy of the aspirations of a great European capital.

On the one hand and except for Piazza dell'Esedra, the adoption of the orthogonal mesh for each sector of the new city turned out to be a first and positive element of urban uniformity, which acted with the solidity of a well-established rule. On the other hand, the uniform architectural image was the result of the slow and collective typological transformation and of an unwritten agreement between architects on the possible languages of architecture. The politicians and technicians of the new regime, mostly military at the beginning, were welcomed in Rome by a strong and consolidated network of architects and engineers who until a few months earlier

● Piazza della Repubblica on the Esquiline, built between 1887 and 1898 by Gaetano Koch.

● Piazza della Repubblica, with the superimposition of the plan of the former Baths of Diocletian, of which it reproduces the shape of the antique exedra after which it was originally named (previously Piazza dell'Esedra).

● Palazzo Farnese (1514–1580), designed by Antonio da Sangallo the younger, Michelangelo, Jacopo da Vignola, and Giacomo della Porta on Piazza Farnese. It is one of the clearest architectural models of the modern *Cinquecentismo*.

● Public and private architecture form the homogeneous fabric of the first modern district for Roma Capitale on the Esquiline hill. At the center the mass of the Ministry of Defense (1876, architect Giulio Podesti); all around the private residential buildings, built along Via Nazionale from 1870. Note how the adhesion of most of the architects to the simplified and standardized ways of the *Cinquecentismo* achieves a great formal homogeneity of the new neighborhoods, albeit uncritically monotonous.

represented the elite of Papal Rome. They embraced the newcomers with the revival of the 16th-century Roman Renaissance language—which we call the *Cinquecentismo* ◖bottom left◗ and which, on close inspection, was to the Rome of the post-1850s what the neo-classical had been to Napoleonic and Austrian Venice, and the neo-Gothic to Victorian London. It was the style of the return to the most convincing and reassuring cultural and formal identity of the city, which gave historical dignity to the pride, which existed even in Papal Rome, of its ruling class. It was the style that represented the linguistic agreement between the architects and the city and continued to represent it even as the speed and size of urban development, as well as the social conditions and expectations of the new "non-Roman" ruling class, changed radically.

To explain the reasons for the continued success and adaptation of the *Cinquecentismo* ◖bottom right◗ to the changing conditions of urban growth, it is not necessary to examine here, one by one, the great personalities of architects and builders, their different leanings, and their impact on the functional and aesthetic quality of the new capital. Almost in unison, Paolo Portoghesi and Carroll Meeks responded with their ability to synthesize. The latter wrote in the already quoted masterwork: "The emphasis on Cinquecento formulas had one very important effect. The vast number of new offices and apartments which went up harmonized to a remarkable extent with the existing structures, giving Italian cities large areas of pleasing unity. This happy amalgamation is particularly exemplified in Rome. Each vicissitude in

Rome's twenty-five centuries of growth and decay has not only obliterated some of the past, but it has also left a fresh deposit, united by the power of tradition and self-confidence, that has miraculously fused into a continuum. Rome is still capable of performing this remarkable feat. It is spirit working upon marble and travertine parallel with that signalized by Eleanor Clark in *Rome and a Villa*; a combination of tough realism in day-to-day matters with an uninhibited emotionalism in matters of art and architecture."[30]

Roman historian and architect, Paolo Portoghesi (1931–2023), in the preface to his book *L'eclettismo a Roma* (1968), tackled the problem of the relationship between architecture and the city. He began by summarizing in a few words the apparently marginal condition of research on architectural language compared to the European conceptual research at the end of the 19th century. He talked about Europe, but he had Rome in his collimator. At the beginning his opinion seemed negative: "Just as historicist philosophy was gaining ground in Europe, architecture would, in an apparent paradox, validate a "two-dimensional" conception of history as a repertoire of interchangeable experiences to be consumed in the likeness of goods. This past architecture, reducible to the present thanks to operations of mechanical resuscitation across procedures of contamination and copy, expresses the bourgeoisie's retreat into positions of conservation and the tendency to dogmatically formalize its behavior."[31]

But let us follow the reasoning to the end: "However, at least two aspects of the eclectic manner can justify a renewed critical interest today. First of all, its ability to carry out tasks of urban design through the deployment of typologies suitable for creating a homogeneous connective tissue at the scale of the city must be reassessed. The aesthetic value of which the individual cells that make up the urban fabric are usually devoid can instead be found very often in that collective work—the urban backdrop intended as the continuous envelope of the urban space."[32]

This is the main point, which Portoghesi developed by getting to the heart of the city's design process based on the linguistic range of eclecticism—in other words, from the ability to translate those historical repertoires into modern ones: "An aesthetic value [that of the urban backdrop] arising from the application of a combinatorial case study based on well-defined structural laws offered by historical repertoires, but above all by the translation process of those repertoires."[33] Finally, he addressed the present, taking as a positive example the experience of the eclectic city that he sees at work in modern Rome: "The return to a conception of urban organism as a *continuum* today proposes in totally new terms the same need to identify structures of reference that allow indirect control of the design."[34]

From the Rome of the late 19th century, therefore, comes a lesson for today: to identify rules, methodologies, and languages that permit indirect control of the design and allow a multiplicity of designers and companies to contribute, with their own individuality, to the realization of the urban continuum. Certainly, now as then, it will be a question of considering the typological innovations and continuities of the buildings. At the same time, it will be essential to give space to linguistic choices that are not ideologically obstructed, and to activate a design coordination of the higher order, i.e., one that establishes the overall design of each new *autonomous part*, thus of every new district of the city. This will imply a design coordination that defines not only the internal hierarchies of the neighborhood, and the alignments of its urban backdrop, but also its functional and social "character," in order to facilitate the creation of cultural conditions deemed desirable for persons and families. As a result, they shall become—hopefully—not only simple inhabitants of new neighborhoods, but also their animators, co-protagonists, interpreters, in brief, the real authors.

In Praise of the *Cinquecentismo* and the Grid

The issue of a superior design coordination, both typological and architectural, of the new neighborhoods was rarely raised in the papal period. To achieve the continuum of the urban scene, as Portoghesi would say, it was enough to adhere to a shared palette of architectural methods and the adoption of traditional building systems. Indeed, in addition to the few building regulations in force, the permanence of artisanal decoration and construction that acted according to historically tested models helped a lot. But the real innovation conceived at the end of the papal reign was certainly the one, already mentioned, led by De Mérode on the Esquiline ◖p. 62◗. To assure the architectural success of his real estate ventures, therefore also its commercial attractiveness, the old rules consisting of the rectangular lots, the strict alignments, and the homogeneous heights of the buildings were deemed to suffice. Indeed, they did. The architectural *Cinquecentismo*, based on the adherence to the architectural principles of Mannerism, proved to be perfectly capable of adapting the Roman "palatial" language—derived from the splendid facades of the princely palaces of the great papal centuries—to the new typologies of the bourgeois city. In

● Block corner on the Esquiline (architect: Gaetano Koch). In the background, Termini train station on Via Giolitti.

other words, that style that could be labeled "late papal" could easily and with little expense give meaning and dignity to a society that was quickly modernizing.

In reality, this process of transferring the "palatial" language to multi-family six-story buildings, typical of both clerical and new professional classes, was a legacy of the papal centuries. The social composition of the city had already started to change in the 18th century and the housing typologies had been transformed appropriately. Most *case a schiera*—the Roman single-family row house with the shop on the ground floor, a couple of domestic floors above the shop, and a small garden in the back—had been remodeled through internal transformations and elevations in order to respond to the new requests for housing by recently immigrated unskilled personnel, made up of simple servants of the Church and the aristocracy, workers in large administrations, and small professionals.[35] The entrepreneurs, without calling real architects but using the tradition of the trade, had merged properties, inserted common stairs, doubled the depth of the buildings and, in the end, had given new architectural form to the facades of the buildings. Medieval and Renaissance single-family row houses converted into multi-story apartment houses. To do so, it was logical to apply the severe geometry of the palatial forms of 16th-century Rome. The old windows, located at the left and right edges of the facades which respected the functions of a bygone complex family life, were closed. Others were opened within the same street walls. They were spaced according to the elementary principles of formal symmetry, mimicking, in a popular dimension, the breadth of the great masterpieces of the Renaissance and Baroque palaces.

The *Cinquecentismo* was not only a cultural choice, it also became the pragmatic language of *Roma Capitale* in transformation. Its clarity, its relative lack of plastic impulses and spatial inventions, seemed to ensure recognizable dignity even for the most modest speculative operation. It is interesting to recall how Rome, in the 18th century, grew demographically without practically leaving the footprint of the Renaissance city. The city literally grew on itself, floor by floor, both respecting the geometry of the existing lots, and profoundly manipulating the building volumes. When the season of the great building expansion of the new capital of Italy began, the regular grid was deemed sufficient to overcome the problem posed by the new dimension of construction operations, and the *Cinquecentismo* style was immediately adopted to interpret the new "mass" typologies in a simple and dignified way. The lots overlooking the squares or the most representative sections of the new districts were more expensive and therefore induced the investors to hire the most eminent architects and commission them to design outstanding buildings for high-class buyers. The more secluded lots, on the furthest edges of the district, were left to a more basic version of the *Cinquecentismo*. Overall, the grid and the wide latitude granted to the choices of every architect, and to the interests of every entrepreneur also ensured, over time, the inclusion of innovative experiments in language: the Neo-Roman, the *Quattrocentismo* (15th century), the Stile Liberty (Italian version of Art Nouveau), the first architecture of cast iron, and other philologically re-proposed historical language.[36]

The Architect of the Third Rome: Gaetano Koch

Despite the speculative turmoil that characterized the first decades of Roma Capitale, designers of great and sometimes of very high quality—genuine heirs to a 19th-century tradition worthy of respect—actively practiced in Rome during these first decades of growth. At that time, there was no real school of architecture in Italy, but mainly graduate engineers and professors of drawing and decoration who received their diploma from the Academies of Fine Arts—in Rome, the Academy of San Luca. Undoubtedly the most celebrated was Gaetano Koch (1849–1910), the son of a family of painters of Tyrolean origin and nephew of Josef Anton Koch (1768–1839). Having moved to Rome with the family, he received the title of engineer and architect in 1872, just as building fever was breaking out in Rome.[37] He had a great mastery of the historical styles, particularly of the reigning *Cinquecentismo*, and, above all, of lucid typological research, both innovative and rational. Or rather it was innovative because it was

● Gaetano Koch. Detail of the side facade of the Palazzo Koch (Via Mazzarino), 1886–1892. The building houses the central headquarters of the Banco d'Italia.

rational. These were Koch's basic qualities, to which he associated a sure ability to organize the building site. In his first years of practice in the technical office of the Società dell'Esquilino, he had the opportunity to design the edificio G between Via dell'Esquilino and Via Gioberti and the edificio B between Via Principe Amedeo, Via Manin, and Via Amendola, as well as the four buildings that made up the urban block defined by Via Principe Amedeo, Via Manin, Via Farini, and Via Gioberti.[38] Koch was instrumental in establishing the typological attributes of the new residential buildings on the Esquiline. He somehow established the model, designing a few buildings as "samples," at strategic points in the orthogonal checkerboard of the neighborhood. At the other extreme, Koch built his greater reputation as an architect through his research on the great palatial buildings, private and public, true modern rewrites of the historic palace: among many others, it is worth mentioning the Palazzo Piombino (1886–1895)—which is now the U.S. Embassy—and the headquarters of the Banco d'Italia ◖ top ◗ on Via Nazionale, known by Romans as Palazzo Koch (1888–1892). But testifying to its excellence were above all his great urban design interventions, the Piazza Vittorio Emanuele (1880–1889) at the heart of the new Esquiline neighborhood and even more so, the already mentioned Piazza dell'Esedra.

Paradoxically, a designer like Koch, so peremptory in his typological and linguistic choices, may be considered as a genuine forerunner of what Gustavo Giovannoni would later define as *ambientismo*. This compositional, both urban and architectural approach, "aimed to achieve harmony with the historical and morphological character of places, through the study and analysis of contexts, characterized by different regional identities."[39] Koch's ability to respond to the complex urban conditions of Rome were spectacularly revealed in his design for the Palazzo Lavaggi-Pacelli, ◖◖ p. 64 right ◗◗ located at 110 Corso Vittorio Emanuele, a couple of steps from Largo Argentina. The primary facade of the building, now the Hotel Tiziano, faces on to the Corso, while its rear front opens on to the narrow Via del Sudario. How did Koch react to those urban conditions? Along Corso Vittorio Emanuele—the first "modern" urban street opened within the historic fabric—he unhesitatingly adopted the most comprehensible strategy of 19th-century *Cinquecentismo*. For him, the new architecture was to heal, with respect for the history of the place and in dignified harmony with it, the deep wound that the wide street inflicted on the living body of the historic city.

The lot available for the project following the demolitions was small and irregular. On the new Corso frontage, Koch designed a five-bay building in perfect 16th-century palace form, but with the facade slightly convex to adapt to the bend in the new street alignment. Convex, in fact, like the Palazzo Massimo alle Colonne (1532–1536), built by Baldassarre Peruzzi (1481–1536) close by on the opposite side of the Corso. From a contemporary perspective, the 16th-century Palazzo Massimo alle Colonne ◖◖ p. 64 left ◗◗ can be read as an "infill," that is, the insertion of a new building into a very ancient *insula*—the Insula dei Massimi. Peruzzi was called upon to rebuild an earlier palace destroyed in 1527 during the Sack of Rome. In an irregular urban context, heavily constrained by pre-existences and history (such as the foundations of a Roman theater), he could not design an absolute typological model, that is, reproducible in every environmental condition. Yet, with his highly refined design skills, he nevertheless left us a methodological model of urban intervention that Gaetano Koch, with the pragmatism and measure that distinguished him, was able to apply precisely in the case of the Lavaggi palace.[40] On the opposite and narrow side, along the ancient street connecting Sant'Andrea della Valle to the Largo Argentina, i.e., Via del Sudario, Koch chose to add three bays and complete the vast monumental elevation of the centuries-old "factory" (an appropriate term because the construction of the palace never really stopped) at the heart of which stands the palace built to a design by Raphael: the Palazzo Caffarelli ◖ p. 66 top ◗, later to become Vidoni-Caffarelli ◖ p. 65 ◗. From its very foundation in 1524 to the 19th century onward, the building constantly absorbed adjacent properties. It eventually expanded to the whole *insula*, rising first one full floor and then two stories, but always using or reinterpreting the architectural module drawn by Raphael. By adding the three bays ◖ p. 66 bottom ◗, Koch guaranteed that the overall palatial elevation would become almost perfectly

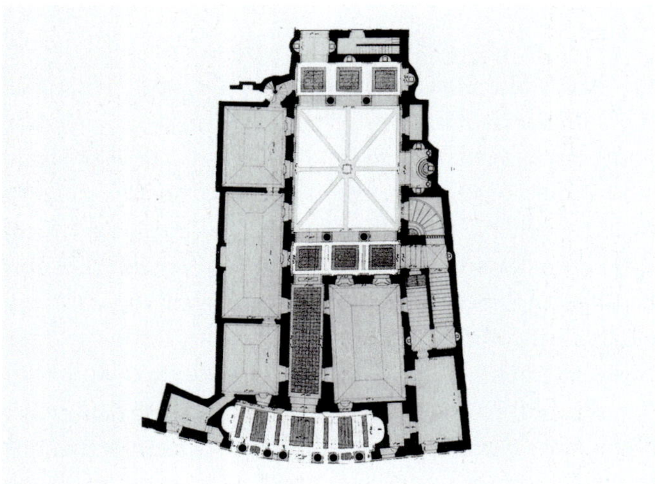

● Baldassarre Peruzzi. Palazzo Massimo alle Colonne, 1516–1536. Front on Corso Vittorio Emanuele II.

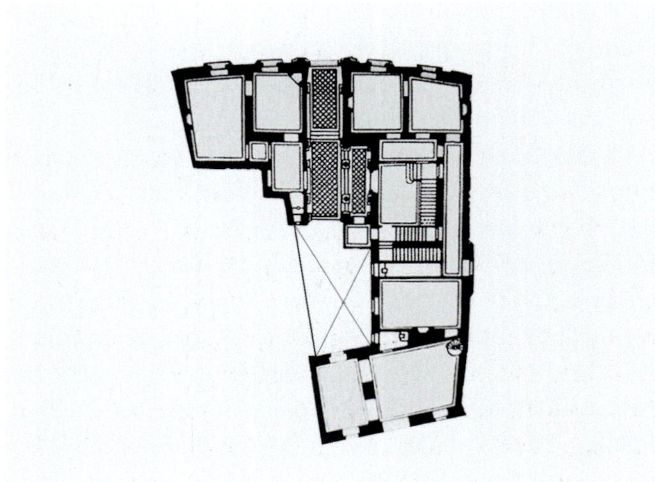

● Gaetano Koch. Palazzo Lavaggi-Pacelli, 1884. Front on Corso Vittorio Emanuele II.

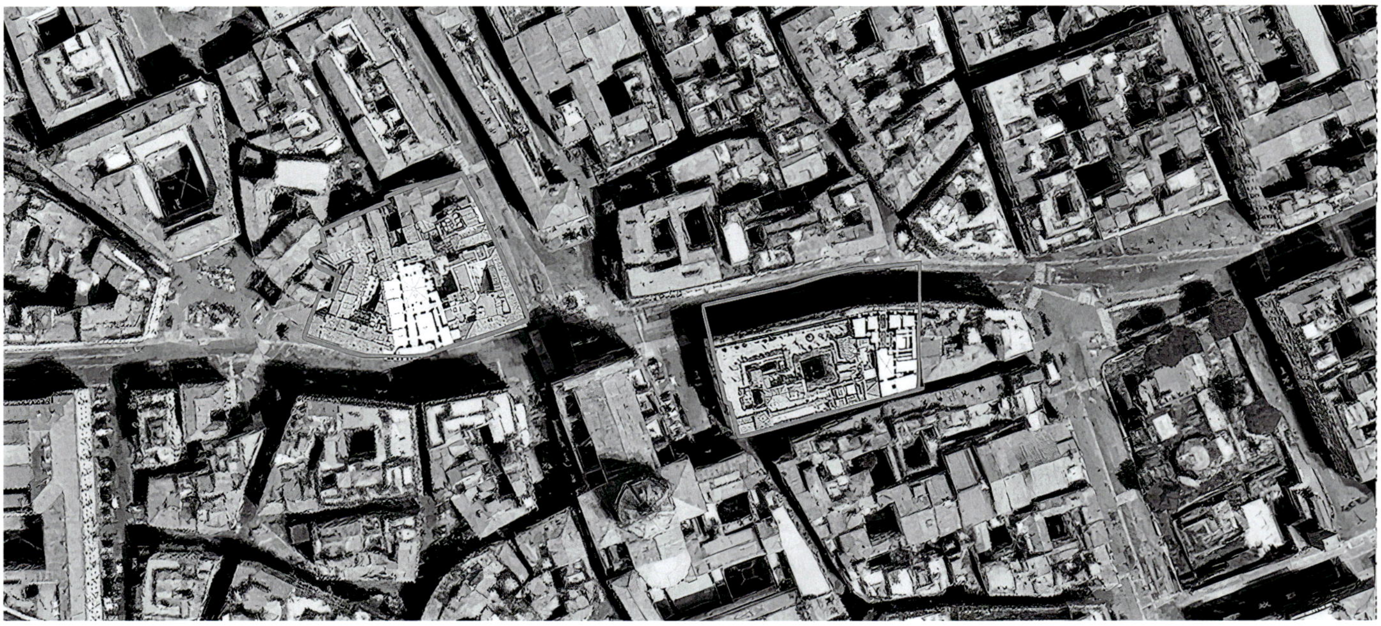

● Comparison of the urban situation of Palazzo Massimo alle Colonne and Palazzo Lavaggi.

symmetrical with respect to the axis of the first section established in Raphael's design. Koch was, in his own way, a revolutionary. In the Insula Caffarelli, he chose to demonstrate that the role of the architect, in such a daring infill, could only be that of the careful interpreter and the wise continuator of the great collective project that preceded him: masonry walls that belong to the buildings of which they are a part, certainly, but even more to the urban space they help define and make meaningful, giving it form and decorating it. In other words, Gaetano Koch chose to entrust self-expression not to the realization of an assertive work, but to the stripping away of all subjective impulses by making his own work consonant with the languages of the surroundings. *Ambientismo*, as Giovannoni would argue thirty years later.

● Gaetano Koch. Palazzo Vidoni-Caffarelli (back side of Palazzo Lavaggi). Front on Via del Sudario.

Carlo Maria Busiri Vici: Theatrical Performance

Carlo Maria Busiri Vici (1856–1925) was another important architect of that era. A contemporary of Gaetano Koch, he was one of the scions of a glorious family of Roman architects still operating today. Contrary to Koch, he was not a civil engineer, but a professor of architectural drawing.[41] Early in his career in the mid-1880s, he designed, and built a singular rental housing building—known as Palazzo Giorgioli ◖p. 67 top◗—at the intersection of Via Cavour, another major "modern" street of the Third Rome, and one of the oldest surviving streets from Antiquity, Via Panisperna. Triangular, the palazzo consists of two architectural fronts of equivalent length, converging on the intersection of the streets as the sides of a ship converge toward the prow. One facade faces Via Cavour, carved out of the ancient fabric and the natural morphology of the hilly ground. The other lines up along the wall of the Roman and medieval street. Busiri Vici was not lured by the temptation to design the building as a ship's prow. On the contrary, each facade is profoundly different, and devoted to interpreting the historical identity of the street of which it is a part.

On the facade facing the modern Via Cavour, he decided to express his spitefulness toward the flat *Cinquecentismo* rampant in the new neighborhoods of the capital. To be sure, those were the years during which the great architects of the moment, after a fifteen-year period of pure *Cinquecentismo*, set themselves the task of inventing the modern architectural language worthy of ancient Rome. The results were, among many, the competitions for the monument to Vittorio Emanuele II, the first king of Italy, and for the Palace of Justice.[42] Accordingly, Busiri Vici modeled the facade on Via Cavour with sculptural emphasis, that is, with giant and fluted Corinthian columns on a monumental ashlar base, deeply recessed walls, as well as large and deep cornices. At the intersection, two paired columns double the sculptural power of the facade and a projecting balcony suggests nonetheless the bow castle of a ship ploughing the ocean. The ocean of history, of course. Emphatic theatricality, but not without effect. Modernity, as seen by a young architect from a backward province, swells with new pride.

The other front was meant to look like a pre-existing element, belonging to another time, and a different urban history. With the same youthful assertiveness with which he responded to the demand for architectural modernity along the new urban artery, Busiri Vici intended to demonstrate his sensitivity to the ancient Via Panisperna and the wounds inflicted by recent demolitions. Stripped of his artist's robes, the young architect became an anonymous but very skilled designer of a wall that, though new, has the scruffy building identity of the more run-of-the-mill *Cinquecentismo*, that allowed the ancient Roman street to maintain its function as a primary urban space. Having decided to restore the more recent scene of the ancient street, he did not agree to rest the reckless

● Gaetano Koch. Palazzo Vidoni-Caffarelli. Front on Via del Sudario in a view by Francesco Ferrari in the 18th century, with the three-bay addition designed by Gaetano Koch in 1884 as the rear front of Palazzo Lavaggi.

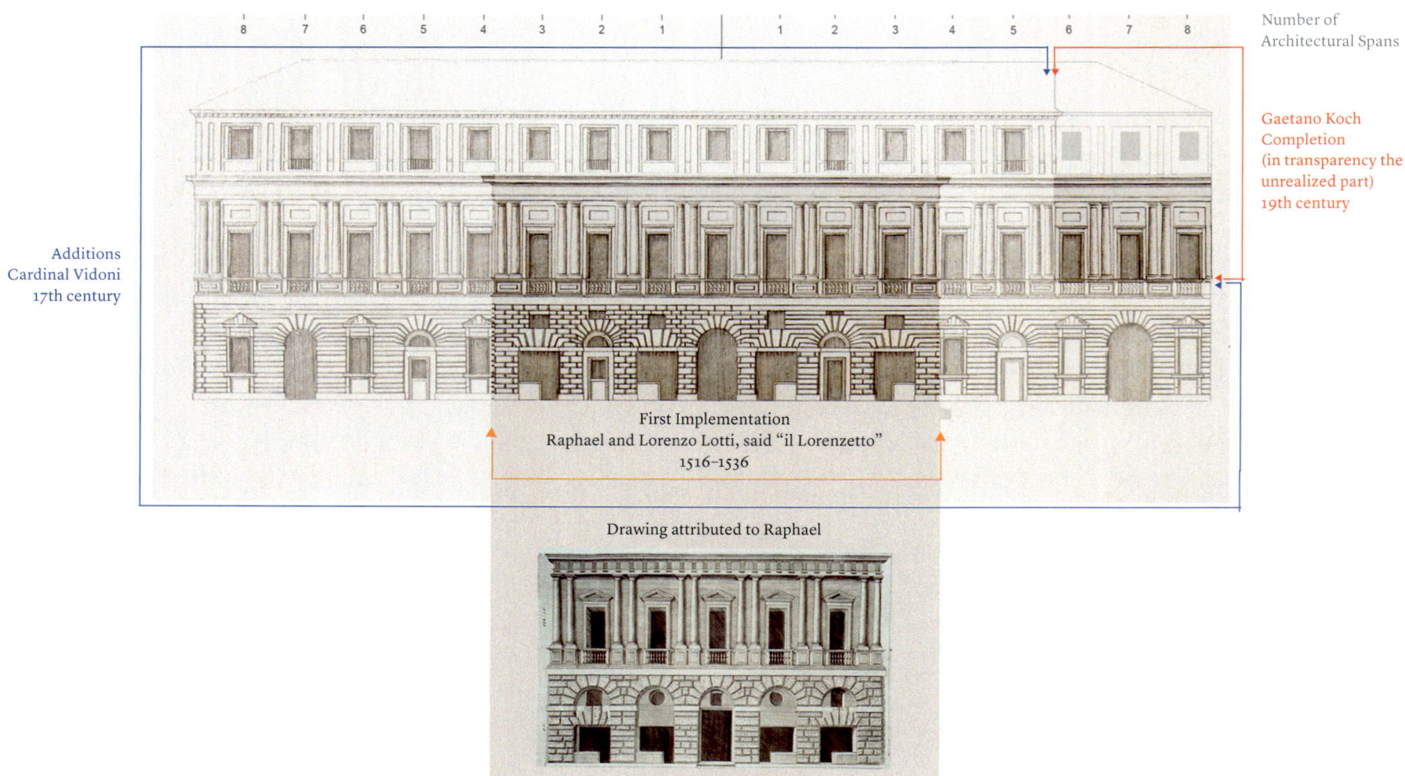

● Gaetano Koch. Palazzo Vidoni-Caffarelli. Historical sequence of the enlargement of the palazzo whose original first part was based on a design by Raphael. The part of the facade added by Gaetano Koch as a rear front of Palazzo Lavaggi is outlined in red.

Cinquecentista building wall on the typical ashlar basement that characterizes the base of almost all the buildings of that type. He set the wall-plastered upper floors of the building on a thickly woven wall of bare brickwork which exposes, above the doors of the entrance and the ground-floor stores, a short series of arches with their associated flatbeds. This was not a bold step toward representing the objective reality of construction, as most 19th-century buildings, including the Palazzo Giorgioli, were built with sack masonry and very few visible brickworks. It was, in fact, a matter of representing, as in a theater, the history of that ancient street. Busiri Vici set up a scene in which ancient Roman *tabernae paiane* ◖ bottom right ◗ lend their surviving masonry to medieval, Renaissance, and post-Renaissance supra-elevations, all merged and reorganized with the simplified lexicon of 19th-century *Cinquecentismo*. As a result, what appeared to be an incomprehensible submission to the architecture of *Cinquecentismo*—which Busiri Vici abhorred—turned out instead to be a virtuosic theatrical action in which the most modest clothes worn by the actors constitute the most valuable element of the staging.

Koch's and Busiri Vici's form of *ambientismo* was really the opposite of what Carducci would have wanted in the lines of his "Metrical Reasons:" environmentalism vs. the metrics of modernity. Rather than environmentalism, the poet wanted artists to jump backward into two thousand years of history and poetic forms—therefore also architectural—to go back to the rhythmic and powerfully archaic roots of our first civilization, and to proudly face the project of modern Rome. Did Carlo Busiri search for those roots and rhythms sought in the walls of the Giorgioli palace, albeit in different forms? To be sure, Carducci felt the need for a classical "primitivism," and thus would have disliked *ambientismo*. As the exploration of distant and "archaic civilizations" generated precisely in those turn-of-the-century years the primitivism of Gauguin and a few years later that of Picasso, so the deep and vast exploration of ancient Rome—which in those years of frenzied construction was enriched with the archaeological knowledge extracted from the soil opened by the new building sites—could really have generated a "classical," rhythmic, archaic, desecrating, and revolutionary primitivism.

Among the other designers who were the protagonists of the first phase of the construction of the Third Rome—let us mention Ettore Bernich (1850–1914), Giulio Magni (1859–1930), and Pio Piacentini (1846–1928)[43]—the figure of Camillo Pistrucci (1856–1927) must be distinguished. He was the author of, among many other buildings, the Palazzo Massimo alle Terme near Termini station (1883–1886). In 1887, his housing project of *case in linea economiche* ◖◖ p. 68 ◗◗ (social row houses) at Vicolo di San Francesco a Ripa in Trastevere, arose as a fascinating ensemble, architecturally modern, and typologically innovative as it offered the option of organizing the apartments with more or fewer bedrooms. It was an advanced modular building not only typologically, but also structurally, at a time when it was necessary to maintain, albeit with a certain freedom of choice, a historically established "masonry" architectural style with continuous facades, at most articulated by false pilasters. On the contrary, here at Vicolo San Francesco a Ripa, modularity was perfectly expressed in the facade by the rhythm of

● Carlo Maria Busiri Vici, Palazzo Giorgioli, 1883–1888, at the intersection of the new Via Cavour (left) and the ancient Via Panisperna (right) with a partial view of Santa Maria Maggiore.

● Carlo Maria Busiri Vici, Palazzo Giorgioli, 1883–1888. Detailed view of the lower floors designed in the manner of ancient Roman *tabernae paiane*.

● Camillo Pistrucci, social row houses in the Vicolo di San Francesco a Ripa (Trastevere), 1887 (graphic restitution). Despite the limits and constraints of the plot obtained within the existing urban fabric, the layout of the typical floor is rationally divided into two bands: one dedicated to a series of modular rooms, the second dedicated to the group of services (kitchen and toilet), and to a family living room, as well as to the condominium stairs.

● Camillo Pistrucci, social row houses in the Vicolo di San Francesco a Ripa (Trastevere), 1887. Regularly punctuated by the masonry pillars, the building is best appreciated in the tangential views from the narrow alley.

masonry pillars highlighted volumetrically by the deeply recessed balconies and walls to reveal the order of the internal distribution and, above all, the structural logic. It may be audacious to jump from 1887 to 1927, the year Mies van der Rohe completed his row house project at the Weissenhofsiedlung in Stuttgart: yet, both projects were built according to the same modular logic, and the same adherence of architectural expression to the logic of the structural system adopted—which for Mies was, of course, the steel-framed structure and for Pistrucci the masonry.

The Borders between the Two Modernities of Rome

Before enrolling in the Faculty of Architecture, I felt that the neighborhoods traced at the end of the 19th century were truly another Rome—a different city, yet one with a strong identity. A subtle repulsion kept us away, a sense of defense that concerned not only the Esquiline neighborhoods near the Termini train station or behind Via Nazionale, but even those closest like the rigid and monotonous checkerboard of Prati di Castello on the southern side of the plane trees of Viale delle Milizie and the poor facades of the military barracks. In those days, the Esquiline seemed even more alien, as it was no longer populated solely by old ministerial employees. A social change had taken place after 1945, it began to accommodate recent immigrants, Calabrians and even more Sicilians. On the Esquiline, the Sicilians traded in fabrics and established their own tailoring workshops, from which years later, the great men's suits of *La Dolce Vita* came out of.[44] An artisanal tailoring workshop in those times was an arcane world where a neurotic attention to detail reigned in a job that we did not understand, where apprentices were treated like frightened servants, male workers ironed with immense irons full of burning embers, and women hand-basted and machine-sewed, bent over and silent. A smell of hot wet cloth and the narrow Sicilian dialect reigned.

Those were the neighborhoods where I learned of the existence of "work," different from what was practiced in my family or those of my friends, where young people would strive to become lawyers, professors, doctors, or bank managers. In the neighborhoods of the Umbertine grids (Esquiline, Prati di Castello), first planned for the liberal professions, there were also many shopkeepers and tailors, milliners, wine warehouses, low-cost restaurants, jewelers, watchmakers, mechanics for rare cars, and porters—many of those which moved to the new districts from the city center and from Trastevere. The difference was not one of wealth or of money. Indeed, there were fabric shopkeepers, tailors, wine merchants, and restaurateurs far richer than our families. Some of those wealthy commercial entrepreneurs had their business in the Umbertine grids but had moved to live with their family in the brightest apartments of the Quartiere Mazzini. Their children attended the same schools as we did and it seemed that they had the same suspicious attitude toward those neighborhoods where the fruitful work of their fathers took place as we did.

I was certainly wrong. The problem was that the invisible antennae of adolescent sensibility captured the historical distance that had opened between the two phases of the modern city, so close, so different, and yet so much part of the same story.

The Fracture

The Umbertine phase ended with the "Great Crisis" and the collapse of the building fever that had started in 1888.[45] The city had grown well beyond the projections of the 1873 and 1883 masterplans. For a long time, the excise belt—beyond which to enter Rome it was necessary to pay a municipal tax for all consumer goods and materials of all kinds—had coincided with the circuit of the Aurelian walls. Therefore, in order not to pay the toll, many building activities were dispersed outside the circle of the ancient walls, therefore outside the territorial limit of the *Piano regolatore* of 1883. The prospect of being able to take advantage of the funds that were given by the central government to those who reclaimed the unsanitary lands of the *agro romano* (countryside to the east and south of Rome) made the situation increasingly absurd. Indeed, the land built in the areas not included in the *Piano regolatore* of 1883 tallied at the beginning of the mayorship of Ernesto Nathan (1845–1921) in 1907 to more than 900,000 square meters; on the other hand, the land to be built inside the city walls, thus contained within the masterplan, reached about 3,500,000 square meters, of which 2,800,000 remained to be built.

While the buildings envisioned by the *Piano regolatore* in Castro Pretorio, Esquilino, Mount Celio, and Prati di Castello advanced very slowly, the neighborhoods outside Porta Pia, Porta Pinciana, and Porta Maggiore, or the working-class district of San Lorenzo rose rapidly beyond the walls and outside the control of the masterplan.[46] From the architectural point of view, the same orthogonal grid design—adapted to the site conditions, the Umbertine architecture, and later, a moderate eclecticism—ensured urban dignity in those "spontaneous" districts, which resulted in often richer and more elegant environments than those within the walls. At the same time, the territorial dispersion weighed heavily and negatively on the public services. In particular, the public transport lines and network infrastructures had been stretched out of proportion.

However, these were not the causes of the dramatic crisis of the late 19th century. In the last twenty years of the 1800s, the new city had been built according to an extremely schematic vision of society, beyond the limit of abstraction. Only two building types had been planned for the new Rome, although each in every possible version: the *villino*, that is, an elegant residence surrounded by a garden, placed in a rarefied grid of low or very low density lots; and *case intensive d'affitto* (intensive apartment buildings for rent), destined for the middle class, employees, and officials, but also traders and employees of the most prestigious services. They consisted of four-story, five-story, sometimes even six-story buildings, with the entrance at street level, an internal courtyard, and *Cinquecentismo*-style plaster facades painted in all possible chromatic variations of ocher, from light brown to golden yellow, going all the way to Pompeian red. However, the construction of the city had created a much richer social palette of intermediate situations and, above all, of necessities not contemplated by the dry offer of two types of buildings.

The capital was a city without modern industrial production, yet it needed workers to build and manage the modern public services, especially those of transport, the industry of vehicle maintenance, the installation of tramway and railroad lines, the production of spare parts, and the distribution of electric and gas energy. Above all, the construction industry had attracted huge masses of precarious workers from neighboring regions, from Lazio, Abruzzo, and Molise. What was being built in the new Italian capital could not fully meet the demand. The classes that needed housing the most remained outside the offer: the middle class which did not consider itself subordinate, but which sought to assert its bourgeois dignity; and a working class that extended downward to include poor families. Many lots remained unbuilt; many buildings were left empty because they were neither sold nor rented.

On the other hand, there were numerous overcrowded apartments, sublet, and shared by more than one family. Many individuals and families who had been left homeless were massed in shapeless shack villages, many of them within the city limits and outside in the *agro romano*. Consequently, the real estate and financial crisis led to people in the construction industry being unemployed. Nearly 30,000 families were forcibly sent back to their towns of origin; the Socialist Party broke away from the bourgeois left, and the Roman political coalitions aligned themselves with national political tendencies: conservative, liberal, and socialist. The Black aristocracy, the papal one, had become *bigia* (gray) as the newspapers wrote. Nobody feared or hoped for the pope's return as ruler of the city. And no one gave the princes of the past the importance and the free hand they had in the first three decades of the Third Rome.

1
About the world exhibition planned for 1942 and now called EUR (Esposizione Universale Roma), see for instance Vieri Quilici, *EUR: una moderna città di fondazione* (Rome: De Luca Editori d'Arte, 2015). See the section on EUR in this volume, 109–115.

2
See for instance, Gianna Piantoni, *Roma 1911* (Roma: De Luca Editori, 1980).

3
The Esquiline is one of the seven hills of Rome. Along with the Macao district, and the areas adjacent to the newly opened Via Nazionale, it is one of the first neighborhoods to be built following the proclamation of Roma Capitale in 1870. The Macao district forms a regular grid immediately to the north of Termini Station. It is now part of the Rione Castro Pretorio.

4
See Allan Ceen, *Roma Nolliana* (Rome: Studium Urbis, 2003).

5
Stendhal, *Promenades dans Rome* (1829) (Paris: Le Divan, 1931). Translated from Italian version: Stendhal, *Passeggiate romane* (Milan: Feltrinelli, edizione digitale, 2019).

6
See for instance, Luciano Villani, *Le borgate del fascismo: Storia urbana, politica e sociale della periferia romana* (Milan: Ledizioni, 2014).

7
The Hunchback of the Quarticciolo was, with his gang, from 1943 to 1945, a hero of the Resistance against the German occupation. He was killed by the police during a criminal action after the Liberation.

8
See Salvatore Santuccio, *Modern Rome and the Cinematic Gaze* in this volume. See also, Jacopo Benci, "'An Extraordinary Proliferation of Layers': Pasolini's Rome(s)," in Dorigen Caldwell, ed., *Rome: Continuing Encounters between Past and Present* (London: Routledge, 2011), 151–186.

9
See Memmo Caporilli (ed.), *Roma. Vedute panoramiche da Monte Mario (1898–1914–1964–2008* (Rome: Marchesi, 2009).

10
See Gabriele D'Annunzio, *Le vergini delle rocce* (Milan: Treves, 1896). In English, *The Virgins of the Rocks*.

11
See Aldo Alessandro Mola, *Giosuè Carducci, scrittore, politico, massone* (Milan: Tascabili Bompiani, 2006). Carducci was the first Italian writer to receive the Nobel prize in 1906.

13
Giorgio Ciucci, *Giuseppe Terragni: opera completa* (Milan: Electa, 1996).

14
Carroll L. V. Meeks, *Italian Architecture, 1750–1914* (New Haven: Yale University Press, 1966), 353.

15
Paul Claudel, *Art poétique; Connaissance du temps. Traité de la Co-naissance au monde et de soi-même. Développement de l'Église* (Paris: Mercure de France, 1905).

16
There is a very large bibliography about Roma Capitale from 1870 to the 20th century. Among the important works are: Gianni Accasto, Vanna Fraticelli, and Renato Nicolini, *L'architettura di Roma capitale 1870–1970* (Rome: Golem, 1971); Flavia Pesci, Federica Pirani, and Gloria Raimondi, eds., *Roma: Nascita di una capitale* (Rome: Museo di Roma, Rome: De Luca Editori d'Arte, 2021; Giorgio Ciucci, ed., *Roma Capitale 1870–1911. Architettura e urbanistica. Uso e trasformazione della città storica* (Venice: Marsilio, 1984); Elisabetta Pallottino, "Building Roma Capitale: Knowing and Interpreting the City of the Past (1870–1925)," *Planning Perspectives*, vol. 37, no.3 (2022), 445–475; *Abitare Roma Capitale: Storia e visioni dal 1871 al prossimo future, AR: Rivista dell'Ordine degli architetti di Roma*, no. 123/124.

17
Claudio Pavone, "Alcuni aspetti dei primi mesi di governo italiano a Roma e nel Lazio," in *Archivio Storico Italiano*, vol. 115, no. 3 (1957), 303.

18
Ibidem

19
See Stefano Caviglia, *La rassegna mensile di Israel*, no. 6 (1986), 117.

20
Before the unification of Italy, the Swiss street vendors who came to Rome to clean the chimneys and sell chestnuts on the streets were called "buzzurri" (from the German "putzer," i. e. cleaner). The word generally meant a slovenly and coarse-mannered person.

21
See Susan M. Dixon, *Archaeology on Shifting Ground: Rodolfo Lanciani and Rome, 1871–1914* (Rome: L'Erma de Bretschneider, 2019). Rodolfo Lanciani was Professor of Roman topography at the Università di Roma from 1878 until 1927. He is mostly known for his *Forma Urbis Romae* (1893, 1901) and the *Storia degli scavi*, a regular summary of Roman excavations that started appearing in 1902. See also Rodolfo Lanciani digital archive: https://exhibits.stanford.edu/lanciani.

22
See Sigfried Giedion, "Sixtus V and the Planning of Modern Rome," in Sigfried Giedion, *Space, Time, and Architecture: The Growth of a New Tradition* (Cambridge, MA: Harvard University Press, 1941).

23
Marina Giannetto, "Roma italiana Roma capitale, Nazione e Unità nazionale nel dibattito parlamentare dal 'decennio di preparazione' ai provvedimenti per la capitale," in *Roma Capitale, 1870–1911: Architettura e urbanistica, uso e trasformazione della città storica* (Venice: Marsilio, 1984). See also Glauco Schetti, *Building the Third Rome: Italy, the Vatican, and the New District in Prati di Castello, 1870–1895* in *Modern Italy*, vol. 24, no.1, February 2019, 63–79.

24
On the masterplans of Rome, see Spiro Kostof, *The Third Rome, 1870–1950: Traffic and Glory* (Berkeley: University Art Museum, 1973).

25
Glauco Schetti, *Building the Third Rome*, op. cit.

26
On the Esquiline and its center Piazza Vittorio Emanuele, see Franco Girardi, Gianfranco Spagnesi, and Federico Gorio, *L'Esquilino e la Piazza Vittorio: una struttura urbana dell'Ottocento* (Rome: Editalia, 1974); Carmelo Severino, *Esquilino 1870–1911: e nel centro del progettato quartiere una vastissima piazza* (Rome: Gangemi, 2020).

27
See the section on Testaccio in this volume, 176–193.

28
See Vincenzo De Meo, Ilaria Giannetti, and Stefania Mornati, *La sistemazione del Tevere urbano. 50 anni di cantiere dalle carte del Genio Civile di Roma (1876–1926)* (Rome: Gangemi, 2022). See also the critical project of reconstruction, Paolo Portoghesi, Pierluigi Eroli, and Claudio D'Amato, *Dopo l'amnesia restitutio et renovatio* (Rome: Gangemi, 1986).

29
When, during Fascism, the destitute families of new immigrants and the poorest families among those expelled from the old quarters were "deported" from the city, they were placed in miserable *borgate*, built precisely along the circumference established by the system of forts, so that they would be beyond the limits of the present and future city and, above all, invisible from it.

30
Carroll Meeks, *Italian Architecture*, op. cit., 304. See Eleanor Clark, *Rome and a Villa* (Garden City: Doubleday, 1952).

31
Paolo Portoghesi, *L'eclettismo a Roma, 1870–1922* (Rome: De Luca Editori d'Arte, 1968), vii.

32
Ibidem.

33
Ibidem. In this text, Portoghesi used the concept of "cell" to suggest the typology of the housing fabric.

34
Ibidem.

35
For more on issues of Roman typology, see Jean-François Lejeune, "Roma non interrotta," in this volume, 6–15.

36
See Irene De Guttry, *Guida di Roma Moderna dal 1870 ad oggi* (Rome: De Luca Editori d'Arte, 2001).

37
On Koch's works, see Carmen Vincenza Manfredi, *L'opera di Gaetano Koch architetto di Roma capitale. Costruzione e trasformazione della città* (Rome: Quasar, 2015).

38
Franco Girardi, Gianfranco Spagnesi, and Federico Gorio, *L'Esquilino*, 45, 59–61.

39
Francesca Romana Stabile, "Shaping Early Twentieth-Century Rome: The AACAR and the Contributions of Filippo Galassi and Gustavo Giovannoni," *Planning Perspectives*, vol. 37, no.3 (2022), 557–558. See also Francesca Romana Stabile,"Gustavo Giovannoni e la cultura dell'*ambientismo*," *Bollettino del Centro di Studi per la Storia dell'Architettura*, I (2017), 135–146.

40
See for instance, Cristiano Tessari and Francesco Dal Co, *Baldassare Peruzzi: il Progetto dell'antico* (Milan: Electa, 1996).

41
Carlo Maria came out of the Academy and worked with his father Andrea (1818–1911), who is better remembered than he is today.

42
See Carroll Meeks, *Italian Architecture*, op. cit.

43
Ettore Bernich is best known for the elliptical Acquario romano (Esquiline, 1885, now seat of the Institute of Architects); Giulio Magni for his Villa Marignoli (1907); Pio Piacentini for the Palazzo delle Esposizioni on Via Nazionale (1883). See Paolo Portoghesi, *L'eclettismo a Roma*, op. cit.; Meeks, *Italian Architecture*, op. cit.

44
Federico Fellini, *La Dolce Vita*, 1960. See Salvatore Santuccio, *Modern Rome and the Cinematic Gaze*, in this volume, 342–355.

45
See for instance Fausto Pitigliani, "La questione delle abitazioni: La crisi edilizia nel 1888," *Rivista Internazionale di Scienze Sociali e Discipline Ausiliarie*, vol. 2, Fasc. 7/8 (July–August 1927), 209–223.

46
Paolo Di Martino, "'Rome Wasn't Built in a Day': Lobbies, Institutions, and Speculation in the 1880s Building Fever," *Urban History*, vol. 39, no. 3 (2012), 471–489.

1873

First *Piano regolatore* of Rome (masterplan), 1873. In red, the first versions of the new neighborhoods. The plan was never approved and was amended in 1883.

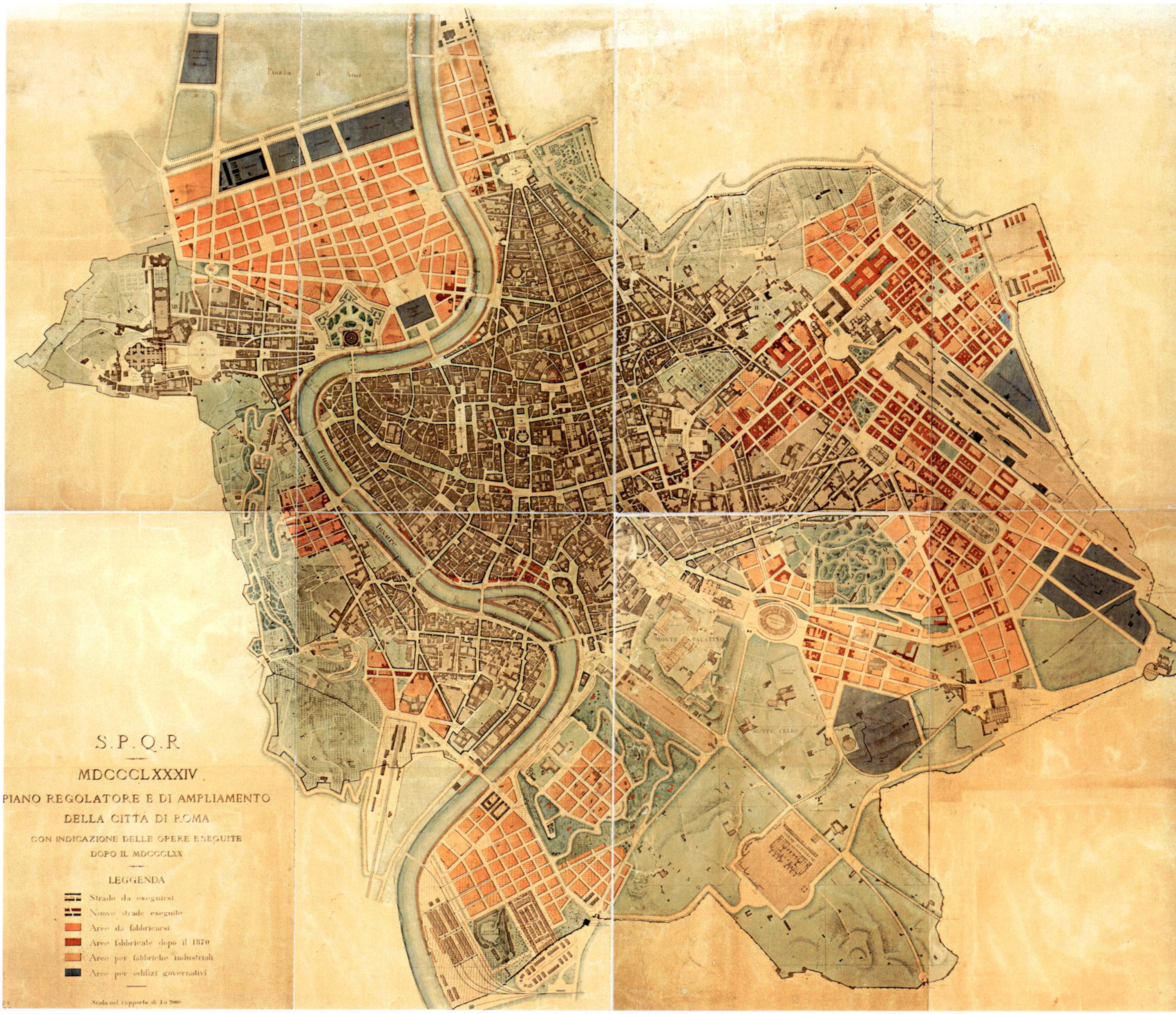

1883

Alessandro Viviani, first official *Piano regolatore* of Rome (masterplan), 1883.
In red, the final version of the new neighborhoods.

1909

Edmondo Sanjust di Teulada, second *Piano regolatore* of Rome (masterplan), 1909. The neighborhoods that originated from the masterplan of 1883 have now been constructed or in construction. In orange, the new neighborhoods for the second phase of urban expansion. Refer to the masterplan of 1931 to see the implemented designs.

1931

Marcello Piacentini, third *Piano regolatore* of Rome (masterplan), 1931. In red and black lines, proposed interventions of demolition and reconstruction within the *centro storico* (partially realized). In black, new public structures. In dark green, areas of residential development with *palazzine* as primary building type. In pink, areas of palazzine. In mustard green, areas for villini. In dark orange, intensive areas of apartments. The masterplan guided the development of the city until the early 1960s, yet with significant modifications in urban form and typological zones.

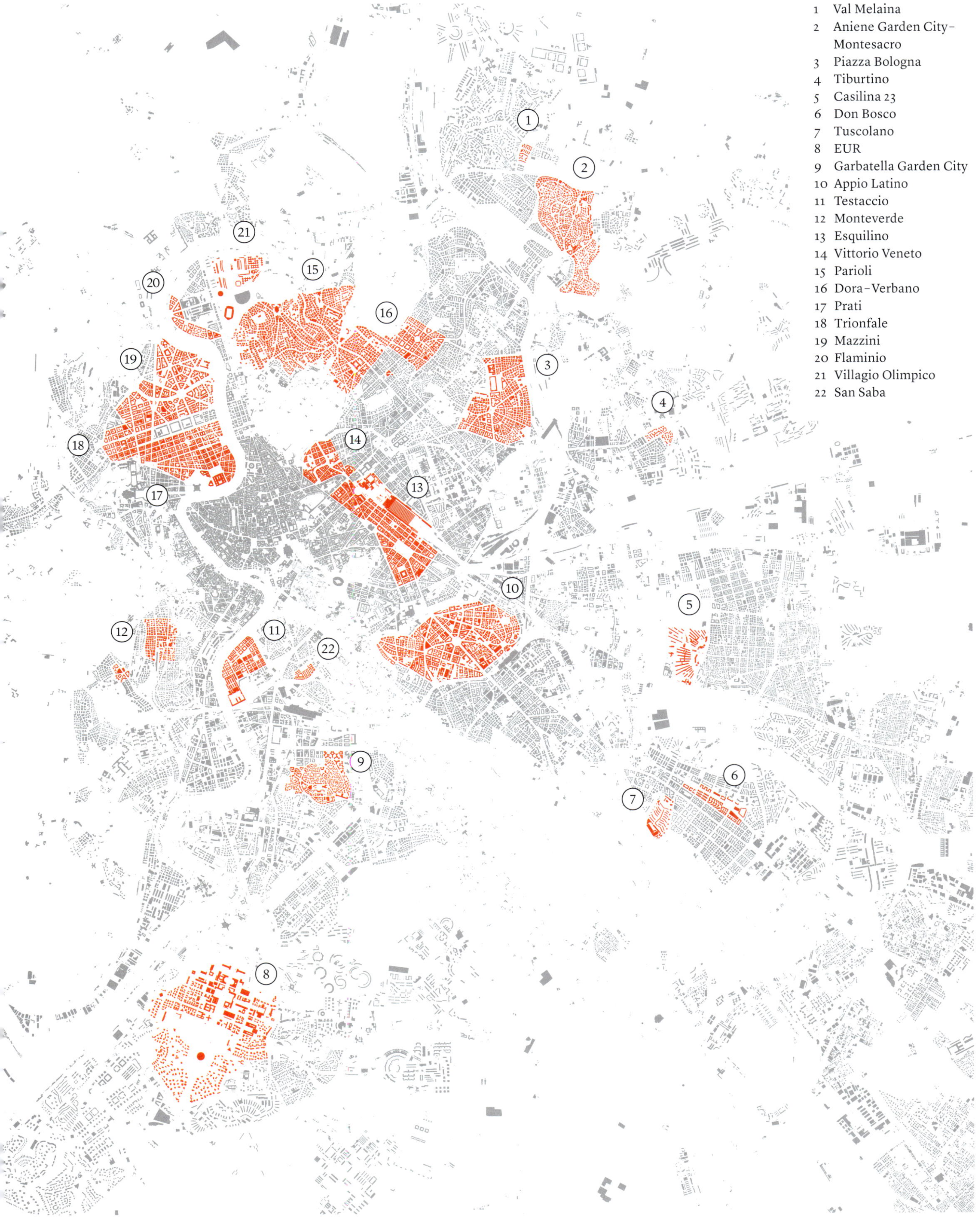

1 Val Melaina
2 Aniene Garden City–Montesacro
3 Piazza Bologna
4 Tiburtino
5 Casilina 23
6 Don Bosco
7 Tuscolano
8 EUR
9 Garbatella Garden City
10 Appio Latino
11 Testaccio
12 Monteverde
13 Esquilino
14 Vittorio Veneto
15 Parioli
16 Dora–Verbano
17 Prati
18 Trionfale
19 Mazzini
20 Flaminio
21 Villagio Olimpico
22 San Saba

● Pietro Aschieri, Palazzina De' Salvi at Piazza Trasimeno, 1930–1931.

II. From Reform to Fascism: 1907–1943

At the beginning of the 20th century, Rome was becoming a different city. The financial crisis of the 1890s was history. The City Hall was no longer in the hands of the old princes and their architects, but of modern men with much broader views. Ernesto Nathan (1848–1921), cosmopolitan, Jewish, born in London, of a fervently Mazzinian Italian mother, was elected Mayor in 1907, and held the position at the head of a diverse alliance of liberal and socialist parties for an exceptionally long period of six years.[1] Nathan brought to Rome his unique blend of Anglo-Saxon and Italian progressive culture. Under his leadership, the system of public schools was not only improved but greatly expanded, with the construction of new buildings, playgrounds and libraries, as well as the first experiment with Montessori methods. In doing so, he strengthened the development of laic education both in the city and in the countryside with the rural school action. Thanks to a popular referendum in 1909, he was able to municipalize the primary infrastructures of the city, from the transportation system to the production and distribution of electricity. Urbanistically as well, there was a different air in Rome. The critics of the first decades of growth had become impossible to ignore. In 1908, Nathan commissioned the Milanese engineer Edmondo Sanjust di Teulada (1858–1936) to elaborate a new *Piano regolatore*, which would move away from the "pirate" vision that had dominated the first decades of *Roma Capitale* to a programmed and organic conception of urban growth. The designer of the new masterplan was an established, non-Roman engineer with extensive international experience. In those years, the professional vision of the city's urbanism and architecture had started to evolve in tandem with important international trends. The architectural culture of the new protagonists—politicians, architects, and technicians—had been formed in the observation of European town planning at the turn of the two centuries. Accordingly, Sanjust's masterplan rejected the systematic use of the urban grid. Most of the new and planned districts—Mazzini/Piazza d'Armi, Flaminio, Parioli, Verbano/Lancellotti, Bologna, Appio—deployed either a star-shaped or half-circular pattern, or were articulated according to the Roman tradition of the trident. Interstitial areas were regularly filled with limited grid figures.[2]

This new phase in building the Third Rome brought forward the European debate between transformation, modernization, and conservation. The development of the modern city and its relationship—both physical and cultural—with the ancient historic cores marked the Italian cultural scene at the turn of the 20th century. Rome was its epicenter. Respect for the historical environment was the reference point for the work of numerous technical and artistic associations, which were engaged in the debate about urban transformations of the capital and other growing cities. Among these groups, the *Associazione Artistica fra i Cultori di Architettura* (AACAR, Artistic Association among the Culturists of Architecture), founded in 1890, assumed a central role in the study, protection, and design of the city.[3] As influential members of the AACAR, the figures of Filippo Galassi (1856–1920) and Gustavo Giovannoni (1873–1947) stand out.[4] They introduced the practice of *diradamento* or careful urban renewal and led intensive research into new urban and architectural models for urban expansion. Through their manifold cultural and institutional activities, their approach to artistic city building, greatly inspired by the writings of Camillo Sitte (1843–1903), shaped the principles of urban and architectural design in the 1910s and 1920s, leaving a long-lasting legacy on Italian urban design.[5]

Giovannoni's Environmentalism

Ambientismo (environmentalism or contextualism) was the name given by Gustavo Giovannoni to his declension of modernity—a declension that was more complex and perhaps more sensitive to the needs of society than the examples analyzed earlier in selected works by Gaetano Koch and Busiri Vici.[6] The development of the modern city and its relationship with the historic cores marked the Italian cultural debate of the first decades of the 20th century, providing a lively discussion on the urban and architectural form, the typologies and occupation of the lots, the compositional language, the construction techniques, and the harmonization with the architectural and artistic environment of the historic places. The vast and diversified urban heritage of the peninsula was conceived as a "collective monument" to be recognized, preserved, and interpreted. Critically, this heritage of "architectural life" extended to include the various expressions of minor architecture. As Giovannoni recalled: "A thousand cities and villages in Italy, such as Verona, Siena, San Gimignano, Pienza, Viterbo, Vitorchiano, Alberobello, Gradara, Ascoli Piceno … present admirable examples of this architectural life expressed in the minor works and in the groupings of buildings … They are part of the broader theme of irregularly picturesque groupings in which the value of the environment and of the spontaneously composed whole is the very essence of architecture."[7]

The discussion on *ambientismo* (contextualism)—primarily led in Rome by Giovannoni and the AACAR—emphasized the importance of historical urban patterns but also that of their necessary modernization. Giovannoni appreciated Haussmann's hygienic rehabilitation of the urban fabric but did not agree with the large and peremptory urban axes for which Paris was admired. The objective was thus to develop more complex strategies and intervene selectively in the urban fabric—by eliminating contributing but less important buildings while building new ones compatibly in order to create new or enlarged public spaces such as streets and squares. Giovannoni labeled this method *diradamento* (thinning out), with the objective of de-densifying the urban context for health and sanitary reasons.[8]

● Gustavo Giovannoni and AACAR, perspective view from Via dei Coronari, of the enlargement of Piazza San Salvatore in Lauro (by demolition of a medieval block), 1911.

Giovannoni's theory was seductively thought out and drawn in plan and perspective, yet extremely difficult to implement. His detailed proposal for the redevelopment of the Rinascimento district ◖p. 79◗ around Piazza Navona was ambitious but would have ultimately been destructive. Interestingly, the widening of Corso Rinascimento and the elimination of Piazza Madama—led under the direction of Arnaldo Foschini—as well as punctual demolitions along Via dei Coronari were realized in the 1930s under the Fascist regime and city government.[9]

Within this context of opening to the emerging international theory and practice of urban design and civic art, the writings and projects of Camillo Sitte (1843–1903), and perhaps more lastingly, that of Josef Stübben (1845–1936), had the greatest role in shaping the thinking of the most influential architects and urban planners of the first half of the 20th century.[10] Likewise, the British culture of planning, and more specifically that of Patrick Geddes, (1854–1932) and Ebenezer Howard's garden city from 1898–1902, were major stimuli for the Roman debate. As Geddes argued, the first task of the modern city planner was to attempt to enter the spirit of the city, its historical essence, and its continuous life. Likewise, John Ruskin had, well before him, asserted that the value of great historic cities did not depend on their palaces and monuments, but on the adornment of their minor dwellings. Hence, between the 1910s and the 1920s, the *ambientismo* became the core principle of the urban and architectural project, identifying and reinterpreting the artistic and environmental features typical of each city, while considering the instances of modern building. In one of his essays from 1913—"Vecchie città e edilizia nuova" (Old cities and new construction)—Giovannoni expounded for the first time on his conception of the figure of the city planner: on the one hand, a humanist and great organizer who must know how to treat the old city with the sensitive hand of the gardener who cautiously thins out the old "urban forest" that has become unlivable over time; on the other hand, a man or woman who is able to transfer to the new city the spatial principles of the old one, considered as the most natural response to the permanent needs of collective life.[11] This cultural orientation materialized in the first decades of the 20th century in various new Roman districts, often for the lower classes, such as San Saba, Aniene's garden city in Montesacro, Ostia Nuova, and the garden neighborhood of Garbatella. All these projects—studied in this volume in the *Quartieri* section—were planned following Giovannoni's theories, taking particular care of the relationship between *vecchie città* (old cities) and *edilizia nuova* (new construction) as in the title of his essay and later, Giovannoni's most important book.[12]

● Masterplan for the redevelopment of the Rinascimento district, 1935. At the center of the plan, Piazza Navona and the future Corso del Rinascimento.

The Cubist Portrait of Rome: Lanciani's *Forma Urbis Romae* (1893–1901)

Rodolfo Amedeo Lanciani (1845–1929) was an Italian archaeologist and a pioneering scholar of ancient Roman topography. Lanciani's major work was the production of a map of antique Rome, whose primary layer was the actualization of the ancient Severan marble plan, known as the *Forma Urbis Romae*.[13] The plan (203–211) originally measured 18.1 meters wide by 13 meters high and was carved into 150 marble slabs mounted on an interior wall of the Temple of Peace.[14] Lanciani's own version of the *Forma Urbis Romae* ◖p. 80◗ consists of a set of 46 detailed maps of ancient Rome, issued from 1893 to 1901, the fruit of almost two decades of archaeological work—"a season of frenetic excavation and publication activity, competing with the city's convulsive building expansion, following site by site, with very limited time and means, the appearance and almost immediate disappearance of entire neighborhoods of ancient Rome."[15] Each map measures 63.5 by 91.5 centimeters, drawn at a scale of 1:1000. Each one outlines antique features in black, early modern features (based on the Nolli map of 1748) in red, and modern features (as of 1893) in blue.[16]

Beyond its enormous scientific value, Lanciani's *Forma Urbis Romae* can be interpreted as a manifesto

● Rodolfo Lanciani, *Forma Urbis Romae*, plate XIV, 1901. In black, antique Rome (First Rome); in red, Nolli plan (Second Rome); in blue, interventions under Roma Capitale (Third Rome).

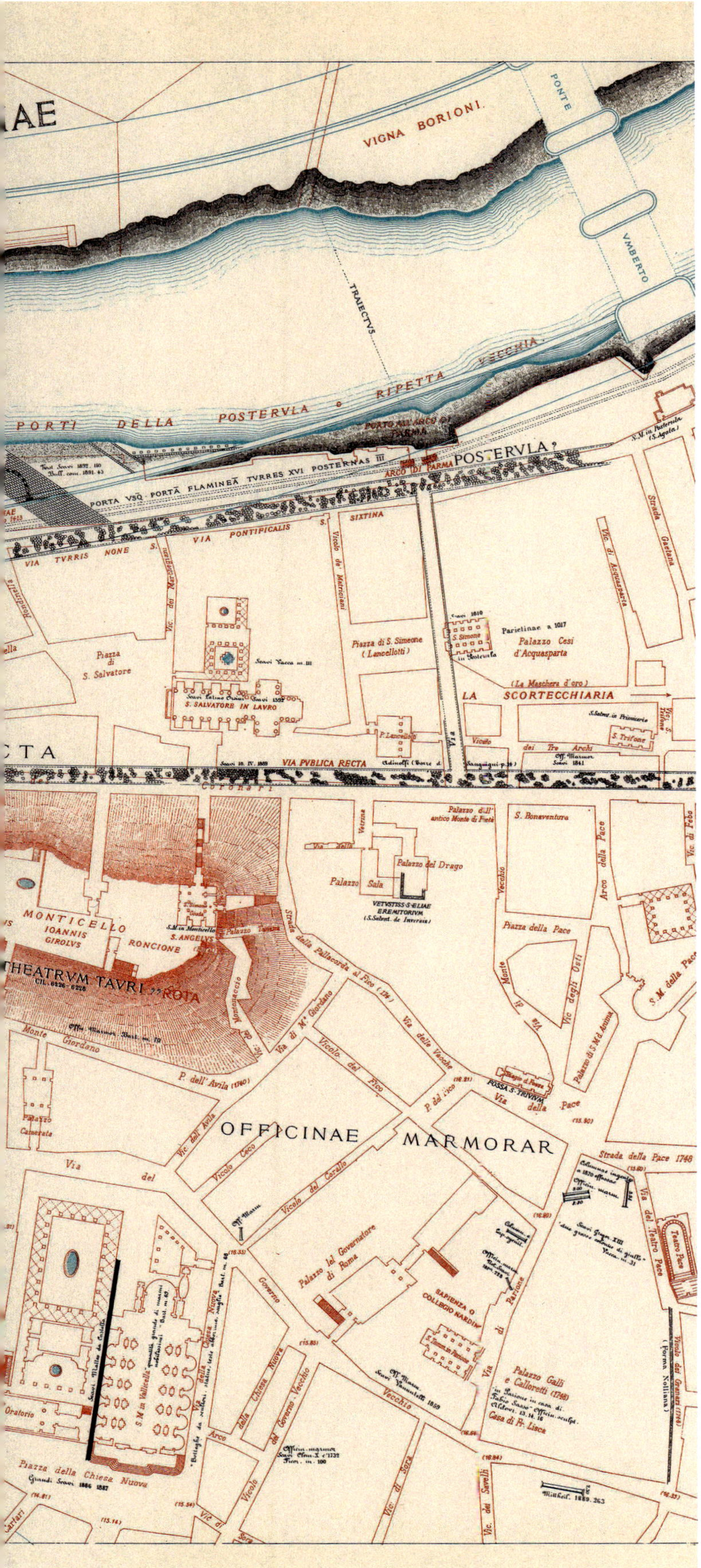

and a revolutionary work of art. Time is annulled and the reader and observer can see, compressed in the same place, superimposed realities that belong to different worlds, millennia apart. The close coexistence, in the two-dimensional reality of the map, of all the material excavated and drawn by Lanciani and his colleagues bring out a new idea of Rome. It reveals an unexpected city, which emphasizes the simplest and barest principles, quasi-primitive, which across each layer of history synthesize the genetic make-up of the urban form: measure and disproportion, order and ambiguity, banality, and unpredictability of the forms traced—no matter in what time—by the innumerable walls and urban spaces between them. They are all thrown on paper as if they were the fruit of a single and arcane design intuition: complex and simple, seemingly randomly composed of forms that are like each other and yet different, varying between broad dimensional and geometric boundaries that depend on materials and construction techniques, but also on the fundamental needs of the human soul: protection, power, representation, and madness.

As discussed earlier, Giosuè Carducci's reflections were undoubtedly prompted by the extraordinary and unrepeatable journey that he saw archaeologists make into the depths of Rome. He indirectly urged architects to extract from the most archaic rhythms of our culture the metrics for designing the new city worthily. Yet, architects were less self-confident than poets. They were academics, sometimes wise and knowledgeable, sometimes conceited. Sometimes, more rarely, they were accurate and even creative echoers of the ferments of novelty, both technological and linguistic, coming from more industrialized countries, and thus more modern. But often, the most thoughtful architects were cautious and sensitive environmentalists.

The International Exposition of 1911 and a New Neighborhood

Three years after the approval of Sanjust's *Piano regolatore*, the 1911 International Exhibition ◀◀ p. 82 ▶▶ opened in Rome to celebrate the 50th anniversary of the unification of Italy. The Exposition included two major urban sections separated by the Tiber, but united by a modern bridge, built in concrete by French engineer Hennebique (1842–1921) and inaugurated in 1911. The International Fine Arts exhibition was located on the hill east of Via Flaminia, in the territory then called Vigna Cartoni—also known as Valle Giulia in reference to Vignola's Villa Giulia, seat of the National Etruscan Museum since

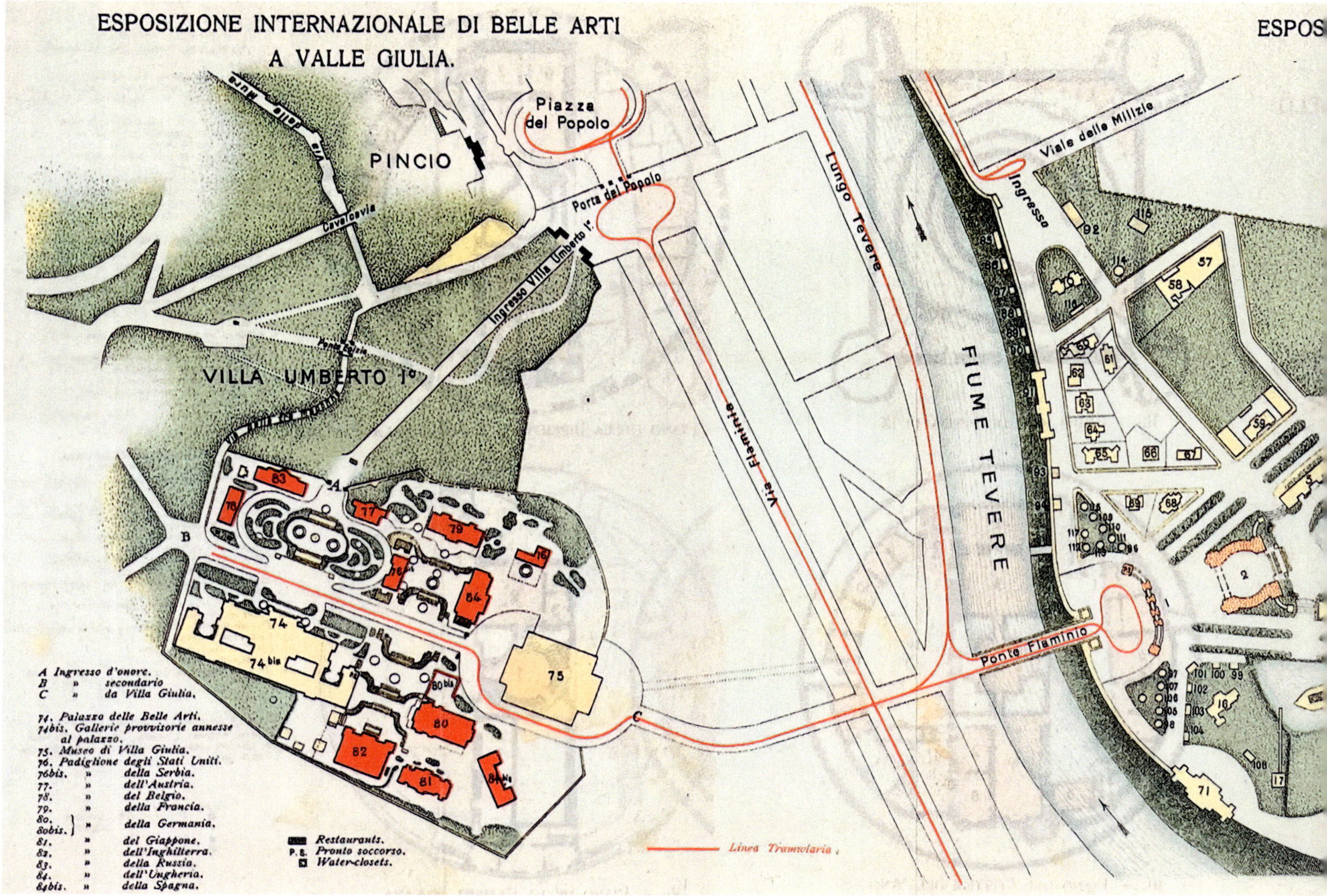

● Map of the 1911 International Exhibition, on both sides of the Tiber. *Esposizione internazionale delle Belle Arti* at Valle Giulia

● Tridimensional plan of the 1911 International Exhibition, with the two sectors on both sides of the Tiber. *Esposizione regionale e etnografica* at Piazza d'Armi (future site of the Quartiere Mazzini).

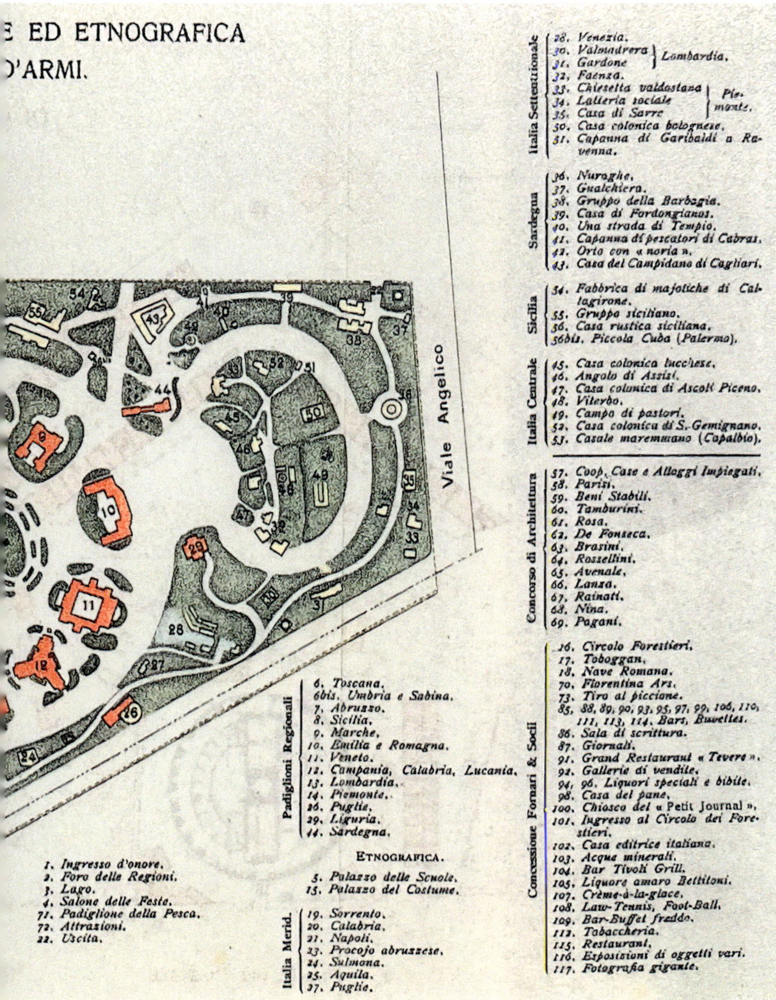

1889—and until then destined for agricultural use. In view of the event, a team of architects led by Cesare Bazzani (1873–1939) drastically transformed the whole area, giving it a public function and creating the new road network. Bazzani built the Palazzo delle Belle Arti (1911–1913), now the seat of the Galleria Nazionale di Arte Moderna (GNAM) ◖◖p. 84◗◗, at the center of a series of national pavilions.[17] The Regional and Ethnographic Exhibition was set up on the other side of the river, in the unbuilt area of Piazza d'Armi, the future Mazzini district extending north of the line of barracks built in Prati on Viale delle Milizie.[18] Its exhibition plan and the architecture of the buildings was the work of Marcello Piacentini (1881–1960) who acted as Artistic Director, with Sanjust among the consultants. As a matter of fact, Piacentini based the structure of the exposition plan on two important avenues—the future Viale Mazzini and Via Prestinari—forming a bi-dent converging on the new bridge at Piazza Monte Grappa, a solution envisioned by Sanjust himself as a variant of the design of the new district included in the *Piano regolatore* of 1909. In addition to the two sectors, there was also an archaeological exhibition at the Baths of Diocletian, an exhibition at Castel Sant'Angelo dealing with topography, numismatics, epigraphy, medieval art, and other objects; as well as Duilio Cambellotti's ground-breaking exhibition on the *agro romano* (countryside to the east and south of Rome).[19]

Following closure, the Fine Arts Exposition at Valle Giulia left a strong and permanent mark on the urban landscape between Villa Borghese and the Tiber. In the following decades, the installation of national academies such as that of Belgium and Japan, Edmund Lutyens' British Academy, and the first School of Architecture created an international cultural center of great prominence. Most other buildings made for the expositions were eventually demolished on both sides.[20] The planning of Piazza d'Armi on the other side of the Tiber immediately became an issue of utmost importance. The whole area was under municipal ownership, which allowed Mayor Nathan and the city council to envision the future district as a radical new opportunity for the design and extension of the Third Rome.[21] In 1908, Guglielmo Calderini, the architect of the Palazzo di Giustizia a Piazza Cavour, had designed a huge housing project ◖p. 85 bottom left◗—30,000, units half of which were reserved for social housing—at the center of the neighborhood, a utopian radial scheme oriented toward the river.[22]

Giovannoni had not been involved in the conception of the *Piano regolatore* of 1909 and was absolutely opposed to the rigid formalism with which the Piazza d'Armi and other new quarters of the city were laid out in the form of a star or a trident. In 1911, he invited Josef Stübben (1845–1936) on the occasion of the International Congress of Architects to be held that year in Rome. The German planner and urban designer was expressly asked to pass judgment on the 1909 masterplan with the evident intention of torpedoing its cultural credibility.[23] Sanjust's reaction was blunt. In response to Stübben's own project, brilliantly inspired by Camillo Sitte's theory, he criticized the technical superficiality of the proposals presented by the AACAR in contrast to his own proposals. He also rejected the idea put forward by Stübben to organize an international competition. In the meantime, despite the controversy, the implementation of the district in the form designed by Sanjust ◖p. 85 bottom right◗ had begun. In 1913, however, Ernesto Nathan's progressive and anti-clerical administration was replaced by a moderate and clerical government. Giovannoni gained more prominence and immediately resumed work on the Piazza d'Armi district to bend it to a more modern and European design concept ◖p. 85 top◗. Piacentini drew up two proposals, not really of high quality, with which he intended

● Cesare Bazzani, facade of the Galleria Nazionale d'Arte Moderna from Villa Borghese and detailed view of the entrance portico, 1911–1913.

to demonstrate that he had also moved from a purely Roman architectural vision to a more international one. Giovannoni's and Piacentini's proposals were by then obliged to consider what had already been built: first and foremost, the bident entrance to the neighborhood from Hennebique's bridge connected to it; lastly, the layout of the central square envisioned by Sanjust, now known as Piazza Mazzini. Summarily, Giovannoni's proposal related to the French-style subdivision with an abundance of irregular blocks. Piacentini's articulated a system of urban greenery and large porticoed squares according to the indications that emerged from the proposals for Vienna by Sitte. Yet, the goal was achieved: in 1915 Giovannoni and Piacentini were both commissioned to draw up the final design of the neighborhood, an improved variant of Sanjust's design which, with few changes, guided the construction of the neighborhood.

Pragmatic Experimentation: Urban Homogeneity and Architectural Variety

The investigation concerning the design ended in 1915, apart from minor adaptations. But what continued instead was the experimentation with a new method of planning and implementing the construction of a new neighborhood in a modern European city as Rome aspired to. The soil of Piazza d'Armi was public property, but it was marshy and subject to frequent flooding. For this reason, it had been left without regret to military uses. To rehabilitate it as developable urban land, it was necessary to extend the high Tiber embankments that were almost completed in the historic section of Rome. This entailed both the raising of all the new streets to an elevation compatible with that of the new embankment and the construction of a general sewer system. To make the different blocks marketable, the city administration took in charge all the infrastructure, including the raising of the streets, the riverbanks, and the sewer network. This progressive policy was implemented for the first time in Rome, and the expense turned to be substantial. To attract private capital in the construction of the high- and medium-quality housing blocks, the lots were put up for sale already equipped with the necessary infrastructure, but at congruous prices, that is, not speculative. The sales prices were calculated in considering only the sums spent by the municipality itself to buy the area, to design it, to infrastructure it, and to manage its construction. It was a global success and, in general, the architectural directions given by Giovannoni and Piacentini to the architects of the private- and public-housing projects promoted in the plan were respected.

As a result, and in addition to the generosity of its urban plan, the Mazzini district owes its spatial quality to the architectural value of most buildings—more specifically, not because they adhered to a single lexical or linguistic model, but because, by respecting the planned alignments and the volumetric regularity required by the masterplan, the architects were able to experiment with typological models and architectural languages that were innovative for the time. To be sure, the urban and

● Gustavo Giovannoni and AACAR, masterplan for the Piazza d'Armi (left of the river) and Flaminio district (right of the river), 1914–1915. In the final Piazza d'Armi plan, the triangular parks were built with apartment blocks; the plan for the Flaminio district (right side of the plan) was built, but substantially modified with the linear trident starting at the landing of the bridge.

● Guglielmo Calderini, bird's-eye view of the masterplan for Piazza d'Armi, 1908.

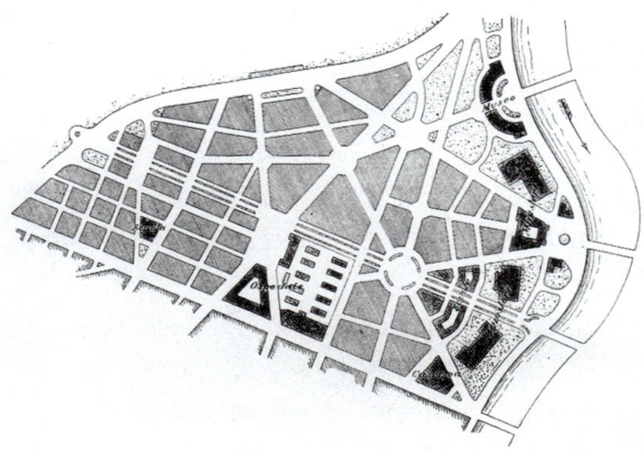

● Sanjust di Teulada, variant of the 1909 *Piano regolatore* for the design of the future Piazza d'Armi district.

the architectural reinforced each other harmoniously because this was an era in which all involved actors—architects, urban planners, administrators, and politicians—shared the idea that the city should consist of a series of external spaces, streets, and squares, conceived as the internal spaces of a common house: the city itself. In other words, urban homogeneity and architectural variety complemented each other because at the beginning of the 20th century, Rome was seen as an airy but compact system of spaces defined by a continuity of dignified building walls or buildings set not too far apart in order not to undermine the unified perception of the rooms of the city—i.e., the streets and the squares.

Finally, the Quartiere Mazzini was also an experiment in urban management. A totally public area whose land was divided into lots according to a unified design was ceded, lot by lot, to private individuals who carried out the provisions of the general design. For this reason, the most beautiful lots, those facing the Tiber, were dedicated to upper-class housing, mostly detached urban villas with gardens. The area immediately behind, still of high value, was assigned to apartment houses for civil servants and clerks; and finally, toward the area farthest from the river, along Via Trionfale at the foot of Monte Mario, the lots were assigned to highly successful interventions for low-cost social housing.[24]

The Birth of the Popular Housing Institute of Rome (ICP)

In 1903, Luigi Luzzatti (1841–1927), a remarkable politician born in Venice to a Jewish family, drafted and convinced the government to sign the law establishing the Istituto per le Case Popolari (ICP).[25] Soon, every major municipality established an institute for popular housing, whose aim was to undertake and/or intensify public intervention in the construction of the modern city. The Roman Institute was created without delay in 1903. Chaired by Luzzatti himself with the support of Prince Prospero Colonna, Mayor at the time, it intimated that the capital of the new state would be considered the field where the campaign for a new model of a humanitarian city was to be won or lost—a modern city projected toward a future of greater social civilization, dignified also by the typological, aesthetic, and constructive quality of the new, large working-class neighborhoods. At the same time, the law spurred the establishment of popular housing cooperatives such as the Cooperative Luzzatti for which, between 1903 and 1920, the architect Vittorio Mascazoni built many units on the Esquiline.

Vigorously supported by Luzzatti, another public housing institute was established in October 1908 to provide housing to the public employees of the State in Rome, the Istituto Cooperativo per le Case degli Impiegati dello Stato in Roma (IRCIS). Until its fusion in 1933 with the INCIS (Istituto Nazionale per le case degli impiegati statali), itself created in 1924, the IRCIS built thousands of modest housing units primarily reserved for employees of lower means. The first realization was both ambitious and huge, in fact the largest coordinated public-housing project of modern Rome. Originally planned by engineer Enrico Bovio but designed and built by engineer Carlo Mongini, a four-block complex of about 900 apartments rose from 1911 along Via Salaria and Via Liegi.[26] The programmatic description by engineer Bovio set the tone for the new generation of apartment buildings in the new Rome: "Neither vast nor squalid phalanstery-style buildings, but buildings of severe architectural beauty, with rotunda and verandas, balconies and loggias.... We absolutely reject all these flat houses, cut with squares, all these buildings that have the appearance of prisons and convents."[27] Accordingly, the architecture of the five-story housing blocks was sober and simple, made up of a repetitive grid of windows extending along all facades, with the projection of rare balconies ◖p. 306◗. It is the setbacks of the volumes and the varied open perspectives from the street to the generous courtyards that created the richness and complexity of the ensemble without any recourse to ornamentation.

The first technical director of the ICP in Rome was Innocenzo Costantini (1880–1962), an engineer born in Osimo, a very old town in the Marche region that had been part of the Church State since Byzantine times. He was the son of a master builder, Costantino Costantini (1854–1937) who, as a self-taught man, had become an architect of rare skill. At the same time another remarkable young man, born in a nearby town in the Marche region, Jesi, entered the ICP in Rome: Quadrio Pirani (1878–1970). He was also the son of a master builder and graduated in engineering in Rome along with Innocenzo Costantini in 1904. A modern man, he was passionate about architectural restoration, as well as photography and cinema.[28] Those two protagonists made it their task to design and build social housing as a progressive practice that bore the fruits of innovative and constant research on the city, its form, typology, construction, and architectural language. Innocenzo Costantini dedicated more than 40 years of his life to the task, brilliantly managing the ICP from 1904 to 1946 through three political regimes and two world wars. For twenty years he worked with Alberto Calza Bini (1881–1957), who took on, among his many positions, that of President of the ICP in Rome.[29] From 1923 to 1943, he was able to restore its finances and confirm its fundamental role in the construction of the modern city. Until his retirement from the ICP, of which he had become General Director in 1917, Costantini was a sure guide for the architects who were engaged in the institute over such a long time. Quadrio Pirani, on the other hand, was essentially the brilliant architect who looked with pragmatic modern sensibility at the reforming concepts coming from Europe and from England above all.[30]

Quadrio Pirani and the New Modernity

Four years after the birth of the ICP, construction started on the workers' district of San Saba ◖bottom◗, on the hill called Piccolo Aventino. The district, which was not included in the masterplan of 1883, established a new and very high civil standard for workers' homes. Above all, it introduced a model of expansion of the city by means of an organic project no longer entrusted solely to the peremptory force of the orthogonal grid. It was a neighborhood that had an author. The engineer and architect, Quadrio Pirani, created the social space of a popular community, directly and linguistically inspired by the Anglo-Saxon garden city and its reform advocates for social architecture. The houses of the first phase ◖p. 235◗ had no more than two floors, each for one or two families, and a small front or back garden. Pirani rejected the Sangallo-inspired *Cinquecentismo* but instead implemented a vernacular architectural style which underlined with very few decorative elements—brick pilasters and band-courses—the structural elements of the building. Pirani's experiment did not stop at the first phase of construction. The foundations turned out to be more expensive and, as a result, he had to depart from the strict reference to English social architecture and abandon the extensive model in favor of a denser use of the land. Alongside the first terraced houses, Pirani designed an articulated set of three- or four-story buildings organized around internal courtyards, open and well ventilated. Likewise, the architectural language took another step forward.[31]

Perhaps responding to Giosuè Carducci's exhortation, Pirani humanized the language of low-cost intensive

● Aerial view of the San Saba district as planned by the ICP (foreground), late 1920s. In the upper left, the Testaccio district.

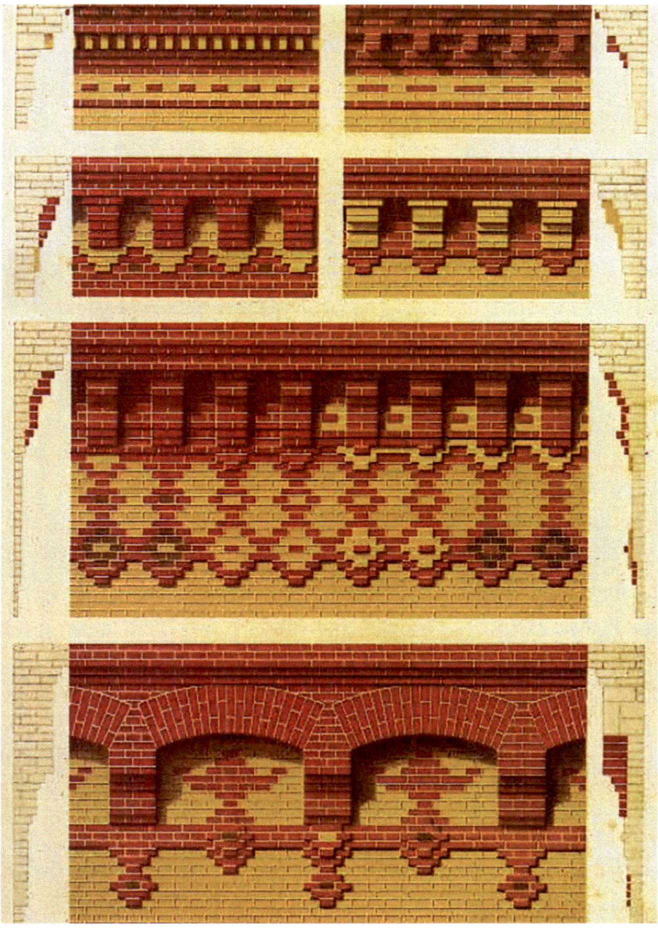

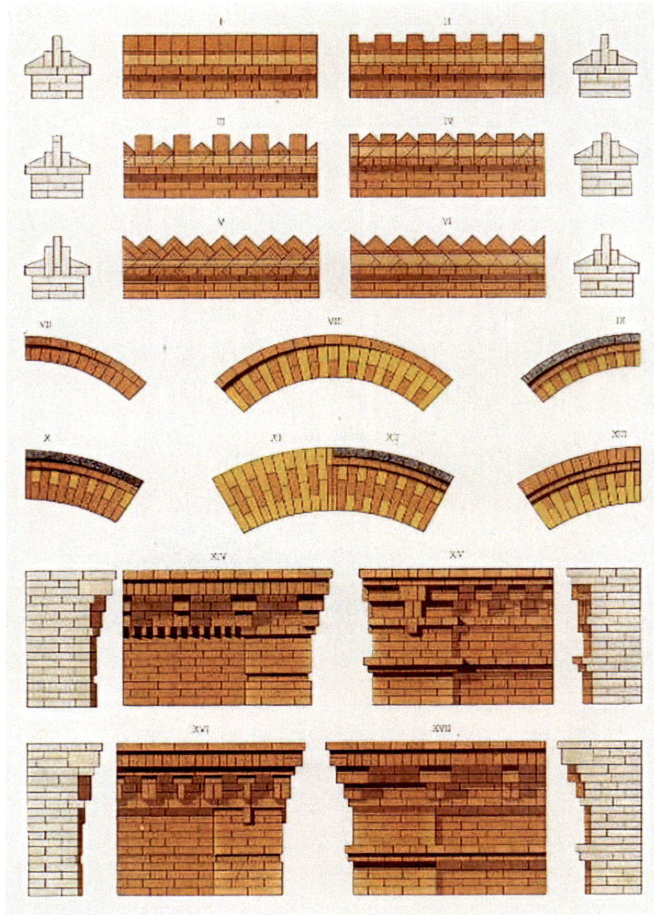

● Traditional details of brick construction as a source of inspiration for Quadrio Pirani (Misuraca & Boldi, 1900).

construction. He left the Renaissance manner behind and challenged the "ancient" as a "modern" man of the early Middle Ages. He adapted the models dictated by classical architecture, replacing marble and stone with bricks laid out in simple chiaroscuro games to mimic, in an almost impressionistic way, all the parts of a canonical order: from the base to the capital of flat pilasters, the large cornices, and the solemn modeling of the architraves. In his rental apartment houses of San Saba, but also those of Testaccio and other districts such as Trionfale where he was actively involved for the ICP, Palladio's and Michelangelo's giant order appears along with the cornices and articulated sill-courses of the windows. The whole composition is like a light and colorful game—the red of the bricks, the beige of the walls—made up of shadows and lights, in which each detail is a naive and refined invention, often surprising in its pictorial ingenuity.

In the 1920s, Pirani became the architect of choice for the large-scale interventions of the IRCIS around Piazza Mazzini (1920–1923, 256 units in two blocks) ◖p. 89 left◗ and, even more significantly, in the new district built around Piazza Verbano ◖p. 89 right◗ on the grounds of the former Villa Lancellotti (1920–1925, 570 units). After having successfully worked on the open-plan type in San Saba and Testaccio, Pirani oriented his IRCIS work toward a block typology in which the powerful distribution of the masses was lightened by the staggering of the buildings in plan and elevation and ennobled by the Otto Wagner-inspired devices, such as the organically frescoed bands under the deep overhang of the cornices. In Pirani's own words, "in relation to aesthetics, we deploy planimetric, altimetric and dissymmetry movement, whose requirements, integrated by the greenery of the gardens, balconies and connecting catwalks, will contribute greatly to creating a harmonious and pleasant decoration. The decorative elements of the facades will be, in part, sought in the elements of the construction themselves and therefore in the use of brick, natural stone, or in the cement conglomerates, integrated with terracotta and notes of color."[32]

With the procedural and linguistic innovations implemented for the ICP and the IRCIS, Quadrio Pirani demonstrated the possibility of affirming a new scale of architectural design—that of large and coordinated building complexes with commercial uses on the ground floor and internal courtyards—and the possibility of entering

● Quadrio Pirani, interior garden of the IRCIS complex in the Mazzini district (Via Nicola Ricciotti), 1920.

● Quadrio Pirani, detail of IRCIS apartments at Via Tagliamento (Quartiere Verbano), 1920.

the fascinating field of innovative linguistic research extended to entire parts of the city. Overall, his work evidenced the definitive detachment of Roman architecture from "passive" historicism and its codified stylistic terms. His research epitomized a kind of measured yet creative "Roman liberty," bathed in Michelangelo and many other memories. What interested Pirani above all was the combined research into the healthy and aesthetic dignity of urban living extended to the less affluent classes. In 1930, at only 52 years of age, and at the height of his maturity as the architect of modern and humanitarian Rome, he retired from the profession. As if, having paved the way for the full modernity of Roman architecture, he decided not to cross that threshold. His mission was accomplished. The time was ripe for new protagonists.

Sabbatini and Humanitarian Experimentation

The Marche dynasty expended further. Innocenzo Constantini's sister, who had married a Pasquale Sabbatini, also from Osimo, had a son named Innocenzo Sabbatini (1891–1983). His uncle, Costantino Costantini, introduced him to architecture, to site planning, and to the new languages coming from other parts of Europe. Innocenzo Sabbatini's training began at the building sites and small Art Nouveau projects carried out in Osimo for the municipality. Then he moved to Rome, apprenticed in the studios of Pio and Marcello Piacentini, and, of course, of Quadrio Pirani. As soon as the war was over in 1918, his older cousin, Innocenzo Costantini, hired him in the ICP's project office. His first commission was the design of the large housing complex Trionfale II, realized between 1919 and 1922, and drawing on Costantini's typological plans. The latter recommended him to deploy the neo-medieval language that Pirani had already adopted in his projects, starting with San Saba. From that project until his departure from the institute in 1931, Sabbatini was the key figure of the extraordinary architectural production of the Roman section of the ICP.[33]

This period was the most prolific and creative in the history of the institute, delivering a rich repertoire of distinctive public housing projects in and around Rome, with modest means and against the backdrop of a severe housing crisis. Under Sabbatini's creative lead, the ICP sought to advance a distinctive, coherent vision for public housing while also producing a singular architectural language that was both modern and unmistakably situated in the traditions and ambience of Rome. During those years, Sabbatini had regular contact with the AACAR and Giovannoni, with whom he collaborated directly at La Garbatella and at Città Giardino Aniene at Montesacro.

Innocenzo Sabbatini (ICP), Casa del Sole, Via della Lega Lombarda, 1929–1930.

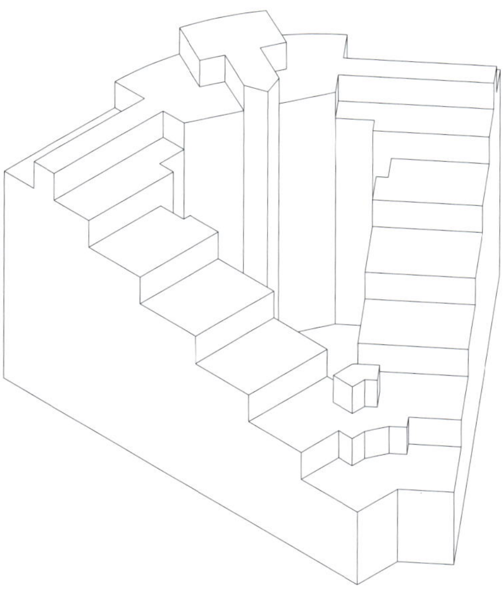

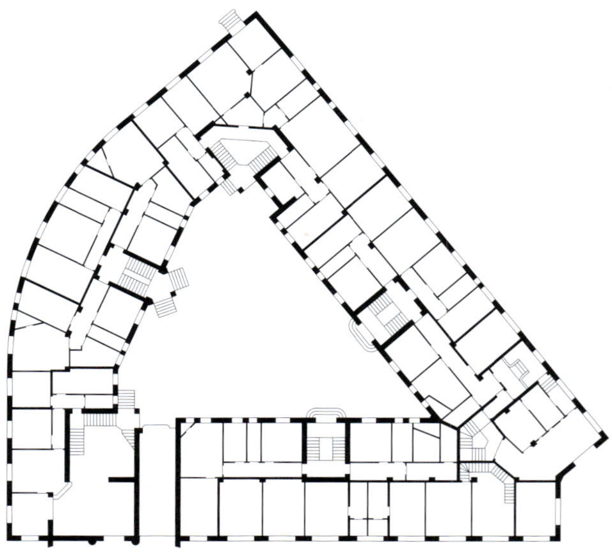

Innocenzo Sabbatini (ICP), Casa del Sole (San Ippolito/Bologna). Typical floor plan and schematic axonometric.

● Innocenzo Sabbatini (ICP), Albergo Rosso, La Garbatella, 1927–1928.

Under Sabbatini's leadership, the ICP rationalized and codified the clever massing of the large super-blocks and the break up of large volumes into multiple elevations. His works evolved toward ever greater compositional precision in his handling of programmatic complexity, while developing a rich and flexible language of simple means and minimal gesture, but also of great effect. The most remarkable examples include the garden-centered blocks around Piazza Mazzini in the Trionfale district, and in the Ippolito II area (at the southern edge of the Piazza Bologna district) where he authored the pyramidal Casa del Sole ◖◖ p. 90, 262 ◗◗ along Via della Lega Lombarda (1929–1930). It is undoubtedly in the Garbatella district that Sabbatini conceived and built his greatest experiments, both on a typological and a linguistic level: a series of innovative housing blocks loosely organized around interior public gardens, the Alberghi suburbani (suburban hotels, 1927–1930), the Cinema-teatro complex (1927–1931), and the Bagni publici e residenza (public baths and residences, 1927) ◖ right ◗.[34]

● Innocenzo Sabbatini (ICP), public baths and residences, La Garbatella, 1927.

Fig. 8. - OSTIA: CASA DI DIANA.

diametro con bordo rialzato. Constatiamo però che il fumo di queste case non ha lasciato alcuna traccia di sè: non nelle murature che non hanno alcuna canalizzazione per esso, non nelle pareti interne ed esterne che non conservano annerimenti di sorta.

STRUTTURA ED ESTETICA DELLE FACCIATE. – Le costruzioni private ostiensi sono tutte in cortina laterizia, sostituita talvolta negli interni e nelle facciate secondarie da opera reticolata con legamenti a mattoni. Mentre internamente riscontriamo abbondanti traccie di intonaco, su queste fronti in laterizio non ce n'è mai traccia: e tutto prova che, almeno nella grandissima maggioranza, gli edifici non dovevano essere intonacati. Del resto, anche a Roma, l'emiciclo del Foro di Traiano, non è intonacato sulla facciata, ma soltanto nelle calotte delle nicchie e gli intradossi degli archi. Anzitutto gli ingressi delle case sono contraddistinti da lesene o colonne in cotto sorreggenti un frontespizio triangolare con una cortina così accurata a mattoni arrotati che non può pensarsi sia stata ricoperta da intonaco (*fig. 3, 4*). Nè intonacati erano certo i listelli di mattone che talvolta rilevano ed accentuano, unica e semplice decorazione la sagoma delle porte e delle finestre. Ma c'è di più: in moltissimi archi

Fig. 9. - OSTIA: CASA DI DIANA VISTA DALLA PIAZZETTA DEI LARI (RICOSTR. ARCH. I. GISMONDI).

delle porte e delle finestre di facciata sia interna che esterna sono rimaste evidentissime traccie di color rosso minio sicchè bisogna ritenere che questi archi fossero dipinti, e poichè la cortina delle parti piene è in mattone talvolta giallo talvolta rosso marrone, è evidente la semplice e sobria policromia di queste facciate ottenuta col materiale stesso della costruzione, lasciando a cortina viva i pieni e rubricando gli archi e gli aggetti della muratura (listelli, lesene, colonne, frontespizi, ecc.).

In conclusione ci sono due tipi di policromia: una ottenuta con la rubricazione (esempi, la casa di Diana (*fig. 9*) e gli Horrea Epagathiana, ecc.); l'altra invece

Fig. 27. - OSTIA: CASA DEI DIPINTI - FACCIATA SUL CORTILE.

Fig. 28. - OSTIA: CASA DEI DIPINTI - RICOSTRUZIONE DELLA FACCIATA SUL CORTILE (ARCH. I. GISMONDI).

● Pages from "Le origini Latine dell'abitazione moderna" (The Latin Origins of Modern Housing) published by the archaeologist Guido Calza in the September 1923 issue of *Architettura e Arti Decorative*. Note the similarities with Pirani's design of an IRCIS courtyard at Piazza Mazzini district ◖p. 89 left◗.

Beyond all the reimagined influences that marked his works, from the rural vernacular, to stripped classical, to Futurism, Sabbatini found a major source in the article "Le origini Latine dell'abitazione moderna" (The Latin Origins of Modern Housing) ◖◖◖ p. 92 ◗◗◗, published by the archaeologist Guido Calza in the September 1923 issue of *Architettura e Arti Decorative*—the periodical edited by Giovannoni and Piacentini.[35] The new excavations in Ostia Antica had unearthed a 2000-year-old "modern city," dense, typologically avant-garde, and innovative compared to the usual Pompeian typologies of which every Roman city was thought to be made. A second article in the following issue of October 1923, of the same title but illustrated with some reconstructive drawings by the Italian archaeologist Italo Gismondi, directed modern architects to use the ancient city as a source of inspiration for devising the modern city, dynamic, dense with activity, collective residences, and public services. Above all, the author suggested that the great residential complexes of Ostia Antica provided the design method and language to be followed. His argumentation was solidly based on the use of the rhythmic sections of a wall structure already strongly expressive, but very freely enriched, only where necessary, with few formal elements taken from the language that might be considered Hellenistic. It was not Carducci's classical "primitivism," severe and freely creative, but maybe the closest to it. At the Garbatella, Sabbatini seems to be inspired by the "dis-proportion Ostiense." And he did so with the confidence and boldness of a free thinker. On the roof of the powerful volumes of the Cinema-Theater, he placed a Tuscan temple quasi reduced to a graphic scheme; and in the building of the Public Baths, he illuminated the interiors with a monumental thermal window while shaping the side walls with the identical sequence of half-vaults and brick lunettes that brilliantly survived at the Insula of Diana in Ostia Antica. Taken as a whole, his works broke down the conservative morphological and typological patterns rampant in Rome in the preceding decades. Yet, he was a shrewd builder and architect for the lower classes, not a Carduccian poet. His buildings and urban complexes were firmly planted in *utilitas*, the Vitruvian category that Quadrio Pirani, perhaps more of a poet than his colleague, already evoked.[36] Undoubtedly, it is with the Albergo Rosso (1927–1928) ◖ p. 91 top ◗ designed at La Garbatella that Sabbatini inaugurated what could be considered as the opening salvo of a fascinatingly singular Roman road to modernist architecture, and this long before the "heroic" phase of *razionalismo* in Rome during the early 1930s. Sabbatini's ICP designs—not least the Albergo Rosso—ushered in a decidedly more modern architectural sensibility in Rome, one that was based on experimental synthesis and critical continuity with the past.[37] The critic and art historian Roberto Papini summed it up in praising the "logical and sound" in the works of the new generation while remaining true to the artistic heritage of Rome: "Rome compels powerful contrasts of chiaroscuro through the accentuated movement of masses, the curve of surfaces, and the choice of materials."[38] Interestingly, the Albergo Rosso was one of the few completed works presented at the First Italian Exposition of Rational Architecture ◖ bottom ◗ in Rome in 1928.

● Nikolay Diulgheroff (Bauhaus Weimar). Poster for the First Italian Exposition of Rational Architecture, 1928.

Rationalism in Rome: A Contextual Avant-Garde

In 1926, a group of young architects from the Milan Polytechnic—Luigi Figini, Gino Pollini, Guido Frette, Sebastiano Larco Silva, Carlo Enrico Rava, Giuseppe Terragni, and Ubaldo Castagnoli—formed the Gruppo Sette (Group 7). The following year, Adalberto Libera, who was one of the first graduates of the Scuola Superiore di Architettura founded in Rome in 1919, replaced Castagnoli. Gruppo Sette's first public action was to publish a series of four controversial essays in the periodical *La Rassegna Italiana* (1926–1927). The articles promoted the new international principles for architecture and referred to the Modern Movement that was growing throughout Europe, with a focus on Le Corbusier, the Deutscher Werkbund, and the Russian Constructivists.[39] Libera and the members of the group endorsed the necessity of a new architecture, however, from the start they intended to develop an Italian way to be modern:

> "Nothing prohibits us from admiring the architectural marquetry of Francesco di Giorgio and the wood engravings of Serlio, and to understand the rhythm, the almost Greek purity of certain factories with walls of glass. There is no incompatibility between our past and our present. We do not want to break with tradition; it is tradition which transforms itself, and assumes new aspects, few people may recognize it.... Other aspects of architecture, on the other hand, despite their absolute modernity, will keep national characteristics in every country, as is already happening. Here there exists a classical foundation. The spirit (not the forms, which is something different) of tradition is so profound in Italy that evidently, and almost mechanically, the new architecture will preserve a stamp which is typically ours."[40]

In 1928, the Group curated the First Italian Exhibition of Rational Architecture which took place at the Palazzo delle Esposizioni in Rome. Forty-one architects from around the country, but with a concentration from Milan, Turin, and Rome, participated and were published in the catalog.[41] The Roman contingent included, among others, Alberto Calza Bini, Giuseppe Nicolosi, Gaetano Minucci, Innocenzo Sabbatini, and Giuseppe Capponi. Even though the Roman group was stylistically very diverse, its implicit target was Giovannoni, Director of the newly created Scuola Superiore di Architettura in Rome, and a handful of professors that included Vincenzo

● Marcello Piacentini, apartment house, Piazza del Viminale, 1918.

● Giulio Gra, apartment house at the entrance of Viale delle Belle Arti, 1929. View from the Risorgimento Bridge.

Fasolo.[42] Giovannoni complained to Piacentini, head of the opposing "innovators" party as if the latter wanted to strike at the teaching line of the school governed by Giovannoni. These were years in which the rivalry between the two founders was clearly emerging. Piacentini had initiated the move away from the Umbertine neo-Renaissance language, opening his work to international currents such as the Vienna Secession for his apartment building on the Viminale (1914–1915) and on Via Germanico in Prati (1920) ◖p. 198 top left◗. In 1928,

● Pietro Bardi, Tavola degli orrori, 1931. The "Table of horrors" was a photomontage that put together newspaper clips, novel, postcards, and photographs of the 1860s with the recent works of "academic" architects. Those included Armando Brasini, Cesare Bazzani, Gustavo Giovannoni, with pseudo-moderns like Marcello Piacentini.

he has just completed the building of the Casa Madre dei Mutilati (Mother House of the War Mutilated), between the Castel Sant'Angelo and the Palace of Justice at Piazza Adriana, making that work the Roman monumental alternative both to 19th-century eclecticism, and to the functionalist message broadcast in Italy by the group of Rationalist architects. The *Cinquecentismo's* tide was also receding quickly in the bourgeois housing market, with Mario De Renzi and Giulio Gra ◖ p. 94, bottom left ◗ among the leading figures of the new generation.[43]

A new movement, Movimento Architettura Razionale (MIAR), was formed two years later to bring all Italian Rationalist architects together and to promote another exhibition. Pietro Maria Bardi (1900–1999) convinced the young modernist architects to set up the 1931 Second Exhibition of Rational Architecture, no longer in an institutional place, but in his own gallery on Via Vittorio Veneto. Bardi was a prominent gallery owner from Milan who moved his business to Rome, having clearly understood that the Italian cultural center, especially for architecture, was now in the capital next to Mussolini. The exhibition opened with the surprising presentation by Bardi of the so-called Tavola degli Orrori (Table of Horrors) ◖ top ◗ in which the works of non-Rationalist architects—those of Marcello Piacentini, Cesare Bazzani, Armando Brasini, Gustavo Giovannoni, Vittorio Morpurgo—were mounted in a mocking and insulting collage of images. Bardi's aim was to replace in the Duce's favor the entire power group of the Roman School, traditionalists and monumentalists as they were, by the Rationalist group. Mussolini himself attended the preview of the exhibition on 30 March 1931, thus giving it the sense of Fascist opportunity and legitimacy. Although the Milanese, Trento, and Como groups dominated the show, Mario Ridolfi, Giuseppe Capponi ◖◖◖ p. 96 ◗◗◗, Pietro Aschieri and Gaetano Minucci were among the Roman architects exhibited in Bardi's polemical gallery. The reaction of Piacentini and the entire Roman School was devastatingly powerful and a series of virulent essays attacked the Rationalists. With the help of the Sindicato Fascista degli Architetti and with the increasing politicization of the debate, the events of 1931 provoked the premature death of the MIAR.[44]

Yet, the "Battle for Modernism" was launched and the 1930s saw the gentle rise of a genuine Roman modernism, anchored on tradition, materiality, and a response to the specific environmental conditions of the city. Its contested appropriation by the Fascist regime led to a wave of public structures such as Luigi Moretti's Casa GIL (Casa della Gioventù Italiana, 1933–1936) ◖◖ p. 97 left ◗◗ at Trastevere; the Casa delle Armi at the Foro Italico (1933–1937 also by Moretti) ◖◖ p. 97 right ◗◗; the post office of Via Marmorata (Testaccio, 1932–1935) by Adalberto Libera and Mario De Renzi; and that of Piazza Bologna (1933–1935) by Mario Ridolfi ◖ p. 265 ◗[45]. On the residential front, the evolution

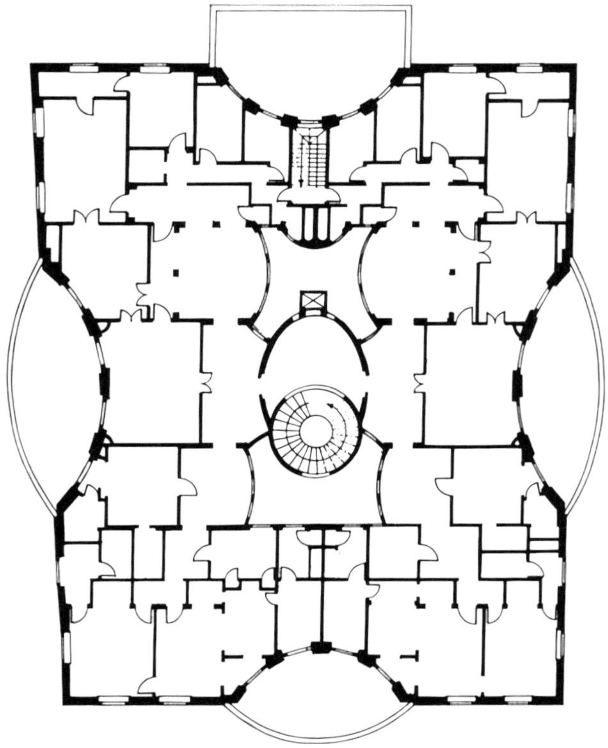

● Giuseppe Capponi, Palazzina Nebbiosi, Lungotevere Arnaldo da Brescia, 1928. Note the facades entirely clad with travertine and the Borromini-like concave/convex design on both facades and interior plans.

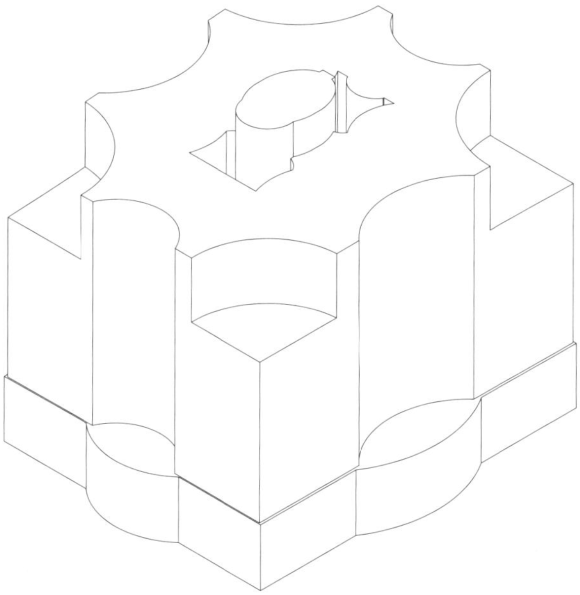

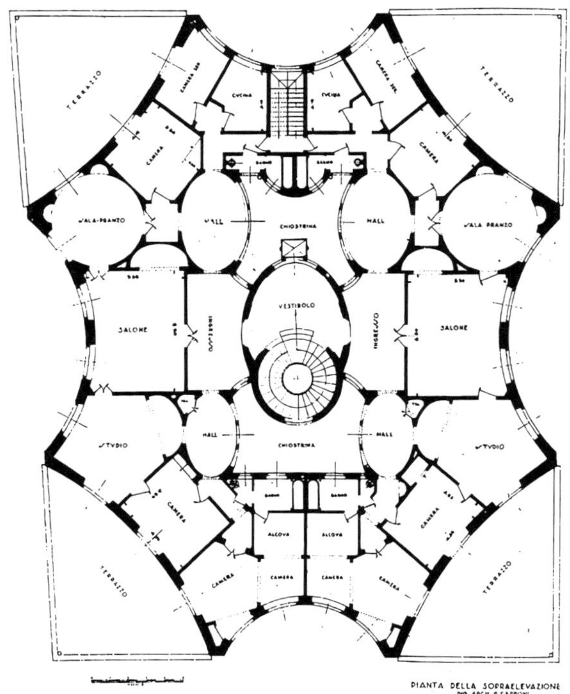

● Giuseppe Capponi, Palazzina Nebbiosi. Plans and schematic axonometric.

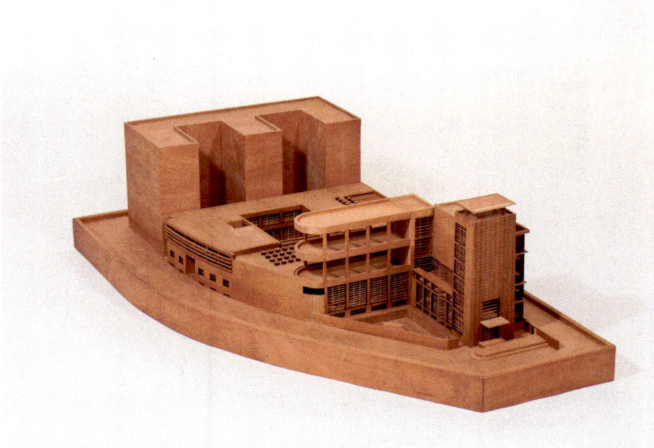

● Luigi Moretti, Casa della GIL in Trastevere, 1933–1936.
Model and front view.

● Luigi Moretti, Casa delle Armi, Foro Italico, 1933–1937.
Model and side facade.

● Luigi Piccinato, project for an apartment house between Via di Ripetta and the Lungotevere in Augusta.
The project dates from 1928/29 but was not realized due to the construction of the Piazza Augusto Imperatore around the Mausoleum of Augustus (Vittorio Ballio Morpurgo). Aerial photomontage of the facade along the Lungotevere in Augusta with the site of the Mausoleum still intact.

● Luigi Piccinato, project for an apartment house between Via di Ripetta and the Lungotevere in Augusta.
Photomontage of the building along Via di Ripetta during the demolition of the houses to free the Mausoleum of Augustus and establish the Piazza Augusto Imperatore (Vittorio Ballio Morpurgo).

● Luigi Piccinato, project for an apartment house between Via di Ripetta and the Lungotevere in Augusta.
Digital reconstruction of the courtyard with Futurist influences, often present in the modern Rome of the 1930s.

● Adalberto Libera, apartment house Casa Nicoletti, Via San Basilio (Barberini area), 1931.

● Adalberto Libera, Villino of the Società Immobiliare Tirrenia, Ostia Lido, 1932–1934 (with the architect standing on the balcony). Ostia was designed as a beachfront garden city in 1916 by a group of architects from AACAR including Vincenzo Fasolo, Tullio Passarelli, Gustavo Giovannoni, and Marcello Piacentini.

was more progressive and well embodied by Luigi Piccinato (1899–1983) ◀◀◀ p. 98 ▶▶▶, Piacentini's most gifted pupil and future co-planner of the new town of Sabaudia, who participated in the Second Exhibition of Rational Architecture with a project that leaked out a straightforward environmentalist matrix. Like the Palazzo Giorgioli by Gaetano Koch, it was a two-front infill project to be inserted into the *centro storico*. On the front facing Via di Ripetta, sandwiched between the Academy of Fine Arts designed by Pietro Camporese il Giovane (1792–1873) and a typical 18th-century apartment house (1931), Piccinato designed a facade without volumetric protrusions, flush with the street, complete with ashlar on the ground floor, and a doorway coordinated with the central balcony supporting a broken tympanum. The other front along the Lungotevere was treated with linguistic elements typical of Rationalist modernity. The windows became larger, with rectilinear balconies devoid of all ornamentation. The facade was not set flush with the street, without classical rustication on the ground floor, but volumetrically articulated. Demonstratively, *ambientismo* continued to mark the Roman urban and architectural practice, even during the rise of the Rationalist movement. The architecture of Giulio Gra (1900–1958), in association with his brother Enrico, was another demonstration of this Roman synthesis. Only a couple of years separate their iconic residential block on Via delle Belle Arti facing the Risorgimento Bridge (1929), the stripped facade of the convent at Via Cairoli (1933), and his last work, the superb Rationalist Condominio Gra at the Lungotevere Flaminio (1934–1939) ◀ p. 229 ▶.[46] Finally, let us mention Libera's first work in Rome, the tall and narrow Casa Nicoletti (Via San Basilio, 1931) ◀ top, left ▶ with its characteristic projecting window frame in travertine, as well as the *villini* in Ostia Lido (1932–1934) ◀ top, right ▶. Yet, it is with the new building type known as *palazzina* that modern architecture will enter the Roman panorama, with the Parioli as privileged terrain.

The Other Legacies: INA and the Scene of the Bourgeois City

The INA or Istituto Nazionale delle Assicurazioni (National Insurance Institute) was a public body established in 1912 to manage life insurance in all its possible forms as a monopoly on the national territory. At the end of the 1920s, the INA decided—and was induced in part—to take a serious interest in the residential problems of the Roman bourgeoisie. The institute was not invested with special humanitarian responsibilities, as, for example, was the Institute for Popular Housing or ICP. INA's interest in housing investment took shape slowly over the course of a few years, especially when, after a reform of national insurance policy, the institute was forced to measure itself against competition. Housing investment became a form of active protection of financial capital. Rome, rapidly expanding, was the ideal terrain for this type of investment, which began in the Piazza d'Armi district and then turned to the Flaminio, and to any neighborhood in the capital where the possibility of a fruitful return on capital invested in building land and construction of some quality emerged. At the same time, the demand for mortgages to buy homes for the growing number of Institute employees was rising. This demand did not only come from the low and middle categories of employees, but also from those of high and very high rank. The two demands added up: the capital invested in real estate transactions served the needs of middle-class people of all levels who worked for the Institute. Likewise, the resurgence of construction activity in the second half of the 1920s generated an increase in requests for financing from private and public companies willing to invest in the residential sector of large cities. The INA management understood that, except for complexes of an intensive and popular character, or located in excessively peripheral areas, construction works could be an excellent instrument of image and propaganda "for the Institute's activities ... for the spread of its name and financial strength and for the collection of new insurance contracts."[47]

If the bourgeois city tends to be unitary, it cannot be homogeneous. On the one hand, it welcomes, by attracting them, the less well-off classes so that they abandon the party of social revolution and enter the bourgeois world with dignity, including economic dignity; on the other hand, it reassures the better off, the rich, and very rich, about the steadfastness and visibility of their social position. Paolo Portoghesi was right when he stated that the bourgeoisie at the threshold of modern times expressed a tendency to "dogmatically formalize its behavior."[48] In the new bourgeois city, the urban scene was and still is the formalization—as an aesthetic or even theatrical representation—of bourgeois social behavior. Despite his inherent critique of the bourgeois city, he argued that at least two aspects of the city as a physical reality of bourgeois ostentation could be the subject of critical interest: first, the search for housing typologies capable of "realizing a connective tissue homogeneous to the scale of the city."[49] In other words, the aesthetic value of the bourgeois city "can be found in that collective work that is the street backdrop, and the continuous envelope of urban space" conceived as a scene made immediately comprehensible by the use of the symbolic, linguistic, and historical heritage of architecture and bourgeois eclecticism. Second, Portoghesi was critically attracted to the "ironic implication" of this architecture, which to him appeared almost grotesque—as if "the now cold and bureaucratic, now passionate and convinced leave-taking from history understood as the past" needed that bath of passionate, ironic last participation in the language—indeed in all languages and all interchangeable with each other—of history."[50]

INA and the *palazzina*: Typology or Pure Image?

The action of the INA in the real estate market paralleled the emergence of a new building type that will become synonymous with the modern bourgeois architecture, i.e., the *palazzina*. One of INA's most fascinating residential complexes was built in the mid-1920s between Via delle Tre Madonne and Viale Bruno Buozzi in the Parioli district of Rome. It consists of ten cleverly composed small buildings on an irregular and very steep terrain, each one of them free-standing and exposing four articulated facades. The buildings were not designed by a renowned academic architect, nor by an ambitious young professional. On the contrary, their creator was a very "bourgeois" architect from the technical office of the INA, Giuseppe Machin, assisted by engineer Massimo Settimi, Head of the office of the Regulatory Plan of Rome, a very reliable technician, but certainly neither a leading, nor motivated figure in the debate on modern architecture.[51] The three most luxurious mansions (Via delle Tre Madonne, 16/18) among the ten form a very theatrical scene, designed in a language immediately understandable. Indeed, it is drawn from the shared historical tradition of the ruling class and incorporates with moderate freedom and imagination the elements of a Renaissance, Mannerist,

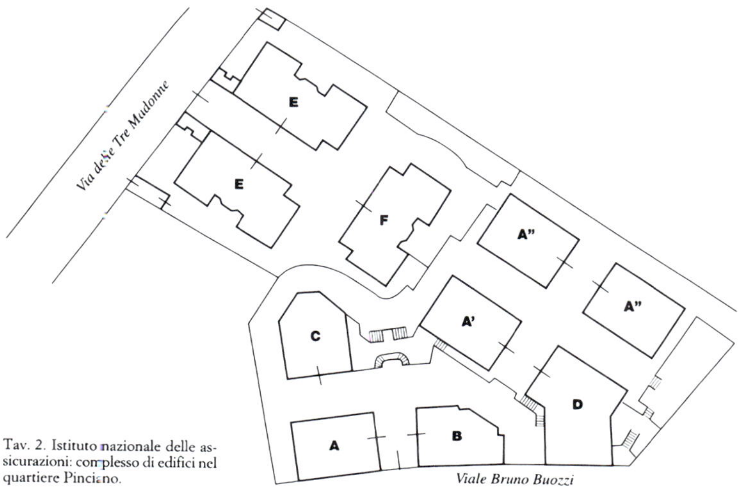

Tav. 2. Istituto nazionale delle assicurazioni: complesso di edifici nel quartiere Pinciano.

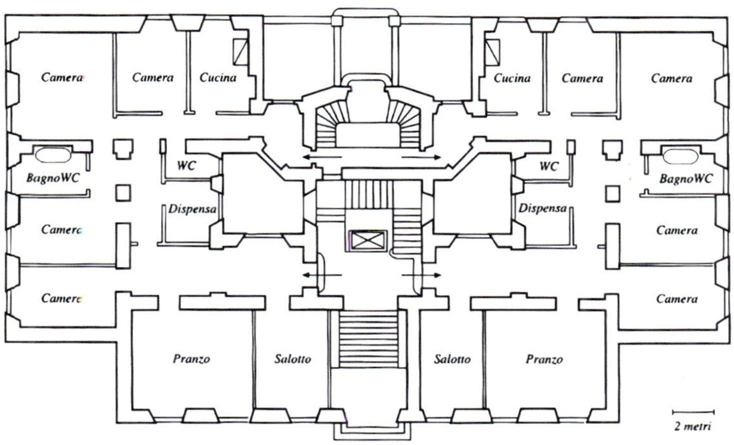

Tav. 12. Istituto nazionale delle assicurazioni: palazzina nel quartiere Pinciano.

● Gino Cipriani (INA), complex of *palazzine* between Via delle Tre Madonne and Viale Bruno Buozzi (Parioli), 1927–1931.
Top: Aerial view, entrance from Via Bruno Buozzi between A and B. Middle: plan of the INA complex in the Quartiere Pinciano (Parioli).
Bottom: typical floor of an INA apartment in the Parioli/Pinciano district.

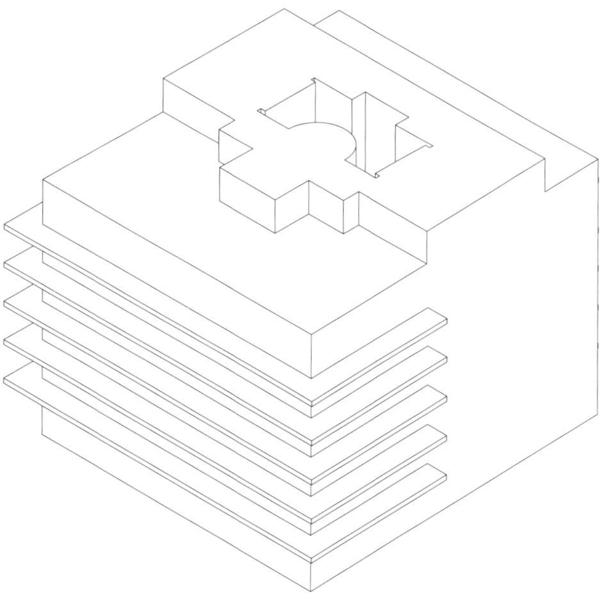

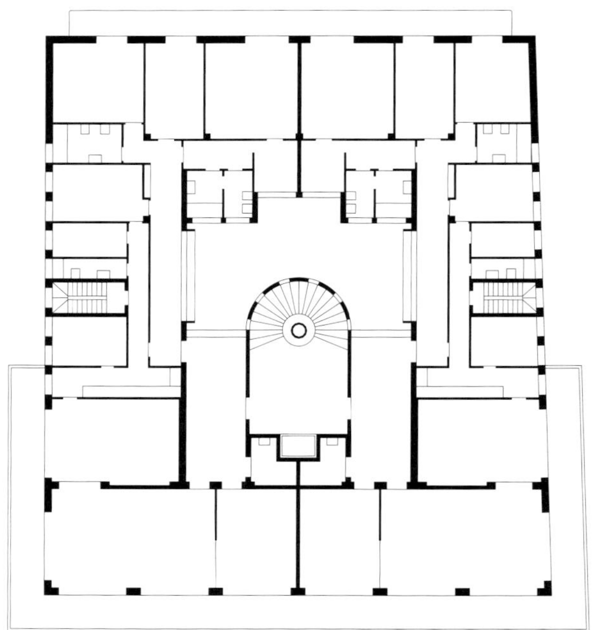

● Mario De Renzi with Giorgio Calza Bini, and Pietro Sforza, Palazzina Furmanik, front on Lungotevere Flaminio, 1935–1940. The photograph shows the original state with the long loggias protected by movable louvers.

almost Baroque repertoire. From the urban space to the architectural wings and the decorative details, the complex wants to be judged by its ability to represent clearly, and to the greatest number of spectators, the character of the protagonists on that stage and to make people naturally imagine the human comedy that goes on between those architectural wings. The three main structures were state of the art in every way: elevators, double bathrooms, central heating, and even a pneumatic mail system. On the other side of the block, Via Bruno Buozzi, the complex of three apartment buildings designed by Gino Cipriani (1927–1931) p.101 was slightly less luxurious but created a sophisticated and well-composed system of street gates, terraces, and double staircases, connecting all apartment buildings with each other and the adjacent streets. The last element of modernity: the sharp difference in street levels allowed the architects to provide the complex with a large underground garage, which was easily accessible from Viale Bruno Buozzi.[52]

Allegedly, this intervention could be considered as the official consecration of the Roman *palazzina* as the residential typology of the modern bourgeoisie in the capital. The *palazzina* typology was still in its nascent state, born in the early 1920s as the adaptation of the large freestanding *villino signorile*—see examples like Villino Cagiati by Garibaldi Burba p.198 bottom left or Villino Allegri by Marcello Piacentini (1917–1920)—to a request for more density and thus a more urban image. This process of early derogation eventually became the rule from 1920 to the mid-1960s. Historically, the urban fabric of Rome consisted of three subsequent typologies: the *casa a schiera* or townhouse; the aristocratic Renaissance and Baroque palazzo organized around one or more courtyards; and the bourgeois multifamily evolution of the palazzo, the *casa in linea*, the basic structure of the modern urban block.[53] The *palazzina* became the fourth and highly successful typology, a multi-family and free-standing one, four to five floors high with one or more apartments per floor, often with a central plan but without a courtyard, and connected to its neighbors with small gardens and other open spaces.[54] From the early 1920s, the *palazzina* was well defined typologically and dimensionally in its permanent characters, thus allowing the architects to pursue their subjective research and partake at the scale of a small urban unit with the modern languages that flourished and evolved for four decades—that is from the variants to the masterplan of 1909 to the new *Piano regolatore* of 1962, the one that abandoned all reference to the construction of the city according to well-established typologies and to a well-defined procedural model of conceiving the urban form. Here, one can argue that the building complex of Via delle Tre Madonne was one of the most successful attempts to use the *palazzina* as a tool to define the principles and the image of a modern urban architecture—in particular, the definition of building complexes sufficiently large and homogeneous to characterize significant parts of the city in a unified way.

Architecturally, the deployment of the *palazzina* as the primary building type of the 1930s and the post-war decades created a very interesting and heterogeneous panorama. Among the most remarkable *palazzine* conceived as individual urban buildings before the Second World War, one can list the Palazzina De' Salvi p.76, designed by Pietro Aschieri in 1930; the Borromini-inspired Palazzina Nebbiosi on Lungotevere Arnaldo da Brescia designed by Giuseppe Capponi (1928) in collaboration with Pier Luigi Nervi; the Palazzine Rea (1934–1936) and Colombo (1935–1937) by Mario Ridolfi and Wolfgang Frankl; the radical "post-antique" Palazzina Furmanik by Mario De Renzi, Giorgio Calza Bini, and Pietro Sforza (1935–1940) p.102; and the Palazzina delle Muse by Ugo Luccichenti at Piazzale delle Muse (1940).[55] Despite their aesthetic differences, the link with tradition that implied two elements of opposite importance remained particularly persistent: the care for the material, and the "durability" of the finishes on the one hand; the search for a solid but moderate urban order on the other.[56]

Futurist Aspirations and the Many Builders of the Bourgeois City

INA's building initiatives were certainly not limited to residential proposals for the upper-middle class. The bourgeois city is organic and diverse; its steadfastness, with respect to history, or politics, lies substantially in its ability to expand downward to eventually absorb those previously excluded. In 1929, the Institute responded to the Governorate's invitation to build "subsidized" housing for public or private employees. INA immediately launched two major interventions for low-cost housing: one at Viale Masaccio near Via Flaminia for about 300 units, and another, larger and conceptually richer, on the opposite side of the city at Via Taranto beyond Porta San Giovanni, for 1300 rooms.[57] These were not central locations, but well serviced with excellent tram and automobile connections. Due to the efficiency of INA's technical office, both projects were completed by the end of 1930 while the scope of Via Taranto was increased to house about 2500 people. The apartments were rented at agreed prices, to

● Gino Cipriani (INA), complex of four *palazzine* at Via Taranto (Appio Re di Roma), 1930. View of the entrance gate. The Futurist-inspired towers can be seen in the distance.

be assigned to those families with few economic resources but still holders of a fixed income. The units were small, made up of two or three useful rooms; some of only one room with essential services; some of four rooms.

The complex at Via Taranto ◖top◗, designed by Gino Cipriani who was responsible for INA's entire building operation, consisted of four large, high-density buildings, each with a central courtyard, that created an organic whole whose outdoor spaces were interconnected both functionally and visually. The individual sections were articulated in various heights and each of the four blocks contributed to the definition of the central urban space—an interior piazza of sort—with projecting nine-story habitable tower-like volumes. A fifth one, placed at the corner of Via Taranto, proudly announced to those coming from Porta San Giovanni the presence and character of the new settlement. The set of buildings forms a complete small town, with its symbols at once archaic and very modern, with its square, its tree-lined avenues, its buildings emerging to give volumetric vigor to the central interior space, which has the role of representing the unity and urban dignity of the newly formed social community, composed of family nuclei from different areas of the suburbs, which found here, even symbolically, signs of their belonging to the modern bourgeois city. Its architecture generated an image of moderate rhetoric, proudly displaying the ancestral topoi of modern architecture, which often, in the specific Italian context, suggested the revenge of the Gothic world over the classical: the tower of medieval castles, the dynamic forms of expressionism, and, of course, those of Antonio Sant'Elia (1888–1916). Is it pure coincidence that in 1930s Rome, these "modern houses" in the form of towers were called *grattacieli* (skyscrapers)?[58] Here, in the youngest, most universal, and yet most provincial capital of Europe, the American Dream, fueled by the tales of emigrants, constituted the distant backdrop of every dream of civil redemption.

While the project was under construction, the INA planned a major expansion nearby, almost 400 new apartments that ended up being more modern, better distributed, and a little larger, with better services and, above all, designed with a simplified language—a quasi-Rationalist aesthetic reminiscent of the complexes of Red Vienna. Yet, the designers did not give up the spatial organization by blocks articulated in volumes of different heights, nor the rhetoric of corner towers. The facades were cleaned of any remaining decorative elements replaced by the articulation of a few balconies supported by bare concrete pillars that move the shadows of some aesthetic interest to the fronts. The quality is not high, but the transition from one language to another was painless and ultimately—especially from a typological and volumetric point of view—respectful of the traditional urban setting.[59]

Analyzed across those projects and many others built during the interwar period, the research on the form of the city was remarkably and pragmatically focused on the achievement of results programmed and verified by strict corporate budgets and deliberately secluded from the great debate on the language of architecture. At the same time, the research on collective housing was not carried out by the INA alone; many other public entities and even large private groups realized what greater attraction they would exert and what increase in value their investments in real estate would gain if they were designed with an organic architectural vision of the whole, understood as a significant and innovative part of the new city. The Unione Edilizia Nazionale, for example, had the task of implementing the projects of employee cooperatives and private citizens; the Società Generale Immobiliare (SGI), for which Mario De Renzi (1897–1967) worked from the beginning and implemented coordinated complexes of apartment buildings, generally of a high standard. Among those, the already mentioned Istituto

● Giulio Gra, low-cost houses for employees of the national railways, Via Etruria and Via Ceneda, 1932–1939. The four-block group reveals strong influences from Red Vienna social-housing complexes.

nazionale per le case degli impiegati statali or INCIS (National Institute for Housing for State Employees), mostly active for the lower-salary market, which was among the protagonists in the construction of the Garbatella, Aniene Città Giardino, and many remarkable projects such as the mixed-use and residential blocks around Piazza Verbano; the Federici Society, which built, precisely to the design of Mario De Renzi, the masterpiece of urban design that is the 650-apartment superblock of Via XXI Aprile in the Bologna neighborhood ◖p. 272–273◗ (known as Palazzo Federici, 1931–1937); the *case economiche per i ferrovieri* ◖top◗ (low-cost houses for employees of the national railways) built between Via Etruria and Via Ceneda (Appio district) as a Rationalist super-block with Viennese inspiration by the Brothers Gra (1932–1939); and above all the IFACP, the Istituto Fascista Autonomo delle Case Economiche Popolari as the ICP was relabeled during Fascism.[60]

Beyond the Boundaries of the Bourgeois City

The activity of the IFACP takes us out of the usual boundaries of the bourgeois city. In the 1920s, the Institute had been concerned, like many other agencies, with the construction of residences for the lower-middle class within integrated and well-designed sections of the bourgeois city (see for instance the Trionfale, Mazzini, Flaminia quarters). Yet, by the early 1930s, due to a change in the law, it faced untenable competition from private companies in the construction of houses for white-collar workers. Consequently, it was substantially directed, almost obliged, to build homes for the less well-off classes, those without a steady job, immigrants unwanted by the regime, as well as deep-rooted inhabitants expelled from the city center following the opening of Via dei Fori Imperiali and other large-scale operations of archaeological excavation.[61] At the same time, an unexpected financial crisis deeply shook its complex relations with the Governorate of Rome. The IFACP risked real closure and an extinction for lack of purpose. Two men were able to change the course: first, Alberto Calza Bini, President, and Innocenzo Sabbatini, General Director of the Institute. Calza Bini's credibility and political skill managed to breathe new life into Costantini's organizational and administrative capacity. The Institute resumed its activities in the 1930s, succeeding in brilliantly organizing housing interventions in favor of the less affluent and excluded classes. It tackled the problem of hyper-economic housing by introducing it as a fundamental theme in the broader research on the form of the modern city—the latter now understood as a complex organism formed of middle-class and non-bourgeois classes, their social behavior and culture different from each other, but all deserving to live within the city with dignity, and to participate with equal merit in the definition of its identity.

The most critical results were two major innovative projects in Val Melaina and Donna Olimpia.[62] Realized in the late 1930s, the basic contradictions between the bourgeois city and the settlements of the excluded implied a significant degree of physical separation. However, having managed to include the focus on housing for the poor in the practice of innovative research on the city constituted an extraordinary achievement in such a difficult era. All of this, almost absurdly, was due to the tenacity and lack of prejudice of precisely the most Fascist of the protagonists of architecture in Italy, Calza Bini, who reversed the policy of excluding the outcasts not only from the city, but even from the list of problems that a modern city had to deal with. Accordingly, if the set of urban design experiments administered by other public agencies and private groups testify to the continuity and autonomy of research into the urban quality of bourgeois residential architecture, IFACP's efforts to find public funding and to fulfill its social mandate anticipated the political vision and logic of the post-World War II housing programs.

The Masterpiece: The Stairs, Galleries, and Courtyards of Donna Olimpia

Gustavo Giovannoni considered the city as a bourgeois organism, and for this reason he went so far as to fully espouse Mussolini's anti-city directives.[63] But, in some of their often contradictory pages, he captured the sense of collective home that in his opinion characterized the medieval city, in which the streets and squares were the real spaces of communal life, the very living rooms that were missing inside the houses of the common inhabitants, i.e., the artisans and workers with numerous offspring and almost always precarious circumstances. But the masterpiece of medieval building was that of the squares whose characteristics Camillo Sitte highlighted quasi-scientifically.[64] Yet, in the bourgeois city of the first half of the 20th century, social life shifted to the private living rooms, dining rooms, or other articulated interior spaces that often in the United States or in the perfect apartments designed by Alvar Aalto at the Hansaviertel in Berlin had taken the place and functions of the inner court of historic homes, from the Roman *domus* to the patios of the Middle East and China. What about the poor and the precarious?

Donna Olimpia's first block of buildings was directly designed by Innocenzo Sabbatini ◀◀ bottom right; pp. 289–290 ▶▶. He certainly sensed the problem; he knew how to empathize with the living conditions of those fortunate enough to get a small apartment in the new settlement. He knew perfectly well the typological and functional consequences of the tight economic constraints of the intervention. He decided to design the collective paths, vertical and horizontal distribution, as the continuation of the public access roads. They would resemble the alleys of an arduous Italian mountain village, serving each house by circling around the steep rise and he designed the staircases, the helicoidal ramps, the courtyards, as the primary places of sociability. Yet, living in a modern city, even on its extreme periphery, is different from living in a medieval center. Donna Olimpia had neither stores nor bars along its interior and public spaces. Eventually, the Governorate built an elementary school along the main public street and a few stores were planned at the foot of the large residential complexes. But they were facing outward, toward the still desolate streets, where it was hoped that sooner or later the city, still a long way off, would arrive with its bourgeois apartment buildings and several inhabitants on fixed wages sufficient to support the essential commercial activities of a modern neighborhood.

● Innocenzo Sabbatini, et al. (ICP), aerial view of the three blocks at Via di Donna Olimpia (Monteverde), 1931–1937. The first phase is to the right; the second phase in the center; the third phase (left) was designed after the war. Now surrounded by a sea of *palazzine*, the complex was initially quite isolated and in the middle of the countryside on the edge of Parco Pamphili.

● Innocenzo Sabbatini, et al. (ICP), blocks at Via di Donna Olimpia. Detail of the porticoed entrance to the courtyard of the central block.

Sabbatini and the whole group of architects and engineers designed the entire complex for ten years straight and built it in almost fifteen years. The first phase was designed in 1931, the second between 1937 and 1938, the third after that date. The war interrupted the construction, which was resumed and finished in 1951. Calza Bini and Costantini found the financing and demonstrated the efficiency of their method of work with the credibility of results achieved with modest budgets. The realized project is beautiful precisely because it is the result of that long travail, and precisely because, in the connection between the different phases, one can analyze and appreciate the adjustments made necessary in acquiring the land, in defining the quantities to be met, and in the growing scarcity of building materials in the times of autarky following the 1935 invasion of Ethiopia. A detailed observation reveals the quiet slide from one architectural language to another along the three phases of design and construction. Everything became simpler, more modern, without losing the compositional and social principles of the enterprise begun on Sabbatini's original drawing board. So much simplicity even induced the designers to call to life some molecule of Futurism or Expressionism which, on the roof of the tallest buildings, is almost unexpectedly revealed, Paolo Portoghesi would say, with a bit of irony. In so doing, the architects seemed to affirm that the taste for suggestive linguistic detail did not belong only to the long vituperated Roman eclecticism but was an ineradicable part of the spirit of every designer who understands that his or her job is the privileged service of caring for the face of cities.

Unlike what the INA planners had done in Via Taranto—a seemingly complete fragment of the city, all introverted, with its tree-lined avenues, its towers, and its central square—the team directed by Innocenzo Costantini and Alberto Calza Bini designed not only the internal spaces and paths, but also the spaces of the future city to come. When the complex of Donna Olimpia was eventually absorbed by the city expanding from Monteverde Vecchio toward the west, it became the heart of the new district and offered a beautiful public square to the new residents: a modern square, brought to life by the vague expressionist posturing of the three buildings that bordered it and by the close comparison of the three different stylistic variants with which the phases of construction faced it. Likewise, the country road that linked the new settlement to Rome, Via di Donna Olimpia, received sufficient care so that, overtime, it appeared as a ready-made public avenue, embellished by a sudden architectural perspective, theatrical enough to claim for that ancient country road the rank of backbone of an entirely new part of the city.[65]

● Mario Sironi, "Italy Between the Arts and Sciences" (*L'Italia fra le arti e le scienze*), Sapienza University of Rome, 1935. The mural fills the backdrop to the stage of the Aula Magna (8 × 17 meters). At the center is the figure of Italy portrayed as the goddess in war gear, flanked by allegorical figures representing the arts and sciences: Astronomy, Mineralogy, Botany, Geography, Architecture, Letters, Painting, and History. In 1950, the fresco was partially repainted to cover up Fascist symbols. A restoration project from 2015 to 2017 removed the overpainting, revealing the original iconography.

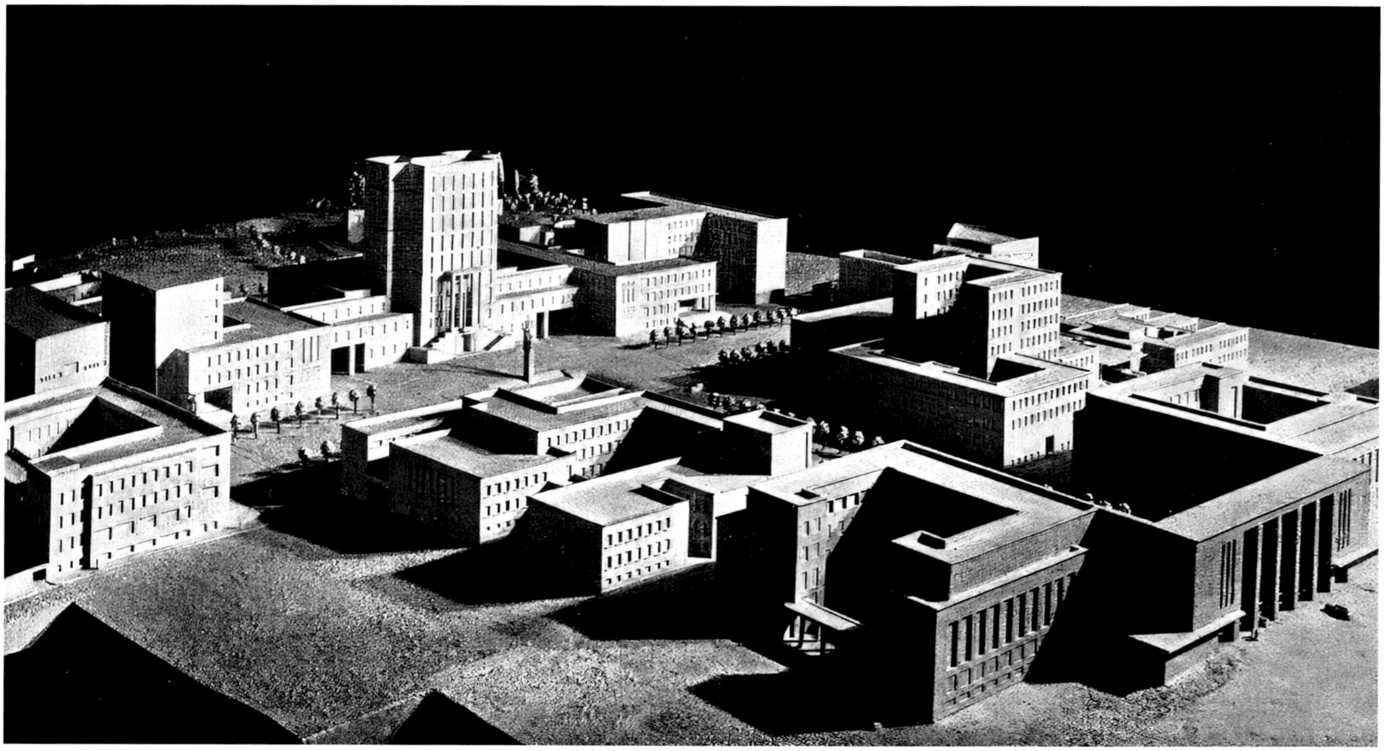

● Marcello Piacentini, et al., model of the Città Universitaria La Sapienza (University City) in its 1933 version. One of the major changes in the final version was the removal of the tower over the Rectorate building. The inauguration took place on 31 March 1935.

● Marcello Piacentini, diagrammatic masterplan of the Città Universitaria in 1940.

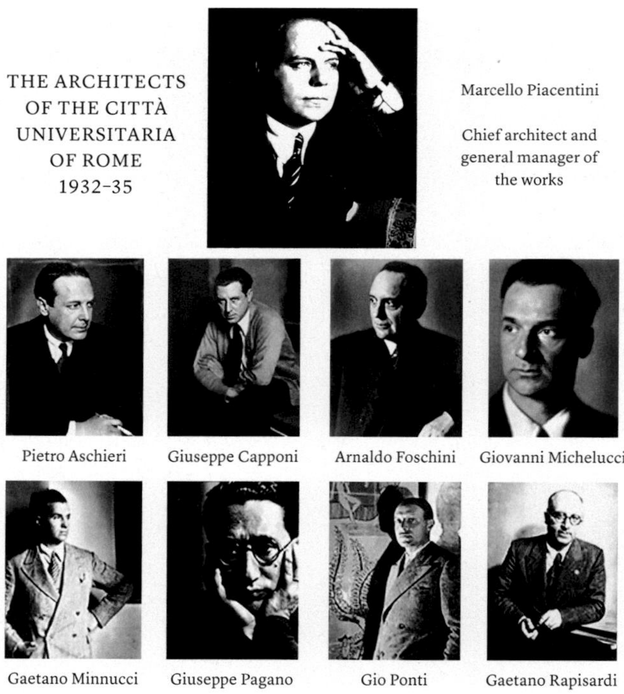

● Chart of the architects involved in the Città Universitaria before 1940.

From the *Città Universitaria* to E42/EUR: The Superior and Authoritarian Architect

The experience of the Piazza d'Armi district, of which the main protagonists were Giovannoni and Piacentini, had imparted two lessons and urged two further objectives. The first lesson was that to innovatively design and civically realize the city it was necessary that the ground of the new neighborhoods be public at the time of their construction. From this requirement stemmed the second lesson: every new part of the city should have an author (understood indifferently as an individual or a small team) capable of combining aesthetic, representational, symbolic, and social needs within an implementation program realistically and technically well grounded. The first of the objectives was to make the author of the overall project equally responsible for the artistic outcome of the architecture of individual buildings. Marcello Piacentini had tasted this role of "indirect authorship" as Artistic Director of the 1911 Universal Exhibition on the very ground of the Piazza d'Armi. He experienced it even more thoroughly in the 1915 San Francisco Exposition, of which he was the sole designer, having been commissioned by Ernesto Nathan, no longer Mayor of Rome but chief representative of Italian participation in the Exposition.[66] In another context, it is also important to remember Piacentini's capacity to design and build all the architectural pieces—including the first skyscraper in Italy, the so-called Torrione INA—of the new Piazza della Vittoria in Brescia (1927–1932).[67] Accordingly, Piacentini was able to reflect on the need for a new figure of the planner to emerge from the ranks of architects and engineers already working: the figure of the "superior architect," author of the masterplan of a new part of the city and the "director" of the architectural development of each of its buildings.[68] Piacentini's vision was a political and authoritarian deviation from the concept of the *architetto integrale*, which Giovannoni had coined in the 1910s: The "integral architect" was to be a leader in architectural and urban design, architectural history, the conservation of buildings and cities, public advocacy, legislation, and education—an all-encompassing notion able to integrate artists', architects', and engineers' skills and interests.[69]

The E42 or Esposizione Universale Roma took place at the end of this journey. Conceived of as a new and very large quarter of modern Rome whose realization was to be decisive for the development of the whole city, it was to see the light of day as a great international exposition planned by Mussolini for 1942 and from whose layout the new and permanent urban district was to develop immediately afterward. The Esposizione Universale of 42, like Piazza d'Armi was to be an opportunity to assert a "national style," which in the late 1930s was the one invented and fine-tuned by Piacentini himself and offered to Mussolini as the "style of Fascism." Moreover, Piacentini succeeded in imposing himself as general planner, genuine *deus ex machina*, who condensed in himself the undisputed authorship of the overall project and that of strict and equally undisputed decision-maker of the basic architectural choices to which all participating designers were asked to adhere. Piacentini's conception of the "superior architect" was not only authorial, but also authoritarian. In all the major urban projects in which he was involved, he assumed the role of a planner who stands apart from the level of ordinary architects—no matter how brilliant and inspired—not because of special artistic qualities, but because of his superior ability to masterfully organize an overall design of urban dimension and to define by broad strokes the language with which to implement its realization through the work of other architects. He chose and controlled them not only for their skill, but also for their willingness to bring

● Marcello Piacentini, view of the Rectorate at the center of the campus, 1933–1935. The bronze statue of Minerva, placed on a pedestal in a water pool, is the work of Arturo Martini.

that language to life with their own linguistic sensibility. This is why the project for the Città Universitaria (University City) of Rome ◖◖◖◖ pp. 107–109 ◗◗◗◗ was such an important occasion and it led him to secure the commission, to join the Fascist Party after ten years of detached "flanking." This was an unusual anxiety for an eminent figure now dear to the regime and already appointed by Mussolini, not many months earlier, as Academician of Italy.[70]

The Improbable Dream: EUR as Seen by Federico Fellini

Within this context, the new University City project was the dress rehearsal for Piacentini's conception and management of the E42 project. He had already defined, in other works, his own *Novecento* language, suggesting to Mussolini, with the help of Margherita Sarfatti (1880–1961) herself, that it was the most suitable for the new Fascist Italy. The University City was precisely the occasion to test its "transmissibility." The result was a great success for Piacentini and the regime, and it guaranteed him the role of Director of the E42 project a few years later. With the Città Universitaria, he succeeded in imposing his own style on a group of highly qualified Italian architects of different linguistic tendencies—suffice to mention Giuseppe Pagano, Giò Ponti, Giovanni Michelucci, and Pietro Aschieri. He knew that his vision would acquire quality and linguistic articulation through the different interpretations that "his" architects would give it, each of them declining it according to his own culture or, even, according to his own brilliant creativity.

Perhaps only Federico Fellini (1920–1993) understood what the great unfinished project of E42/EUR meant to Piacentini. A new city, imagined, designed, founded, and arisen in the late 1930s, while, at each step of the way, the economic crisis, Hitler's madness, Mussolini's incapacity, the resistance of the young, and the envy of the old seemed to conspire to push its realization away, turning it into an unattainable dream. Federico Fellini, in a short film about EUR, responded to the film director Luciano Emmer, saying, "Its empty houses, uninhabited houses, its buildings created for ghosts. Or for statues .... I like the sensation of provisional .... It has the charm of a mad dream interrupted."[71] Dream? Can we talk about dreams when it comes to the programs of an eternal winner who was always disenchanted, pragmatic, concrete to the point of cynicism like Piacentini? Yes, although it is also true that in those years, in the gloomy deterioration of the general situation, the pragmatic, the undefeated Piacentini was competing with destiny to complete or at least safeguard his major projects: not only his urban and architectural projects still under construction in many Italian cities but also projects to reform urban planning, the design of the Italian city, and the profession of the architect.

Italy's Superior Architect Competing with History

The National Urban Law written by Virgilio Testa, which made the urban design know-how of Piacentini and his group the legal basis for national planning, and which, despite its imperfections, is still the current national law, was brought for Mussolini's signature on 17 August 1942.[72] They were engaged in a race against time to achieve, before the upcoming catastrophe, an outcome considered fundamental to their program. Determination, political flair, the ability to dissimulate in the face of the now unbearable loser, Mussolini, and his most sordid clique: all this testified to the pragmatic realism of Piacentini and his group. He was not a man of easy illusions, results counted. But this was not to be with the E42 Esposizione. In his vision, its realization should not only have been the most glorious achievement of his work as an architect and the definitive affirmation of the category of "superior architects," with him as the supreme one. Given this "supra-architectural" and existential goal, the E42 project could not, like some others, be put aside to await the return of better times; it had to go ahead at all costs or rather pretend to go ahead until its superior architect had achieved his very lofty goal. First, it was promptly renamed from E42 (Esposizione 1942) to EUR (Universale Esposizione Roma), implying that it was completely changed in nature and purpose—in Piacentini's words, Città Internazionale del Sapere (International City of Knowledge).[73] With an astonishing leap backward of more than 60 years, he made his own the positivist and resurgent program of the liberal and conservative Minister Quintino Sella, who in 1871 replied to the question of what the program of the government of the new Italy was for Rome: "One does not stand in Rome without having cosmopolitan purposes .... Yes, a cosmopolitan purpose we have in Rome: that of Science."[74] In the space of a few words written by Piacentini in a private letter, EUR was reimagined from being a monumental affirmation of the imperial spirit of Fascism, to a new city of cosmopolitanism—of the international culture and science of those who would govern Italy after Mussolini.

Yet, it was necessary to move quickly. As early as 1941, Piacentini had coordinated a draft and a revised

● Marcello Piacentini, et al., axonometric plan of the E42 world fair as proposed, wood marquetry. The spirit of the plan was maintained after the Second World War, yet with significant urban and architectural modifications.

version of the *Piano regolatore* of 1931, known as the General Variant and designed according to the urban planning principles of the law that Testa was preparing. The elements were all in place and perfect for Piacentini to officially become "the sole director of architecture in Rome."[75] He would assume the official role of Edile, a new institutional figure that he coined himself, modeled on the equally named magistracy of ancient Rome. It would have the task of supervising the drafting of the *Piano regolatore* and all detailed plans at a bigger scale, the *Piano particolareggiato*. It would have control over the public and private buildings in the capital and be shielded from all interference and control by other agencies. Basically, it was a matter of extending to the whole city those powers that Piacentini already held at EUR.[76] Although the proposal for the Edile di Roma aroused great resistance, it raised the stakes higher.

It was the first months of 1943, a fateful year. Germany had suffered the disaster of Stalingrad; the Allies had landed in Africa and were preparing to invade Italy. The cities were suffering heavy bombardment from American and British flying fortresses. There was neither architect nor planner in Italy who was not already thinking about the need to face a great and strenuous reconstruction after the end of the war. In the early months of 1943, the aerial bombardment of Italian cities intensified. Piacentini's thoughts turned to the post-war period, the reconstruction of the bombed cities, the recently passed National Urban Law, and the city plans envisaged by the law, which would regulate their growth. To provide an adequate response to these new challenges, he envisioned the establishment of a new professional organization, the Gruppo di architetti, ingegneri, urbanisti (GAIU, Group of Architects, Engineers, Urbanists), that he would chair. He invited about thirty professionals to join it, Giorgio Calza Bini and Mario De Renzi in Rome, but also Alberto Alpago Novello (1889–1985) in Milan, and many other professionals and university professors. The fall of Mussolini in 1943 interrupted everything.

Fascist or Bourgeois City?

The search for a more organic and unified architectural definition of large urban interventions for the design of modern Rome—with Piacentini as the major leader and protagonist—took place during the Fascist period, but not really in function of the ideology of Fascism. Or at least not solely in function of it, although it often clothed itself in its ideality. To be sure, major settlement programs, whether those of land reclamation in the Pontine area—Littoria, Sabaudia, and others—and throughout the country, or of large urban spaces, or new neighborhoods, could not even be imagined unless they were presented to Mussolini as a realization of Fascist and imperial culture, as it was presented in the last years of the regime. It was the culture of the new bourgeois city that tended to assert itself. Bourgeois, modern and, on some occasions, humanitarian.[77] Far removed from the avant-garde and imperialist claptrap of even the many architects involved in those enterprises. All of the research on the city made use of the Mussolinian aspiration to make the city the mirror of the regime, but it retained its character as European-oriented research on the form of the modern city. In Rome in the late 1920s and early 1930s, the destinies of architecture were officially all entrusted to the debate, or better to the struggle between the young Rationalists and the academics of the Roman School of Architecture. At the same time, important institutions of a public character were continuing, in a truly exemplary way, the research on the organic design of normal, bourgeois-like residential parts of the city without any stentorian verbal—let alone linguistic—reference to the dominant political ideology and to the dominant architectural ideologies.

● View of the EUR partially constructed and abandoned during World War II, 1953. From left clockwise: Palazzo della civiltà romana (G. Guerrini, E.B. Lapadula, M. Romano); Restaurant (E. Rossi); Palazzo degli Uffici (G. Minnucci, Gio Ponti); Piazza Imperiale (Francesco Fariello, Saverio Muratori, Ludovico Quaroni, and Luigi Moretti); Palazzo dei Congressi (Adalberto Libera); Palazzo Mostra della Romanità (Pietro Aschieri, Domenico Bernardini, Cesare Pascoletti, Gino Peressuti); Palazzo dell'Autarchia e del Corporativismo (Mario De Renzi, Gino Pollini, Luigi Figini). Center: Palazzo delle Poste (BPPR); bottom center: Basilica of St. Peter and St.Paul (Arnaldo Foschini).

1
On Ernesto Nathan, see Fabio Martini, *Nathan e l'invenzione di Roma: Il sindaco che cambiò la Città eterna* (Rome: Palombi Editori, 2021); Emanuele Zammit and Luca Guazzati, eds., *Ernesto Nathan: L'inventore di Roma capitale* (Rome: Tipheret, 2021). For Parts 2 and 3, see also Piero Ostilio Rossi, *Roma. Guida all'architettura moderna 1909–2000* (Bari: Laterza, 2000).

2
On the masterplans of Rome, see Spiro Kostof, *The Third Rome, 1870–1950: Traffic and Glory* (Berkeley: University Art Museum, 1973). See also Gianni Accasto, Vanna Fraticelli, and Renato Nicolini, *L'architettura di Roma capitale 1870–1970* (Rome: Golem, 1971), 311–314. Even before Nathan's election, the technical office of the City of Rome had drawn up a draft masterplan that was no longer guided by the systematic application of the grid layout.

3
The AACAR was founded on 23 January 1890 on the initiative of the architect Giovanni Battista Giovenale (1848–1934) and a group of 24 promoting members, almost all architects who established the early modernity in Rome. Gustavo Giovannoni was a member from 1903 and was the president after 1910. Marcello Piacentini and his father Pio were also members.

4
Richard A. Etlin, *Modernism in Italian Architecture, 1890–1940* (Cambridge, MA: The MIT Press, 1991); see vol. 37 (2022) of *Planning Perspectives*, titled "The Art of Preserving and Building Cities in Italy (1860–1930): Legacies and Actors," and in particular, Francesca Romana Stabile, "Shaping Early 20th-Century Rome: The AACAR and the Contributions of Filippo Galassi and Gustavo Giovannoni," *Planning Perspectives*, vol. 37, no. 3 (2022), 551–581; Marina Docci and Maria Grazia Turco, "L'Associazione Artistica fra i cultori di Architettura in Roma 1890–1930," *Bollettino del Centro di Studi per la Storia dell'Architettura*, no. 5 (2022).

5
Camillo Sitte, *Der Städte-Bau nach seinen künstlerischen Grundsätzen* (Vienna: Carl Graeser, 1889). In English, *City Planning According to Artistic Principles*, translated in George Collins and Christiane Crasemann Collins, *Camillo Sitte and the Birth of Modern City Planning* (New York: Rizzoli, 1986).

6
See the first part of this essay "The Pirate Times: 1870–1900," 40–70.

7
Gustavo Giovannoni, *Questioni di architettura* (Rome, 1929), 191, quoted by Francesca Romana Stabile, in "Gustavo Giovannoni e la cultura dell'*ambientismo*," *Bollettino del Centro di Studi per la Storia dell'Architettura*, no. 1 (2017).

8
See Giovanni Spizuoco, "Patrick Geddes e Gustavo Giovannoni: Conservative surgery e 'diradamento edilizio' per la tutela della città storica," *Eikonocity*, no. 2 (2018), 81–97. Also see Richard A. Etlin, *Modernism in Italian Architecture*, op. cit., and Guido Zucconi, ed., *Camillo Sitte e i suoi interpreti* (Milan: FrancoAngeli, 1993).

9
See Gianfranco Spagnesi, ed., *Il Quartiere e il Corso del Rinascimento* (Roma: Istituto dell'Enciclopedia italiana, 1994; Antonio Cederna (edited by F. Erbani), *I Vandali in casa: Cinquant'anni dopo* (Bari: Laterza, 2006).

10
Camillo Sitte, *Der Städte-Bau nach seinen künstlerischen Grundsätzen*, op. cit.; Josef Stübben, *Der Städtebau—Handbuch der Architektur* (Stuttgart: Kröner, 1907). On Camillo Sitte and its influence, including on Giovannoni, see Guido Zucconi, ed., *Camillo Sitte e i suoi interpreti*, op. cit.; Chuck Bohl and Jean-François Lejeune, eds., *Sitte, Hegemann and the Metropolis: Modern Civic Art and International Exchanges* (London: Routledge, 2009). It is worth mentioning that the AACAR organized the conference of the Mayor of Brussels in January 1902, Charles Buls (*L'esthétique des villes*), in which he presented the theory of Sitte and its application to the center of Brussels. The AACAR adopted Sitte's concepts: see for instance, "Sugli odierni criteri edilizi con speciale riguardo alla transformation di Roma," in *Annali della Societa degli Ingegneri e degli Architetti italiani*, XX (1905), 177–199; "Considerazioni sull'architettura e sui piani di ampliamento delle città," *Annuario dell'Accademia di S. Luca, Roma*, (1911), 109–120.

11
In English, see Steven W. Semes, Jeff Cody, and Francesco Siravo, eds., *New Building in Old Cities: Writings by Gustavo Giovannoni on Architectural and Urban Conservation* (Los Angeles: Getty Conservation Institute, 2024).

12
Gustavo Giovannoni, "Vecchie città ed edilizia nuova," *Nuova Antologia* (1 June 1913), 449–472; Gustavo Giovannoni, *Vecchie città ed edilizia nuova* (Turin: Utet, 1931); see also *Gustavo Giovannoni, tra storia e progetto* (Rome: Quasar, 2018); Giuseppe Bonaccorso and Francesco Moschini, eds., *Gustavo Giovannoni e l'architetto integrale* (Rome: Accademia di San Luca, 2019).

13
Rodolfo Lanciani, *Forma Urbis Romae* (Rome: Quasar, 1990). On Lanciani, see Domenico Palombi, *Rodolfo Lanciani: l'archeologia a Roma tra Ottocento e Novecento* (Rome: L'Erma di Bretschneider, 2006).

14
Gianfilippo Carettoni, ed., *La pianta marmorea di Roma antica: Forma Urbis Romae* (Rome: Ripartizione del Comune di Roma, 1960).

15
Filippo Coarelli, "Introduzione to Rodolfo Lanciani," in Roberto Lanciani, *Forma Urbis Romae*, 2.

16
Andrea Carandini's *The Atlas of Ancient Rome: Biography and Portraits of the City* (Princeton: Princeton University Press, 2017), first published in Italian as *Atlante di Roma antica, vol. 1–2* (Milan: Electa, 2012) is a systematic update and an expended reformulation of the information and maps contained in Lanciani's *Forma Urbis Romae*.

17
See Michele Giorgini and Valter Tocchi, eds., *Cesare Bazzani. Un Accademico d'Italia* (Perugia: Electa Editori Umbri Associati, 1988). Bazzani had a remarkable career, including designing the National Library in Florence, the Stazione Maritima in Naples, and many works in Forlì and Rieti. See also Maria Vittoria Marini Clarelli, "La Galleria Nazionale d'Arte Moderna," in Marcello Fagiolo and Alessandro Mazza, eds., *I Monti Parioli e il "Nuovo Campo Marzio" della cultura internazionale* (Rome: Artemide, 2022), 478–487.

18
Its name suggested that the area was at the disposal of military exercises; it was therefore owned by the armed forces, present in the barracks that delimited to the south the neighborhood of Prati di Castello.

19
See Sabrina Spinazzé, "Cambellotti e la Mostra dell'agro romano del 1911 alle radici dell'espressione artistica tra impegno sociale e primitivismo," 119–132, see https://www.academia.edu/12398536/Cambellotti_e_la_mostra_dellAgro_Romano_del_1911_Alle_radici_dellespressione_artistica_tra_impegno_sociale_e_primitivismo. See also Michelangelo Sabatino, *Pride in Modesty* (Toronto: University of Toronto Press, 2010).

20
On the 1911 exposition, see Gianna Piantoni, *Roma 1911* (Rome: De Luca Editori d'Arte, 1980); Stefania Massari, ed., *La festa delle feste. Roma e l'esposizione internazionale* (Rome: Palombi Editori, 2011); Stefania Massari, *Roma 1911 nella rassegna illustrate della esposizione* (Rome: De Luca Editori d'Arte, 2011); Mario Sanfilippo, *La costruzione di una capitale. Roma 1911–1945* (Rome: Silvana, 2002). Also important was the Mostra archeologica (archaeological exhibition) set up within the Baths of Diocletian.

21
In 1890, Guglielmo Calderini had presented a "Memoir for the Government" on the costs, best examples, and possible typologies for social housing. A few years later, he proposed the Piazza d'Armi area as a field of experimentation and demonstration of how, by acting on public areas, outstanding urbanistic, architectural, and humanitarian results could be achieved. See Gianni Accasto, Vanna Fraticelli, and Renato Nicolini, *L'architettura di Roma capitale 1870–1970* (Rome: Golem, 1971), 275.

22
Nuova Antologia, 1908. See also Antonino Terranova, "Architettura e urbanistica per Roma. Dal Palazzo di Giustizia al quartiere di Piazza d'Armi," *Controspazio*, no. 9, September 1972. Sanjust had to consider that the municipal administration would have to trade the area in the hands of the Armed Forces for an equivalent one, equally vast and well accessible.

23
Vanna Fraticelli, *Roma, 1914–1929: la città e gli architetti tra la Guerra e il fascismo* (Rome: Officina Edizioni, 1982).

24
See Lucio Valerio Barbera, "Il deposito Vittoria dell'Atac a Piazza Bainsizza nel quartiere Delle Vittorie di Roma," in *L'architettura della città. The Journal of the Scientific Society Ludovico Quaroni*, no. 11 (2017), 19–51.

25
This book uses the abbreviation ICP consistently to refer to the Istituto per le Case Popolari. Please note that the abbreviation IACP (Istituto Autonomo Case Popolari) is also used in the literature. From 1931 to 1945, the Institute was renamed IFACP (Istituto Fascista Autonomo per le Case Popolari).

26
See Livio Toschi, *L'Istituto cooperative per le case degli impiegati dello stato in Roma: 1908–1933*, (Rome: Galleria A. A. M., 1986). Construction took place from 1913 to 1915. See the section on Parioli in this volume: 302–311.

27
Errico Bovio, quoted in Livio Toschi, *L'Istituto cooperative per le case degli impiegati*, 3.

28
See Livio Toschi, *Costantino Costantini (1854–1937) e Innocenzo Costantini (1881–1962). Progetti e realizzazioni* (Osimo: Industrie grafiche Errebi, 1984).

29
Among other responsibilities during his career, Alberto Calza Bini was President and Fascist of the first hour, Secretary of the Fascist Architects Union, great friend of Marcello Piacentini, Dean of the Faculty of Architecture in Naples, and the president of the newly founded Istituto Nazionale di Urbanistica (National Institute of Urban Planning, INU). See Sarah Catalano, *Alberto Calza Bini Architetto (1881–1957)*, Dissertation Università degli Studi di Palermo, Department of Architecture, 2011.

30
On the range of ICP realizations between 1903 and the 1950s, see Alberto Calza Bini, *Il fascismo per le case del popolo. L'opera dell'Istituto per le Case Popolari in Roma nel primo quadriennio dell'amministrazione fascista* (Rome: IACP, 1927); IACP, *Cinquant'anni di vita dell'Istituto Autonomo per le Case Popolari della Provincia di Roma* (Rome: IACP, 1953); Tommaso Dore, Alessandro Nocera, and Maria Vittoria Rinaldi, *L'archivio storico iconografico IACP. I progetti delle case popolari a Roma dal 1903 agli anni '50* (Rome: ATER del Comune di Roma, 2010); P. Capolino, ed., *Case romane. La periferia e le case popolari* (Rome: Prospettive Edizioni, 2009).

31
See the Inserto Quadrio Pirani in Livio Toschi, *L'istituto cooperative per le case degli impiegati*, op. cit.

32
Quadrio Pirani, quoted in Livio Toschi, *L'istituto cooperative per le case degli impiegati*, 5.

33
On Sabbatini, see Bruno Regni and Marina Sennato, *Innocenzo Sabbatini: architettura tra tradizione e rinnovamento* (Rome: Kappa, 1982); Lorenzo Ciccarelli, "Innocenzo Sabbatini and the Construction of Modern Rome," in Carmen M. Enss and Luigi Monzo, eds., *Townscapes in Transition: Transformation and Reorganization of Italian Cities and Their Architecture in the Interwar Period* (Bielefeld: transcript Verlag, 2019), 247–260; Aristotle A. Kallis, "Rome's Singular Path to Modernism: Innocenzo Sabbatini and the 'Rooted' Architecture of the Instituto Case Popolari (ICP), 1925–1930," *Papers of the British School in Rome*, vol. 85 (2017), 269–301.

34
Adam Nathaniel Furman and Aristotle A. Kallis, "Magnificent Seven: Sabbatini's Housing," *RIBA Journal* (5 February 2015).

35
Guido Calza, "Le origini Latine dell'abitazione moderna," *Architettura e Arti decorative*, no. 1 (September 1923), 1–18; Guido Calza and Italo Gismondi, "Le origini Latine dell'abitazione moderna," *Architettura e Arti decorative*, no. 2 (October 1923), 49–63.

36
On La Garbatella, see the special section in this volume, 248–259.

37
Aristotle A. Kallis, "Rome's Singular Path," op. cit., 6.

38
Quoted by Richard A. Etlin, *Modernism in Italian Architecture*, op. cit., 272, from Roberto Papini, "Architetti giovani in Roma," *Dedalo* 12 (1932), 148.

39
Gruppo Sette, "Architecture I (1926)," "Architecture II: The Foreigners (1927), *Oppositions*, no. 6 (Fall 1976), 89–102; Gruppo Sette, "Architecture III: Unpreparedness- Incomprehension-Prejudices," "Architecture IV: A New Archaic Era (1927)", *Oppositions*, no. 12 (Spring 1978), 91–98. In Italian: Gruppo 7, "Architettura 1," *La Rassegna Italiana* (December 26), 849–854; Gruppo Sette, "Architettura II: Gli Stranieri," *La Rassegna Italiana* (February 1927), 129–137; Gruppo 7, "Architettura III: Impreparazione, incomprensione, pregiuduzi," *La Rassegna Italiana* (March 1927), 247–252; Gruppo 7, "Architettura IV: Una nuova epoca arcaica," *La Rassegna Italiana* (May 1927), 467–472.

40
Gruppo Sette, "Architecture," *Oppositions* no.6, 91–92.

41
See the 27-page catalogue: Adalberto Libera and Gaetano Minnucci, eds., *Esposizione Italiana di Architettura Razionale. Roma VI* (Rome: De Alberti Editore, 1928).

42
The Scuola Superiore di Architettura di Roma was created by decree on 31 October 1919, following a protracted political and cultural debate initiated after 1870. For a detailed history, see "La nascita della Scuola Superiore di Architettura" at "https://www.architettiroma.it/lordine/archivio-storico-dellordine/la-nascita-della-scuola-superiore-di-architettura/

43
On the Rationalist movement, see Giorgio Ciucci, *Gli architetti e il fascismo. Architettura e città 1922–1944* (Turin: Einaudi, 2002); Richard A. Etlin, *Modernism in Italian Architecture*, op. cit.; Dennis Doordan, *Building Modern Italy* (New York: Princeton Architectural Press, 1989); David Rifkind, *The Battle for Modernism. Quadrante and the Politicization of Architectural Discourse in Fascist Italy* (Venice: Marsilio, 2012).

44
On Pietro Bardi, see Francesco Tentori, *Pietro Maria Bardi: primo attore del Razionalismo* (Turin: Testo & immagine, 2002).

45
See David Rifkind, *The Battle for Modernism*, op. cit.

46
See Fabrizio Aggarbati and Carla Saggioro, *Giulio Gra: Opere e progetti 1923/1939* (Rome: Edizioni Kappa, 1991).

47
Francesco Bartolini, *Roma Borghese: la casa e i ceti medi tra le due guerre* (Bari: Laterza, 2001), 113–114. The book is not well known to architects and yet essential for understanding the degree of autonomy of the research on the architecture of the bourgeois city, Rome, during the two Fascist decades.

48
Paolo Portoghesi, *L'eclettismo a Roma, 1870–1922* (Rome: De Luca Editori d'Arte, 1968), VII.

49
Ibidem.

50
Ibidem.

51
Giuseppe Machin (no dates available) is also known for the INA building in Lecce, a curved structure built across from the excavation of the Roman theater.

52
See Ettore Maria Mazzola, "Il complesso di palazzine INA di Gino Cipriani in viale Buozzi," in Marcello Fagiolo and Alessandro Mazza, eds., *I Monti Parioli*, op. cit., 336–343. Also see Gino Cipriani's biography in Charles Bossu and Sabine van Sprang, *The Academia Belgica in Rome. Building for the Arts and Sciences in the Eternal City* (Brussels: Mercatorfonds, 2023).

53
See Jean-François Lejeune, "Roma non interrotta," in this volume, 6–15.

54
Carlo Mezzetti and Fabio Lanfranchi, *Il disegno della palazzina romana* (Rome: Kappa, 2008); *Metamorfosi: Quaderni di architettura*, nos. 1–2 (1985); Alessandra Muntoni, *Roma tra le due guerre, 1919–1944*, chapter 9, "La Roma delle palazzine' degli anni venti agli anni quaranta" (Rome: Edizioni Kappa, 2010), 361–404; Ricardo Agarez, "Giles Worsley Travel Fellowship: The Making of the Roman Palazzina," *Papers of the British School* (Cambridge, UK: Cambridge University Press, 2015).

55
Pier Luigi Nervi had his office in Palazzina Nebbiosi. On Palazzina Furmanik, see Anna Irene Del Monaco, *Modernità postantica. La palazzina Furmanik di Mario De Renzi* (Rome: La Sapienza, 2016).

56
For a typological analysis, see Emanuel Christ and Christoph Gantenbein, "Typology Transfer—Towards an Urban Architecture," *Typology: Hong Kong—Rome—New York—Buenos Aires* (Zurich: Park Books, 2012). See also Alessandro Mazza, "Astrazione e memoria: la palazzina ai Parioli fra le due guerre," in Marcello Fagiolo and Alessandro Mazza, eds., *I Monti Parioli*, 310–329.

57
Therefore, by today's standards, for 1300 people, but by the standards of the time it was designed for about 2000 people.

58
See the section on Monteverde in this volume, 282–291.

59
The real estate activities of the INA remain to be investigated and published. The INA Assitalia Historical Archive covers the period from 1912 (the year the company was founded) to 2013. The Historical Real Estate Fund (1912–1992) contains both administrative and technical documentation of the INA's architectural and urban realizations: https://heritage.generali.com/archivi/archivio-storico-ina-assitalia/

60
For the activities of the SFI, see the inventory realized by Paola Puzzuoli (2009), *Società generale immobiliare-Sogene. Proprietà fondiaria e immobiliare. Serie A-Proprietary fondiaria e operazioni finanziarie 1862–1948*, at https://search.acs.beniculturali.it/OpacACS/inventario/IT-ACS-GEAST0407-0000001#n. See the neighborhood sections on Parioli, Bologna, Flaminio, Bologna for more details about all those realizations. For activities after 1945, see the third section of Barbera's essay "1945–1960: From the Reconstruction to the Olympics."

61
See for instance Spiro Kostof, *The Third Rome, 1870–1950*, op. cit.; *L'invenzione dei fori imperiali: demolizioni e scavi, 1924–1940* (Rome: Palombi Editori, 2008).

62
In this volume, see section on Monteverde, 282–291, and section on Aniene Montesacro, 240–247.

63
The date of 26 May 1927 marked a momentous turning point in Fascist urban policy. In his notorious Ascension Day speech, Benito Mussolini argued that metropolitan industrialization induced the "sterility of the population." A year later, in his article "Sfollare le città," the Duce outlined the regime's radical goals to limit metropolitan growth by re-equilibrating city and countryside and "ruralizing" the country. See for instance, Danilo Breschi, *Mussolini e la città. Il fascismo tra antiurbanesimo e modernità* (Milan: Luni Editrice, 2018); Diane Ghirardo, *Building New Communities: New Deal America and Fascist Italy* (Princeton, NJ: Princeton University Press, 1989).

64
Camillo Sitte, *Der Städte-Bau nach seinen künstlerischen Grundsätzen*, op. cit.

65
Attributed here to Sabbatini, there remains some imprecision regarding the authorship of the Donna Olimpia complex, particularly as regards the different phases of construction: for some clarification, see Anu Kaisa Koponen, "From Utopias to Roman Residential Realities: the Golden Era of Roman social housing 1919–1932," in *Planning Perspectives*, 16 November 2024. For the superblocks produced by INA, INCIS, and ICP, see Christ and Gantenbein, *Typology: Hong Kong—Rome—New York—Buenos Aires*, and on the particular cases of Via Melaina and Donna Olimpia, see Luciano Villani, *Le Borgate del fascismo: Storia urbana, politica e sociale della periferia romana* (Milan: Ledizioni, 2020), http://books.openedition.org/ledizioni/99.

66
Piacentini chose not to fragment the different pavilions assigned to Italy, but to concentrate the presence of our country in a real "Italian Citadel," a kind of scenic and yet realistic reproduction of an "Italian place," a civilized urban space of a hypothetical but typical town, in which the entire range of the historical and stratification of its urban construction would be made visible.

67
On Piacentini in Brescia, see Renato Pacini, "La sistemazione del centro di Brescia dell'architetto Marcello Piacentini," *Architettura*, XII, December 1932, 649–673; Roberto Behar, ed., *The Architecture of Politics: 1910–1940* (Miami Beach, FL: The Wolfsonian, 1995).

68
Guido Zucconi, "Dal capitello alla città. Il profilo dell'architetto totale," in Guido Zucconi, ed., *Gustavo Giovannoni. Dal capitello alla città* (Milan: Jaca Books, 1997), 9–68.

69
See Steven W. Semes, Jeff Cody, and Francesco Siravo, eds., *New Building in Old Cities*, op. cit.

70
On the Città Universitaria, see "La città universitaria di Roma," Special supplement to *Architettura*, Roma, 1935; Alessandra Muntoni, "La Città Universitaria di Roma (1933–1935)," in Alessandra Muntoni, *Roma tra le due guerre* (Rome: Edizioni Kappa, 2010), 87–126; Guia Baratelli, *La città universitaria di Roma. Costruzione di un testo architettonico* (Milan: Silvana Editoriale, 2019).

71
See Luciano Emmer, director. *Fellini e ... EUR*, 1972 (https://www.youtube.com/watch?v=2ZqoevcbxhY); see also Salvatore Santuccio, *Modern Rome and the Cinematic Gaze*, in this volume, 342–355.

72
For more explanation of the National Urban Law and its importance, see Barbera, "From the Reconstruction to the Olympic Games: 1945–1960," 122–150 in this volume.

73
Letter of Piacentini to Vittorio Cini, 18 August 1942, in Enrico Guidoni, "L'E 42, città della rappresentazione. Il progetto urbanistico e le polemiche sull'architettura," in Maurizio Calvesi, Enrico Guidoni, and Simonetta Lux, eds., *Urbanistica, architettura, arte e decorazione. E 42. Utopia e Scenario del Regime*, vol. II. (Venice: Marsilio, 1987), 17–73.

74
Ibidem.

75
See Paolo Nicoloso, *Marcello Piacentini. Architettura e Potere: una biografia* (Udine: Gaspari Editore, 2018), 260.

76
Ibidem. It is worth noting that in the same year (1941) the first *Piano Regolatore della Metropolitana di Roma* was established. The task was entrusted to the engineer Vito Perrone, Director of the Higher Office for the Metro and Foreign Railways of the Ministry of Transport, and it was carried out in agreement with the technical offices of the Governorate. In fact, shortly before this plan, work had begun on line B (unusual choice to label the first line built on the Rome metro with the letter B). It was dug from Piramide to Termini between 1938 and 1941 and inaugurated after the Second World War in the section between EUR and Termini in 1955. The development of this line toward Lido di Ostia along the Via Imperiale (today Via Cristoforo Colombo) was detailed in the variant to the 1942 PRG which focused precisely on the development of Rome toward the sea.

77
See Diane Ghirardo, *Building New Communities*, op. cit.

Giovanni Guerrini, Ernesto La Padula, and Mario Romano. Palazzo della Civiltà del Lavoro (also Palazzo della Civiltà Italiana), EUR, 1938–1953. Winner of the competition in 1937, the structure was abandoned almost finished in 1943 and completed in 1953. With its four identical facades on high ground, the Palazzo is one of the most iconic structures of modern Rome. The text on the facades reads: "A People of Poets of Artists of Heroes of Saints of Thinkers of Scientists of Navigators of Transmigrators."

Palazzo della Civiltà del Lavoro, view of the arcades on the ground floor. The abstracted classical architecture refers directly to the metaphysical painting of Giorgio de Chirico.

Adalberto Libera, Palazzo dei Ricevimenti e dei Congressi, EUR, 1938–1953. Winner of the competition in 1938, the structure was abandoned almost finished in 1943 and completed in 1953. Behind its Rationalist columns, the iconic cubic structure, entirely covered with marble slabs, rises 45 meters and forms the central exhibition hall.

Adalbero Libera, Palazzo dei Ricevimenti e dei Congressi, marble theater on roof terrace.

Giovanni Guerrini, “La nascita di Roma” (The Birth of Rome), sketches for the Ostia Antica-inspired black-and-white mosaics, EUR, 1938–1940. The mosaics can be seen in front of the Salone d’Onore of the Palazzo degli Uffici, EUR.

Adalbero Libera, Palazzo dei Ricevimenti e dei Congressi, interior view of the central exhibition cube.

Saverio Muratori, Palazzo Sturzo—Ex-Headquarters of the Christian Democracy Party, EUR, 1955–1958. Fruit of the architect's research on typology and construction in Rome, the rectangular palazzo building, surrounded by arcades on the ground floor, consists of two square structures connected by a wide passage and a courtyard (10 × 18 meters). References to the Roman, Renaissance, and Baroque history of the city are everywhere, particularly to the brick facades and vaults of Palazzo Farnese and structures by Borromini.

Ludovico Quaroni and Saverio Muratori, general view of the Piazza Imperiale and central axis of EUR, Via Cristoforo Colombo. The obelisk of Marconi was commissioned to the sculptor Arturo Dazzi to commemorate the physicist and inventor Guglielmo Marconi. Threatened with demolition in the post-war era, it was eventually inaugurated for the Olympic Games of 1960. The 92 panels that cover it represent scenes of dance, songs, prayers, and animals, interpreted as hymns to the discoveries of Marconi.

Ludovico Quaroni and Saverio Muratori, Piazza Imperiale, EUR, detailed views.

● Ludovico Quaroni and Mario Ridolfi, et al., 1949–1954. Street of the INA-Casa Tiburtino district.

III. From the Reconstruction to the Olympic Games: 1945–1960

Marcello Piacentini survived professionally after the war in a quasi-miraculous way. First, with the strong support of the Vatican and of Giulio Andreotti, the new star of the dominant Democrazia Cristiana (Catholic political party) after the war; second, because the new and established professional figures such as Pier Luigi Nervi (1891–1979) and historian Enrico Calandra (1877–1946) testified in his favor. Not only did he survive, but he succeeded quite well. He continued to be a professor and he was again elected Dean of the Faculty of Architecture in 1951 until 1954. Professionally, he was able to fully complete the opening and the construction of Via della Conciliazione ◖ bottom ◗ on axis with St. Peter and inaugurated for the Holy Year of 1950. Moreover, he resumed a coordinating role in restarting planning and construction at EUR when Virgilio Testa (1889–1978) became its President.[1] To be sure, by the end of the war, the Rome Faculty of Architecture had lost its central role, but the most important professors, except for Gustavo Giovannoni who died in 1947, were still those of the post-World War I period. Arnaldo Foschini (1884–1968)—architect of the Basilica dei Santi Pietro e Paolo at EUR, the monumental entrance portico to the Città Universitaria (1935), and one of the authors of the reconstruction of the Corso del Rinascimento (1930s)—became Dean for a critical period of the reconstruction (1945–1951); then there was Vincenzo Fasolo (also Dean from 1954 to 1960). The only professor who was dismissed was Enrico Del Debbio, but an amnesty law by Palmiro Togliatti allowed him to be reinstated. Overall, the faculty was the same as in 1942, although the professors had no professional posts comparable to the pre-war period.[2]

● Polish soldiers overlooking the opening of the Via della Conciliazione in progress from the dome of St. Peter. The *spina* has already been destroyed and reconstruction is in progress.

In the late 1940s, while Head of the Rome School of Architecture, Arnaldo Foschini played a critical role in the urban and architectural program of post-war reconstruction, known as the INA-Casa (1949–1963). The INA-Casa plan, established to increase workers' employment while building new public housing, was the brainchild of Minister of Labor and Social Security Amintore Fanfani. Formerly a member of the Fascist party, Fanfani was situated to the left of the Christian-Democrat party, and was driven by a Catholic view of capitalism that encouraged and supported the role of the State to temper the "amorality and excesses of market-capitalism."[3] Funded by the Marshall Plan, the aspiration of the INA-Casa program was "to give workers a civilized home, studied in ways so that each can feel in its own and where each man can feel himself a citizen of a new community."[4] At the same time, the plan had fundamental economic goals. The logic and principles of the plan implied to build houses in a traditional and non-industrialized way, without the use of heavy cranes or special machines, and thus suitable to give work to large amounts of "workers," including the unskilled.[5] Along with the engineer Filiberto Guala (who chaired the Implementation Committee and managed the funds), Foschini acted as manager of the architectural and urban aspects, and in so doing was able to "reinvent" a national role for the Faculty of Architecture of Rome.

Foschini's first critical decision was to call on the best students before the war: Mario Ridolfi (1904–1984), who was teaching at the Istituto Tecnico Industriale (Industrial Technical Institute) and Adalberto Libera (1903–1963) who had returned to his native Rovereto during the war. Foschini was aware of Libera's studies on the *casa esatta* (exact house) ◖◖ p. 124 ◗◗—"the exact construction, i.e., the good reconstruction, the reconstruction that Italy and the current civilization require"—whose results had been published in a single volume in 1945.[6] Likewise, Ridolfi was the coordinator of the *Manuale dell'architetto*

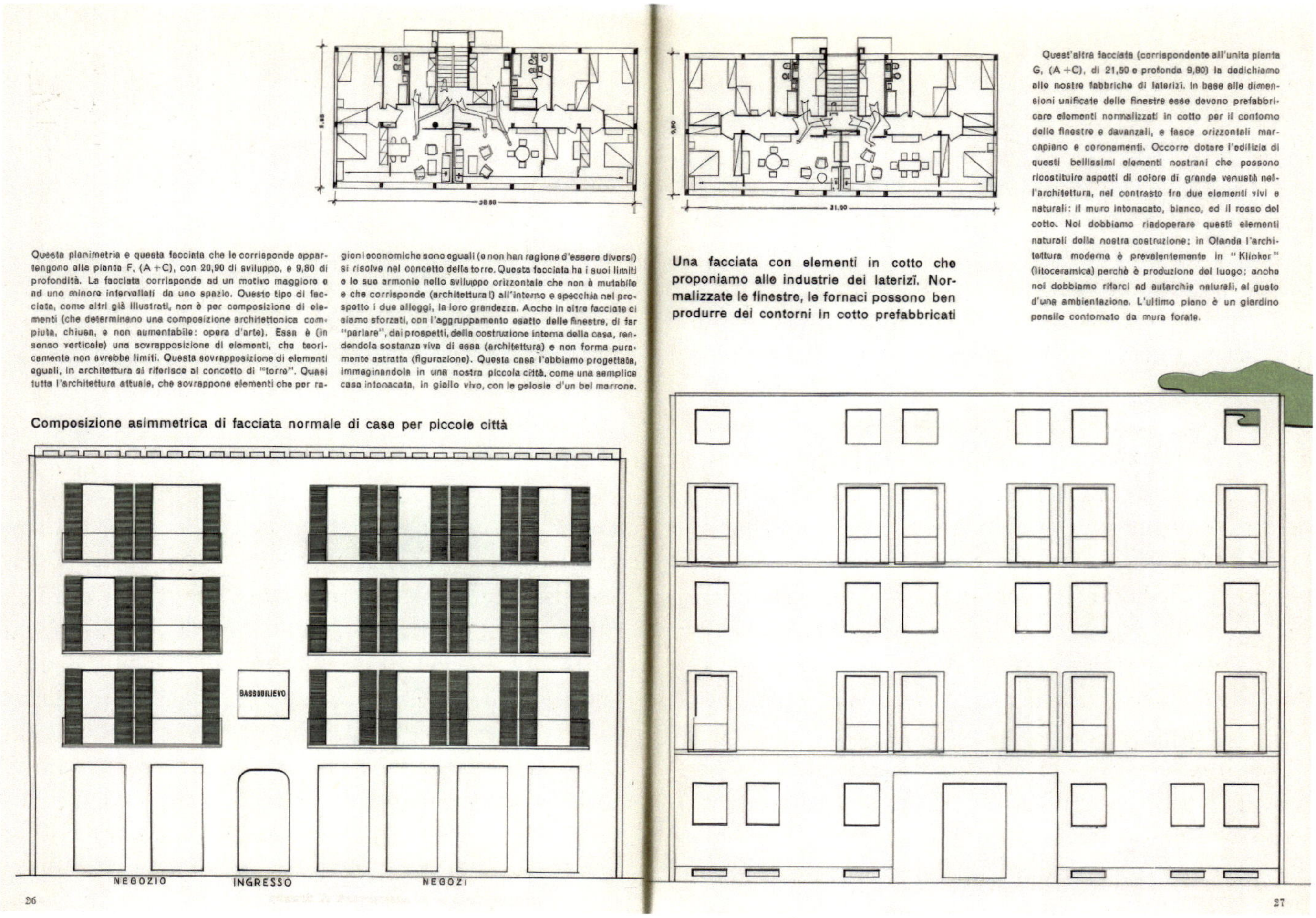

● Adalberto Libera, et al., first and only issue of the publication *Verso la casa esatta*, Milan, 1945, cover and typological studies.

(Manual of the Architect), published in 1946. Foschini gave them the task of drawing up small manuals with the guidelines to be followed in the making of INA-Casa projects. The Institute published two design manuals in 1949 and 1950.[7] These manuals combined normative rules, examples of projects both good and bad, and were richly illustrated with diagrams and photographs. Together, the first and second manuals comprise a theory and method of interior, architectural, and urban design for architects working during the first seven years of the plan. Overall, they promoted a humane type of urbanism, in contrast to the geometric rationalism of Fascist low-cost housing in the peripheries, with winding streets, changing perspectives, and a vernacular approach to materials that favored labor-intensive techniques: "The house should contribute to the formation of the urban environment, keeping in mind the spiritual and material needs of man, of a real man and not an abstract human being; a man, that is, who neither loves nor understands the unending repetition and monotony of the same type of dwellings ... He does not love the arrangement of a chessboard, but rather those environments that are both cozy and dynamic."[8]

With this program which placed a ban on modern construction sites and rejected international architecture and the use of steel, Neorealism was born in architecture, with its language primarily extracted from the rural world. Interestingly, the action of the INA-Casa, which in the post-war period brought Italian architectural research back into the mainstream of humanitarian and popular culture and to the dimension of the neighborhood, had its roots in those decidedly bourgeois and popular experiences that continued to develop during the Fascist period alongside, and basically indifferent to, the rhetoric of the regime. INA's tradition and experience in the field of coordinated residential interventions in the middle-class city, carried out during the Fascist period, represented a unique managerial and technical expertise that would positively influence the programs of post-war reconstruction. It is this precisely little-known experience that allowed INA-Casa to rethink and design the city following Fascism.

At the Roots of Neorealism

It is certain that Piacentini's direct and indirect disciples—Ludovico Quaroni (1911–1987), Luigi Piccinato (1899–1983), and almost all the architects and urbanists engaged in the reconstruction after the war were afraid of unwillingly applying to the post-war city the visions and views of the ruling classes to which they belonged by birth and education. Though very young during Fascism, they had cultivated a growing impatience with the regime's culture but had participated with their masters in outlining the aesthetic character of the ideal modern Italian city: a definitively, and for that matter, splendidly, bourgeois city. After the war, those young architects who were on their way to becoming masters logically adhered to Neorealism—a movement which in cinema, in art, and in literature had found in popular spontaneity the language to represent, and honor, the genuine identity of mass Italian society, of the poor, struggling, and hopelessly innocent popular society of that time. After the Second World War, Rome underwent great transformations and a major territorial expansion, mostly due to the immigration of peasant masses attracted by the "mythical image" and job opportunities offered by the capital. In this way, a strong link was established between the architecture of the time, and the immigrants who represented the workforce and at the same time were the main beneficiaries of economic and popular building interventions.

To be sure, during the Fascist period too, many of the architects most engaged in the contest for the language of modernity had considered spontaneous, popular, and rural architecture as an alternative source to the linguistic models battling each other for cultural dominance. Giuseppe Pagano (1896–1945), Piacentini's most tenacious opponent, had curated a major photographic exhibition on rural architecture at the Sixth Milan Triennale in 1936 ◀◀ bottom ▶▶. The exhibition, *Architettura rurale italiana*, consisted of 62 large black-and-white photos all taken and chosen by Pagano himself, the result of a passionate journey through the many faces and cultural roots of rural Italy. Years earlier, Piacentini himself did not hesitate to express his attention to spontaneous architecture. But in Pagano, there was no trace of interest in the picturesque or pictorial values of so-called minor Italian architecture.[9] As he stated in the introduction to the exhibition, "this study represents the result of a survey of the Italian rural house undertaken with the aim of demonstrating the aesthetic value of its functionality."[10] For Pagano, the most conscious and best-armed standard bearer of the dragnet of Rationalist architecture, intended to assert that the unadvanced technological reality of most construction sites in Italy could not be a sufficient excuse to justify the eclectic trappings or classicist motions of most architecture, because it was always and only in the material, economic, and technical reality of construction that its aesthetic values be sought.

54 · DIVERSI TIPI DI LOGGIATI RURALI AD ARCO E A PIATTAFORMA ORIZZONTALE NELLE CASE DI TOSCANA, DEL LAZIO, DELL'UMBRIA E DELLA CAMPAGNA DI SALERNO

ni, per quanto rare, sono di una elevata intensità (pioggie tropicali) e richiedono provvedimenti adatti. La copertura del tetto a tegola non permetterebbe mai senza dispersioni un tale concentramento delle acque, come invece avviene nelle forme di tetto derivanti dal trullo. La parentela col trullo nelle case a cupola o a padiglione non viene soltanto ricordata dal tipo di copertura ma anche dalla stessa pianta delle case: anche esse sono composte di singole cellule con tetto separato, e solo la casa con tetto a botte dimostra una pianta unica ad un asse allungato, mentre le case con tetto a cupola e a padiglione hanno i singoli elementi a pianta perfettamente quadrata come quella del trullo. Cosi le varie bel- 61

● Giuseppe Pagano and Guarniero Daniel, view of the exhibition and page from the book *Architettura rurale italiana*, 1936. The selected page shows examples from the Lazio region.

It is also noteworthy that Gustavo Giovannoni published his seminal *Vecchie città ed edilizia nuova* (Old cities and new construction) in 1931, the very year of the Second Exhibition of Italian Rational Architecture. To be sure, he was already tired of the subjective and often arbitrary use of elements of the historical language of architecture that he had promoted for many years, and, at the same time, he felt far removed from adhering to the language of Rationalism. His project of garden city on the Aniene river was being built and, faced with the decorative proposals that the builders and designers of the villas intended to carry out despite the required economy of the construction, he made a series of suggestions. In a few words, he advised them "… to suspend the exterior work having completed the basic framework, in order to leave the walls raw with the brown color of the tufa and the purplish color of the pozzolano, or to cover them with a rustic, dark-colored floated plaster, uniform on each cottage and little different from cottage to cottage, so as to impart solidity of mass."[11] And he urged the reluctant planners of the housing cooperatives to refrain from applying unnecessary and grotesque decorations. Instead, he recommended to deploy "pergolas, gates, trellises, flower beds, and the most suitable species … because the sun is very generous and can thus offer a serious competition to plasterers and painters."[12] Likewise in 1930, the AACAR had published two volumes titled *Architettura minore in Italia/Roma* with a strong focus on the volumetry and opening to nature that characterized the architecture of minor towns and quarters.[13] To be sure, these initiatives already announced one of the fundamental elements of the linguistic choice that would preside, twenty years later, over the design, not only of Quaroni and Ridolfi's Tiburtino IV, ◀◀ p. 127 ▶▶ but of all the other neighborhoods of Rome's Neorealist season.

Tiburtino and the Rural

Much has been written about the architecture of Neorealism, especially about a handful of works of strong poetic intention realized in a very short time within the first seven years of the INA-Casa program.[14] The most iconic of the new post-war districts in Rome, the Quartiere Tiburtino, was designed between 1949 and 1954 by a team of architects led by Ludovico Quaroni and Mario Ridolfi, and including Wolfgang Frankl, Carlo Aymonino, Carlo Chiarini, Marco Fiorentino, Federico Gorio, Maurizio Lanza, Sergio Lenci, Piero Maria Lugli, Carlo Melograni, Giancarlo Menichetti, Giulio Rinaldi, and Michele Valori.[15] Commenting on the project in *Casabella*, Aymonino wrote that it had "the character of a village, archaic and free, as something more intimate than the chaos of the periphery of the metropolis."[16] And further: "from the very beginning of the project for the district, the accepted idea was to move beyond a Rationalist type of composition, dictated by uniform orientations, constant distances, and the repetition of a few building types … in order to obtain a unity by means of the superposition of always different perspectives formed by a succession of diverse spaces brought together by a renewed value of the street."[17] The team successfully pursued the picturesque, "with the studied happenstance of many different types of facades and roofs, with the use of balconies for their sculptural functions, with the extension of the first flights of stairs on the exterior of the building in order to reinforce their character of being constructions that had arisen spontaneously at successive moments in time."[18] As Bruno Reichlin has commented, Wolfgang Frankl, a member of the team and a former student of the Stuttgart School in Germany, was passionately interested in minor architecture. It is well known that he scrutinized and drew the towns and villages of central Italy in search of design ideas.[19]

However, the experience of the Tiburtino district was immediately and explicitly criticized by some of its main protagonists and Ludovico Quaroni himself. In the short essay "Il paese dei Barocchi," published in *Casabella-continuità* in 1957, Quaroni commented on the INA-Casa neighborhood of Tiburtino and substantially downplayed the importance of the entire experience of Neorealism in architecture:

> "The country of the Baroques—so he labeled, very ironically, the idea of the city behind the INA-Casa projects—the Country of the Baroques is not the result of a solidified culture, or of a living tradition: it is the result of a state of mind … The state of mind that sustained us in those days, in which, for each of us, here in Rome, we were only interested in doing something that was detached from certain errors of a certain past to which we reproached the sterility and failure on the human level."[20]

"A state of mind": Quaroni used the expression twice in succession as he referred to the need for a human, poetic, and liberating architectural and urban expression, as far away as possible from the monumentalism and rationalism that had dominated the scene for more than a decade before the war. Hence, the reference to the language of spontaneous architecture deployed in words and buildings by the masters of Neorealism was not an affirmation

● Ludovico Quaroni, Mario Ridolfi, et al., street of the INA-Casa Tiburtino district, Block B, houses with terraces and workshops.

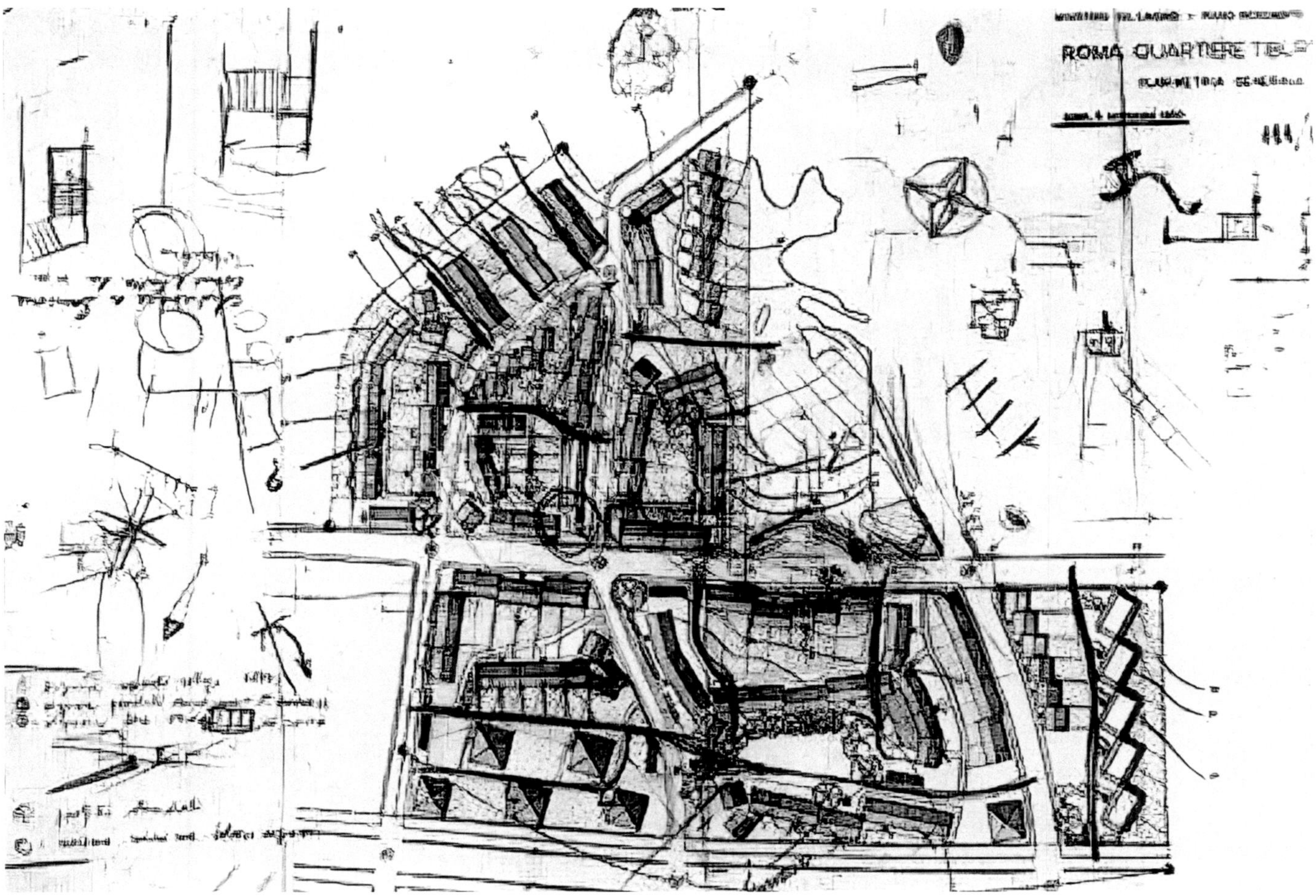

● Ludovico Quaroni, Mario Ridolfi, et al., draft masterplan of the INA-Casa Tiburtino district, 1949.

of the inevitable relationship between functionality and aesthetics, as Giuseppe Pagano would have wished, but an escape from the battleground between the representative city of bourgeois values and the new industrial city of the future.

At Tuscolano the Turreted Medieval City Looms

In the INA-Casa district of Tuscolano II ◀◀◀ p. 129–130 ▶▶▶, designed and built from 1950 to 1960 by Saverio Muratori (1910–1973) and Mario De Renzi (1897–1967)—with Lucio Cambellotti, Giuseppe Perugini, Dante Tassotti, and Luigi Vagnetti—, one does not recognize the fruit of that state of mind, of that liberating poetic intention, only partially achieved, that guided Quaroni and Ridolfi to seek in the apparent planimetric randomness of the Tiburtino project the spatial and environmental miracle of spontaneous settlements. On the contrary, one can read Muratori's and De Renzi's careful search for a method of urban composition that prescinds from the lexicon of Neorealism, although adopted without hesitation. In fact, the tuff in rows is also very visible here and a simple plaster wraps the building volumes concluded, at the top, by vast sloping roofs like those of the granaries of the ancient peasant courts. Likewise, the urban structure is clearly grafted onto the decade-long research concerning the form of the modern Italian city, therefore, on the interpretation, or rather actualization, of the compositional principles of the ancient city.[21]

Tuscolano II is a walled city. Its outer boundary is marked by a regular and well-spaced sequence of eleven towers, sized in relation to the scale of the settlement, and positioned to the right and left of a great urban wall—a long and slightly bent residential barre of six habitable floors above a commercial ground floor. The main gateway to the new district opens in the center of that large urban wall. The space in front of the gateway is known as Largo Spartaco—a square like those that were formed in front of the gates of medieval cities, where merchants and buyers from neighboring towns convened on market days. However, the lack of enclosure and the fact that only the crypt of the church designed by Muratori (Chiesa dell' Assunzione di Maria SS, 1954–1970) was built resulted in an urban space with good intentions but without quality. Past the gate, in the area bordered by the towers and the residential wall, there is a long street-square, inspired by the ancient cities of Italian culture. Among those, the square in Fabriano in the Marche; the linear square in Ferrara, on the side of the cathedral; the piazza-road of Udine on the eastern border of the Republic of Venice; and finally, the central street of Ragusa, now Dubrovnik in Croatia. Its towers proudly mark its boundaries and in the center of the regular fabric lies the most beautiful piazza-street in the history of Mediterranean architecture. On an island opposite Dubrovnik stands Curzola, a smaller town, narrow, defended by its towers and traversed by a sequence of spaces that form an articulated piazza-street, at the center of which stands the church of San Marco.

Here, the similarity of the generating geometry of Curzola and that of the Tuscolano neighborhood is really striking. To be sure, the fabric of Curzola is very compact; the houses form a dense structure, and the open spaces are very limited. A series of narrow cross streets are grafted almost perpendicularly to the main piazza-street, slightly undulating to avoid the infiltration of the winds that can be very cold in that part of the Adriatic. Similarly undulating are the alignments of the minor residential group of houses which Muratori and De Renzi, adopting modern rules of spacing, grafted onto the central street-square known as Via Sagunto. However, the end results are neither alleyway nor square. The spines and even more so the street-square itself suffer from a spatial fragmentation created by parking spaces ◀ p. 130 ▶, parking lots, and metal fences that do not allow real pedestrian occupation and eventually make the potential public space impossible to perceive.

In 1950, Muratori obtained the charge of the important course Caratteri dell'Architettura (Characters of architecture) at the Faculty of Architecture in Venice, where he began to fine-tune his method of analyzing the city—a long-range scientific investigation that resulted in his remarkable *Studi per una operante storia urbana di Venezia*.[22] To be sure, his knowledge of Venice extended to its exemplary architectural tradition spread over the very wide geographical space of the Adriatic and the coast of Croatia. It is reasonable to speculate that he visited them all, Dubrovnik, Curzola, Spalato, and others. In that context, Tuscolano II may have been the first outcome of the research he had just undertaken, and which would lead him, in the end, too far from the world—wishfully poetic—of architecture. If Quaroni immediately abandoned the Neorealist experience that he embraced as a moment of necessary detachment from the past, Muratori never partook in Neorealism understood as a poetic approach to a truer social Italy. In some of his statements he seems closer to the by then distant position of Giuseppe Pagano, who was interested in the aesthetic value of the functionality of minor historical fabrics. Muratori sought in them "the cyclically permanent human, therefore functional ...

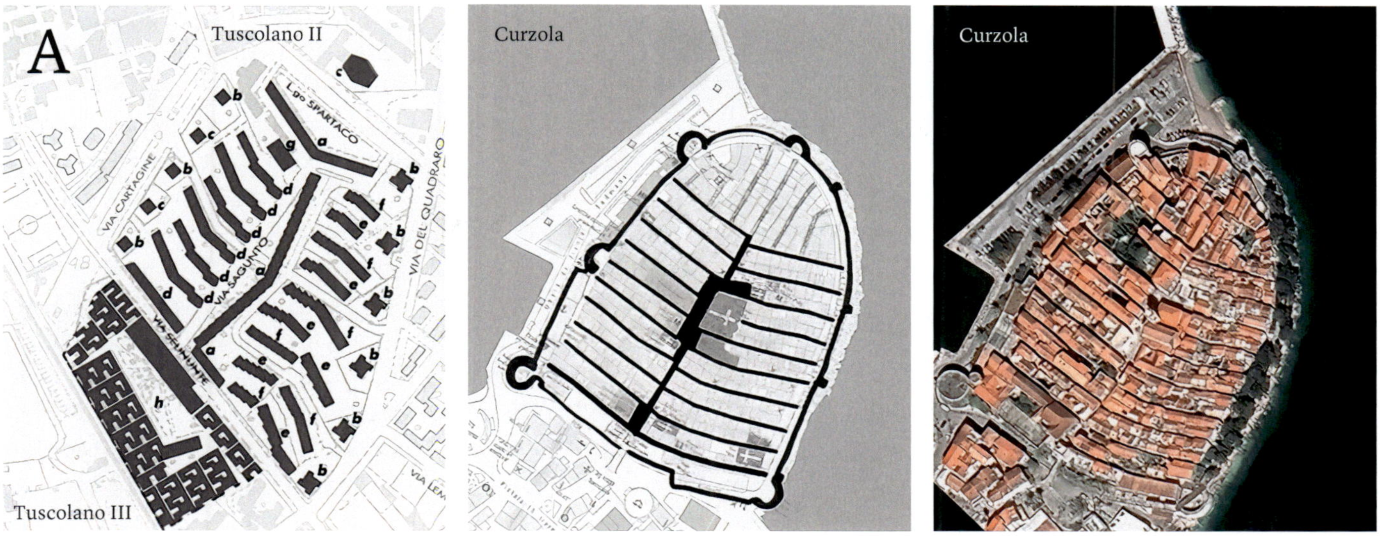

● A left: plan of the INA-Casa Tuscolano II district, 1950–1960. A middle: plan diagram of the town of Curzola, Croatia. A right: aerial view of Curzola. B: aerial view of Dubrovnik, Croatia.

therefore moral and aesthetic laws of architecture. And of the city."[23] In 1954, Muratori moved to Rome where he taught architectural composition at the Faculty of Architecture until his death in 1973. He continued his research on typology and the formation of the urban fabric, this time in Rome, and in 1964 he published another exceptional volume, *Studi per una operante storia urbana di Roma*.[24]

However, the Tuscolano project was a collective work, and it is important to underline the critical role played by Mario De Renzi (1897–1967) who signed the project of the new working-class neighborhood as an equal. De Renzi was an *enfant prodige* of early modern Roman architecture, a character at once outspoken and shy, without any ideological bias, but always the best at articulating whatever architectural language he intended

● Mario De Renzi, Saverio Muratori, et al., INA-Casa Tuscolano II district, 1950–1960. Current view of Via Sagunto. The fragmentation created by the uncoordinated combination of parking spaces, parking lots, and metal fences is clearly visible.

to employ. He trained professionally in the studio of Alberto Calza Bini, a period which served as a trampoline for his first great achievements. Too often obscured by his contemporaries Luigi Moretti and Adalberto Libera, his hand was in fact present in all the true masterpieces and innovative projects of the Roman school. In 1925, he designed the Case d'abitazione per i dipendenti di Roma (1925), a splendid block in *barocchetto* style at the heart of the Mazzini district ◖◖ p. 222 top ◗◗; in the same language, the social-housing complex facing the Piazza Perin del Vaga, part of the Flaminio II ICP complex (1925–1927); and the Rationalist and metropolitan "mega-block," known as Palazzo Federici at Via XXI Aprile near Piazza Bologna (1931–1937) ◖◖◖ p. 266 top, 268, 270 ◗◗◗ ◖◖ p. 271, 344 ◗◗. With Adalberto Libera as co-designer he built the post office in Via Marmorata, considered one of the great masterpieces of Italian rational architecture; and with Giorgio Calza Bini (Alberto Calza Bini's son), the very modern and elegant Palazzina Furmanik (1935–1941) ◖◖◖ p. 102 ◗◗◗.[25] And here, in the Tuscolano project, begun in 1950, it is as if he took his youngest co-protagonist Saverio by the hand so that the path of systematic research, just begun by that young talent, would not come to a halt in the difficulties and complexities of an imposing multi-handed urban project.

Libera's Unità Orizzontale at Tuscolano: The Greek Reference

As mentioned earlier, Adalberto Libera became, along with Mario Ridolfi, Foschini's right-hand man in the technical direction of the INA-Casa program. While the first INA-Casa booklet showed mostly plans with distributive layouts of single residential units, the second focused on the urban form of the new neighborhoods. For Libera, the minimal internal dimension of the dwellings was to be compensated by the common public spaces for the social interaction of all residents. In contrast with most examples dealing with multi-story buildings, the second part of the booklet presented what could be considered as the draft version of Libera's Unità Orizzontale ◖ right ◗, built between 1950 and 1954 as Tuscolano III for about 1000 residents. Whereas Tiburtino and Tuscolano suggest, as we have seen, a reinterpretation of rural and medieval urban structures, Libera's horizontal city made direct reference to antique Greek urbanism such as Olynthus in northern Chalcidice (432–348 BC). It consists of a one-story horizontal grid whose basic block or module is made of four adjacent dwellings, each one articulated around a small private patio. A network of narrow alleys with outdoor niches connects the houses and provides resting places for the residents. On the street that runs along the complex, defined by a continuous stone wall and closed perimeter, are shops and a vaulted concrete gate which provides access to a pleasant internal garden. At the southern edge of the green, Libera placed a two-story residential barre posted on pilotis and whose apartments are accessed along an open-air gallery.[26]

The Original and Dramatic Sin in the Love of Spontaneous Languages

In 1959, the season of Neorealism that had given life and identity to the first working-class neighborhoods had waned. Mario Ridolfi himself, the sincerest of the authors of Roman Neorealism and the true leader of the movement, had always kept other paths well open, as witnessed by the elevation of the Villino Alatri (1952)—originally built by Vittorio Ballio Morpurgo in 1928—which marked a symbolic break between the past and the present of Rome's bourgeois culture.[27] More importantly, the residential tower buildings INA-Assicurazioni ◖◖◖◖◖◖ pp. 132–133 ◗◗◗◗◗◗ on Viale Etiopia (Mario Ridolfi and Wolfgang Frankl) were built in the period between 1949–1956 and became a different symbol of post-war Italy in fervent reconstruction.[28] Yet, as Bruno Reichlin stated, if these towers seem to negate all or nearly all that the architects accomplished in the Tiburtino, why did Paolo Portoghesi—and many Italian architectural critics agreed—define the project as "the masterpiece of post-war Italian architecture?"[29] Is it because the towers represent the most complete expression of "truth of construction" in architecture as Guido Canella and Aldo Rossi put it: "what remains is the fact that it documents the most profound contribution of an architect to that progressive culture that, in the period following the war, was so dedicated to bending its means of expression to the representation of reality."[30] Or is it rather the realistic expression of the low level of technological modernity in Rome? Beyond the semantic debate, Ridolfi and Frankl transcended the substantially anti-urban character of their contemporary Tiburtino project, bringing to full maturity the previous experiences on the tower house and the studies on the building types prepared for the UNNRA (United Nations Relief and Rehabilitation Administration) and for the INA-Casa. Moreover, Ridolfi and Frankl proved to be particularly attentive to the emerging issue of psychological well-being but also to controlling the project in every phase and in every element, managing a poorly mechanized building process but with a great availability of manpower. The Tiburtino IV, Ridolfi and Quaroni's Neorealist neighborhood par excellence was finished in 1954. It was thus conceived and built at the time that its authors and the whole Roman architectural culture, faced with other languages and other themes, already embraced the search for the architecture of modernity.

It can thus be said, provocatively therefore, that there never existed a Neorealist phase of Roman architecture, but only an intense time of research in which some of its protagonists selected certain themes as the most suitable to experiment with, among others, languages drawn from or inspired by the popular and spontaneous ways of Italian culture. Inevitably, one can see in those projects the reflection of a culture that was rural rather than urban, exactly as so many Italian literati—Giovanni Pascoli, Ippolito Nievo, Giovanni Verga, Pier Paolo Pasolini—but also some great Italian linguists—such as Bruno Migliorini or Tullio De Mauro—taught us. In the years following the end of Fascism, the passionate quest to express oneself—in literature, painting, film, architecture—by recovering, and sometimes reinventing, the most natural and spontaneous language of popular culture, was dictated by the need to wash away any residue of nationalist rhetoric, steeped in instrumental historical myths and the collective pride of which racism had been the inevitable, final, and tragic imposture. But it is precisely the elaboration of the political concept of race, of

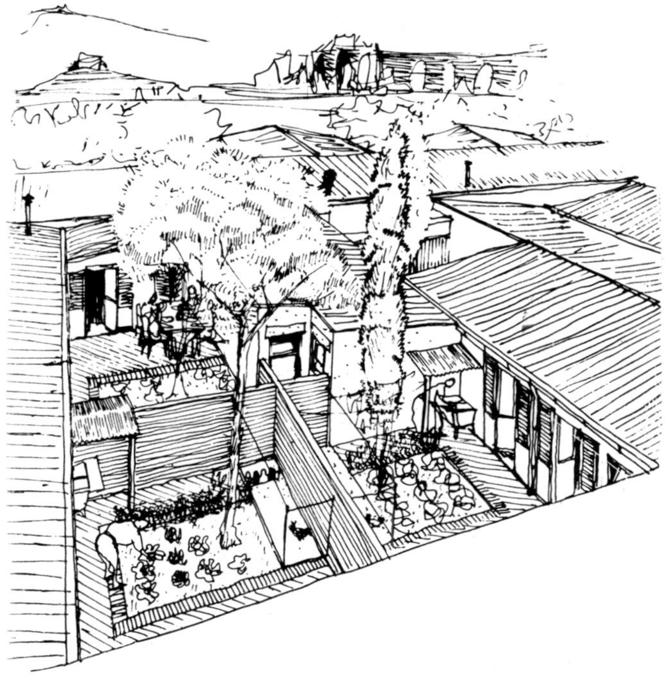

● Adalberto Libera, Unità di abitazione orizzontale or INA-Casa Tuscolano III, 1950–1954. Perspective sketch of the patio houses.

national superiority—that is, of those born in a place—that has introduced, since the dawn of modernity, the need to refer to the oldest spontaneous and primordial language to regain the identity of the nation. It is worth recalling that for Johann Gottlieb Fichte (1762–1814), the German philosopher who continued Kant's thought and initiated Idealism, those who speak the same language are connected to each other by a multiplicity of invisible ties through mere nature, long before human art intervenes. Likewise, the language that creates the multiplicity of invisible bonds of a nation must be that which existed before human art appeared i.e., the spontaneous language. Fichte went further and argued that, even if an original language is spoken in only a few villages, it will be necessary to go and find it, spread it, and even if it is poor in terms and meanings relative to the contemporary world, it will be necessary to reinvigorate and develop it because only the original language will enable the nation to realize itself and find freedom. Paradoxically then, Neorealism—a search for the original rural language that now lives only in a few villages, but which our post-World War II humanist and humanitarian planners cultivated for a brief time as an antidote to the linguistic nationalism of the past regime—contained the unquenchable seed of the ideological vertigo of nationalism, of the supremacy of one nation over others, of one race over all others. To be sure, it is hard not to see that those architects wanted to express, both architecturally and typologically, the pride of being born far from the metropolises, among the fences

● Mario Ridolfi and Wolfgang Frankl, towers of the INA-Assicurazioni complex at Viale Etiopia, 1949–1955.

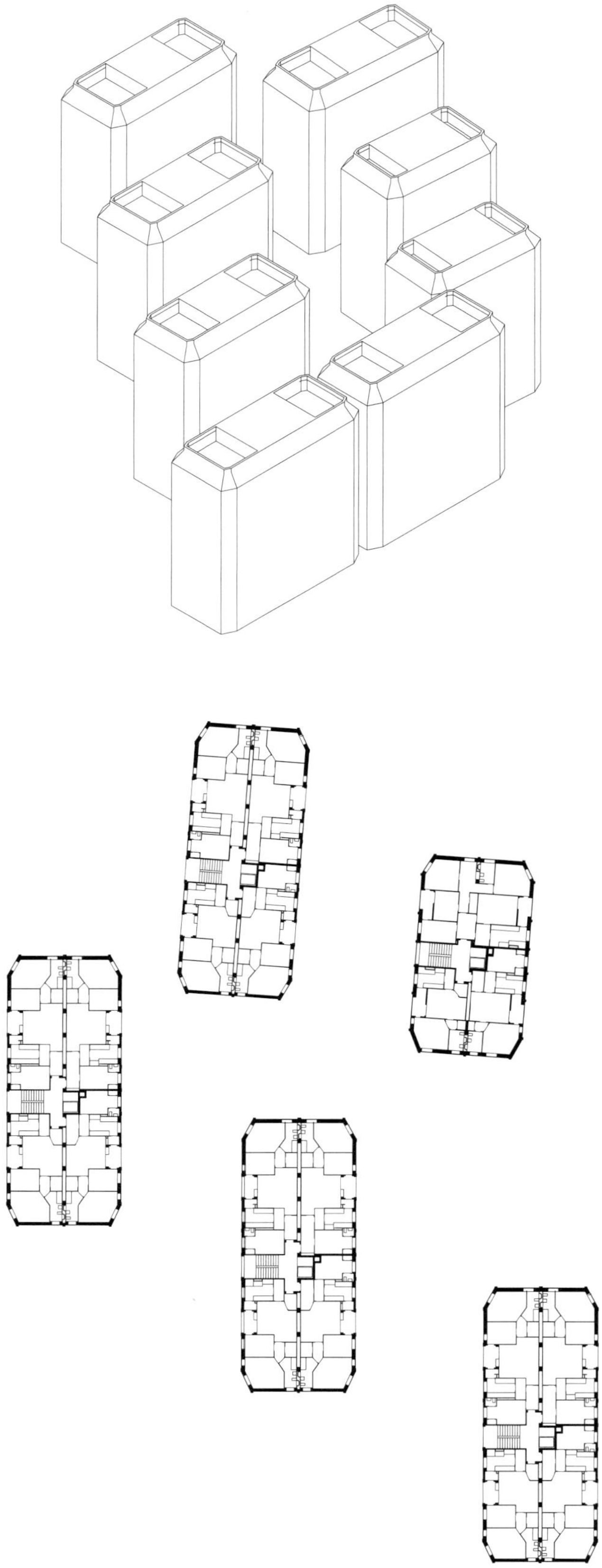

● Mario Ridolfi and Wolfgang Frankl, INA-Assicurazioni complex. Schematic plans of the five original towers and axonometric of the whole complex.

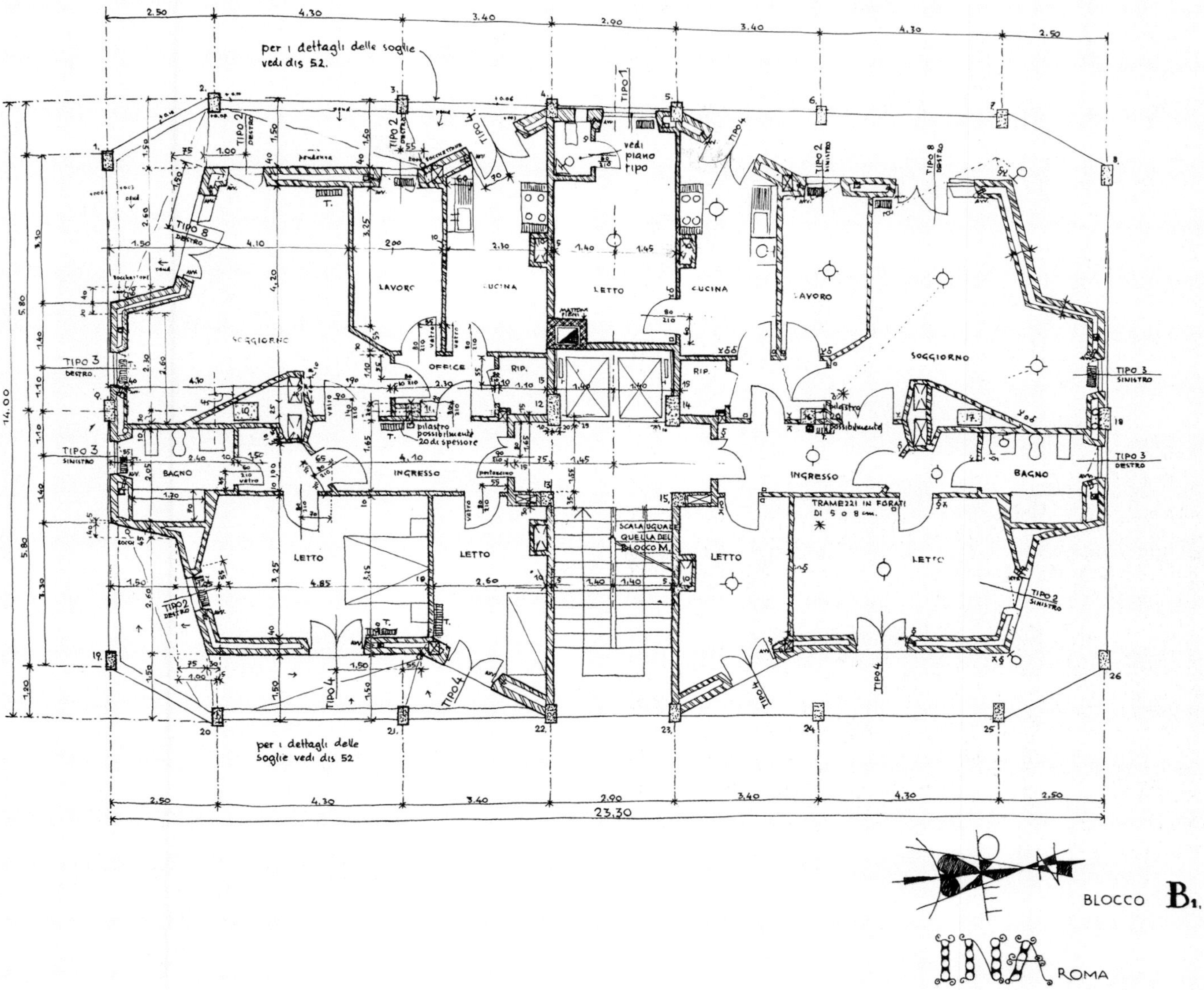

● Mario Ridolfi and Wolfgang Frankl, INA-Assicurazioni complex. Plan of the attic floor, tower B1, 1953–1956.

● Mario Ridolfi and Wolfgang Frankl, INA-Assicurazioni complex. Interior street.

of the open countryside, in the primordial—and therefore what was considered healthy—culture of farms and fields swaying with crops under the sun. Those young post-World War II Romans were educated and intelligent designers, and above all, they had gone through a dramatic time during their youth. They had by then matured into a sensibility that intuitively led them to seek the architecture of their time—and of future times—away from easily distorted traditions.

Victory and Death of Avant-Garde Architecture, Modern and Heroic

It is in 1947, when Italian cities were preparing for recovery and the Allied troops were completing their demobilization, that Luigi Moretti (1906–1973) conceived the Palazzina Il Girasole (1947–1950) ◖right; p. 302, 307 bottom◗, that masterpiece of modern bourgeois architecture that would radically alter the genteel tastes of Rome's middle and upper-middle classes. From before the war, Moretti knew how to be the best and most unpredictable at every opportunity. His linguistic invention was superior to that of all his peers, cultivated in a conception of architecture which made him a great heir to the Galli da Bibiena: architecture as a cultured spectacle of itself and its entire history.[32] Before the war, he was one of the architects projecting the Piazza Imperiale at E42 and the unbuilt Cinema-Teatro scheduled to occupy the western edge of the square, but his reputation came largely from his Rationalist works at the Foro italico and the Casa della GIL near Porta Portese in Trastevere. In times of reconstruction, Moretti was only one of the many Roman modernist architects who did not show any interest, not even a mild one, in Neorealism.

Similarly, the works designed by Ugo Luccichenti (1898–1976) represented the perfect paradigm and the most complete repertoire of modern Mannerism in Rome. Ugo Luccichenti was a prolific builder of modern high-income *palazzine*, designed with great care for typologies, *mise-en-oeuvre* of materials, and details—as Mario Manieri Elia wrote, "with unscrupulousness, experimentalism, will to succeed, and profound professional discipline, all characteristic traits of his strong personality."[33] His first apartment building, Palazzina Bornigia at Piazzale delle Muse, was designed in 1939.[34] His career ended with the unfortunate decision to participate in the design of the Hotel Cavalieri Hilton at Monte Mario, a project that was unanimously badly received in light of its disastrous impact on the landscape and city skyline.[35] On a

● Luigi Moretti, Palazzina Il Girasole, 1947–1950. Facade on Via Bruno Buozzi, Parioli.

more positive note, his name remained associated with a major building complex in Rome that, in the second phase of the triumphant life of the Roman *palazzina*, achieved—not unlike the complex of Via delle Tre Madonne before the war—a convincing and extraordinary composition of urban-scale houses. The large housing block he designed at Piazzale delle Medaglie d'Oro on the Monte Mario ridge—known as the Belsito housing complex (1950–1953) ◖◖◖ p. 135 ◗◗◗◗—is a work that simultaneously disproved and exalted the role of the Roman *palazzina* as a possible basic element for the organic design of the modern city. It disproves it because typologically it is not really a set of *palazzine*, but rather a large multifunctional urban block—it originally included the famed cinema Belsito—that defines unitarily the front of a large square in the intensive bourgeois periphery of Rome. Yet, and to succeed in the undertaking without falling into the monotony of many working-class 19th-century neighborhoods, Luccichenti chose to articulate the architectural surface of the large building as the apparent sequence of small buildings, as if it were a set of delightful bourgeois dwellings spread out from each other, and enriched by external staircases alluding to the modernity of the duplex type in Le Corbusier's immeubles-villas.[36]

Interestingly, Ugo Luccichenti had a younger brother, Amedeo Luccichenti (1907–1963) who led a parallel and prestigious career in a partnership with Vincenzo Monaco (1911–1969). Their focus was equally on residential *palazzine* for the middle to high bourgeoisie, many of them standing in the Parioli district as landmarks of post-war optimism and modernity. Among the most famous is the duo of adjacent buildings known as Palazzine Antares (1948–1951) ◀◀ p. 136 left ▶▶ on Via di San Valentino and Palazzina Palladium (1950–1952) on Via Archimede, right on the hill overlooking the future Olympic Village. These were very high-density buildings, which excelled with the elegant compositional simplicity of their street fronts.[37] Also of interest is the Palazzina Giammarusti (1953–1954) ◀ p. 136 bottom right ▶ facing the Largo Messico and whose facades displayed prominent outdoor staircases linking residential floors in duplex. Monaco and Luccichenti were deeply involved in the building of the Villaggio Olimpico, and were the architects of the new Fiumicino airport, inaugurated in 1960 for the Olympic Games.

Thus, for about twenty years after the end of the war, the *palazzina* became the privileged typology for the linguistic experimentation of Roman modernity for the bourgeoisie. Paradoxically, the best architects, almost all sons of the School of Architecture in Rome, succeeded where the extraordinary protagonists of Gruppo Sette, of MIAR, and of the two exhibitions of Italian Rational Architecture in 1928 and 1931 had somewhat failed. Avant-garde architecture seemed to have won, but it is the high bourgeoisie that adopted it for its generous plans, multiple facades, large terraces, and integration within a new conception of urban blocks and streets. Why wonder then if the strong repulsion that the generation that came of age in the 1960s showed toward the so-called *palazzinari*—a term that includes architects, speculators, entrepreneurs, or even inhabitants of the Roman *palazzine*—did not depend precisely on the widespread, elitist, and therefore also intellectually conformist, adherence to this concept of the avant-garde? However, by the 1960s, the Roman bourgeoisie had long recognized in the elegant modern Mannerism elaborated by its best architects, the architectural guise with which to illustrate its dwellings, to distinguish its neighborhoods from pre-war and poorer ones. In the varied directions of post-war modernism, the Roman bourgeoisie no longer perceived any trace of the avant-garde but felt the fragrance of the new and satisfied stability achieved after Fascism and after the war.[38] However, as Davide Spina has shown in his study on the Società Generale Immobiliara (SGI), historians have concentrated their research and analysis on those architects—Albini, Ridolfi, Moretti, Monaco and Luccichenti, and many others—responsible for the best buildings, formally and typologically brilliant and built and studied in a craftsman-like fashion. As a result, little attention has been paid "to the opposite side of the coin: the conditions of work and production in larger, profit-driven outfits and, beyond this, speculative building in general, which accounts for the majority of the housing stock constructed in Italy from 1945 onwards."[39]

● Ugo Luccichenti, Belsito housing complex with cinema, 1950–1953. Facade on Piazzale delle Medaglie d'Oro.

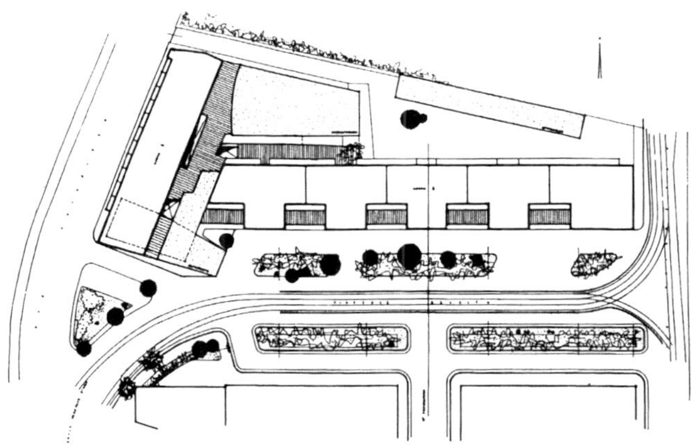

● Ugo Luccichenti, Belsito housing complex, site plan and elevation on Piazzale delle Medaglie d'Oro.

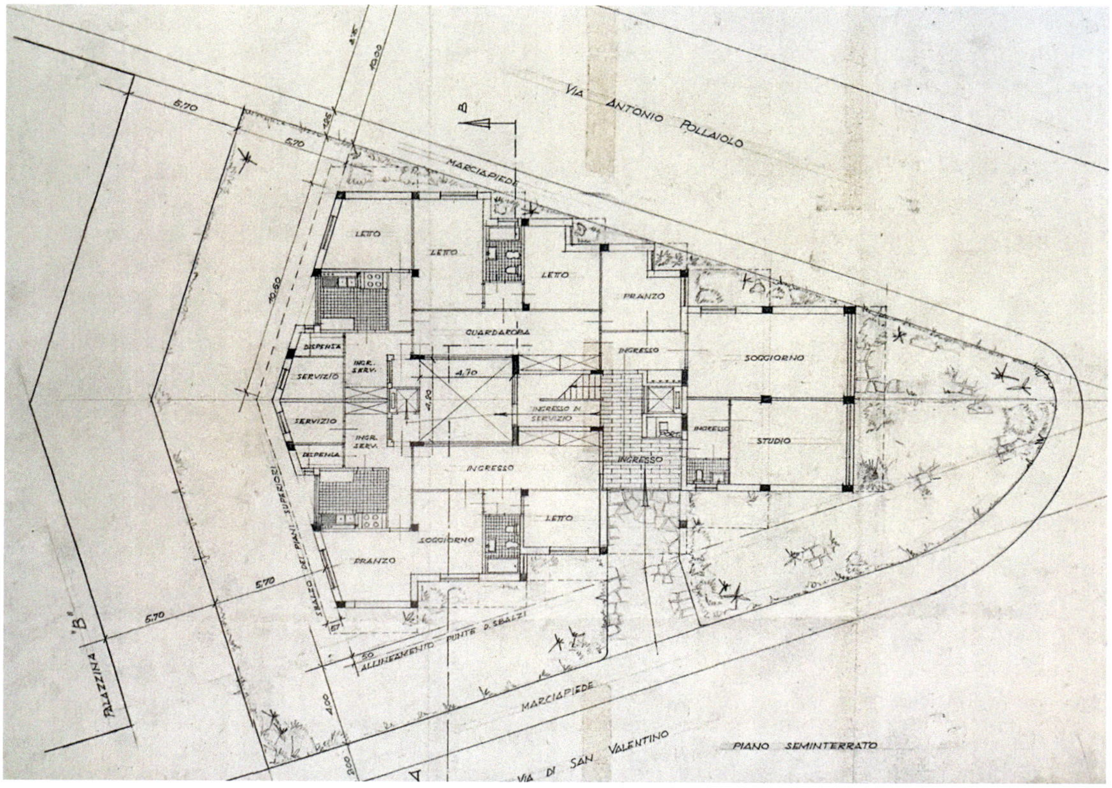

● Vincenzo Monaco and Amedeo Luccichenti, Palazzina Antares. Plan of the entry level.

● Vincenzo Monaco and Amedeo Luccichenti, Palazzina Antares, 1948–1951. On Via di San Valentino (Parioli), the palazzina overlooks the Villaggio Olimpico and the Auditorium Parco della Musica.

● Vincenzo Monaco and Amedeo Luccichenti, Palazzina Giammarusti, 1953–1954. Facade on Largo Messico (Parioli).

A Plan for Imperial Rome or An Imperial Plan for Rome

We are now on the threshold of the 1960s. The city has changed and grown dramatically. The great Roman planners must once again measure their influence on the strategic choices of the new political forces, the new municipal administration, and the new central government. A new *Piano regolatore* has begun its long and arduous elaboration with the goal of securing a different and brighter future for the capital of Italy. To be sure, between 1939 and the end of the Fascist regime in 1943, the entire community of leading Roman architects gathered around the old families of professionals and the Faculty of Architecture in Rome—with Piacentini, Giovannoni, and Virgilio Testa at their head—had already been engaged, directly or indirectly, in the failed attempt to set up the planning principles for the new masterplan to be finished precisely in 1942. It was a collective effort, intense, labored, and in many ways innovative despite the political exaltation.[40] The masterplan, which was never completed, intended to implement all the main goals that political, representative, and modernist urban planning had elaborated and proposed for Rome over 70 years: from the idea of expanding the capital to the Tyrrhenian Sea to making it the capital of science and a monument of national pride; in brief, an Imperial city.[41]

Even though the disavowal of the Piacentini era was now public and widely shared, there is no hiding the fact that the masterplan of Rome laboriously elaborated in the 1950s and very early 1960s had its roots in the proposals, designs, and visions that were confronted, but not concluded, during the preparation of the failed project of 1942. As its heir, the new *Piano regolatore* of 1962 was the first to be drawn up and approved, amid many battles of opposing interests, according to the new urban planning law of 1942. As discussed earlier, the law—put forth by Piacentini—required that every new urban addition be designed and directed by a "superior architect," responsible for the general form of the settlement, as well as the architectural features of each building, the efficiency of the infrastructural network, and the services. Critically, it was the first plan in Roma Capitale to no longer entrust the identity and unity of the new neighborhoods to the use of codified building types: *villino* (free-standing house, *casa in linea* (apartment building), and *palazzina*. Each neighborhood was to be realized as a new work of urban art with a strong identity.

However, the new urban planning law signed by Mussolini did not solve the problem of ownership of the land to be urbanized: the model applied for the Quartiere Mazzini and the EUR, based on the unquestioned authority of a superior architect, could not be successfully replicated without the full public availability of the buildable areas. The studies and proposals for the masterplan of 1942 rested on a special governmental decree that stipulated that all areas included in the plan would be compulsorily expropriated by the public administration. The decree had to be confirmed by a law within two years of its signing, but as the war intensified on Italian soil, it was never signed, much to the delight of many landowners. The principle remained, but was not effectively regulated by the new planning law. In the early 1960s, the elaboration of the new *Piano regolatore* inevitably turned into a huge struggle with the large landowners, who led and hindered the laborious path toward its approval. Fiorentino Sullo,

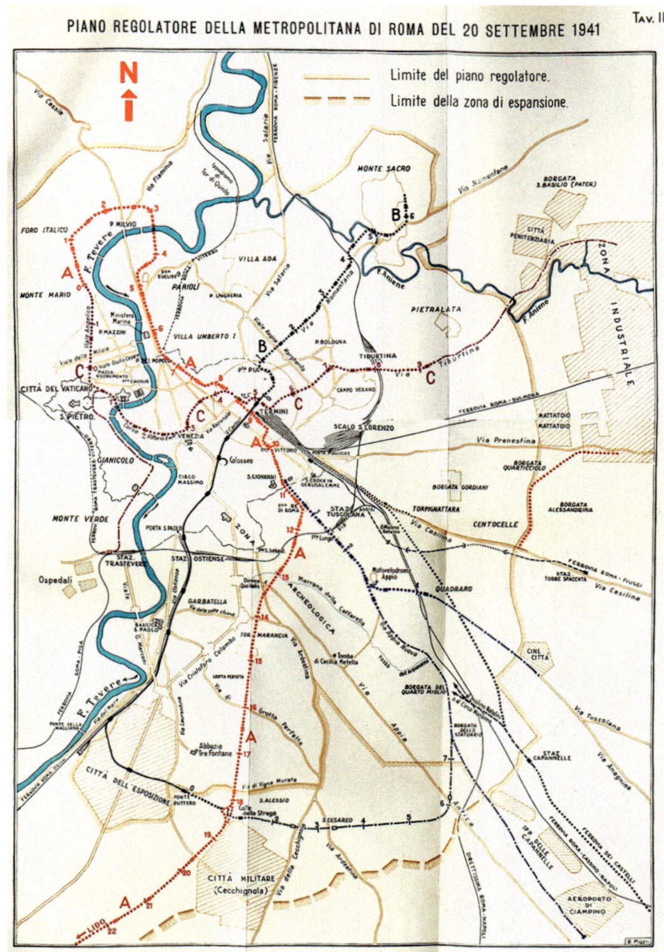

● Governorato di Roma, masterplan of the Metro network, September 1941. Line B was dug from Piramide to Termini between 1938 and 1941 and inaugurated after the Second World War in the section between the EUR and Termini in 1955. In the 1941 masterplan there are subway lines A, B, C, and additional unnamed lines. The plan came at a time of strong urban expansion which began and was interrupted by the outbreak of the Second World War, and which mainly envisaged an expansion of the city toward the sea. Built or projected sections of the lines proposed in 1941 are now part of the Lines A and C.

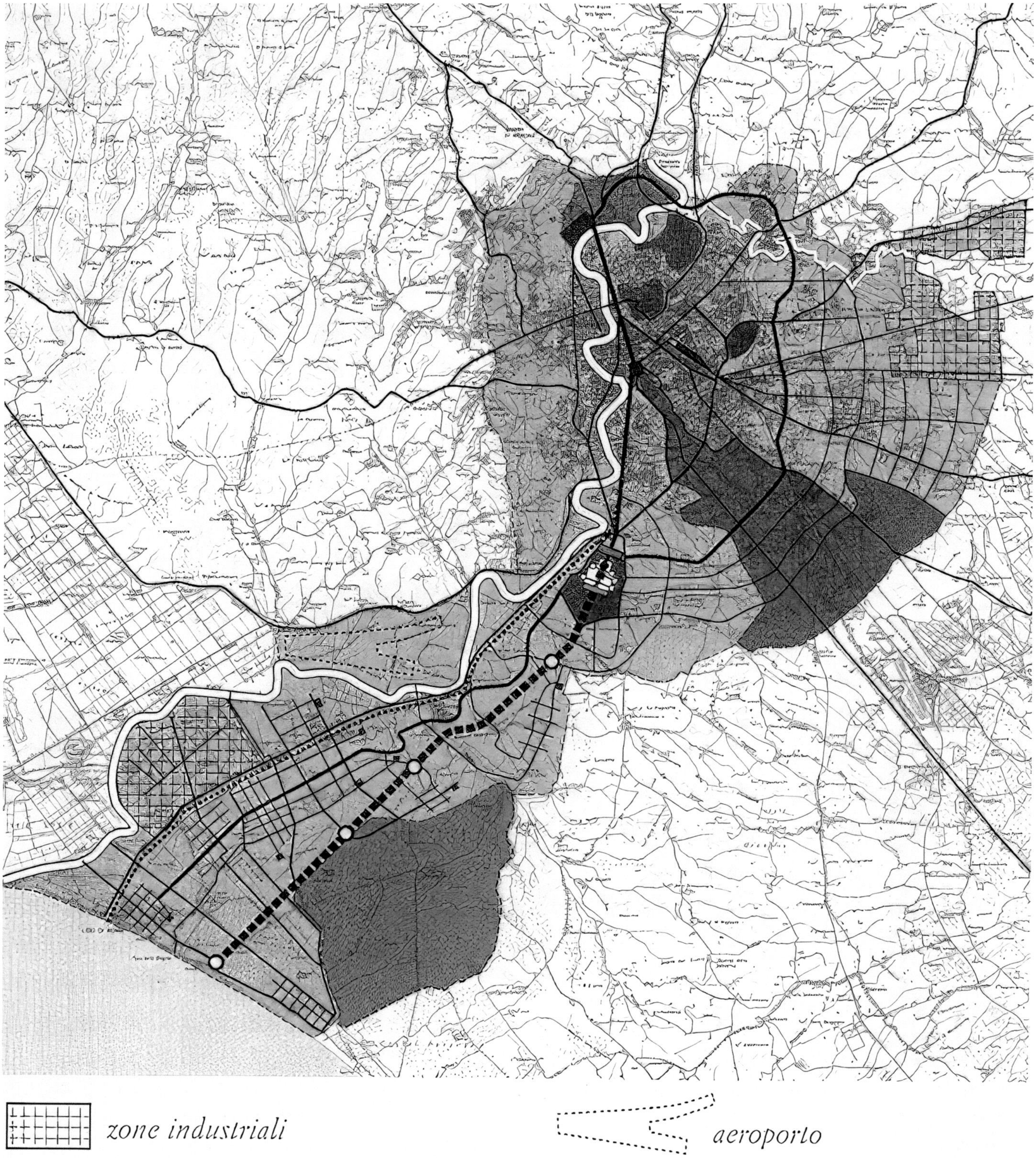

● Gustavo Giovannoni, Marcello Piacentini, et al. *Piano regolatore per Roma Imperiale* (Masterplan for Imperial Rome), 1941. Development scheme toward Ostia Antica, Ostia, and the Tyrrhenian Sea.

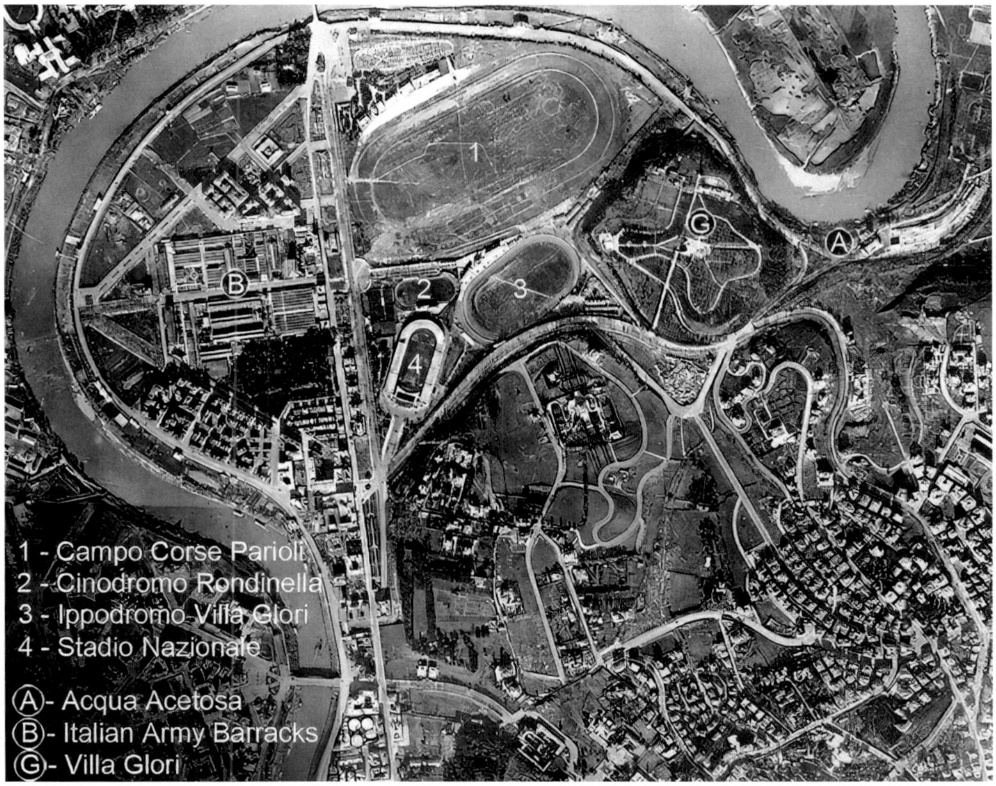

● Map of the Via Flaminia and Parioli hills, 1934. To the right of the Stadio Nazionale and tangent to the Villa Glori (the future Piazza Euclide), one can see the scenic and curving Viale Parioli, the major structuring infrastructure of Parioli, before connecting to the series of boulevards linking to the Verano cemetery.

Minister of Public Works in the early 1960s, fought aggressively in favor of the expropriation process, but he lost the battle. Yet, he succeeded in passing a less far-reaching law that applied the principle of compulsory expropriation only to the areas selected by municipalities for the construction of housing of an economic or popular character. It was a good result, but the law was only applicable to areas that were not contiguous with each other and dispersed in the periphery contributed in no small way to making Rome a shapeless constellation of irreconcilable and uncoordinated diversities. At the same time, a completely illegal city came to life, spread out in the wide interstices between infrastructure and legally built areas. The illegal city was built without any rules or permits, the genuine protagonist of Rome's growth. By 1985, an illegal city of a million inhabitants had grown in the meshes of the legal city.[42]

From the Flaminia Promenade to the Monti Parioli

The last phase of preparing the 1962 masterplan coincided with the decision to host the Olympic Games of 1960. Curiously enough, the history of the area where the Villaggio Olimpico was built runs parallel to that of the Quartiere Mazzini, on the other side of the Tiber, and replicates some of its basic features. The natural and topographic conditions were quite similar. It was a low-lying area subject to an almost permanent overflow of the river, wet for much of the year. Nevertheless, it was part of a natural landscape that despite its condition carried a great beauty. Overlooking it are the last reliefs of the larger system of Roman hills, i.e., the Parioli and the Villa Glori. Along its western edge runs the ancient Via Flaminia ◖ top ◗, which, in a straight line from Piazza del Popolo, reaches the Ponte Milvio, Rome's historical gateway to the north. From time immemorial, the first slopes facing the Tiber at the foot of the Parioli Hills were the site of farms, archaic, and then Christian communities that, in later times, gave way to simple popular trattorias, the destination for Sunday outings. Stendhal, in the 1820s, wrote in his *Passeggiate romane*: "Were it not for the fear of fever, nothing would be more pleasant than to live there in the summer?"[43] Despite the pleasant landscape and its proximity to the city's ancient center, the idea of making it a residential area was certainly not taken seriously until after 1945.[44]

Considering the popular success of the area as a recreation place, the *Piano regolatore* of 1883 included

● Giovanni Battista Falda, Fonte dell'Acqua acetosa, 1665.

the proposal for a tree-lined *passeggiata* (promenade) along Via Flaminia, while the site of the present Olympic Village was targeted to become a popular area for playing fields. A planning addendum also envisaged that a branch of the Passeggiata Flaminia be extended to turn and run at the foot of the Parioli hills. The promenade was to extend to the Acqua Acetosa ◖ top ◗—an ancient spring that had always been a destination for pleasant pilgrimages for Romans and had been transformed into a tiny architectural jewel by an artist of the Baroque age, likely to be Andrea Sacchi in association with the architect Marcantonio Rossi.[45] In 1908, the Campo Corse Parioli was built on the plain for galloping races. The grandstands, designed by Marcello Piacentini and inaugurated by King Vittorio Emanuele III in 1911 on the occasion of the International Exposition, were one of the first Roman constructions in reinforced concrete along with the Ponte Risorgimento. In the same year, 1911, Piacentini built a new stadium between the Via Flaminia and the new Flaminia promenade. An important project for the time, modeled on the stadiums of ancient Hellas, it was given the name of Stadio Nazionale (eventually demolished in the late 1950s).

The concept of a wide and planted promenade caught the attention of the city administration which immediately began the process to expropriate the area—it belonged to the family of engineer Vittorio Glori, who also owned the hill that still bears that name, Villa Glori. The grand Flaminia promenade was soon envisioned as the first section of one of the greatest infrastructural interventions in modern Rome. The construction of Viale Parioli, directly connected to the Passeggiata Flaminia and climbing up the Monti Parioli in a scenographic curvilinear avenue, took place on the initiative of the owners of the land interested in the creation of the new major artery. Their project involved the construction of elegant *villini* along the planted avenue. Viale Parioli, extended into Viale Liegi, became the fulcrum of a sequence of boulevards articulated with an orderly sequence of squares—known today as Piazza Ungheria, Piazza Buenos Aires, Piazza Regina Margherita, Piazza Galeno, Piazza Sassari—and leading all away to the Verano cemetery. This urban sequence became the backbone of the new and large bourgeois quarters of the Parioli hills, to the northeast of the ancient city, entirely located outside the constraints of the newly approved masterplan and, above all, outside the city's customary belt: buildings, therefore, were exempted from taxes on materials. The Parioli racecourse was dismantled in 1926 and replaced by the Capannelle racetrack to the south of Rome. During Fascism, it became the Dux Course, a vast area for gatherings and paramilitary exercises of the Gioventù Italiana del Littorio.[46]

Foro Italico and Luigi Moretti's *Forma Ultima Fori*

Meanwhile, on the other side of the Tiber, work had begun on the Foro Mussolini (now Foro Italico) ◖ p. 141 top ◗, the vast urban project of the Fascist regime devoted to the practice and rhetoric of sports training of the Italian youth. Located at the foot of Monte Mario and Raphael's Villa Madama (1518–1527), the Foro was built according to a masterplan of 1927 designed by Enrico Del Debbio (1891–1973). The centerpiece was Del Debbio's Palazzo H (1932), seat of the Fascist Academy of Male Gymnastics ◖ p. 141 bottom ◗, and connected on an axis with the Stadio dei Marmi (1932). The bright red of the Academy, the 60 marble statues of athletes bordering the marble stadium, and the Futurist obelisk dedicated to Mussolini became the instant icons of the complex.[47] In 1936, the young Luigi Moretti designed the monumental entrance to the complex and one of the masterpieces of modern Italian architecture: the Casa delle Armi (Fencing Academy) at the southern entrance of the Foro Mussolini ◖◖ p. 97 right ◗◗.[48]

In those convulsive years of the war, when events were precipitating and the uncertainty of the future was pushing Rome's great architects to imagine new programs for the post-war period, Luigi Moretti began to work with the Italian National Olympic Committee (CONI) to draw up large-scale plans to complete the Foro Mussolini as the capital's main sports center. His was a wide-ranging territorial vision of this northern section of Rome, destined to flow into the design of the city that Piacentini and Giovannoni were assembling as a mosaic of detailed plans (*piani particolareggiati*) to be entrusted to "superior personalities" such as Luigi Piccinato, Giorgio Calza Bini, Lenti, Apolloni, Enrico Del Debbio, Mario Paniconi, and a few others.[49] Moretti produced more than one proposal. The

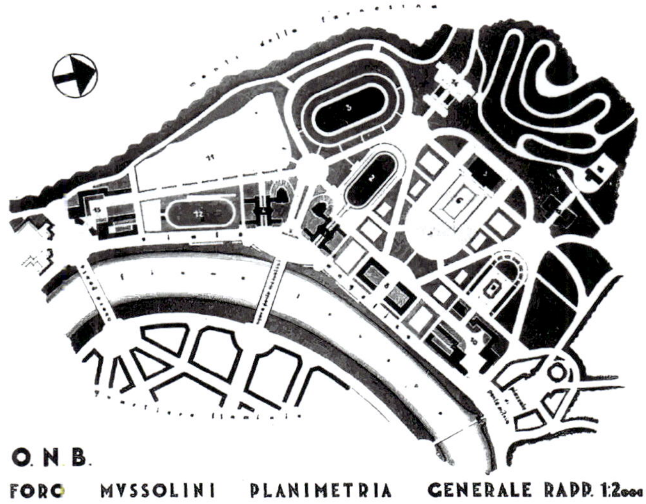

● Enrico Del Debbio, final masterplan of the Foro Mussolini, now Foro Italico, 1932.

● Enrico Del Debbio, Academy of Physical Education and Gymnastics, 1927–1932. The Stadio dei Marmi and its 60 statues are located behind the Academy.

most interesting, complete, and final one—which he called, in Latin, *Forma Ultima Fori* (1941) ◀◀ p. 142 ▶▶—went so far as to include the entire area of the future Olympic Village and was presented to Mussolini in the form of a large model. The project provided a deviation of the Tiber to create a large artificial island which was de facto extending the sports complex into the Flaminio neighborhood. The new bridge designed by Armando Brasini (1879–1965), which was to replace the Ponte Milvio as the northern entrance to the capital, was in construction and its future connection with the Flaminio district and the Parioli was not yet designed.[50] Moretti prepared a convincing solution: the new boulevard axis would immediately regain the ground down from the monumental bridge and be transformed into a kind of large public square, symmetrical and monumental, around which the new sports facilities—the dome of a sports palace is noticeable on the model—and large buildings with vast courtyards and probably surrounded by porticoes would be located. In 1939, Rome had submitted its bid to host the Olympic Games in competition with Tokyo and made the preliminary decision to build the Olympic Village exactly where it would later be built for the 1960 Games. So, the central part of Moretti's *Forma Ultima Fori* visible on the now lost model can be considered as the first version of the Olympic Village, twenty years before its realization.

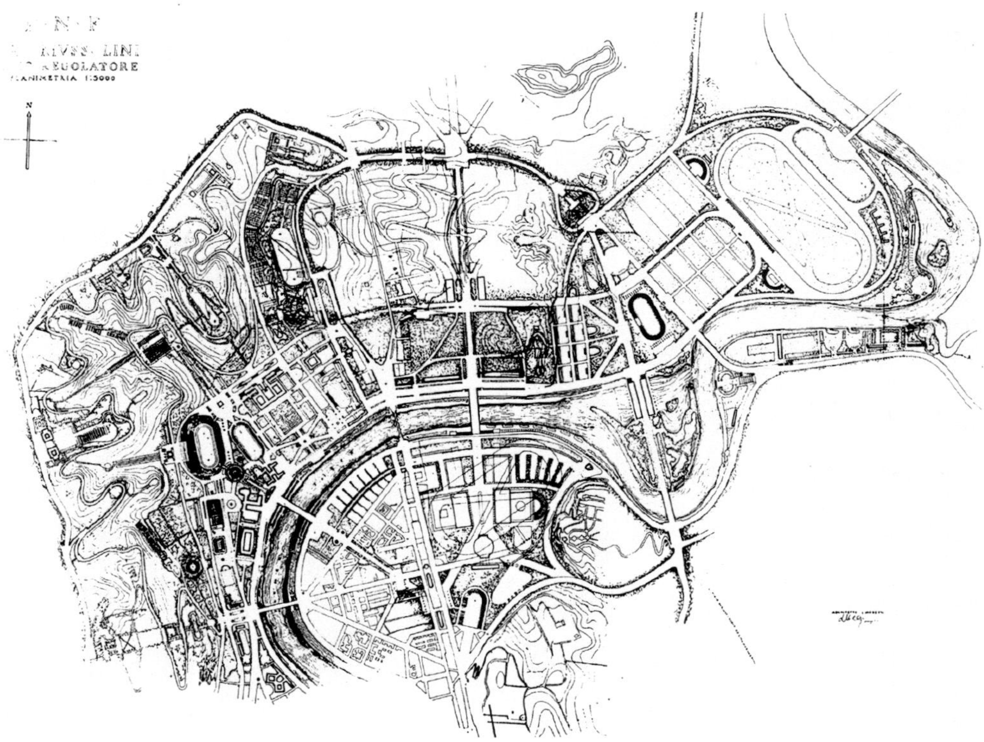

● Luigi Moretti, masterplan and model known as *Forma Ultima Fori*, 1941. The unrealized project integrates the existing Foro Italico (to the left with the Olympic Stadium. In the center of the plan is the proposed new north-south axis that connects the hills to the area of the future Olympic Village).

The Failed Competition of 1948–1949

In the aftermath of the war, the City of Rome owned the area but had no resources to initiate any development. The public housing construction program, INA-Casa, would not be established until two years later in 1949. In the meantime, private building activity had restarted at an increasingly triumphant pace. As a result, the city council decided to enter the residential market for Rome's bourgeoisie by allocating the Parioli Field area for the erection of a new neighborhood on public land. To do so, the municipality announced a competition in 1948. It was won by Claudio Longo (1912–1997) ◖bottom◗, but its implementation was a failure. Only six lots were contracted and built as a series of tall buildings lined up in a comb-like fashion along Viale Tiziano, running parallel to Via Flaminia between Piazzale delle Belle Arti and Ponte Milvio. The rest of the area was deserted, and the field of shacks continued to expand and swallow up part of the Villa Glori Racecourse.[51] Longo's project embodied, for the first time after the war, what a purely bourgeois neighborhood built without public subsidies could be. Once realized, it would have consisted of a kind of Rationalist translation of the minimal principles of the garden city: a fabric of small buildings somewhere between the typical Roman *palazzina* and the *villino*, each surrounded by a bit of greenery, but without the sought-after planimetric variety and the picturesque civic image that Giovannoni pursued. The small volumes of Claudio Longo's project were arranged according to a simple grid guided by the alignment of the temporary viaduct connecting to and from the new Flaminio bridge, which would be replaced, ten years later, by Pier Luigi Nervi's double viaduct on piers. Only as it approached the slopes of the Villa Glori hill did the fabric of small residential buildings lose regularity to almost conform to the hill morphology.[52]

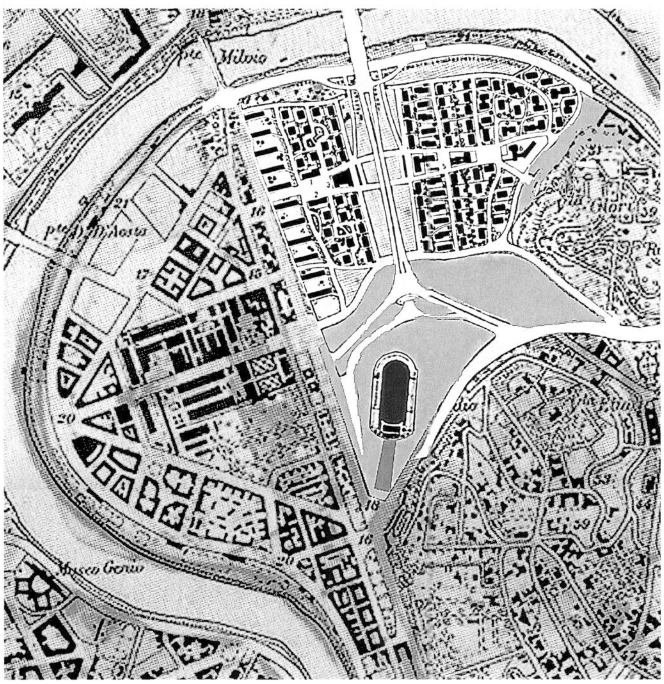

● Claudio Longo, winning entry of the competition for a housing district on the Parioli Fields (now Olympic Village), 1948–1949.

The Indifferent Architects of the Olympic Village

Arguably, 1960 can be considered as the official date of birth of the new era of Roman urbanism. It was the year of the Olympic Games and the inauguration of the *Villaggio Olimpico*. The Olympic Village definitively interrupted the continuity of research on urban architecture that had taken off, with effort and toil after 1870, and had gained momentum, coherence, and form in the first 50 years of the twentieth century. To be sure, the project lent itself perfectly to asserting an architectural and political trend over the others. It was not only a neighborhood to be built on a public area—therefore to be designed with great freedom, without proprietary constraints—it was also and above all a true showcase through which a very large international audience would be able to appreciate, through architecture, the modern face of the capital and of Italy as a whole. Today, more than 60 years after its inauguration, the Olympic Village stands as a demonstration of the contradictory richness of the Roman School of Architecture, thus of its great vitality even in the post-war era. The fact that such an important project was not entrusted to any of the already established stars of the Faculty of the School of Architecture in Rome—Piccinato, De Renzi, Quaroni, Muratori, Ridolfi, Fiorentino, or to other younger students of theirs—marked a momentous rupture in the history of modern Rome. Consequently, it is Luigi Moretti, Vittorio Cafiero, Vincenzo Monaco, Amedeo Luccichenti, and Adalberto Libera who designed and built the Olympic Village. They were all pupils of the Rome School of Architecture, however, none of them belonged to the established academic body of the post-war faculty.

In his anthology of post-war Italian architecture, Manfredo Tafuri defined the two opposing ranks of Roman architects in the post-war era.[53] On one side were Quaroni, Piccinato, and many others who were working to lay the foundations of a civilized development of the urban community and the elimination of the frightening deficiencies of the city's urban economy. These were the "committed" architects. On the other side were the allies of capital and speculation, those architects who had an interest in maintaining the status quo as much as possible, in covering with an elaborate technicality the permanence of structures that had so far allowed the widespread building and urbanistic malpractice and caused the most shameful social imbalances. These were the "indifferent" architects and they included the entire group that was responsible for the design and construction of the Olympic Village. Paradoxically, the bourgeois Rationalism of those indifferent architects appeared to Tafuri to be more in step with the functional and technical needs of a progressive civilization than the systematic doubts, research, and linguistic deviations of the committed architects.

In fact, the bourgeois Rationalism of the indifferent architects convinced Giuseppe Togni, a great industrial executive who had become Minister of Public Works in 1957 and remained so until 1960. He was a successful and efficient politician who in those few years managed to realize very important public works: in Rome in particular, he started and completed all the facilities for the 1960 Olympics—Palazzi dello Sport, Velodrome, the Corso Francia Viaduct, the so-called Via Olimpica that united the Foro Mussolini (or Foro Italico) with the reborn EUR, another important Olympic pole, as well as the Fiumicino airport. Moreover, it was Giuseppe Togni who in 1957 chose and commissioned the five designers of the Olympic Village. Certainly, he all but ignored the indifference of the Olympic Village's planners to the fate of society's civil and political progress; therefore, he could not be concerned with the profound cultural contradiction in Italian society pointed out by Tafuri. For the minister, that group of talented architects represented, simultaneously, a guarantee of modernity and, above all, of professional efficiency. The Olympic Village was built as a residential settlement of INCIS, i.e., the National Institute for the Housing of State Employees, and lent, for a few weeks in 1960, to the Olympic Committee (CONI) as a village for the athletes. The minister, CONI, and INCIS needed great professionals who would meet the schedule while ensuring the aesthetic modernity and functionality of the new works. The timetable was tight, yet all the designers chosen for the Olympic works, engineers, and architects, met the deadlines perfectly. Some of them, such as Amedeo Luccichenti and Vincenzo Monaco, were simultaneously engaged in the design of the new Fiumicino airport. In the same period, Luigi Moretti and Adalberto Libera were commissioned by INCIS to build another neighborhood for state employees in Decima, an area on the road to Ostia. Among the designers of the village, only

● Pier Luigi Nervi, double viaduct of Corso Francia, 1959.

Adalberto Libera became an academic architect. In 1962, he was called to join the Faculty of Architecture in Rome where he ended his career as an innovator in the teaching of architectural design.[54]

As for Pier Luigi Nervi (1891–1979), the Olympics marked his national and international apotheosis as one of the greatest structural architects and engineers. First, he designed the circular Palazzetto dello Sport and the new Flaminio stadium, both of which were inaugurated in 1960 and crowned the Olympic Village. At the urging of the designers of the housing village, he was commissioned to resolve the connection with the monumental bridge designed by Armando Brasini and completed in 1951. His solution was to raise the Corso Francia ◖ top ◗ as a high-speed viaduct supported by a string of masterfully shaped concrete pillars. In so doing, he freed the ground from traffic and was able to unite both sides of the Olympic Village.[55]

Precedents and Innovation

It would be interesting to find out whether a hierarchy emerged within the group of designers, even though they all consented to each of them overseeing a block of housing. Moretti has often been cited as a potential coordinator, yet, according to Paolo Melis, author of a complete biography of Monaco and Luccichenti, it is among the drawings of the two Rationalist architects that various elaborations of the overall design of the Olympic Village appear, as if they had assumed the role of coordinating the general plan of the settlement before distributing the parts to be designed down to the architectural detail. To be sure, coordination took place and the results are obvious: standardized ribbon windows for most buildings; traditional floor-to-ceiling windows, equally standardized, even though used in smaller numbers; unification of the interplay between exterior walls clad with ceramic battens and exposed concrete stringcourses; the brick grid drums around the stairwells that stick out on the roofs of many buildings; and more importantly for the image of the neighborhood, a free-standing ground floor on pilotis.[56]

Yet, it is in the typological choices that the authorship of the five designers can be detected and that the cultural continuity with their youthful works and projects was largely affirmed. Leaving aside minor variations in the number of floors, the building types present in the Villaggio Olimpico are four: two of clear derivation from the history of modern European architecture, and two truly innovative. The most common is the in-line building type known as "A", used in three- or four-story buildings but almost identical in terms of interior distribution (Libera, Cafiero, Monaco, Luccichenti, Moretti). Its source lies in Mies van der Rohe's in-line house at the 1927 Weissenhofsiedlung in Stuttgart, with one major variation, that is the introduction of service terraces on the side of the kitchens—a necessity in Italy as an outdoor space of convenience. Otherwise, both the adoption of ribbon windows and the setback of the columns from the plane of the facades were ostentatious quotations from the Rationalist precedent. Libera had certainly studied it when he participated, with a large delegation of young Rationalist architects, in the International Exhibition held in 1928 in the very spaces of the Weissenhofsiedlung. The other building type of clear historical ascendancy is the tallest building in the entire district, with five stories above the pilotis and the only type with elevators. It consists of two linear structures parallel to each other to form a "triple-body building," with an internal and continuous lighting and ventilation space, interrupted only by the staircase and elevator groups. It is the most imposing building, dedicated to smaller apartments. Its resemblance to the Immobile CX designed in 1938 by Cesare Cattaneo (1912–1943), the youngest of the group of Rationalist architects in Como, is quite remarkable.[57] Certainly, Libera knew him and appreciated his precocious design ability as well as his exact and poetic way of designing typologically innovative and linguistically abstract structures. Comparing the plans and sections of the two buildings—Cattaneo's one was not built—dispels any possible doubt. So here too, Libera's personal, human, and cultural experience may have determined the group's choices.

The first and most famous of the two innovative building types was undoubtedly the one known under the name of *crocette (palazzine a croce)*—a continuous two-story fabric of apartments on pilotis, open on square interior spaces, and organized in the shape of a cross around the general distribution stairs. In fact, this type was built in two similar versions, one by Libera, the other, perhaps more refined, by Moretti. To be sure, the type was a development, almost an abstract exaltation, of the Tuscolano Horizontal Housing Unit designed by Libera a few years earlier. If one analyzes some of Moretti's hand sketches, it becomes apparent that he wanted to share the reworking of Libera's truly innovative idea and perhaps even urge its author to design a profound revision. The second innovative typology seems the least important, almost marginal, and perhaps useless in the economy and general design of the neighborhood: it consists of a small number of square buildings, only five, two stories above pilotis, placed almost as if to guard the Olympic Village on the side facing Viale Tiziano. They seem to suggest that the bourgeois type par excellence in Rome—the *palazzina*—could also generate a low-cost, efficient, very well-distributed building type (four apartments per floor, two bathrooms per apartment), but without architectural frills. One wonders which of the five designers was the inventor of that rational, economical, and even severe building type in its absolute lack of private or service terraces: a building type never again used, or attempted, by any Roman or Italian architect. I would like to be able to say that this was an act of demonstration by Monaco and Luccichenti and with Moretti's blessing: almost a demonstrative signature of what two hardened *palazzinari* could have done if engaged more often and systematically in the design of affordable housing districts.[58]

On the inauguration of the Olympic Village, a pamphlet of a journalistic and laudatory nature—an interview with the village's five designers—was published.[59] Almost everyone dwelt, however, on the choice of resting each building on a free-standing floor supported by pilotis, truly an absolute novelty in Rome, especially for an area so close to the historic center and the neighborhoods of early modernity, such the Mazzini and Flaminio districts. As Libera stated "... the solution of the buildings on pilotis offers an infinite series of perspectives in all directions, with sudden and very different panoramas, with unpredictable views ... while the green turf here and there interrupted by roads and paths with irregular course, by bushes, by plants and the pilotis themselves, determines in plan a texture on which the eye never tires."[60] The decision

● Transparencies and pilotis, Villaggio Olimpico.

to use pilotis was therefore presented as the most effective concept to achieve a horizontal visual continuity at ground level ◖top◗. Luigi Moretti was much more pragmatic and after agreeing with Libera and his colleagues that the architecture of the village would be immersed in a park to connect with the hill of Villa Glori, he added: "We have oriented ourselves towards the adoption of the buildings raised from the ground level also because of the consideration that the apartments on the first floor are generally disqualified … Thus, with a modest additional expense, an intelligent administration of public money could be realized."[61]

Good Architecture but Poor Urbanism

In conclusion, the Olympic Village can be seen as a successful neighborhood: very good architects, a strong link to the modern tradition of architecture, some not insignificant typological innovations, and the creation of an urban landscape made of deep glimpses through the horizontal plane of the ancient floodplain soil, restored but still somewhat verdant. Libera, Cafiero, Luccichenti, Monaco, and Moretti must have designed the complex with passion, fun, and pleasure.[62] They must have discussed, with great taste and competence, the selection and design of typologies, the unification of architectural details and materials, to create a modern residential settlement: pilotis, depth of horizontal views, ribbon windows. On the other hand, they did not apply themselves with the same depth and expertise to the conception of the urban form: do the urban spaces in the neighborhood have characteristics that distinguish them from one another? Are they real squares? Are the courtyards varied in shape and size? Is there a real center or did they think that a functional spatial hierarchy was not necessary? Or did they think that the center was not needed because around it was, already well established, the city with its neighborhood centers? Why ostentatiously give the tallest buildings the specific task of shielding, indeed separating the new neighborhood from the city? Arguably, the center was supposed to be marked by the church in a truly central location, but unfortunately, it was not built where it was planned, but rather in a leftover space close to the viaduct. It is a nice modern building, but nowadays, can a church, apart from its location and architectural quality, really make the center of a modern neighborhood? To be honest, it is much later, when Renzo Piano designed the three-theater complex of the Auditorium Parco della Musica (inaugurated in 2002), that a genuine series of urban spaces—the long arcades, the shops, and the cavea-like open-air theater—were created and made unrestrictedly public.

Back to the Future: The Great Ruin of the New Rome

An early trip to EUR in 1945, with my somewhat grown-up band of brats in a little truck of the kind that replaced tram services right after the war, excited me as a great discovery and an amazing exploration. EUR in those days was, to a boy's imagination, a genuine field of miracles, a city of unfinished squares, empty buildings, and unreal architecture made up of large, skeletal concrete frames, cornices, and turgid columns, all abandoned on the ground like newborn ruins. Therein our shouts echoed, with laughter and great awe, in the emptiness of marble halls. Above all, it was a deserted district, no peers of different urban ethnicity owned it or stood between us and the place, only shepherds and flocks placidly animating the great deserted yard. Yet, in those very Roman days, there were men and animals which, twice a year, would camp out in the meadows of Monte Mario and prepare to cross Piazza Mazzini in the last hours of the night, pushing with them toward the *campana romana*, an endless tinkling of faint bells lying on a thick, gray, muffled trampling: transhuman, nomadic ethnicity, loose from urban constraints and yet as integral to my city as a punctual comet is part of our solar system.

However, the city to be explored and experienced, the city that attracted me and made me slip into itself imperceptibly more and more each day was the one that I walked through daily and could look at whenever I wanted from the heights of the hills to the right and left of the Tiber, but which also spoke to me about itself from school texts, from the lessons of the best professors, and from not a few of the books that my mother placed silently on my small study table—books that I often ignored for months, but which I eventually began to leaf through and read intensively. All this cultivated my natural disposition, which was that typical of the very young, to make knowledge and emotion coincide directly. It allowed me to nourish, with the very tools of research, the sensory and intuitive perception of reality and to throw into the furnace of mythical elaboration all the materials provided by science. This is why I was later interested in drawing, an activity that frequently takes on a cognitive function and elucidates, in an unparalleled way, what exists, or has existed, or will exist. Just as much, drawing does not ask for explanations, nor does it give any. Like music, drawing directly transforms the most analytical and precise gaze, as well as the most demanding technique it needs to exist, into the privilege of saying what cannot be said in any other way and to bring to life in distinct form the fruitful but otherwise ambiguous, confusing, and inexpressible world of creative subjectivity. That is why, from the moment I encountered it, Piranesi's *Ichnographia Campi Martii antiquae urbis* (1762, also known as *Campus Martius*) has mesmerized me: not so much

● Contemporary aerial view of the Olympic Village from the north, with cultural and sport context.

● Giovanni Battista Piranesi, Ichnographia Campi Martii antiquae urbis, also known as Campus Martius, 1762.

because of its prophetic visionariness or its dilation of the world of architecture toward an exhilarating future revealed by a mythical past; but because of it being the result of an instantaneous transformation of study and research into a creative drive, as if all historical, archaeological, or philological knowledge was the necessary fuel for an inexhaustible workshop of creativity, as greedy and innocent as a child's instinct. From boyhood to adolescence and beyond, little fragments of knowledge, brought to me by rivulets from different sources, accumulated in my consciousness. And while the drawing techniques of the architect, even if rudimentarily deployed, enriched my capacity for knowledge, the fantastic traversal of the city—my first tool for perceiving and learning about reality—gained even more intellectual weight. Even today, I have the awareness that when I least expect it, the physical transect of the city continues to take advantage of all my residual perceptive capacities to build on my current and few historical certainties, real or imaginary journeys into the space and time of Rome, moments of unashamed emotion perhaps too intense for my age.[63]

EDITOR'S NOTE

Following our first conversations in Calliol, Daniel Solomon, Anna Irene Del Monaco, and myself agreed that the core of the book would be written in Italian by Lucio Valerio Barbera. An ambitious and quasi-impossible table of contents was agreed upon to develop a history of Modern Rome in three chronological phases: from 1870 to the mayorship of Ernesto Nathan; from 1907 to the fall of Fascism; from 1945 to the Olympic Games and the Villaggio Olimpico. The first section, somewhat autobiographical, was written by Lucio Barbera. The second and third ones were first transcribed from hours of conversations between Lucio Barbera, Anna Irene Del Monaco, and me. These Italian drafts were then re-written by Barbera. My work as editor was first to edit the translation into English then to both reduce it in length and to add essential elements to facilitate the understanding of the text for non-Roman and non-Italian readers; thirdly to add the apparatus of footnotes fundamental to the reading; last to assemble and edit the iconography following Lucio Barbera's indications. On the request of Lucio Valerio Barbera, I include the following comment:

Dear Jean-François, first, I want to thank you for the work you have done on my text, to edit and shorten it to make it attractive and easier accessible for a, hopefully, wide audience. I am truly amazed by the ability you have shown to not only tighten the text, but also—in this tough exercise—to not completely extinguish the sense of autobiographical narration that sustains the original. For this reason, and from now on, I will call you Diodorus Siculus, perhaps the greatest among those who knew how to write an epitome from a complex text, producing, however, a work of value. Also interesting is the ending of the piece, made by recomposing, with wit and art, pages from the first part of the original and perhaps, if I'm not mistaken, other pages of mine taken from I don't know where.

(L. B., J. F. L)

1
See Paolo Nicoloso, *Marcello Piacentini. Architettura e Potere: una biografia* (Udine: Gaspari Editore, 2022).

2
On Gustavo Giovannoni's role after the war, see Giuseppe Bonaccorso, "L'architetto integrale and Gustavo Giovannoni's Role in Education and Cultural Dissemination," *Planning Perspectives*, vol. 37, no.3, 2022, 477–495. On Foschini, see https://siusa.archivi.beniculturali.it/inventari-pdf/lazio/Foschini_inventario.pdf; Gregory Paola, "L'architettura di Arnaldo Foschini e il Corso del Rinascimento," in Gianfranco Spagnesi, ed., *Il Quartiere e il Corso del Rinascimento* (Rome: Istituto dell'Enciclopedia Italiana, 1994), 173–225. On Del Debbio, see Maria Luisa Neri and Paola Raffaella David, *Enrico Del Debbio* (Viareggio: Idea Books, 2006).

3
Stephanie Zeier Pilat, *Reconstructing Italy: The INA-Casa Neighborhoods of the Postwar Era* (London: Routledge, 2014), 50.

4
Quoted from Luigi Beretta Anguissola, *I 14 anni del piano INA-Casa* (Rome: Staderini, 1963), cited by Stephanie Zeier Pilat, op. cit., 29.

5
Paola Di Biagi, *The INA-Casa Plan and Italy in the Fifties. The Great Reconstruction* (Rome: Donzelli, 2010). In 1949, Amintore Fanfani signed the Legge Fanfani that enabled the INA-Casa program. It provided the financing for a massive housing program that created 350,000 new dwellings across Italy from 1949 to 1963. See also, https://tulliaiori.com/downloads/riservato/2002%20inacasa%20cantierecostruzione.pdf

6
Adalberto Libera, et al., *Verso la casa esatta* (Milan, 1945), 3. The architects involved included Pietro Giulio Bosisio, Adalberto Libera, Gio Ponti, Pierangelo Pozzi, Eugenio Soncini, Giuseppe Vaccaro, Carlo Villa, and Guido Beretta. The publication's objectives are well described on page 3: "These pages are open to everyone, all useful ideas will be expressed and presented to you, they must be the bulletins of the campaign for reconstruction. Gradually, from subsequent studies, from attempts, from incessant work, from everyone's passionate collaboration, yes it will outline the 'exact house,' the exact construction, that is, the good reconstruction, the reconstruction that Italy and current civilization require."

7
Manuale dell'architetto (Rome: CNR, 1946); INA-Casa, *Suggerimenti, norme, e schemi per la elaborazione e presentazione dei progetti: Bandi dei Concorsi* (Rome: F. Damasso, 1949) and INA-Casa, *Suggerimenti, esempi e norme per la progettazione urbanistica: Progetti tipo* (Rome: F. Damasso, 1950). Also see Riccardo Renzi, "Adalberto Libera and the Domestic Dimension of Being Together. The Horizontal Housing Project in the Tuscolano Area," *Firenze Architettura*, no. 1, 2016, 76–81.

8
Stephanie Zeier Pilat, op. cit., 69, cited from *Suggerimenti*, 1950, 10–11.

9
Giuseppe Pagano, *Architettura rurale italiana* (Milan: Ulrico Hoepli), 1936.

10
Giuseppe Pagano, *Architettura rurale italiana*, op. cit., 6.

11
Gustavo Giovannoni, *Vecchie città ed edilizia nuova* (Turin: Utet, 1931), 140.

12
Ibidem.

13
AACAR, Architettura minore in Italia/Roma, vol. 1 and 2 (Rome: C. Crudo e C. Editori, 1930).

14
The literature on Neorealism is extensive. Most useful resources are Stephanie Zeier Pilat, *Reconstructing Italy*, op. cit.; Paola Di Biagi, *The INA-Casa Plan and Italy in the Fifties*, op. cit.; Bruno Reichlin, "Figures of Neorealism in Italian Architecture (Part 1)," *Grey Room*, 05, Fall 2001 and Bruno Reichlin, "Figures of Neorealism in Italian Architecture (Part 2)," *Grey Room*, 06, Winter 2002, 110–133.

15
"Quartiere Tiburtino a Roma," *Urbanistica*, 21, no. 7, 1951, 24–25; Carlo Aymonino, "Storia e cronaca del quartiere Tiburtino," *Casabella continuità*, no. 215, November 1955, 18–43.

16
Carlo Aymonino, *Casabella*, no. 215, April 1957, 20.

17
Ibidem.

18
Ibidem.

19
Marcel Meili and Markus Peter, interview with Wolfgang Frankl in "Durch die Abruzzen nach Rom: Eine architektonische Reise," photocopied document distributed during research trip for the Ecole Polytechnique Fédérale de Zurich, 1993, 111–125, quoted by Bruno Reichlin, "Figures of Neorealism in Italian Architecture (Part 1)," 86.

20
Ludovico Quaroni, "Paese dei Barocchi," *Casabella continuità*, no. 215, April 1957, x. Note the play on words between Paese dei Balocchi "Country of Toys" (a reference to Pinocchio) and Paese dei Barocchi "Country of Baroques."

21
See Stefania Mornati and Filippo Cerrini, "Il quartiere Tuscolano a Roma (1950–60)," in Sergio Poretti, Riccardo Capomolla, and Rosalia Vittorini, eds., *L'architettura INA Casa (1949–1963) Aspetti e problemi di conservazione e recupero* (Rome: Gangemi, 2004).

22
See Saverio Muratori, *Studi per una operante storia urbana di Venezia* (Rome: Istituto Poligrafico dello Stato, 1960).

23
Giorgio Pigafetta, *Saverio Muratori architetto: teoria e progetti* (Venice: Marsilio, 1990); Anna Bruna Menghini and Valerio Palmieri, *Saverio Muratori: didattica della composizione architettonica nella Facoltà di Architettura di Roma, 1954–1973* (Bari: Politba, 2009); Giancarlo Cataldi, ed., *Saverio Muratori architetto a cento anni dalla nascita* (Florence: Aíon, 2014).

24
Saverio Muratori and Centro studi di storia urbanistica, *Studi per una operante storia urbana di Roma* (Rome: Consiglio nazionale delle ricerche, 1963).

25
See Maria Luisa Neri, *Mario De Renzi: architettura come mestiere 1897–1967* (Rome: Gangemi, 1992).

26
See Riccardo Renzi, "Adalberto Libera and the Domestic Dimension of Being Together," 76–81.

27
On Ridolfi, see Renato Nicolini, ed., *Mario Ridolfi architetto. 1904–2004* (Milan: Electa, 2005); Francesco Cellini and Claudio D'Amato, *Le architetture di Ridolfi e Frankl* (Milan: Electa, 2005); Francesco Moschini and Luciana Rattazzi, *Mario Ridolfi. La poetica del dettaglio* (Rome: Kappa, 1997); Federico Bellini, *Mario Ridolfi* (Bari: Laterza, 1993).

28
See Bruno Reichlin, "Figures of Neorealism in Italian Architecture (Part 2)," 110–133.

29
Ibidem, 117, from Paolo Portoghesi, "Dal neo-realismo al neoliberty," *Comunità* 65 (1958), 69–79.

30
Guido Canella and Aldo Rossi, "Architetti Italiani: Mario Ridolfi," in *Comunità* 41 (1956), 50–55; and Paolo Portoghesi, "Dal neo-realismo al neoliberty," *Comunità* 65 (1958), 69, quoted by Bruno Reichlin, "Figures of Neorealism in Italian Architecture (Part 2)," 112.

31
See Johann Gottlieb Fichte, *Reden an die deutsche Nation*, 1807–1808; in English, *Addresses to the German Nation* (Cambridge: Cambridge University Press, 2008).

32
The literature on Luigi Moretti is vast. See Federico Bucci and Marco Mulazzani, *Luigi Moretti. Works and Writings* (New York: Princeton Architectural Press, 2002); Cecilia Rostagni, *Luigi Moretti*, 1907–1973 (Milan: Electa, 2008); Bruno Reichlin and Letizia Tedeschi, *Luigi Moretti: razionalismo e trasgressività tra barocco e informale* (Milan: Electa, 2010); *Luigi Prisco and Franco Storelli, Luigi Moretti e la casa della GIL a Trastevere: lo spazio ritrovato* (Rome: Palombi Editori, 2020); Filippo Lambertucci, *Luigi Moretti: Piazza Imperiale e Cinema teatro* (Milan: UNICOPLI, 2001).

33
Mario Manieri Elia, "Il contributo di Ugo Luccichenti," in *Metamorfosi*, no. 15 (1990), 33–38.

34
On Palazzina Bornigia, see Mauro Marzo, *Case con vista. Mario De Renzi, Ugo Luccichenti, Mario Ridolfi a Roma. 1935–1940* (Naples: Clean, 2019); also see Filomena Pierdomenico and Mario Piersensini, eds., *Ugo Luccichenti architetto* (Rome: Officina Edizioni, 1980).

35
See Davide Spina, "Grand Hotel," in Adam Jasper and Stefan Neuner, eds., "Grand Gestures," *gta papers 4* (Zurich: gta Verlag), 127–151.

36
On the Belsito complex, see Giorgio Muratore, "Un maestro romano: Ugo Luccichenti," *Rassegna di Architettura e Urbanistica*, nos. 89–90 (1996), 110–115; Gianluigi Mondaini, "Palazzina 'Organismo' Città, il complesso residenziale a Roma-Belsito di Ugo Luccichenti e le case ecologiche a Berlino di Frei Otto", *Rassegna di Architettur e Urbanistica*, nos. 89–90, 139–146.

37
See Paolo Melis, *Vincenzo Monaco, Amedeo Luccichenti: opera complete* (Milan: Electa, 2017).

38
See Davide Spina, "The Bureaucratization of Architecture in Post-War Italy: SGI under Aldo Samaritani, 1945–73," *Architectural History* 65 (2022), 81–104.

39
Ibidem, 81–82.

40
See Andrea Bruschi, "Roma 1960. Le trasformazioni urbane e il 'piano delle Olimpiadi'," in Andrea Braschi, Anna Irene Del Monaco and Anna Giovannelli, eds., *Città e Olimpiadi Roma 1960, Barcelona 1992, Beijing 2008, London 2012* (Rome: Edizioni Nuova Cultura, 2011), 15–44.

41
That capital city project, or what remains of it in the documents, really looks like the unfinished portrait of a city that is not real (Imperial Rome) but nevertheless designed and composed, with precision and decision, of solid members of a real modern European city. Because of this organic ambiguity, it is remembered by many different names that, when added together, illustrate the political, professional, and cultural ambitions that were concentrated in it. Its contemporary name is aseptic and technical: *1942 variante al piano regolatore del 1931*. Yet, at the time, it was really baptized by its authors as the Plan of Imperial Rome. Luigi Moretti, precisely one of the future authors of the Olympic Village, wanted to go even further by calling it The Imperial Plan of Rome, making the idea of Empire the exclusive patrimony of the Eternal City.

42
See Italo Insolera, *Roma moderna: da Napoleone I al XXI secolo* (Turin: Einaudi Editore, 2011). In English: *Modern Rome: From Napoleon to the Twenty-First Century* (Cambridge: Cambridge Scholars Publishing, 2018).

43
Stendhal, *Promenades dans Rome* (1829) (Paris: Le Divan, 1931). Translated from Italian version: Stendhal, *Passeggiate romane* (Milan: Feltrinelli, digital edition, 2019).

44
For the interpretation of Piranesi's vision of Via Flaminia and its historic-geographical context, see Marcello Fagiolo, "Il 'Nuovo Campo Marzio' e la Valle delle Nazioni," in Marcello Fagiolo and Alessandro Mazza, eds., *I Monti Parioli e il "Nuovo Campo Marzio" della cultura internazionale* (Rome: Artemide, 2022), 20–33.

45
See Alessandro Cremona, "La Passeggiata Flaminia e l'Acqua Acetosa: proposta per un parco pubblico irrealizzato," in Marcello Fagiolo and Alessandro Mazza, *I Monti Parioli*, 188–205.

46
On the Parioli district, see neighborhood section in this volume, 302–311; and see Marcello Fagiolo and Alessandro Mazza, *I Monti Parioli.*

47
See Maria Luisa Neri and Paola Raffaella David, *Enrico Del Debbio*, op. cit.

48
Roberta Lucente, *Luigi Moretti: Casa delle armi al Foro italico* (Turin: Testo & Immagine, 2002).

49
See Andrea Bruschi, "Roma 1960. Le trasformazioni urbane e il 'piano delle Olimpiadi'," 15–44.

50
Luca Brasini, *L'opera architettonica e urbanistica di Armando Brasini: dall'Urbe Massimi al ponte sullo stretto di Messina* (Rome: Pagnotta, 1979).

51
Andrea Bruschi, "Roma 1960. Le trasformazioni urbane e il 'piano delle Olimpiadi'"; Piero Ostilio Rossi, *Roma. Guida all'architettura moderna 1909–2000* (Bari: Laterza, 2000).

52
Ibidem. In contrast, the masterplan designed by Saverio Muratori was vague and difficult to envision three-dimensionally. Hence, it is hard to place this project within the wide-ranging theoretical system—both typological and morphological—that Muratori elaborated in the series of critical projects for INA-Casa neighborhoods designed together with De Renzi.

53
Manfredo Tafuri, "La vicenda architettonica romana, 1945–1961," *Superfici*, 5 April 1961, 20–42.

54
On the more general history of the debates regarding the Olympic Games and, in particular, the relationship to Mussolini's Foro Italico, see R. G. B. Bosworth, "Rome: Sport, Blood and Histories," in *Whispering City: Modern Rome and Its Histories* (New Haven: Yale University Press, 2011); see also David Maraniss, *Rome 1960: The Olympics That Changed the World* (New York: Simon & Schuster, 2008).

55
On Nervi, see Carlo Maria Olmo, Cristiana Chiorino, Christophe Pourtois, and Elisabetta Margiotta Nervi, *Pier Luigi Nervi: Architecture as Challenge* (Milan: Silvana/Brussels: CIVA, 2010).

56
See Piero Ostilio Rossi, *Roma*. op. cit.

57
Rosanna Fiocchetto, *Cesare Cattaneo, 1912–1943: la seconda generazione del razionalismo* (Rome: Officina, 1987).

58
Palazzinari can be translated as building speculators, but by extension can also be applied to the architects who worked for those developers. In general, the term refers to the construction of *palazzine* as the specific building type of the post-WWII era and more often than not has a negative value.

59
INCIS, *Villaggio Olimpico di Roma* (Rome: INCIS, 1960).

60
Ibidem.

61
Ibidem.

62
I cannot fail to notice the sign of Luigi Moretti's peremptory touch. In an early version, documented by a beautiful model reproduced in many publications, the houses in line of the Olympic Village are all long rectilinear, between 160 and 180 meters. In the final solution, many of the in-line buildings, on both sides of the Corso Francia viaduct, are developed according to a polygonal line in three segments. It is the result of a typical Moretti intervention under influence from Baroque precedents and the bent symmetrical barres defining Piazza Grecia are certainly his invention. See Piero Ostilio Rossi, *Roma*. op. cit., 233–234.

63
Lucio Valerio Barbera, "La casa di Roma," in Andrea Bruschi, ed., *Roma Architettura e città negli anni della Seconda Guerra Mondiale* (Rome: Quaderni di Ricerca e Progetto, Gangemi, 2003), 64–81. On the Campus Martius see in particular John Connors, *Piranesi and the Campus Martius: The Missing Corso. Topography and Archaeology in Eighteenth-Century Rome* (Milan: Jaca Books, 2011); John Wilton-Ely, *Piranesi* (Milan: Electa, 1994).

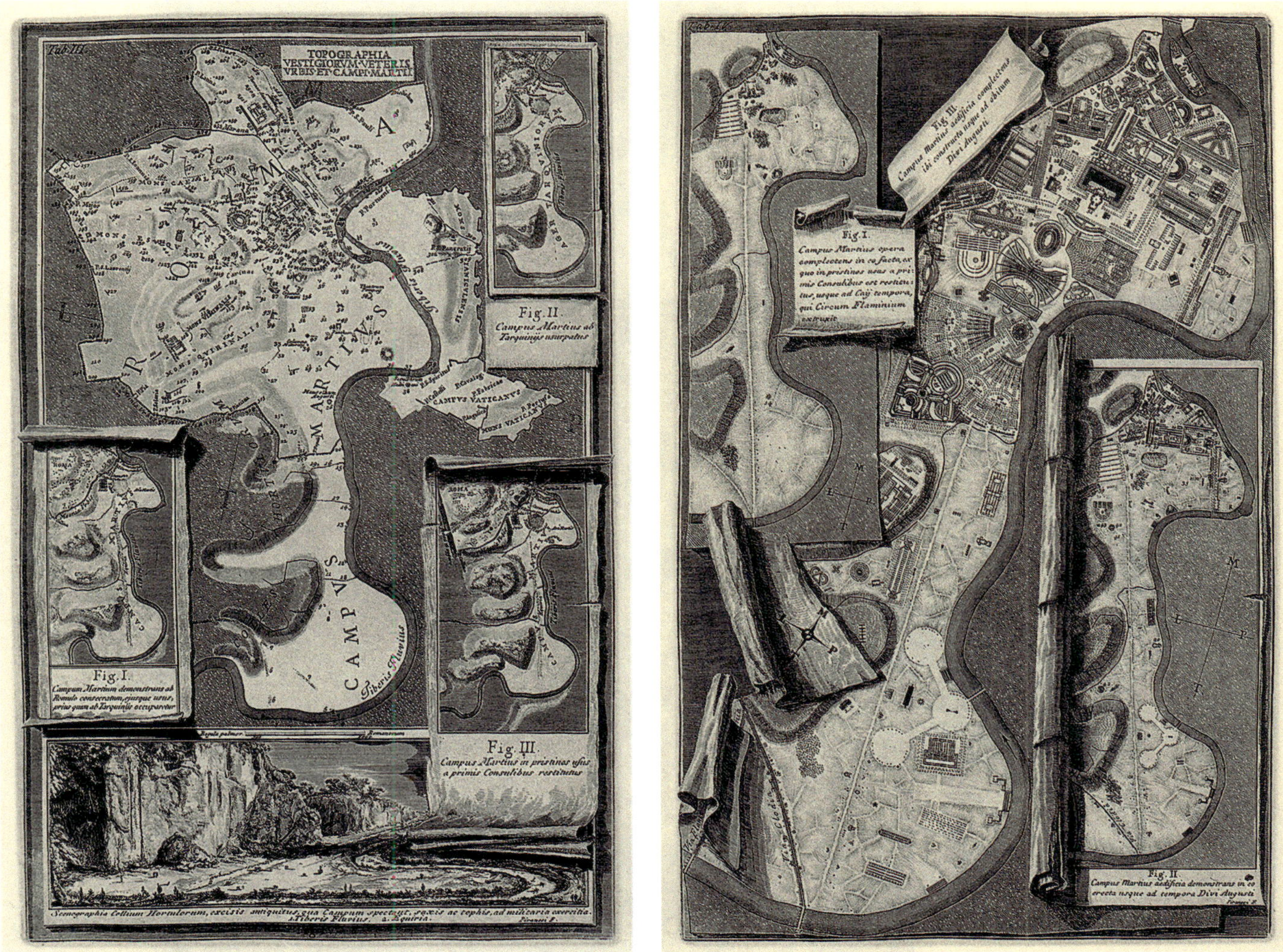

● Giovanni Battista Piranesi, Campus Martius of Ancient Rome, 1762. The maps clearly show the axis of Via Flaminia and its connection to the Ponte Milvio. The impressive topography of the Monti Parioli is suggestively represented in the perspective at the bottom left.

Neighborhood Typologies: Reform Blocks, *Palazzine*, and Metropolitan Density

Jean-François Lejeune

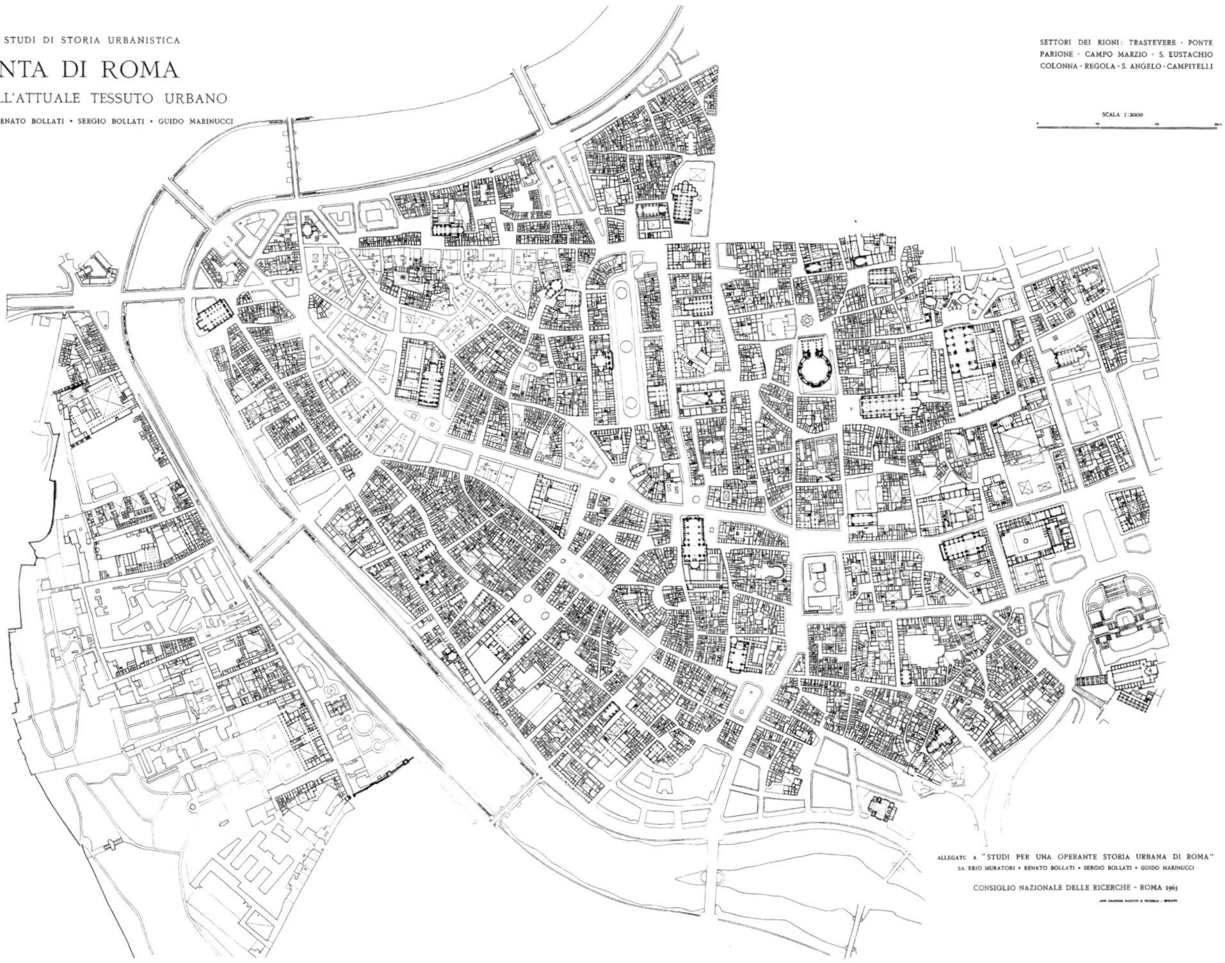

● Saverio Muratori, typological plan of Rome (Campo Marzio and Via di Ripetta in Trastevere), 1963. The plan clearly shows the two building types: *casa a schiera* and palazzo.

"We would like to discover, like an imaginary tourist of the twenty-first century, several urban instances and places that may not nowadays be of the greatest interest but certainly will in the future ... For example, entire neighborhoods, today appreciated perhaps for just one 'monument' such as the Palazzo delle Poste at Piazza Bologna and its surrounding streets; other districts like the Parioli, one of the most staggering examples of typological homogeneity where countless structures and fragments of high-level architecture are hidden, still practically and completely unexplored; or other quarters where speculation has been pushed over the years to the very limits: the Appio-Tuscolano, the Casilino, the Africano, or even that of Monte Mario, a fiefdom of famous real estate companies. All of these will necessarily become the object of adequate and emblematic reflection. It is now essential not to erase from collective memory the most compact, the most authentic, and most significant part of contemporary Rome. These urban spaces and architectures should and will become sites of thoughtful research, of refined attention, and of sophisticated cultural walks. And this *Forma Urbis*, after all, is the one to which we are most attached and in which we are interested, more than anywhere else, to place the emphasis and focus of research—research that, in the case of Rome, has been spreading scholastically on excessively worn-out places, and on questions of academic philology that are not always convincing. We believe ... that the urban planning and urban culture from the fifties to the seventies have sinned out of schematism and moralistic reduction. Therefore, we are not interested in repeating tiredly that ours is a modern city 'without quality,' a city without values, a city devoid of meaning, therefore worthy, at the limit, of a senseless destruction. To the contrary, we believe that the city of Rome—that has been stratified according to canons that are perhaps questionable but undoubtedly adhered to a precise social and cultural dynamic as did the Antique, the Renaissance, the medieval city, and the baroque city—is extremely rich in quality."[1]

Giorgio Muratore

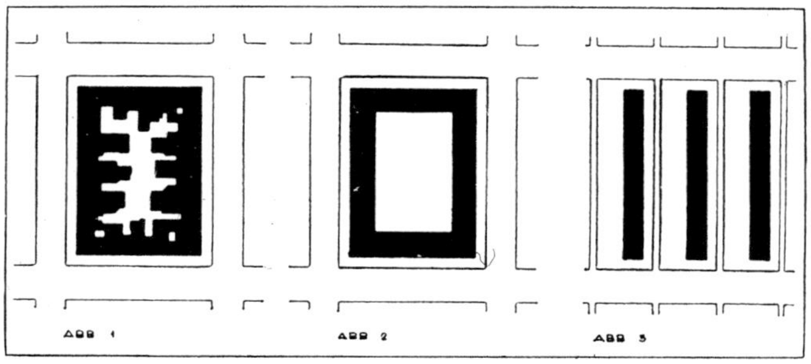

● Walter Gropius, diagrams of the advocated modernist evolution of the urban block, from enclosed to open.

In 1929, in the pages of the periodical *Das neue Berlin*, Walter Gropius published a set of three diagrams which, according to his biased opinion, summarized the evolution of the urban block ◖ above ◗ from history to modernity: the "medieval block"—in reality a mixed-use block that synthetized housing and work; the second block with a large courtyard or garden at the center, which drew on an early concept of zoning privileging the residential and which has become known as "reform block"; and then the "Zeilenbau" which in essence makes the traditional block disappear.[2] The arguments for such a "necessary" evolution ranged from hygienic and urbanistic to political and implied a linear concept of progress. In a series of studies and articles that culminated in his outstanding book *Urbanity and Density in 20th-Century Urban Design*, Wolfgang Sonne dismantled Gropius' argument and analyzed the development of the reform block, country by country, and from the 1890s to the 1940s. In doing so, he demonstrated that the reform block—a perimeter block which introduced light, air, and greenery with a large courtyard or garden while still defining the public street with continuous facades—was not an accidental urban strategy but had been developed in most industrialized countries as a fundamental morphological tool of urban design.[3]

In the early 1890s and 1900s in Berlin, Alfred Messel and Albert Gessner pioneered the typology for both the lower and middle classes. Other architects like Paul Wolf, Paul Mebes, and Bruno Möhring in Berlin, and especially Fritz Schumacher in Hamburg expanded the use of the reform block, that was given increasing importance thanks to its widespread promotion in the 1908–1910 Greater Berlin Competition. However, it is Camillo Sitte who, from Vienna, in an article titled "Metropolitan Green," gave a more theoretical vision of the importance of the green courtyard at the heart of the modern block: "The 'sanitary greenery' should not be found amidst the dust and noise of the streets, but rather in the sheltered interiors of large blocks of buildings, surrounded on all sides."[4] Sitte experimented with the concept in his masterplan for Marienburg, now Ostrava in Moravia, but it is the Red Vienna program of social housing that embodied the most extent application of the reform block and Sitte-inspired strategy of medieval-modern urban design.[5] Among many, Hendrik Berlage and Michel de Klerk in Amsterdam Zuid, Kay Fisker in Copenhagen, Eriel Saarinen in Helsinki, Per Olf Hallman and Sigurd Lewerentz in Stockholm designed and built some of the most remarkable and hygienic modern blocks of the pre-1940 era for the working class. Addressing the context of Southern Europe, Wolfgang Sonne correctly argued that "because of the climate it was not necessary to bring some more light into the apartments ... there was also no need to build large courtyards."[6] As an exception he cited the famous *Casa de las Flores* in Madrid (1929–1933, Secundino Zuazo Ugalde) but surprisingly did not mention the most significant example in the South, the case of Metropolitan Rome, and the innovative housing quarters—many based upon the reform block model—that were developed there before, during, and after the Fascist regime.

The origin of the present book resides precisely in the progressive discovery—through a series of long walks inside and outside the Aurelian walls, many of them with co-author Daniel Solomon, and intensive bibliographic research—of the new neighborhoods that arose from the masterplans of 1873, 1883, 1909, and 1931 and where more than half the Roman population lives and works. Modern Rome — or as in the title The Other Rome to distinguish the "lived-in" city in contrast with the historic center increasingly invaded and given over to tourists—was made of an assemblage of high-density districts, quite compact and whose identity does not reside in the "monumental" but rather in the everyday—or the ordinary—of their residential fabric and urban spaces. The overall quality of that urban fabric (we could call it also 'vernacular') exposes an astonishing degree of both continuity with and evolution from the "basic housing types" (*edilizia di base*) that made up Rome from the medieval times to the first two decades following the Second World War. These were scientifically identified, from the 1950s, by architects and historians Saverio Muratori and Gianfranco Caniggia: firstly, the *casa a schiera* or townhouse ◖ p. 155 top ◗, typically built on a 5-meter module in both dimensions of the lot; the Renaissance *palazzo* ◖ p. 155 bottom ◗, often established by the combination of previous townhouses, the opening of a courtyard and a significant increase in façade height; and the *casa in linea* ◖ p. 155 bottom ◗, a type which emerged in the late 18th century by the consolidation of two or more townhouses then transformed into a multi-family apartment structure that somewhat "imitates" the *palazzo*

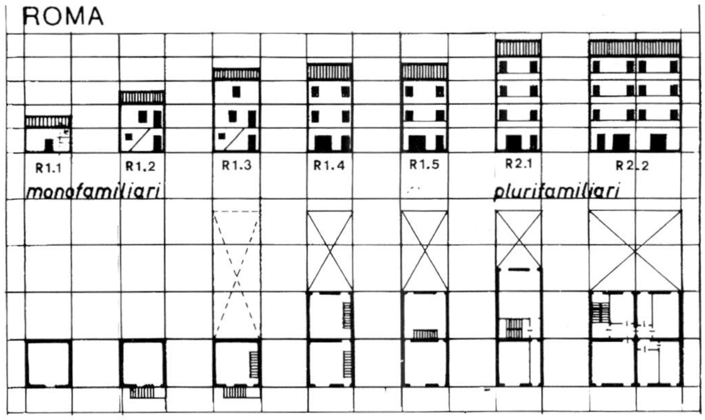

● Gianfranco Caniggia and Gian Luigi Maffei, mutations of the basic typology in Rome (*casa a schiera*, townhouse). The diagrams show the evolution of the earlier family-based townhouses which were the single building type used to start the reconstruction of the city after 1200. The last example shows the process of aggregation to produce apartments from the early 1800s.

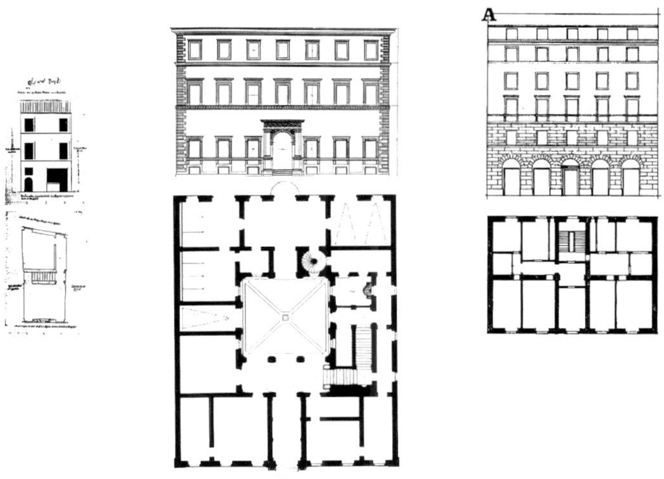

● Three fundamental building types in Rome: *casa a schiera* (townhouse), *palazzo* (Renaissance palace), *casa in linea* (apartment building). The three types share a basic dimensional module of +/- 5 meter and are presented here at the same scale.

and opened it up to what would become the primary bourgeois typology. From 1870 onward, a rich and innovative process of aggregation was to parallel the permanence of those types and eventually enrich the morphological characteristics of the new districts.[7]

It is within this evolutionary context that one must frame and celebrate the diverse and innovative application of the international concept of the reform block, as discussed earlier, and its use for various classes of citizenry, with an emphasis on the industrial and administrative working class. It is in the district of Testaccio (the only one in the *Piano regolatore* of 1883 for industrial workers) that Giulio Magni (1859–1930) built 30 low-cost apartment structures for the recently born Istituto per le case popolari (ICP, 1909–1913) in a series of semi-open blocks centered on a garden interior. In the following years, Quadrio Pirani continued the work of the ICP with a series of brick-faced blocks centered on large gardens (1914–1917), an operation completed in the 1920s by Innocenzo Sabbatini along the Lungotevere Testaccio and Via Marmorata across from the Aventine. From 1920 to the early 1930s, Pirani and Sabbatini were responsible as well for scores of reform blocks commissioned by the ICP and the IRCIS in the new neighborhoods of San Saba, Trionfale, Piazza Verbano, Flaminio, Donna Olimpia in Monteverde, and the garden cities of Aniene Montesacro and Garbatella. Most of those projects had their origin in Sanjust di Teulada's masterplan of 1909 ◖p. 73◗, conceived and approved during the enlightened administration of Mayor Ernesto Nathan. The Swiss architects and professors at the ETH Zurich Emanuel Christ and Christoph Gantenbein summarized their typological studies of Modern Rome:

> "The urban model is, in other words, always fundamentally the same: the block with an inner courtyard. What is interesting, however, is the tenacity with which typological research was pursued for decades—not with the goal of molding the courtyard as an inferior space, but of extracting spatial, functional and aesthetic qualities from this courtyard. A wonderful inventiveness has spawned a full range of proposals that break open the hermetically closed form of the development in favor of a spatially rich system."[8]

For most historians and critics, the *Piano regolatore* or masterplan of 1931 developed under the direction of Marcello Piacentini was primarily associated with the problematic demolitions and isolation of monuments in the historic center. However, the 1931 masterplan was the last one to be conceived according to the planimetric and spatial conventions of urban design in Rome, and that determined the urban form—street system, parks and squares, infrastructures—of the expected urban developments. The whole urban expansion until 1960 was eventually guided by Piacentini's masterplan even though there were unavoidable changes in the built urban patterns. Overall, the masterplan increased the density of the urban blocks, including the reform ones with large gardens, from an average of five to six floors to about ten floors, known as *intensivi* (intensive). Within this evolving context and in response to increasing housing needs, the ICP directed by Alberto Calza Bini and the new financial pattern of development of subsidized private housing had to direct the production toward blocks of higher density. Architects like Innocenzo Sabbatini, Mario De Renzi,

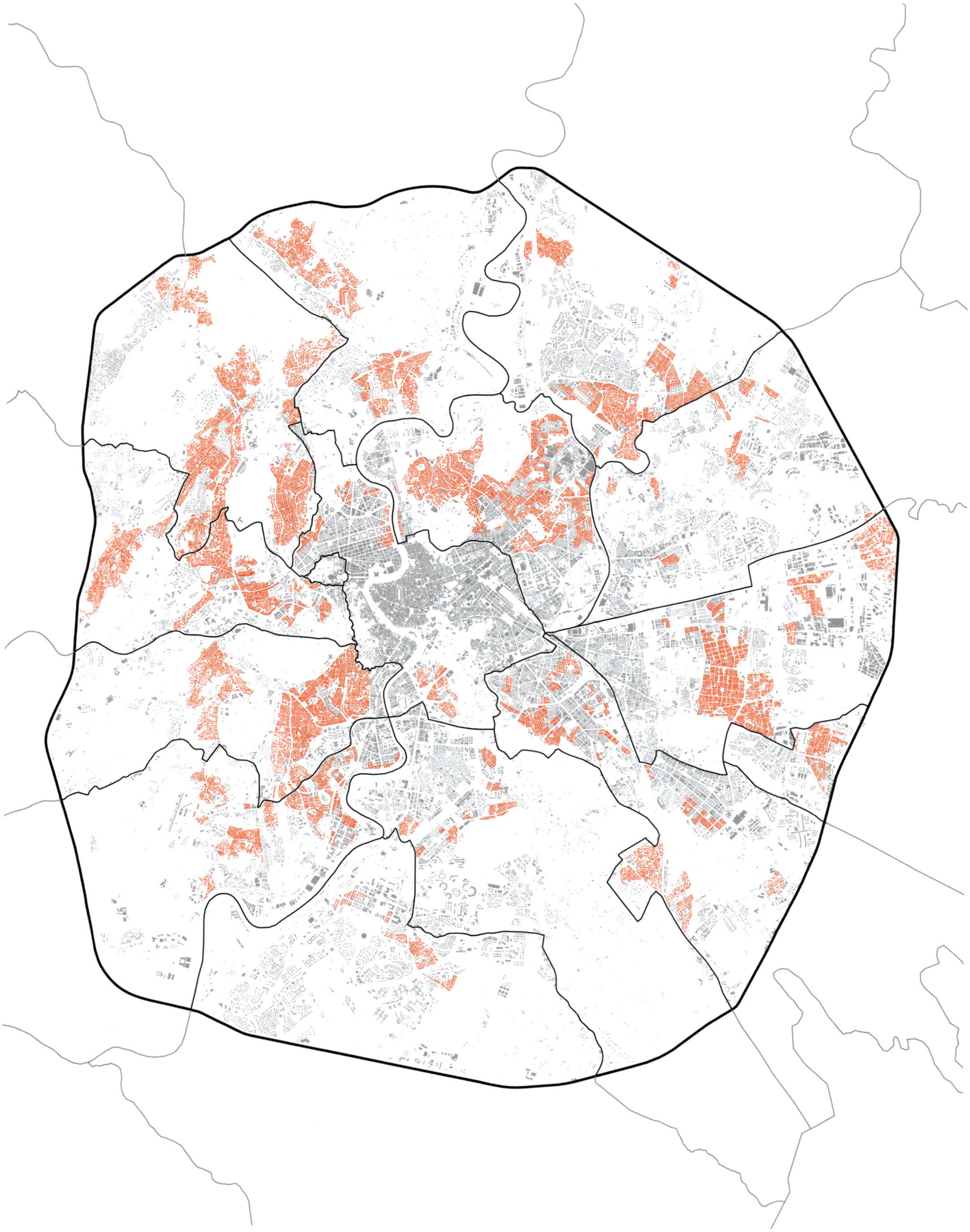

● In red, the distribution of the *palazzina* type across Rome. In black the route of the Grande Raccordo Anulare (GRA), the ring road of Rome. Until 1960, the GRA marked the limit of the built area but since then development has expanded into the countryside.

● Piazza delle Provincie and Piazza Istria, two examples of 1930s development in Rome. Notice the significant height permitted by the masterplan of 1931 as well as the Rationalist, almost unornamented, architectural language.

Giulio Gra, and Gino Cipriani explored the limits of the reform block and various avenues of experimentation, arriving at the design of partially discontinuous blocks made up of combined fragments of fabric (Garbatella), new modes of typological aggregation exploiting various schemes of solar orientation, cross-ventilation, and organization around audacious vertical circulations (Donna Olimpia), and toward the super-block approach epitomized in the Palazzo Federici near Piazza Bologna.

To be sure, if the reform block found in Rome an astonishing variety of application, it was not the only 'invention.' In 1920, a royal decree recognized the legality of the *palazzina* as a new building type for lots initially attributed to *villini* (a single-family house mainly planned to occupy topographically complex areas of the city). As the name suggests, the *palazzina* is a free-standing multi-story building with a central circulation articulating apartments opening on the four facades. In parallel with the high-density *intensivi*, the masterplan of 1931 adopted the *palazzina*, particularly well suited to the topographically complex terrain of districts like Parioli, Monteverde, or Trieste. Over the years, the *palazzina*—"the building brick of Rome" in the words of Fransiscus van Kessel—eventually spread throughout the entire territory of Rome's periphery, being used by small and large builders as the most practical way to build upper-middle class and low-cost—often illegal—housing. Heavily criticized until recently as an instrument of private speculation—even given way to the word *palazzinaro* (building speculator)—the *palazzina* is a uniquely Roman typology which has allowed the coexistence of the private with the public and carried ultimately the bourgeoisie's aspirations to modernity.[9]

During the 1930s, the vernacular influences—derived from the Lazio countryside like at Trionfale or from the Baroque tradition like in Garbatella—gave way to a more rational and metropolitan architecture and image, characterized by flatter surfaces, terraces and horizontal balconies, a sort of middle-class Italian version of the streamline Moderne/Art Deco popular in Vienna, Madrid, Paris, and in the United States. It is this "vernacular modern" architecture that dominated[10] the last decade of residential architecture—whether public or private or hybrid—under fascism and gave its unique identity to neighborhoods centered on such squares as Piazza Bologna, Piazza Re di Roma, Piazza Istria ◖ top right ◗, Piazza delle Provincie ◖ top left ◗, and Piazza Ragusa. Following the Second World War, the INA-Casa program of reconstruction and absorption of new populations emigrating from the Italian south embraced a renewed approach to the rural vernacular—Neorealism—combined with influences from Scandinavia and the Mediterranean. Teams of architects coordinated by Ludovico Quaroni, Mario De Renzi, Saverio Muratori, and Adalberto Libera introduced new typologies like towers, patio houses, and new modes of aggregation of the *case a schiera* in the design of new neighborhoods like Tuscolano, Tiburtino, Valco San Paolo, and Tuscolano.[11] In close distance from the latter, yet largely unknown, the church of San Giovanni Bosco gave its name to one of the most unique low-middle class and high-density neighborhoods of the Roman suburbs, built by Gaetano Rapisardi in the 1950s, which represents one of the most emblematic and most coherent moments of the variegated Roman panorama of those same years. In the words of Giorgio Muratore, it is "an alternative urban model to the multi-articulated morphologies of the Tiburtino [and the Tuscolano], a neo-monumental antidote to the rampant organicism, it represents a further element of continuity and methodological permanence with the architectural

● Vincenzo Fasolo, Tullio Passarelli, Gustavo Giovannoni, and Marcello Piacentini, masterplan of the seaside garden city of Ostia Nuova (now Ostia Lido), 1916. The plan for the new city was implemented during the 1920s, albeit with significant evolution of the architectural language. It was later integrated within the city of Rome and guided by the masterplan of 1931 signed by Marcello Piacentini.

culture of the late 1930s."[12] In contrast to Red Vienna or Weimar era Berlin, the full extent of the social program of housing in 1900–1960 Rome remains relatively unknown, but with fruitful promises of further and detailed investigations.[12] Moreover, and in spite of the overall negative criticism, the critical importance of the private sector—particularly the Società Generale Immobiliare (SGI) and its links to the Vatican—offers an open field of urban and architectural research that has been barely tapped.

The selection of neighborhood portraits that constitute the second part of this volume did not aim at being exhaustive but most representative of the coexistence of public and private development, while at the same time emphasizing the quality of architecture and urban design. Except for the Esquiline and Via Vittorio Veneto districts that were built from 1870 within the Aurelian walls, the studied districts form a sort of a "ring" around the historic center and include Testaccio, Prati and Trionfale, Mazzini, Flaminio, San Saba, Aniene Montesacro, Piazza Bologna, Piazza Mincio and Piazza Verbano, Monteverde Vecchio, Appio Latino, Parioli, Tiburtino, Tuscolano, and the Villaggio Olimpico. All those districts did, one way or another, originate from the masterplans of 1873, 1883, 1909, and 1931. In contrast, the original garden city of Ostia Nuova ◖ top ◗ (planned in 1916 by Vincenzo Fasolo, Gustavo Giovannoni, Marcello Piacentini, Tullio Passarelli, and now incorporated within the City of Rome), and the low-density faraway *borgate* (such as Primavalle or Trullo) built by the ICP from 1930 to 1937, were all outside of the masterplans and thus not featured. The latter manifested the first real attempt at social segregation from their instauration under the Fascist regime. However, it is important to argue that, even though these many of these *borgate* were built for the very poor, far from the city and lacking the material strength of their equivalents within the city itself, they continued to respect, albeit too informally, the urban principles that this book has attempted to define and advocate. Finally, and as explained by Salvatore Santuccio in his essay on the "Modern Rome and the Cinematic Gaze", the EUR district became during its 1950s one of the much-sought after area for the middle-high and high bourgeoisie. However, in contrast with the rational vision of Piacentini for the EUR core, the postwar residential area made of *palazzine* lacked the structural quality for analysis with the context of this book.

● Two views of the Borgata Primavalle constructed in the 1930s. Despite of its isolation and the precarious quality of construction, the projects demonstrated a will to maintain an urban civic structure.

1
Giorgio Muratore, "La nuova 'forma' della città," in *Forma Urbis* (Rome: Clear, 1988), 15–19; reprinted in Alessandra Capuano, ed., *Giorgio Muratore, Roma Scritti Scelti* (Rome: Centro Studio Giorgio Muratore/La Sapienza, 2023), 150–151.

2
Walter Gropius, "Die Wohnformen. Flach-, Mittel- oder Hochbau," in *Das neue Berlin*, vol. 1, no. 4, 1929, 73–80.

3
Wolfgang Sonne, *Urbanity and Density in 20th-Century Urban Design* (Berlin: DOM Publishers, 2017), 50–117; Wolfgang Sonne, "Dwelling in the metropolis: Sitte, Hegemann, and the international dissemination of reformed urban blocks 1890–1940," in Charles Bohl and Jean-François Lejeune, eds. *Sitte, Hegemann and the Metropolis: Modern Civic Art and International Exchanges* (London: Routledge, 2009), 249–273.

4
Camillo Sitte, "Großstadt-Grün" [1900], in Camillo Sitte; Christiane Crasemann Collins and Klaus Semsroth, eds., *Der Städte-Bau nach seinen künstlerischen Grundsätzen*, (Vienna: Böhlau, 2003), 247. In English, see George R. Collins and Christiane Crasemann Collins, *Camillo Sitte and the Birth of Modern City Planning* (New York: Rizzoli, 1986), 219. Quoted by Sonne, "Dwelling in the Metropolis," 251.

5
See in particular Eve Blau, *The Architecture of Red Vienna, 1919–1934* (Cambridge, Mass.: The MIT Press, 1999).

6
Wolfgang Sonne, *Urbanity and Density*, op. cit., 95.

7
On typological history and research, see e.g. Saverio Muratori, *Studi per una operante storia urbana di Venezia* (Rome: Istituto Poligrafico dello Stato, 1960) and Gianfranco Caniggia, "Permanenze e mutazioni nel tipo edilizio e nei tessuti di Roma (1880–1930)," in Giuseppe Strappa, ed., *Tradizione e innovazione nell'architettura di Roma Capitale 1870–1930* (Rome: Edizioni Kappa, 1989).

8
Emanuel Christ and Christoph Gantenbein, "Typology Transfer–Towards an Urban Architecture," *Typology: Hong Kong–Rome–New York–Buenos Aires* (Zurich: Park Books, 2012).

9
Among the now growing literature, see Fransiscus Johannes van Kessel, *The Building Brick of Rome–On the Intricacies of the Roman Palazzina Typology*, 2016, https://issuu.com/frankvankessel/docs/the_building_brick_of_rome

10
Valco San Paolo (1949–1950) is an interesting simulation of urbanity, unfortunately not completed according to the original plans.

11
Giorgio Muratore, "L'architettura italiana del secondo dopoguerra: occasioni di continuità, dalla ricostruzione all'espansione," *Modelos alemanos e Italianos para España en los años de la postguerra* (Pamplona: Escuela Técnica Superior de Arquitectura Universidad de Navarra, 2004), 56.

12
See Eve Blau, *The Architecture of Red Vienna*, op. cit.

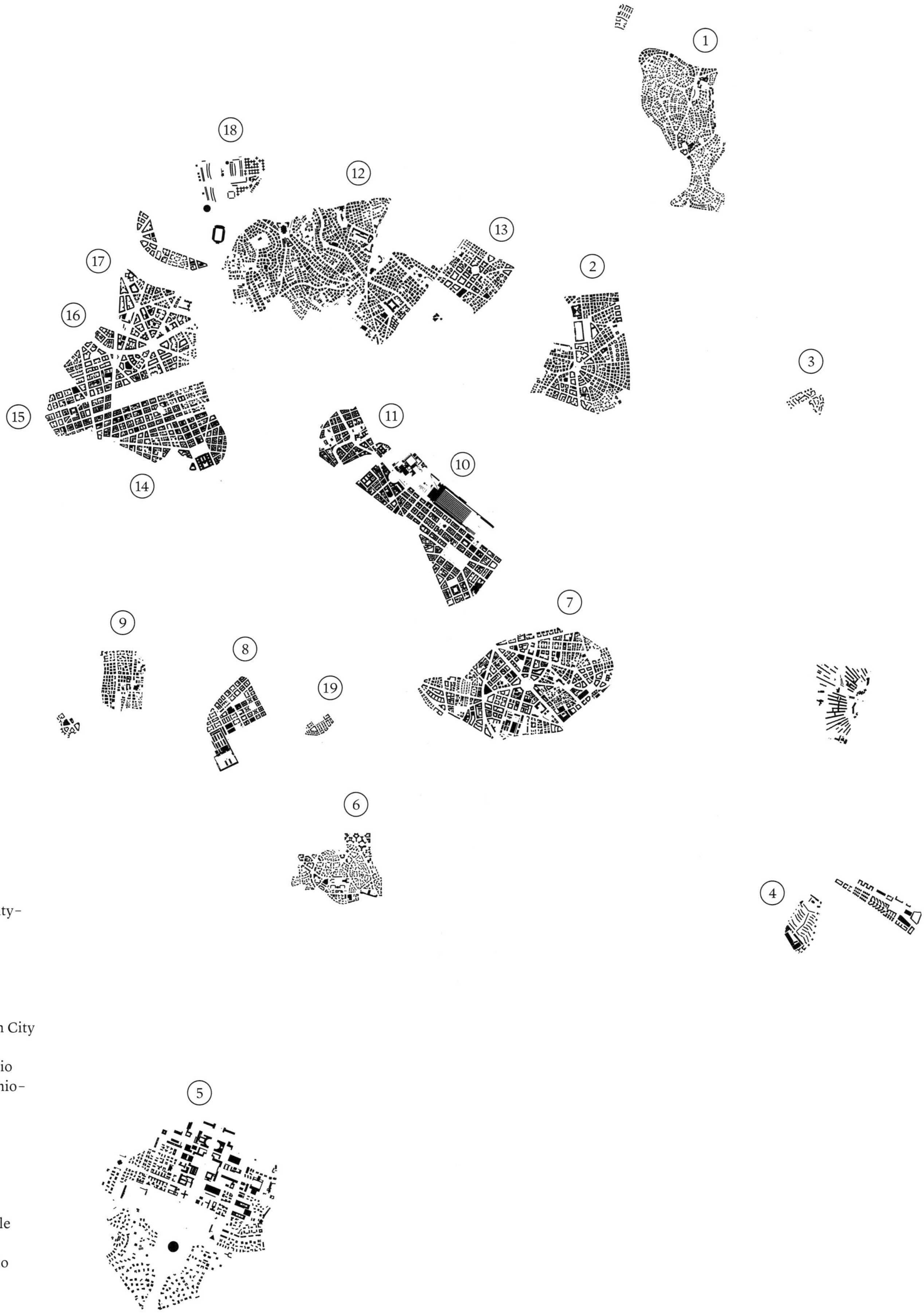

1 Aniene Garden City–Montesacro
2 Piazza Bologna
3 Tiburtino
4 Tuscolano
5 EUR
6 Garbatella Garden City
7 Appio Latino
8 Quartiere Testaccio
9 Monteverde Vecchio–Donna Olimpia
10 Esquilino
11 Vittorio Veneto
12 Parioli
13 Piazza Verbano
14 Quartiere Prati
15 Quartiere Trionfale
16 Piazza Mazzini
17 Quartiere Flaminio
18 Villagio Olimpico
19 San Saba

Neighborhood Portraits

Anna Irene Del Monaco, Jean-François Lejeune,
commentaries Daniel Solomon

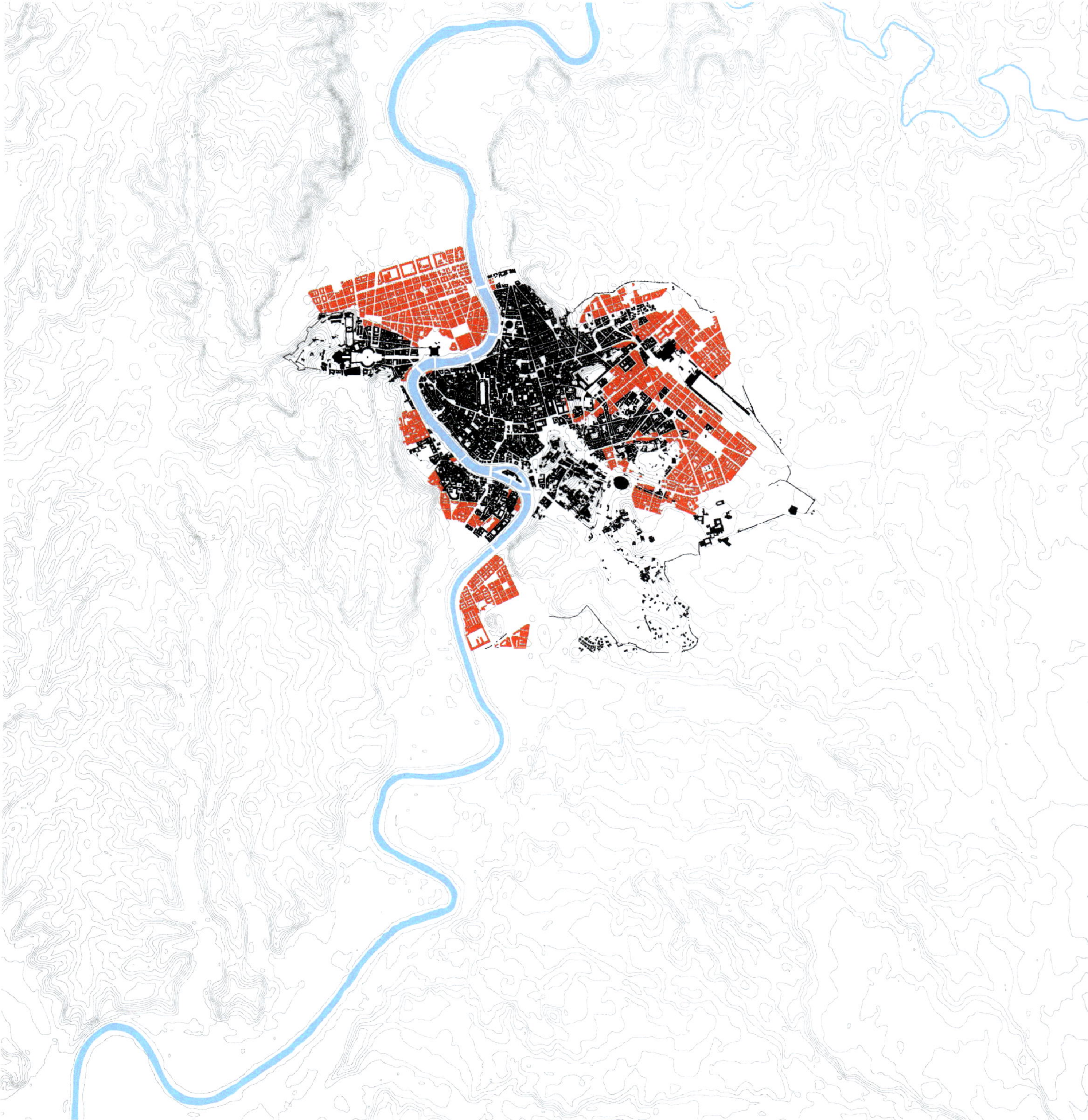

Rome
1873–1910

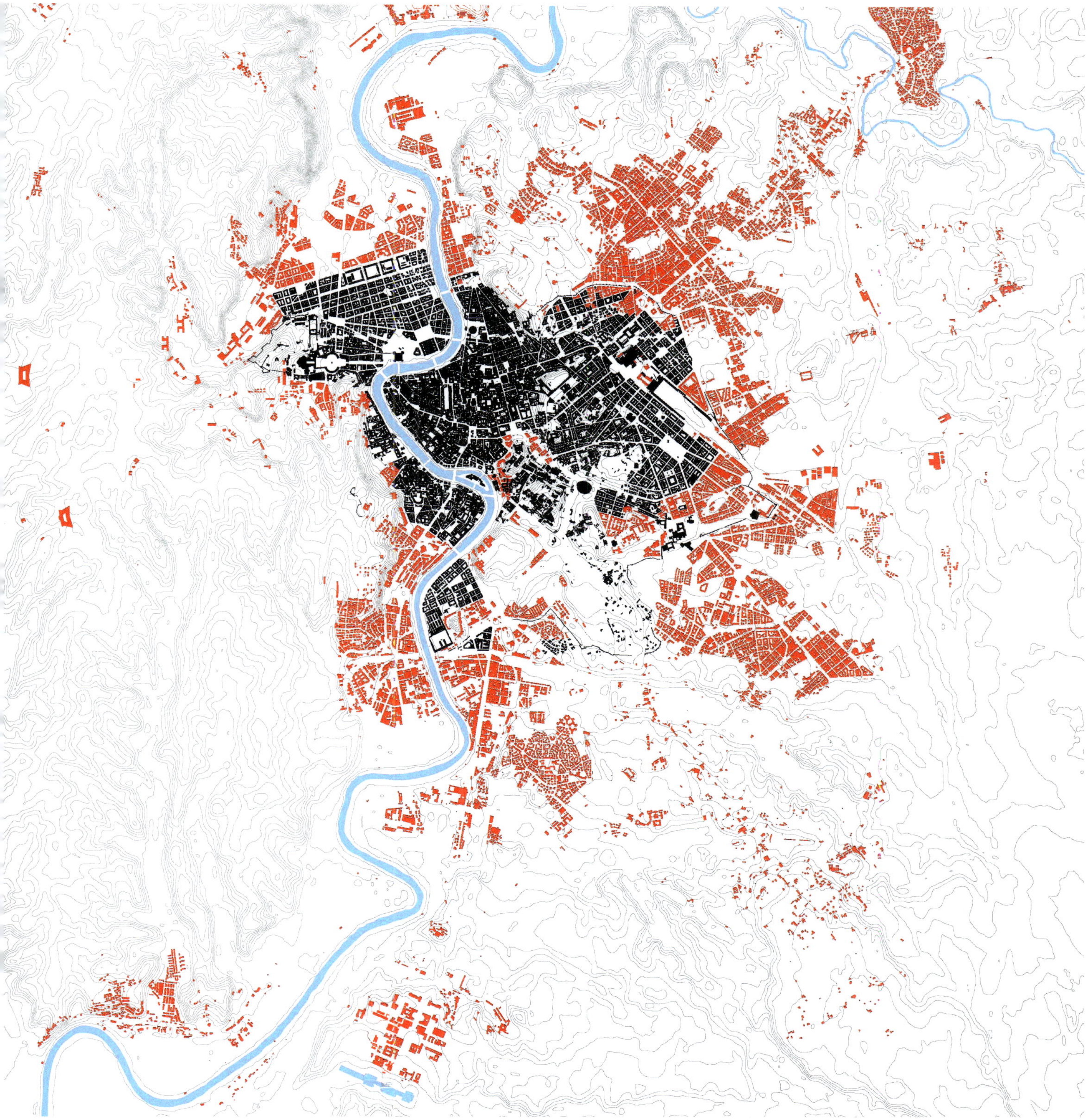

Rome
1922–1940

ESQUILINO—VITTORIO VENETO

Alessandra Ciacciofera, *Inter Urbes et Colles. Via Bissolati, Rome: Ragioni della forma di una strada dell'architetto Marcello Piacentini* (Rome: Università degli studi Rome Tre, 2017), http://hdl.handle.net/2307/40680

Franco Girardi, Gianfranco Spagnesi, and Federico Gorio, *L'Esquilino e la Piazza Vittorio: una struttura urbana dell'Ottocento* (Rome: Editalia, 1974).

Carmelo Severino, *Esquilino 1870–1911: e nel centro del progettato quartiere una vastissima piazza* (Rome: *Gangemi*, 2020).

TESTACCIO

Enrico Puccini and Giovanni Duranti, *Testaccio: il quartiere operaio di Rome Capitale, 1870–1930* (Rome: Palombi Editori, 2012).

Francesca Romana Stabile, *Testaccio, il quartiere operaio di Rome Capitale dal 1870 agli interventi dell'Istituto per le Case Popolari* (Rome: Quasar, 2023).

Maria Letizia Accorsi, *Da unità sistemica a configurazione episodica. I giardini pubblici di Testaccio* (Rome: Quasar, 2018).

QUARTIERE PRATI
QUARTIERE TRIONFALE

Mario De Renzi, *Una casa d'Abitazione in Via Andrea Doria in Rome*, "Architettura e Arti Decorative," fasc. XIII anno X, 1931.

Vanna Fraticelli, *Roma, 1914–1929: la città e gli architetti tra la Guerra e il fascismo* (Rome: Officina Edizioni, 1982).

Bruno Regni and Marina Sennato, *Innnocenzo Sabbatini: architettura tra tradizione e rinnovamento* (Rome: Kappa, 1982).

Glauco Schetti, "Building the Third Rome: Italy, the Vatican, and the New District in Prati di Castello, 1870–1895," in *Modern Italy*, vol. 24, no. 1, February 2019, 63–79.

PIAZZA MAZZINI—
QUARTIERE DELLA VITTORIA

Piero Ostilio Rossi, *Roma. Guida all' architettura moderna 1909–2000* (Bari: Laterza 2000), 23–24.

Lucio Valerio Barbera, "Il deposito Vittoria dell'Atac a Piazza Bainsizza nel Quartiere Delle Vittorie di Rome," in *L'Architettura delle Città - The Journal of the Scientific Society Ludovico Quaroni*, no. 11, 2017, 19–51.

Valentina Montellanico, "Barocchetto Romeno e razionalismo: due stili a confronto nel quartiere Della Vittoria," https://www.academia.edu/34680985/Barocchetto_Romeno_e_razionalismo_due_stili_a_confronto_nel_quartiere_Della_Vittoria_cod_0021

QUARTIERE FLAMINIO

Alberto Calza Bini, *Il fascismo per le Case del Popolo. L'opera dell'Istituto per le Case Popolari in Rome nel primo quadriennio di amministrazione fascista*, Rome, 1927, 39–63.

Carlo Cecchelli, "L'architettura alla Terza Biennale romana," in *Architettura e Arti Decorative*, IV, July-August 1925, 528–545.

Cristina Cocchioni and Mario De Grassi, *La casa popolare a Rome. Trent'anni di attività dell'ICP*, Rome, 1984, 86, 90, 100–101, 217–219.

SAN SABA

Alessandro Briotti, *Il quartiere San Saba e l'Aventino* (Rome: Kappa, 1988).

Francesca Romana Stabile, *Il quartiere San Saba e la casa popolare a Rome. Il Progetto di Quadrio Pirani per l'Istituto Case Popolari in Rome, 1906–1923* (Rome: Quasar, 2024).

ANIENE GARDEN CITY—
MONTESACRO

Michele Bianchi and Elena Ogliani, *Città Giardino Aniene. Il rapport privilegiato tra costruito e spazio aperto* (Rome: Nuova Cultura, 2024).

Alessandro Galassi and Biancamaria Rizzo, *Città Giardino Aniene* (Bologna: Minerva Edizioni, 2013).

Sara Fabrizi, *La storia di Montesacro. De la preistoria ai giorni nostri* (Rome: Typimedia Editore, 2020).

GARBATELLA GARDEN CITY

Antonella Bonavita, Piero Fumo and Maria Paola Pagliari, *La Garbatella: Guida all' architettura moderna* (Rome: Palombi Editori, 2010).

Innocenzo Costantini, "Le nuove costruzioni dell'Istituto per le case popolari in Rome. La borgata giardino Garbatella," in *Architettura e arti decorative*, November 1922, 119–137.

Vanna Fraticelli, *Roma, 1914–1929: la città e gli architetti tra la Guerra e il fascismo* (Rome: Officina Edizioni, 1982).

Francesca Romana Stabile, *La Garbatella a Rome. Architettura e Regionalismo* (Rome: Quasar, 2020).

PIAZZA BOLOGNA

Maria Luisa Neri, *Mario De Renzi: architettura come mestiere 1897–1967* (Rome: Gangemi, 1992).

Eva Masini, *Piazza Bologna. Alle origini di un quartiere "Borghese"* (Milan: Franco Angeli, 2013).

PIAZZA MINCIO
PIAZZA VERBANO

Dario Barbieri, *Per la grande Roma. Formazione e sviluppo delle grandi città modern* (Rome: Società editrice di arte illustrate, 1927), 90, 220–224.

Piero Ostilio Rossi, *Roma. Guida all'architettura Moderna 1909–2000* (Bari: Laterza, 2000), 35–38.

Domitilla Dardi, *Il quartiere Coppedè. Un'isola di originalità architettonica nella Rome del primo Novecento* (Milan: Newton Compton, 1999).

Rossana Bossaglia and Mauro Cozzi, *I Coppedè* (Genova: Sagep, 1982).

MONTEVERDE VECCHIO
DONNA OLIMPIA

Ana Kaisa Koponen, "From Utopias to Roman Residential Realities: the Golden Era of Roman Social Housing 1919–1932," in *Planning Perspectives*, November 2024, 1–37.

Nina Quarenghi, *Un salotto popolare a Rome. Monteverde (1909–1945)* (Milan: Franco Angeli, 2016).

Luciano Villani, *Le borgate del fascismo: Storia urbana, politica e sociale della periferia Romena* (Milan: Ledizioni, 2014).

APPIO LATINO

Fabrizio Di Marco, "Tipi e paramenti all' antica nell'opera di Vittorio Morpurgo," in Benedetti Simona, Flavia Benfante, et. al. *Forme dell'abitare a Roma. Echi dell'antico nell'architettura del primo Novecento* (Rome: Gangemi, 2023), 353–364.

Sara Fabrizi, *La storia di Appio. San Giovanni. Dalla preistoria ai nostri giorni* (Rome: La Storia di Roma, 2019).

PARIOLI

Marcello Fagiolo and Alessandro Mazza, eds., *I Monti Parioli e il "Nuovo Campo Marzio" della cultura internazionale* (Rome: Artemide, 2022).

Antonio Thiery, ed., *Rome Salaria. La città delle ville* (Rome: Palombi, 2001).

Livio Toschi, *L'Istituto cooperative per le case degli impiegati dello stato in Rome: 1908–1933* (Rome: Galleria A.A.M., 1986).

TIBURTINO

Pippo Ciorra, "Quartiere Ina-Casa sulla via Tiburtina," in *Ludovico Quaroni 1911–1987. Opere e progetti* (Milan: Electa, 1989).

Paola Di Biagi, *The INA-Casa Plan and Italy in the Fifties. The Great Reconstruction* (Rome: Donzelli, 2010).

Rinaldo Capomolla and Rosalia Vittorini, "Il quartiere Tiburtino a Rome (1950–1954)," in Rinaldo Capomolla, Rosalia Vittorini, and Sergio Poretti, eds., L'architettura INA Casa (1949–1963). *Aspetti e problemi di conservazione e recupero* (Rome: Gangemi, 2002), 68–81.

Piero Ostilio Rossi, *Roma. Guida all' architettura Moderna 1909–2011* (Bari: Laterza, 2012), 90–113.

TUSCOLANO

Clementina Barucci and Marco Falsetti, *Gaetano Rapisardi Architetto 1893–1988* (Rome: Capisano, 2022).

Stefania Mornati and Filippo Cerrini, "Il quartiere Tuscolano a Rome (1950–60)," in Sergio Poretti, Riccardo Capomolla, Rosalia Vittorini, eds., *L'architettura INA Casa (1949–1963) Aspetti e problemi di conservazione e recupero* (Rome: Gangemi 2004).

Daniele Carfagna, *L'architettura tra le case. Abitare lo spazio aperto nei quartieri INA-CASA* (Florence: Alinea Editrice, 2012).

Gaia Remiddi and Antonella Greco, eds., *Adalberto Libera. Guida a 45 Architetture* (Rome: Palombi, 2003).

VILLAGGIO OLIMPICO

INCIS, "Villaggio Olimpico quartiere di Rome, Rome," in *Edilizia Popolare*, no. 35, 1960.

Piero Ostilio Rossi, *Roma. Guida all'architettura moderna 1909–2011* (Bari: Laterza, 2012).

Gaetano Koch, semi-circular arcades on the ground floor of the Exedra buildings, Piazza della Repubblica, 1888–1889. At the center is the Fontana delle Naiadi (Fountain of the Naiads) sculpted by the Palermo artist Mario Rutelli, 1901–1912.

Esquilino—Vittorio Veneto 1870–1950

Italy's influential Minister of Finance of the new Italy, Quintino Sella, championed the idea that the new Rome had to turn its back on the papal town and be built as far as it could be—both physically and functionally—from the historic center and the Vatican. The result was the new Esquiline district whose rectangular gridiron of streets and its "white collar" unitarian architecture caused the destruction of most 17th–20th historic villas and gardens. Yet, these changes were necessary to transform the city into a modern capital and reflected the urbanistic trends developed in the late 19th century in Berlin, Vienna, Barcelona, and other capitals like Paris. The Esquiline, never really liked by the Romans, appears today as a quite extraordinary urban construction. Its grid may be alien to the spirit of Rome, but its architecture is uniquely Roman, and the bourgeois "neutrality" of the district at the time of its foundation has become a key to its contemporary multicultural potential. Initiated at the turn of the century, the development of Via Vittorio Veneto and its surroundings was equally damaging to the heritage, but its urban design structured along the curvilinear boulevard opened the way to a more organic yet highly rational plan epitomizing the spirit of 1930s Rome. In 1931–1932, work began on the opening of Via Barberini as a connecting artery between the square of the same name and the Largo di Santa Susanna, and simultaneously on the creation ex-nihilo of Via Leonida Bissolati, connecting the same Largo to Via Vittorio Veneto. This large-scale urban operation—mostly completed by the time of the Second World War—was one of the best and most accomplished interventions in the city of Rome to be conceived by Marcello Piacentini. Twenty years later, the upper section of Via Veneto, close to Porta Pinciana, became the symbol—now gone—of the economic boom of the late 1950s—known as the "Italian Miracle"—a time of societal change and excess epitomized in Fellini's *La Dolce Vita*.

Architects

Gino Coppedè
Vincenzo Fasolo
Ugo Giovannozzi
Gaetano Koch
Mario Loreti
Giulio Magni
Angiolo Mazzoni
Marcello Piacentini
Pio Piacentini
Achille Sfondrini
Giuseppe Vaccaro

Following the advent of Rome as the new Capital in 1871, a large-scale neighborhood was planned and established on the Esquiline hill, one of the seven hills on which Rome was born, to provide accommodation for the administrative white-collar class that was relocating to Rome from all over Italy. Interestingly, the first train station (engineer Salvatore Bianchi) was inaugurated in 1874 on the edge of the neighborhood in front of the ruins of the Baths of Diocletian. At the same time, and according to the project of Belgian prelate François-Xavier de Mérode, Via Nazionale was opened as the first modern boulevard to connect the station and the half-circular Piazza della Repubblica in the direction of Piazza Venezia and the historic center. Located on the central axis of the new Esquiline district (coinciding with the 16th-century Via Sistina or Strada Felice), the Piazza Vittorio Emanuele II became the beating heart of the modern neighborhood. Surrounding this largest square in Rome, the monumental mixed-use buildings with porticoes were designed by architects Gaetano Koch, Giulio Podesti, and Giovanni Riggi. However, as speculation and greed characterized these early decades of the Third Rome, the Esquiline lost most of the richness of its history—in particular, its aristocratic villas and gardens. As a result, the geometric regularity of the housing blocks and the extensive use of the 16th century elegant and sober palazzo-style, also known as *Cinquecentismo*, established the character of the first bourgeois quarter in the formerly papal city. The image evolved in the 1920s with the introduction of modern Baroque motifs and the deployment of a vernacular language borrowed and adapted from rural models in the Lazio. Also important were the first building cooperatives for workers, such as those built by Giulio Magni on Piazza Santa Croce in Gerusalemme. In the 1930s, the Roman version of streamline Moderne/Art Deco marked by the horizontal emphasis of long curving balconies and terraces emerged increasingly toward Porta Maggiore (Via Principe Umberto and Via Principe Eugenio). After the Second World War, the Esquiline gradually became the multi-ethnic area of Rome par excellence, given its proximity to Termini station. This change in the social fabric had initially led the area into a situation of degradation and hardship before some urban planning interventions slowly improved it. Due to the proportionate mix of public and private buildings and the regularity of its urban fabric, the Esquiline is potentially able to face the difficult challenge represented by the multi-ethnic presence of many communities, but also develop culturally and urbanistically as a pole of attraction for the entire city. Among important public buildings built in the district: the Palazzo delle Esposizioni (Pio Piacentini, 1883) on Via Nazionale; the Roman Acquario (Ettore Bernich, 1887), now the seat of the Ordine degli architetti in the park of Piazza Manfredo Fanti; the Palazzo delle Casse di Risparmio Postali (Luigi Rolland, 1914) in Piazza Dante; the Istituto Poligrafico e Zecca dello Stato (State Mint, 1911), restructured as museum and housing; the Ufficio d'Igiene e Sanità (Hygiene and Health Institute, 1929), in part destroyed in 1962 and then partially rebuilt in 2018 as Fondazione Elena e Claudio Cerasi (Palazzo Merulana); and last but not least the Teatro Costanzi, the Roman opera house (Achille Sfondrini and Marcello Piacentini, 1880–1958).

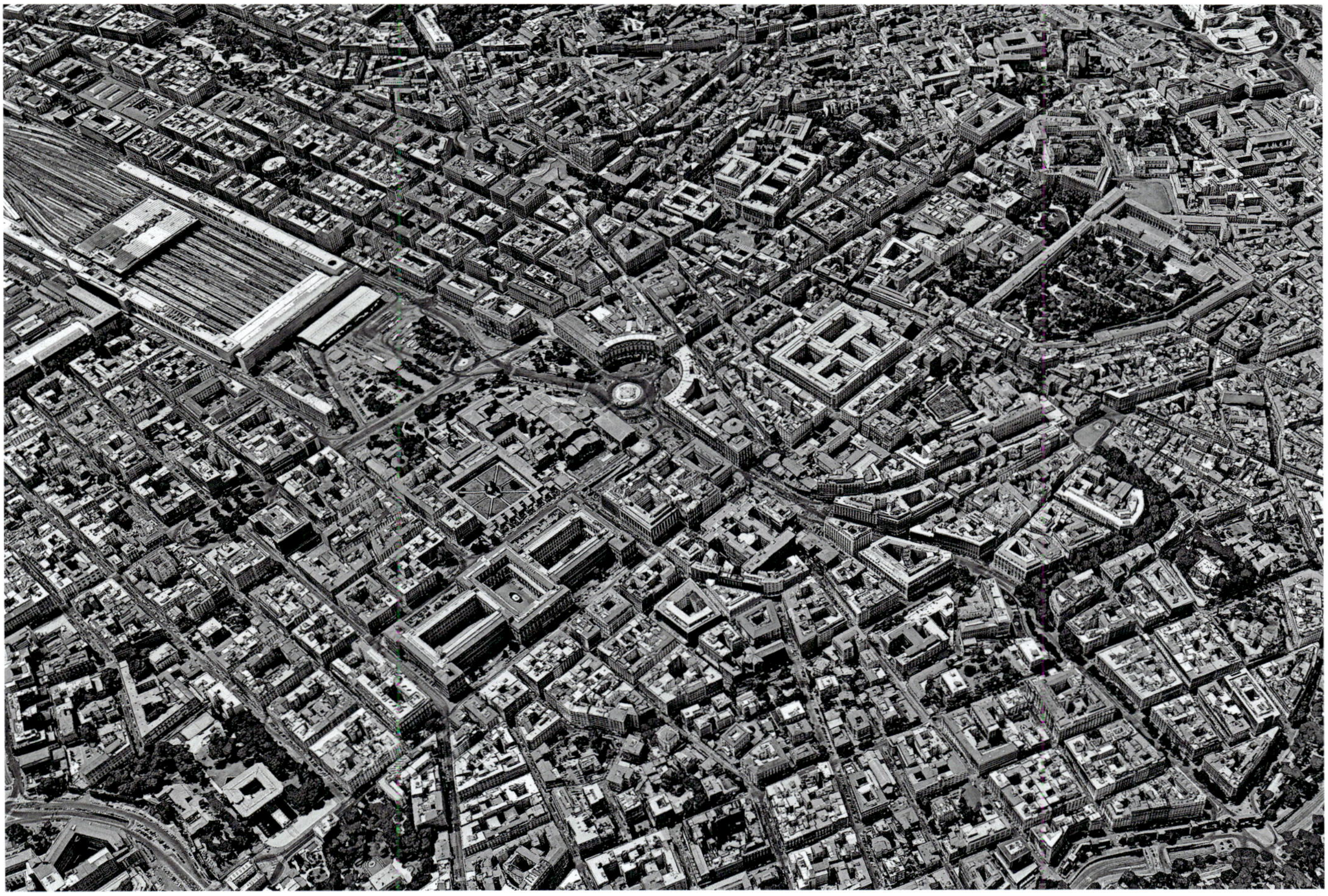

Aerial view. From the upper left clockwise: Termini station and Piazza dei Cinquecento; the grid of the new Esquiline with Piazza Vittorio Emanuele II and Santa Maria Maggiore; the straight axis of Via Nazionale starting at the half-circle of Piazza della Repubblica; Palazzo del Quirinale; Piazza Barberini (bottom right) as the starting point of the curvilinear Via Vittorio Veneto to Porta Pinciana and Villa Borghese; Porta Pia as the endpoint of Via del XX Settembre and the series of ministries.

Marcello Piacentini, facade on Piazza Beniamino Gigli, 1956–1960. The Teatro dell'Opera or Teatro Costanzi was first built by Milanese architect Achille Sfondrini (1836–1900) from 1879 to 1881 in neo-Renaissance style with a frescoed ceiling by Annibale Brugnoli. Piacentini directed the first transformation (new rooms and increased capacity from 1926 to 1928). The same Piacentini guided the final restructuring and the new facade design in *Novecento* (classical-modern) style.

Pio Piacentini, Palazzo delle Esposizioni, Via Nazionale, 1880–1882.

View of Via Torino with the church of Santa Maria della Vittoria as terminating vista. In the other direction the street ends on Santa Maria Maggiore.

Detail of the facade of 121 Via Torino, the residence of Mayor Ernesto Nathan and where he died. See the plaque to the left of the entrance gate. The eclectic Baroque apartment house is a striking departure from the neo-Renaissance image of most facades in the Via Nazionale neighborhood.

Angiolo Mazzoni, southern facade of the Stazione di Roma Termini, Via Giolitti, c. 1938–1943. The architecture of the long wings (following the demolition of the previous station designed by Salvatore Bianchi) makes direct reference to the antique aqueducts and more generally to the *Pittura Metafisica* associated with Giorgio de Chirico. The station front facing the Baths of Diocletian and Piazza dei Cinquecento was built by the team: E. Montuori, L. Calini, A. Vitellozzi, M. Castellazzi, V. Fadigati, and A. Pintonello (completion in 1950).

Vincenzo Fasolo, apartment building for municipal employees (later part of the ICP holdings), 1926, Via Napoleone III. The large apartment building reflects the change from the neo-Renaissance toward a more vernacular approach: setbacks from the street edge, division in sections of varied height, asymmetry, etc.

Art Deco building at the intersection of Via di Porta Maggiore and Via Bixio. Notice the curvilinear balconies and the combination of exposed brick and stucco on the facades.

Vincenzo Fasolo, apartment building for municipal employees. Facade along Via Napoleone III (1922–1924).

Rome of the 1930s

Via Vittorio Veneto was laid out at the end of the 19th century, following the subdivision of the ancient and magnificent Villa Ludovisi, to connect Via del Tritone to Villa Borghese. The street, now at the heart of the Ludovisi district, starts at Piazza Barberini and ends, uphill and after two large curves, at Porta Pinciana across from Villa Borghese. A series of monumental stairs connect the street to the surrounding streets mainly laid out on a grid-like pattern. The street is one of the widest in Rome, 40 meters wide with sidewalks wider than 10 meters overall. The street is lined with a succession of important buildings which retrace the evolution of architectural style from the 1890s to World War II. The first buildings were mostly the Renaissance-inspired work of Gaetano Koch who designed the Hotel Majestic (1896, known for the frescoes by Domenico Bruschi), the Palazzo Balestra (1891), and the freestanding villa Palazzo Margherita Piombino (1886–1890), now the American Embassy—behind which is the Palazzo Grande (1622), the last remnant of the Villa Ludovisi with the 16th-century Casino dell'Aurora located nearby next to Villa Maraini (Swiss Institute of Culture). Other important structures are the Ambasciatori Palace Hotel (Carlo Busiri Vici, 1900–1902) with, in its center, three stories of loggia-like projecting balconies on top of the porticoed entrance. Next to it, Marcello Piacentini and Giuseppe Vaccaro designed the Albergo degli Ambasciatori, a remarkable curved structure which mixes influences from Borromini and Antiquity (the Colosseum, the Tomb of Eurysaces at Porta Maggiore).

Marcello Piacentini and Ugo Giovannozzi, header buildings at Largo Santa Susanna. Left: Ugo Giovannozzi, Palazzo Assicurazioni La Fondiaria di Firenze, c. 1937–1940, Via Barberini and Via Bissolati. Right: Marcello Piacentini, Palazzo Fiat (1937–1948, former Cinema Flamme, 1948–1949), Via Bissolati, and Via di Santa Susanna.

Mario Loreti, Hotel Mediterraneo, Via Cavour, 1937–1942. Conceived to open for the E42 Exposition, the hotel was, at 50 meters, the highest in the city at the time. Its architecture combines Rationalism (see the unique square windows) and an exceptional Art Deco interior.

On the right side starting from Piazza Barberini stands the Palazzo Parlante by Gino Coppedè (1927) with its third-floor inscription containing a dedication and date in Latin. It is followed by two powerful structures by Marcello Piacentini. The first, in collaboration with Giuseppe Vaccaro, is the former Palazzo delle Corporazioni (also known as Palazzo Piacentini–Vaccaro, now the Ministry of Economic Development), the L-shaped building with its curved facade on Via Veneto and built between 1930 and 1932. The main entrance consists of a large portal with bronze doors, designed by Giovanni Prini, with eight panels depicting "the activities of Italian workers" (Liberal Arts, Plastic and Lyrical Arts, Commerce, Banking, Sea Transport, Air and Land Transport, Agriculture, Industry). Above is the balcony, with a continuous frieze in red marble, the work of Antonio Maraini depicting the "Seven Corporations." Facing the staircase at the end of the entrance hall is the stained-glass masterpiece *La carta del lavoro* (Jobs Act, 1931) by Mario Sironi. Next and making the corner with Via Leonida Bissolati is Marcello Piacentini's Banco Nazionale del Lavoro, with the sumptuous treatment of the brick facade and the remarkable angle balcony supported by sculptural workers (1931–1937). Closing on Porta Pinciana, the Beaux-Arts-style luxurious Hotel Excelsior by architect Otto Maraini (1905–1908) and the Grand Hotel Flora (1897, original structure by Andrea Busiri Vici, later transformed) epitomized the apotheosis of *La Dolce Vita*.

Marcello Piacentini and Giuseppe Vaccaro, detail of entrance to the Albergo degli Ambasciatori (now Grand Hotel Palace), Via Vittorio Veneto 70, 1927. The fresco cycle in the salon dining room—a 1920s version of *La Dolce Vita* showing the architects, the owner, and other representatives—is the work of Venetian painter Guido Cadorin (1892–1976).

Marcello Piacentini and Giuseppe Vaccaro, model of facade of the Albergo degli Ambasciatori, 1927.

Mario Sironi, stained-glass composition *La carta del lavoro* (Jobs Act, 1931), illuminating the main staircase of Palazzo Piacentini-Vaccaro (1929–1932, now the Ministry of Economic Development, MISE; originally the Ministry of the Corporations), Via Vittorio Veneto. It is a large triptych with the large allegorical figures on the right and left in connection to Labor: Industry, Crafts, Liberal Professions. In the center is an urban landscape with a crowd of characters with powerful and statuesque shapes. The background is dotted with railway arches, industrial chimneys, and airplanes in flight against the background of the blue sky. In the center, turreted Italy presents the Labor Charter.

While Via Veneto was in development, the area between Piazza Barberini and the Largo Santa Susanna had remained semi-rural and undeveloped. The masterplan of 1931, signed by Marcello Piacentini, incorporated his proposal to build two new streets, Via Barberini and Via Bissolati and create a modern mixed-use business district generated from Santa Susanna and connecting Piazza Barberini and Via Veneto. Piacentini was responsible for a series of modern-classical structures such as the Cinema Barberini next to the palace (1930), the Palazzo dell'INA at Via Leonida Bissolati 23 (1936–1944), the Palazzo Fiat (the former Cinema Flamme) at the intersection of Via Bissolati and Via di Santa Susanna, and the aforementioned Palazzo delle Corporazioni, also known as Palazzo Piacentini-Vaccaro.

Via Vittorio Veneto at the location of Palazzo Piacentini-Vaccaro or Palazzo delle Corporazioni (right).

Gino Coppedè, Palazzo Coppedè, Via Vittorio Veneto, 1927. Often named Palazzo "Parlante" (speaking) for the numerous inscriptions on the facades.

Marcello Piacentini, Banca Nazionale del Lavoro (1931–1937), balcony and sculptural works at the intersection of Via Bissolati and Via Vittorio Veneto.

Pietro Lombardi, Fountain of the Amphorae at Piazza Testaccio, 1926.

Quartiere Testaccio 1883–1930

In studies selected for this volume, an interaction of circumstance and strategy provides some sublime moments of urban grace. A clear example is the planned workers' neighborhood of Testaccio. Its plan is a relatively rudimentary affair, making use of the widely spread convention of the non-hierarchical orthogonal grid of small blocks, reminiscent of the cardo and decumanus of ancient Roman settlements. At Testaccio there are two grids, each derived from the orientation of the antique portuary structures that pre-existed and the inexorable edge condition of the site—the river and the Via Marmorata along the Aventine hill. They meet at the center of the neighborhood, and their 20-degree mismatch creates a handsomely shaped public space, Piazza Santa Maria Liberatrice. The streets that open on the northwest side of this piazza align with the streets that open on its southeast side, but with a bend in the street alignment caused by the shifted grids. These bent streets provide moments of spatial magic that rival the illusionistic manipulations of space in the most revered Baroque architecture such as Borromini's San Carlo alle Quattro Fontane and Balthasar Neumann's Vierzehnheiligen: spaces that are simultaneously finite and infinite. Looking eastward from the western side of the piazza, the streets have both a closed vista and an open vista. The bent alignment creates closure denoting a finite place, but after the bend, the street heads off somewhere unknown and unknowable, to the infinite firmament. Borromini and Neumann knew exactly what they were doing with unknowable sources of daylight poking around corners and from behind arches, but the spatial quality of the neighborhood appears to be the unanticipated by-product of pragmatic process. That it was probably not fully intentional should not prevent us as students of urban design from appreciating and learning from the memorability and beauty of the plan and other serendipitous accidents in the district, such as the animated and cross-generational Piazza Testaccio, undoubtedly the best square in all of modern Rome. (D. S.)

Architects

Giovanni Bellucci
Carlo Broggi
Innocenzo Costantini
Giulio Magni
Camillo Palmerini
Quadrio Pirani
Innocenzo Sabbatini
Carlo Tonelli

In Antiquity, the area of Testaccio, immediately west of the Aventine but included within the Aurelian walls, was the place where most of the Tiber trade took place. The main documented structures included the Porticus Aemilia and the Horrea Galbana. The Porticus, whose remains along the river were excavated in the second half of the 19th-century, was 487 meters long and 60 meters wide. Divided into 50 vaulted naves, it was intended for the storage of goods. The Horrea Galbana consisted of a series of alimentary warehouses, organized around three large rectangular courtyards with arcades. Over the centuries, the remains of thousands of broken clay amphoras and other detritus were piled up, eventually creating the artificial Monte Testaccio or Monte dei Cocci, about 30 meters high. Until the 1870s, the area was vulnerable to the Tiber floods, and mainly inhabited by farmers and shepherds. However, the space between Monte Testaccio and the walls was public and commonly used by the citizens as a recreation ground outside the city fabric—a traditional destination for holiday trips and for the typical *ottobrate romane* (wine celebrations during the month of October).

Laboratory of Urban Transformation

After 1871 and the designation of Rome as the capital of the new Kingdom of Italy, the district of Testaccio became a laboratory of urban transformation, a strategic node for the development and modernization of the city. The *Piano regolatore* (masterplan) of 1873 drafted by Alessandro Viviani proposed developing Testaccio as an industrial and working-class neighborhood to provide small industries, worker's housing, and a variety of workshops and warehouses. Ten years later, Viviani updated the plan and the resulting 1883 *Piano regolatore* confirmed the construction of public housing immediately adjacent to a new slaughterhouse. The complex of the slaughterhouse and the livestock market, known as Mattatoio, was built between 1888 and 1891, on a project by the municipal architect Gioacchino Ersoch. As outlined in the plan of 1883, the new district was aligned along two axes whose orientation related directly to the antique structures that preexisted in the area. The grid of square blocks followed the orientation of the courtyard slave quarters of the Horrea Galbana; the other rectangular grid paralleled the river and the Porticus Aemilia. Construction of the Lungotevere Testaccio, part of the system of new riverbanks designed by engineer Raffaele Canevari, started in 1887 and opened the way to the creation of a new urban facade. A square was proposed at the intersection of the two grids, which was eventually enlarged and became Piazza Santa Maria Liberatrice, now faced with the church built in 1909 by architect Mario Ceradini.

Alley within the former Mattatoio (slaughterhouse), now part of the Roma Tre University.

Mario Ceradini, Church of Santa María Liberatrice, 1909.

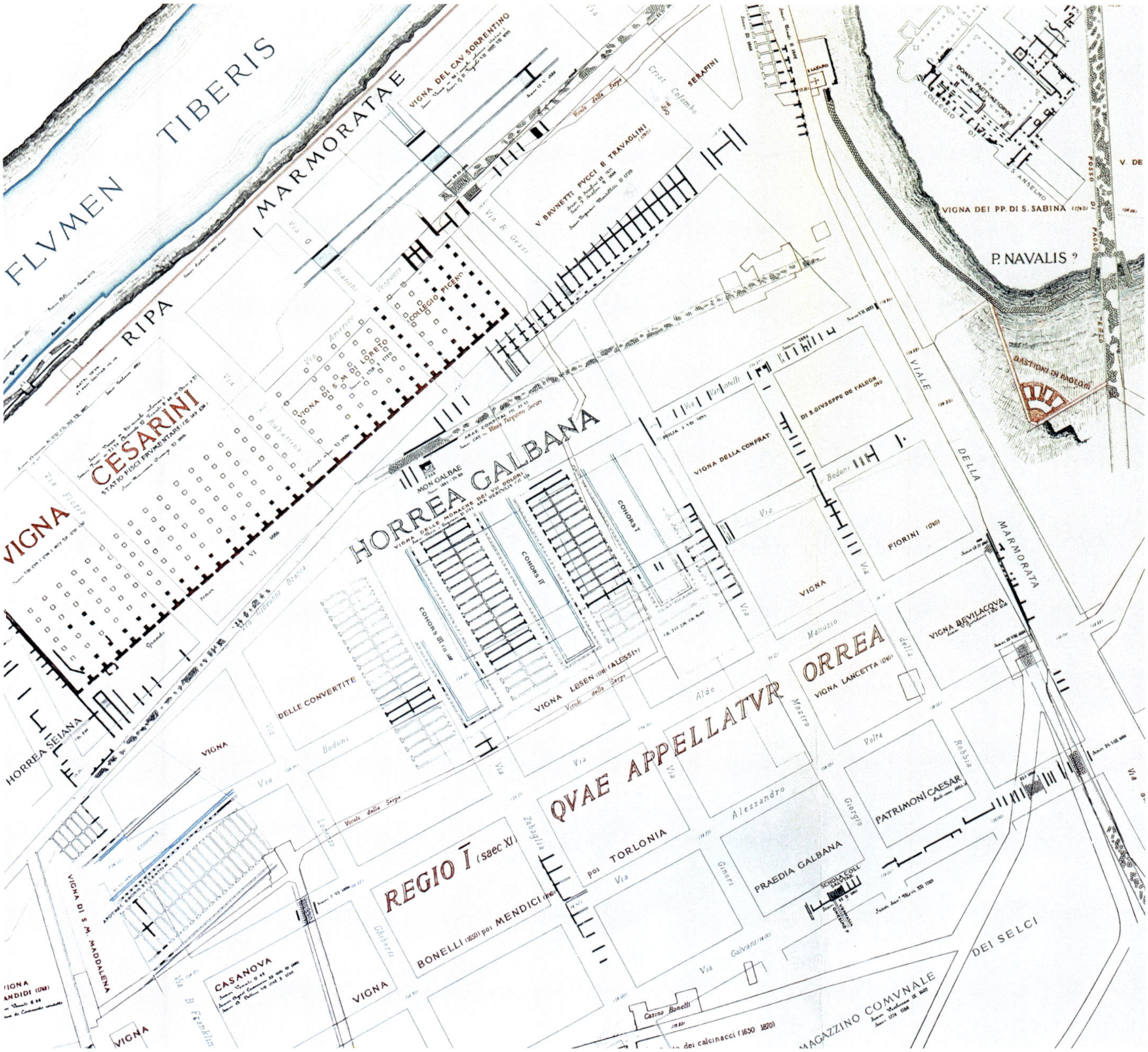

Rodolfo Lanciani, *Forma Urbis Romae*, 1901. Plate XL showing the area which is now Testaccio. In black: Roman structures; in red: structures and roads (until 1870); in blue: the new streets of Testaccio.

General view of Piazza Testaccio with housing blocks by Carlo Tonelli in the background.

Aerial view of the Testaccio district, with the Tiber to the left, Piazza Santa Maria Liberatrice in the center, and Piazza Testaccio on the right. The edge of the Aventino hill is visible in the upper-right corner.

Figure ground plan of the four main phases of the construction of Testaccio.

Axonometric drawing looking north, with the Tiber to the right, Piazza Santa Maria Liberatrice in the center, and Piazza Testaccio to the left. The edge of the Aventino hill is visible in the lower-left corner.

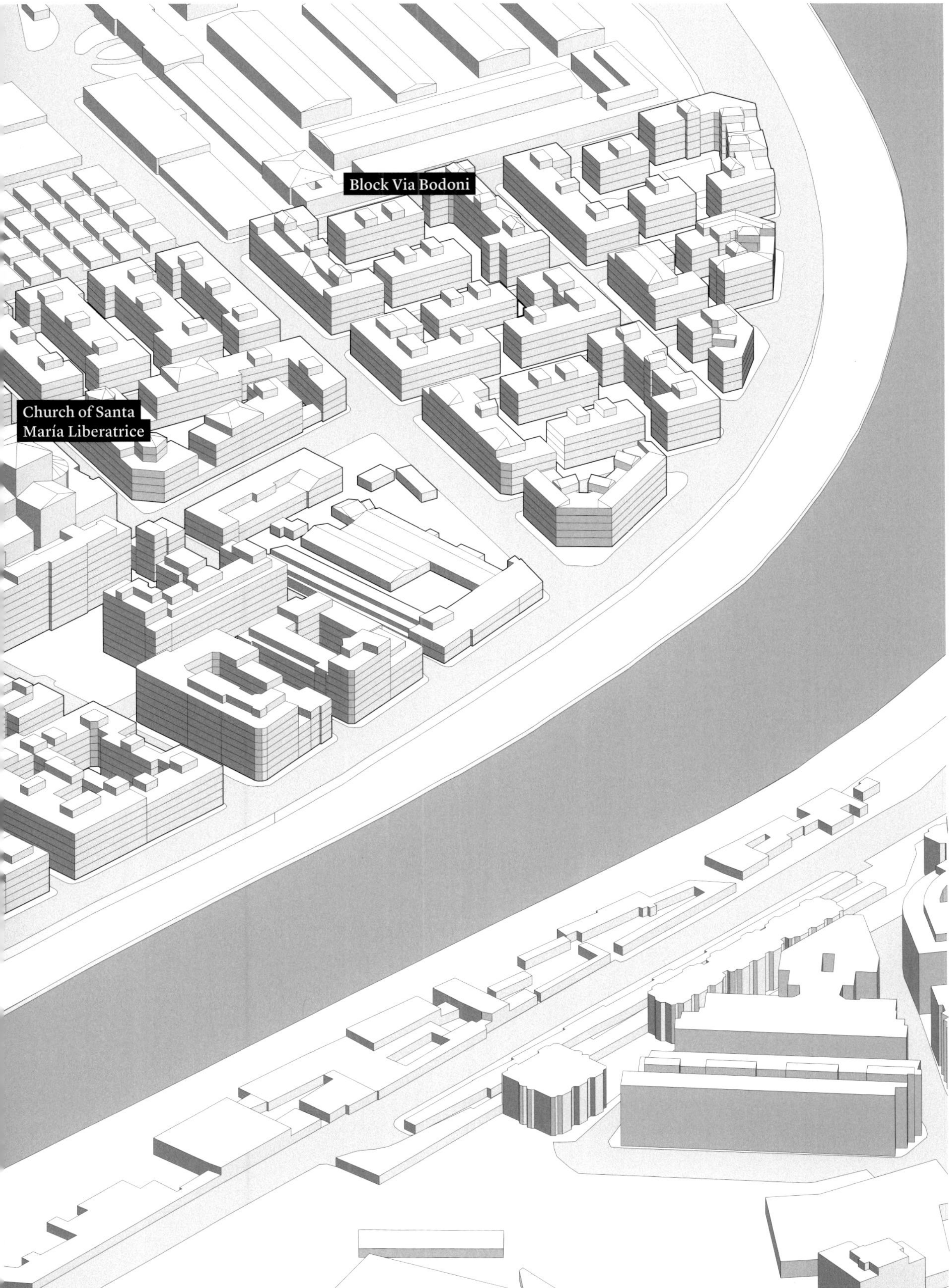
Block Via Bodoni
Church of Santa
María Liberatrice

Quartiere Testaccio, figure ground plan with block typologies.

Between 1883 and 1906, private and caritative cooperatives constructed the worker's housing grid of square blocks–53 by 53 meters—adjoining the Via Marmorata at the bottom edge of the Aventino. Architect Carlo Tonelli developed a unique series of experimental typologies that maintained the continuity of the streets at ground level while opening the upper floors as U-shaped courtyards, whose articulation provided improved illumination and ventilation of the apartments. In the early 1900s, to give voice to the inhabitants of the populous district, the Committee for the Economic and Moral Improvement of Testaccio left one block empty to build a square. In 1935, Piazza Testaccio, formerly known as Piazza Mastro Giorgio, became the setting of the public market. Eighty years later, the market was relocated, and the square was redesigned as an active and popular public space, framed on its edges by trees and benches, with the beautiful Fountain of the Amphorae, designed by architect Pietro Lombardi in 1926, was at its center. At the beginning of his career, the architect Lombardi (1894–1984) worked in the studios of Armando Brasini and Marcello Piacentini. Along with his design for the Fontana delle Anfore to be installed in Testaccio, he won a national competition in 1925 for conceiving nine fountains in seven of the traditional quarters (*rioni*) of Rome. In 1935, the Fountain of the Amphorae was transferred from the center of Piazza Testaccio to the Piazza dell' Emporio at the foot of the Aventino. In 2015, it was returned to the center of the square, its original location.

View of the block and entrance passage.

Carlo Tonelli, housing block at the intersection of Via Aldo Manuzio and Via Ginori, 1887.
Axonometric and second-floor plan.

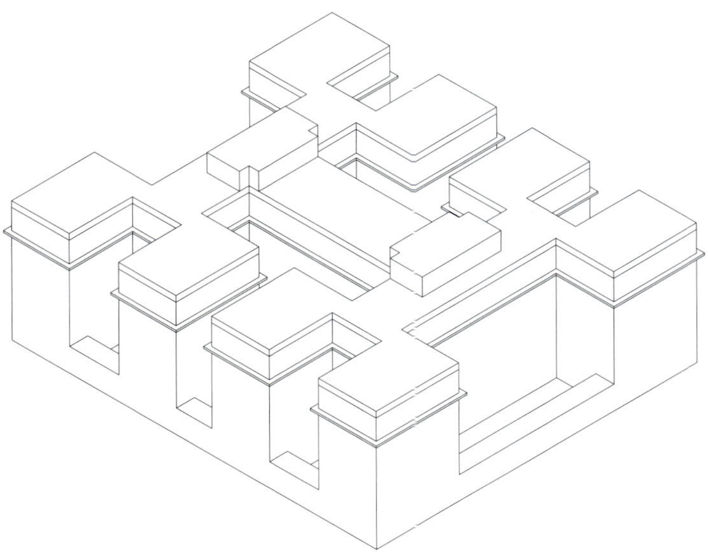

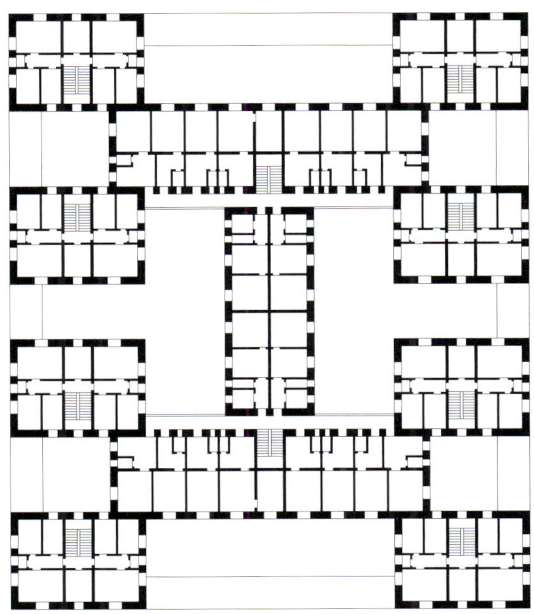

First Phase by the Istituto per le Case Popolari (ICP)

From 1907 and following the election of Mayor Ernesto Nathan (1907–1913), the Istituto per le Case Popolari (ICP) took over from the private and caritative sector. The first phase of construction consisted of an intensive complex of thirty structures, located in the bend of the river directly west of the church, i.e., the triangle defined by Via Galvani, Via del Mattatoio, and the Lungotevere. The project was entrusted to the architect Giulio Magni. The perspective image illustrates the eleven blocks, divided into thirty buildings, that were built quickly (1909–1913) with a highly rational approach to urban morphology, typology, and architecture. The architect adopted the concept of the semi-open block, a hygienic alternative to the closed 19th-century equivalent, which provided better ventilation and lighting. This open-court building block interrupted the continuity of the facades while maintaining the built perimeter at the level of the sidewalk. Most blocks were made up of two C-shaped buildings facing each other across an inner courtyard. Within the larger blocks, the Cs were complemented by two detached additional buildings, set back from the street and framed with front courts or gardens. The exception was a central block at the edge of the slaughterhouse made up of four parallel bar-like structures, the continuity of the street being maintained by the insertion of walls and gates. The rigorous design of Magni's facades corresponds to the various articulations of the open courtyard. Their architectural *partiture* refers to the classical language of Roma Capitale: symmetry in the openings defined by simple frames, the ashlar stone that marks the base and the corner sections, the hierarchy of the floors underlined by the string course, and the crowning cornice.

Giulio Magni, ICP, interior courtyard housing, Via Franklin, 1909–1913.

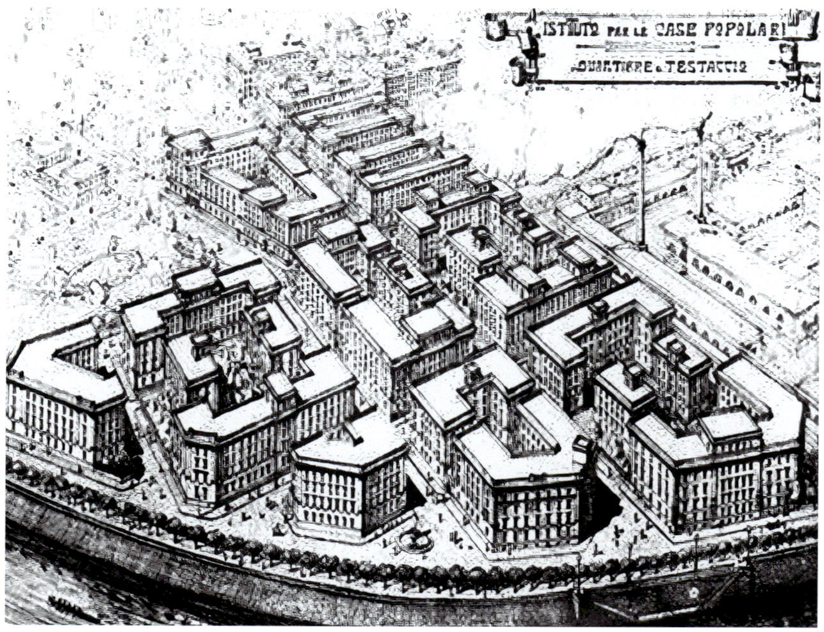

The perspective illustrates the eleven blocks, divided into thirty buildings, that were designed by Giulio Magni, ICP, and built between 1909 and 1913.

Giulio Magni, ICP, Block Via Bodoni, 1909–1913. Axonometric and plan.

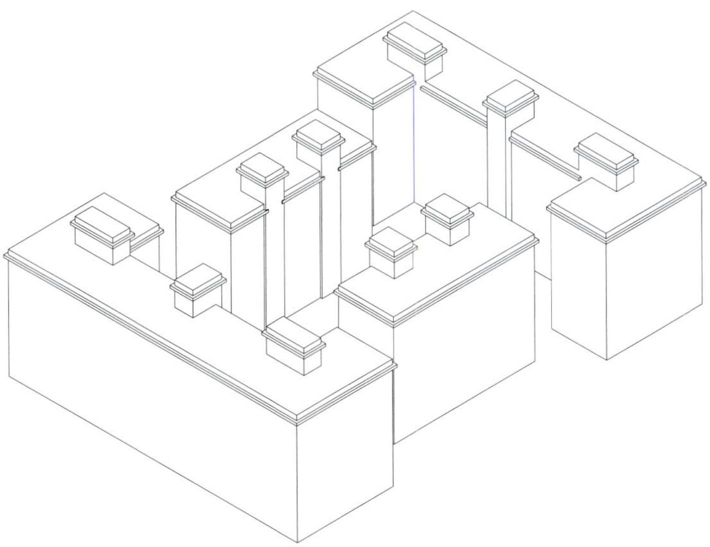

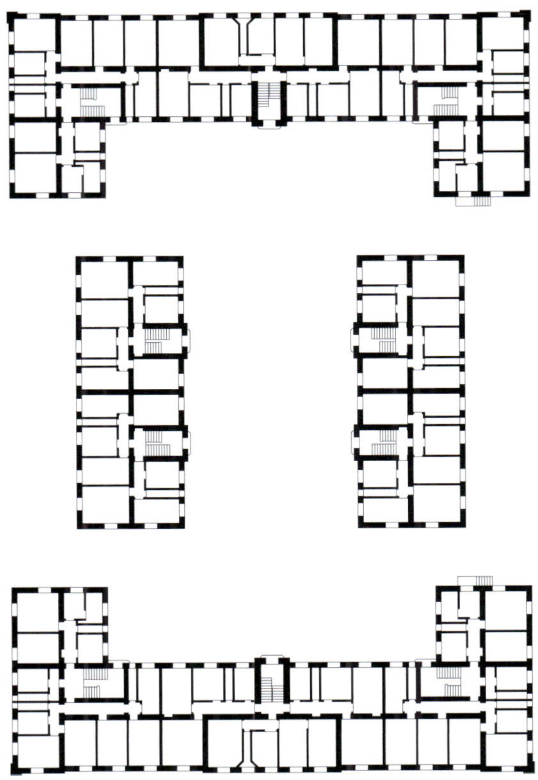

Other Phases of Public Housing, 1914–1929

From 1914, the ICP embarked on a second phase of public housing, building a series of blocks containing 395 apartments within the grid parallel to the river. The blocks overlooking the Lungotevere and the central Piazza Santa Maria Liberatrice were the works of the architects Quadrio Pirani and Giovanni Bellucci. They displayed significant improvements in the quality of public housing in Testaccio. They introduced the concept of the reform block with a large semi-public inner garden, accessed through a series of gates—in some cases they created an opening or a lower volume between adjacent buildings—that in turn give access to the individual staircases. As in San Saba, Pirani used a strong ashlar base, but replaced the stuccoed facades with walls, lintels, and other details in Roman brick. Of particular scenographic effect are the colossal brick pilasters that mark street intersections in front of the park.

Quadrio Pirani, ICP, Block XXXII, 1911–1917. View of the interior courtyard.

View of the Lungotevere Testaccio toward the north. In the sun, Block XXX (Quadrio Pirani, ICP, 1911–1917); to the right, Block XXXII (Quadrio Pirani, ICP, 1911–1917).

Quadrio Pirani, ICP, Block XXXIII, 1911–1917. View of interior courtyard.

Further interventions of the ICP involved other architects and a growing diversity in architectural and urban expression. In the 1920s, Innocenzo Sabbatini and Camillo Palmerini brought in the new trends already developing in other districts such as Trionfale and Piazza d'Armi. Making use of elements of the *barochetto* language, they developed a complex volumetry that broke the previous cubical image established by their predecessors. They recessed street corners above the strong base, introduced terraces at various levels, curved the street corners, and extruded staircase volumes in the manner of Borromini, thus creating a plastic environment magnified by Rome's stunning effects of light and shadows. These choices contributed to establishing the bourgeois connotations of the neighborhood edge along its most visible front facing the Aventino. At the same time, elements of a more metaphysical Roman-classical language appeared, such as the grouping of three elevated columns at the intersection of Via Marmorata and Via Vanvitelli, a half-block designed by Sabbatini in front of the Aventino.

Innocenzo Sabbatini, ICP, Block XXVIb, 1928. Intersection Via Marmorata and Via Vanvitelli.

Innocenzo Sabbatini, ICP, Block XXVIa, 1928. Intersection Via Marmorata and Via Branca.

Camillo Palmerini, ICP, Block XXXI, 1927–1929. Northwest intersection of Via Giovanni Branca and Via Romolo Gessi.

Carlo Broggi, Edificio Cremlino, 1924–1926. The building complex overlooks the Piazza dell'Emporio and the Lungotevere Testaccio, marking the entrance to the district from the Trastevere and the Sublicio bridge. In contrast with the strict roof lines of the district, Broggi deployed an articulated score of three-dimensional volumes that somewhat recalls the skyline of the Baroque Trident. Plan and massing structure.

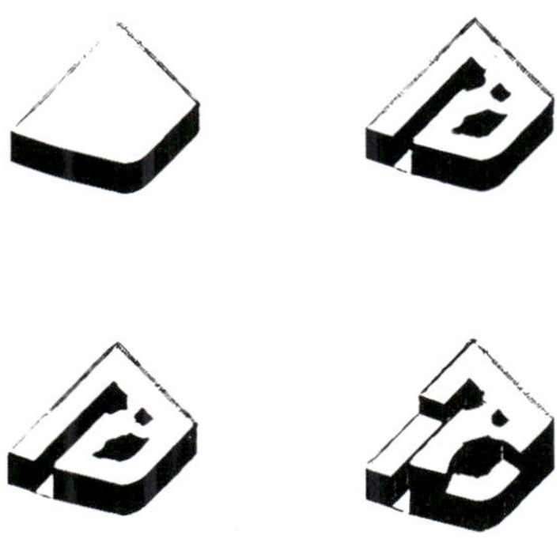

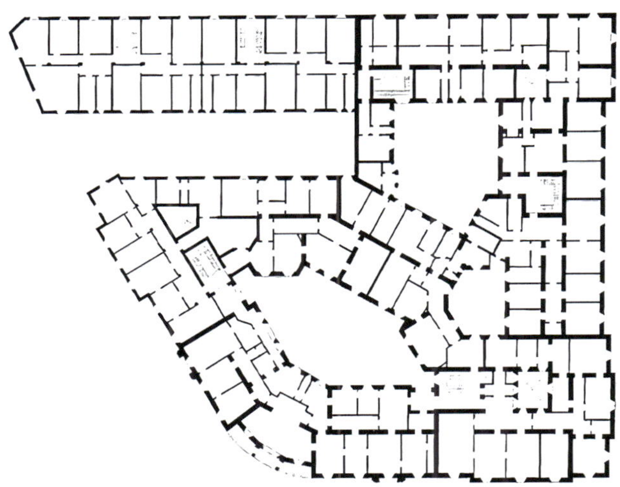

Adalberto Libera and Mario De Renzi, post office, Via Marmorata, 1933–1935.

View of Via Romolo Gessi. The block in the background articulates the intersection between the two grids of the district and thus faces the Piazza Santa Maria Liberatrice.

View of Via Ruggero di Lauria at the heart of the Trionfale district, on an axis with the cupola of St. Peter. To the right, at the intersection with Via Andrea Doria, one of the ICP apartment blocks (Innocenzo Sabbatini).

Quartiere Prati 1883–1930 Quartiere Trionfale 1911–1927

In the shadow of the Vatican the neighborhood of Prati represents the "Continuous City", i.e. the traditional city of blocks and streets, in all of its physical, temporal, and social dimensions. Roman grandeur for middle-class bureaucrats—most of Prati—and the working class—the Trionfale section of Prati. The degree to which these quite magnificent places were ignored in the literature of 20th-century planning and in the extensive documentation of Fascist-era architecture is quite notable. Even Spiro Kostof never mentions Prati. Perhaps scholars ignore Prati and other neighborhoods like Mazzini because they do not know what to make of them—even though things are gradually changing. Can one extol their virtues without compromising oneself with the brush of Fascism? Perhaps one should just look at them, look closely, or better, live in these places for a while, which I have had the good fortune to do. The word that describes the most Roman of Roman qualities is grandeur—the grandeur of Antiquity, the grandeur of the popes, the amazing grandeur of the fabric of the historic center studded with the palazzi of the great dynastic families. With the construction of Prati, Testaccio, Garbatella, and other districts studied in this volume, ordinary working people became the legatees of Rome's historic grandeur, and for whatever horrors Italian Fascism brought to Italy, this much they got right. (D.S.)

Architects

Pietro Aschieri
Garibaldi Burba
Luigi Ciarrocchi
Marcello Piacentini
Mario De Renzi
Innocenzo Sabbatini

Prati del Castello: The Beginnings

During the Roman Empire, the area located north of the Mausoleum of Hadrian, now Castel Sant'Angelo, consisted of vineyards and fields. The only access was the Ponte Sant'Angelo which led to the funerary monument and Pope's fortress. Until the early 1880's the whole borough was a vast floodable expanse of fields, meadows, pastures, and wetlands, with just a few farmhouses on the slopes of Monte Mario further to the north. In 1873, Belgian prelate Xavier de Mérode, who owned a great portion of the area, signed an agreement with the municipality to start the construction of a new district, but the masterplan published that year failed to start construction. Ten years later, the masterplan of 1883 designed by Alessandro Viviani conceived of the new district of Prati del Castello in two interrelated sections. The first section formed an irregular grid and was articulated around three large squares forming a triangular figure: next to the Castel Sant'Angelo, the Piazza Cavour facing the *palazzaccio* (Justice Palace) built between 1889 and 1911 under the direction of architect Guglielmo Calderini; the Piazza della Libertà on the river edge and connected to a new bridge leading to Piazza del Popolo on an axis with the Pincio; and third, the Piazza del Risorgimento traced at the foot of the Vatican walls and connected to the Via Trionfale which marked the western edge of the district. That street took its name from the Antique *Via Triumphalis*, which remained in use for centuries by pilgrims arriving from the north.

Aerial view of Prati, with from the bottom left counterclockwise: Piazza San Pietro, the Borgo, the Castel Sant'Angelo, the Palazzo di Giustizia and Piazza Cavour, the Prati neighborhood, Piazza del Risorgimento.

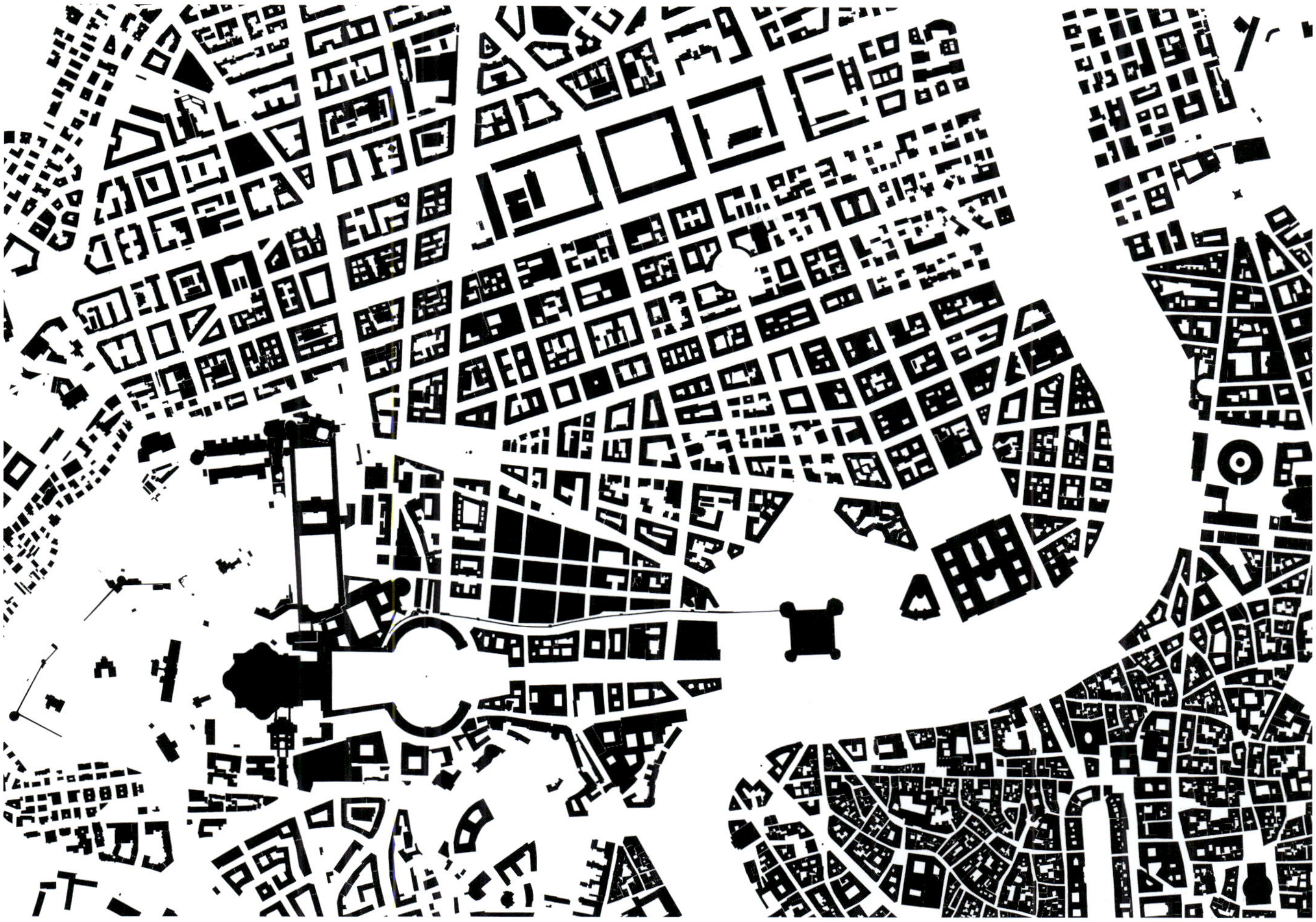

Figure ground of the Prati neighborhood with the Trionfale district (upper left corner). Clearly visible are the Vatican, Piazza San Pietro, the Borgo district, the Castel San Angelo, and the Palazzo di Giustizia.

Topographical map of the Suburban of Rome taken from the "Maps of the New Census and Trigonometrically Outlined in the Proportion of 1:15,000, 1870." Detail of the area north of the Vatican, now the Prati and Mazzini areas. Running north-south at the center is the Viale Angelico.

Marcello Piacentini, apartment house, Via Germanico, 1919–1921. The structure shows strong Central European influences (Vienna).

Housing block at Via Germanico and Via Paolo Emilio.

Garibaldi Burba, Villino Cagiati, 1902. Intersection of Via Virgilio Orsini and Via dei Gracchi. The *villino* is one of the most interesting cases of eclecticism and a major example of Stile Liberty (Italian equivalent of Art Nouveau) in Rome. The building has exceptional majoliche, frescoes, and wrought iron.

From the Piazza del Risorgimento, a trident of streets projects east and creates a connection to the Castel Sant'Angelo, to Piazza Cavour, and to the Tiber along the commercial boulevard Via Cola di Rienzo. Along its wide sidewalks, a square piazza was eventually built as a market, while the two-block-long Piazza Cola di Rienzo became the location for retail, cinemas, cafés, and other informal functions. The second section north of Via Cola di Rienzo formed a regular grid whose main axes were parallel and perpendicular to the historic Corso. The only exception to the orthogonal grid was the oblique Via Ottaviano, which departed from Piazza del Risorgimento as the continuation of Via di Porta Angelica (Viale Angelico) running alongside the physical limit of the Vatican walls. At the center of the district, Viviani introduced the first of a series of circular squares that over the years would characterize the neighborhoods of modern Rome, i.e., Piazza dei Quiriti. The State fringed the northern line of the district with the construction of a series of new barracks and the tree-lined Viale delle Milizie was designed to create a transition into the further Mazzini district.

View of the circular Piazza dei Quiriti. At the center is the Fontana delle Cariatidi, the work of sculptor Attilio Selva, 1928.

Entrance of condominium building.

Entrance and courtyard of the housing block at Via Germanico and Via Paolo Emilio.

Pietro Aschieri, Palazzina de' Salvi, 1930. Piazza della Libertà.

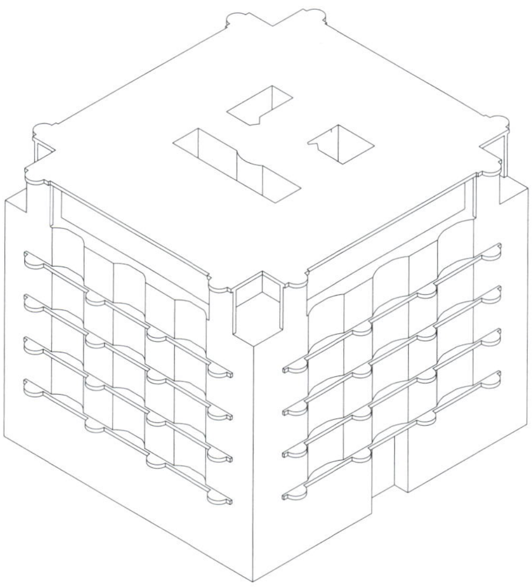

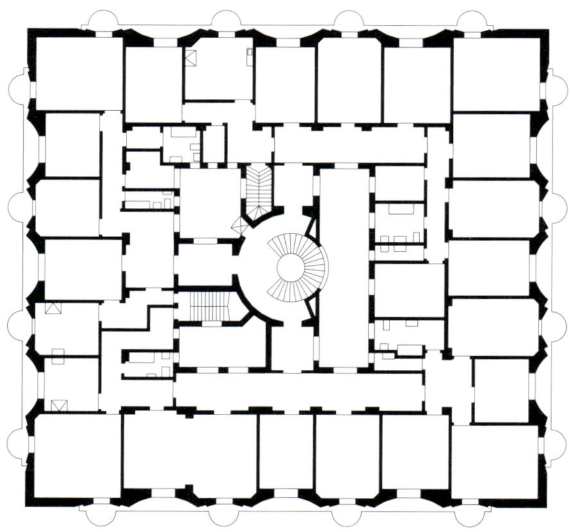

Pietro Aschieri, Palazzina de' Salvi, axonometric and typical floor plan.

Private Building Types

The development of Prati started in a piecemeal manner with various building types: apartment buildings (*case in linea*) in an unpretentious neo-Renaissance style, detached *palazzi* such as Palazzo Blumensthil (1890, Luca Caramini), and exuberant Arts and Crafts *villini* such as Villino Cagiati by Garibaldi Burba (1902). The borough, however, remained marginal because of the lack of infrastructure, and De Mérode himself financed the creation of a temporary iron bridge near the Porto di Ripetta, later dismantled after the inauguration of Ponte Umberto I. Following the real estate crisis of the mid-1890s, most of the district was built during the two first decades of the 20th century. It attracted professionals, particularly, law firms and government employees, but interestingly, a growing number of artists and writers—in particular Futurist artists like Giacomo Balla, Filippo Tommaso Marinetti, and others—who found in its newness and metropolitan character a privileged place of residence. The urban fabric of *case in linea* was limited to 24 meters in height—corresponding to six/seven floors including the ground floor—with a continuous corniche across the different parcels and structured around semi-private courtyards. Most buildings were organized around a courtyard whose dimensions vary from an enhanced lightwell to a garden occupying the entire block—for instance the so-called Palazzone along Via Leone IV.

The fountain in Piazzale degli Eroi is the terminal exhibition of the Peschiera Aqueduct. Initiated under Mussolini, it was inaugurated in 1949 (ahead of the Giubileo, the Holy Year of 1950). Extended various times until 1980, it provides 90 percent of the water in Rome.

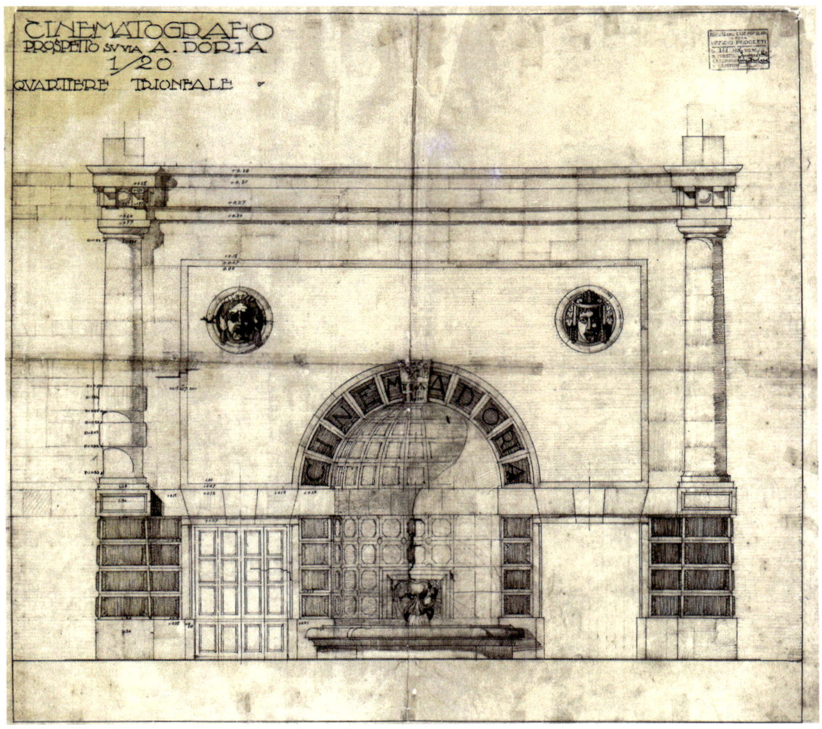

Innocenzo Sabbatini, Cinema Doria, 1926, at Via Andrea Doria. The cinema is carefully inserted between the ICP apartment houses. It opens at the back in the block interior garden.

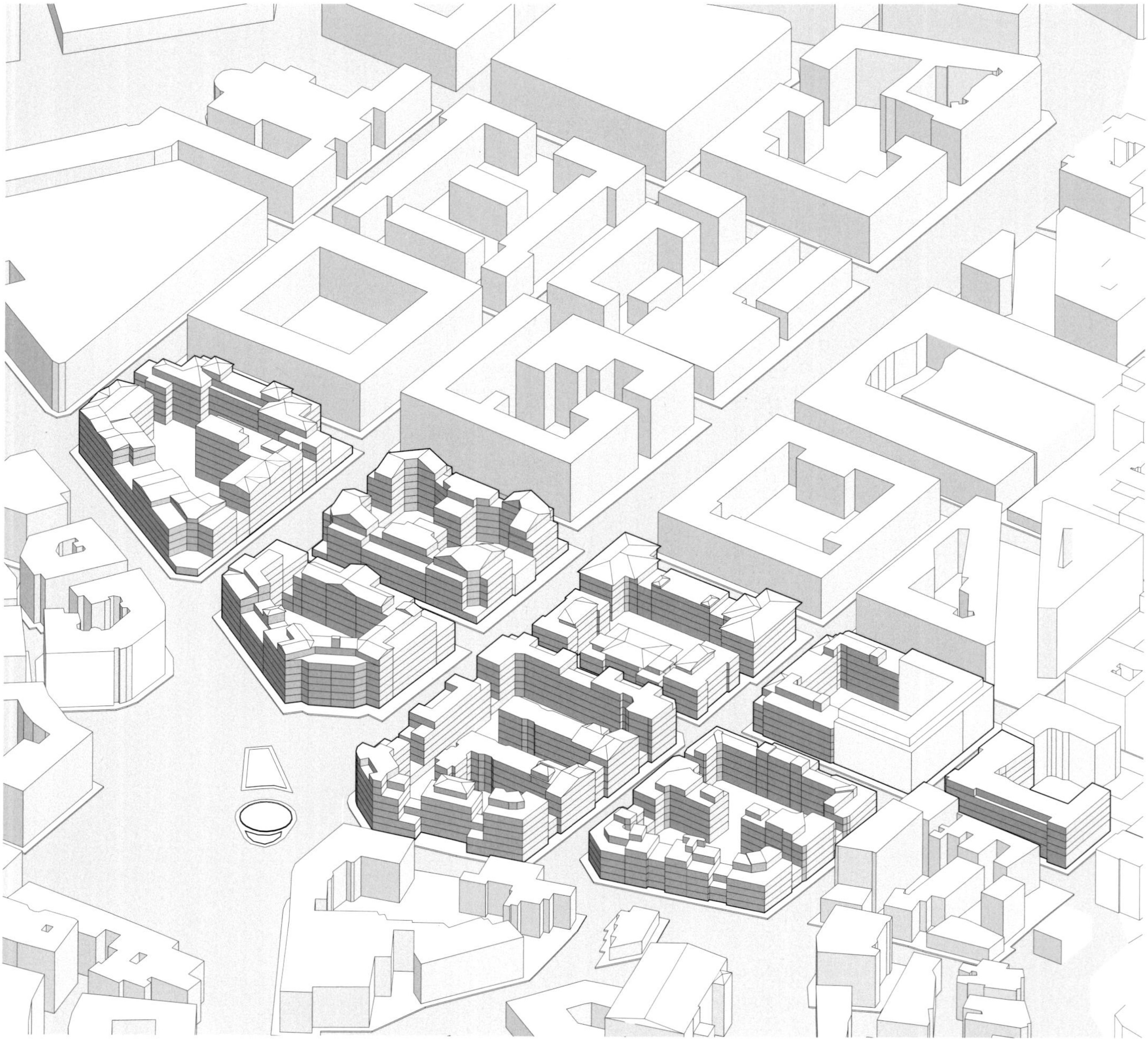

Aerial view (axonometric) of the eight-block development for the ICP (Innocenzo Sabbatini). The district was built on both sides of Via Andrea Doria (center, in diagonal).

Figure-ground plan. In black, the ICP housing blocks and to the right, the ICP building by Mario De Renzi.

Period photograph of the pedestrian section along Via Pomponazzi (between Via Andrea Doria and Via Tommaso Campanella).

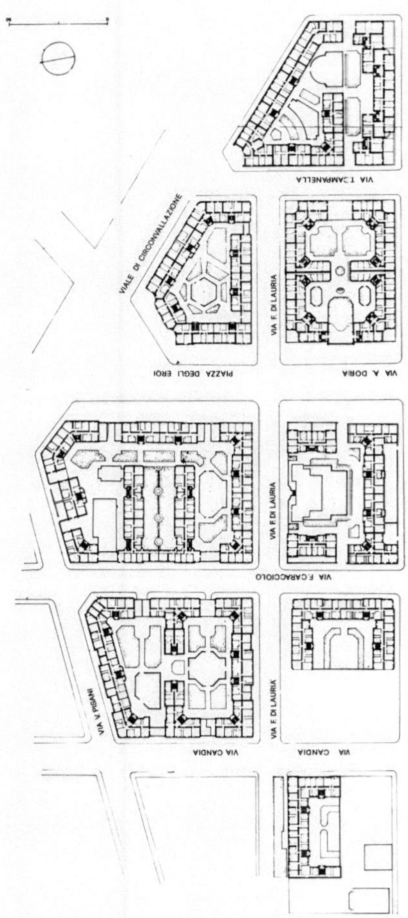

Innocenzo Sabbatini, detailed floor plan of the ICP housing blocks.

Trionfale as Integrated Social Housing Quarter

To the east of the proposed tree-lined Viale Angelico, Sanjust's masterplan included a Paris-inspired radial scheme for what would become the future Quartiere Mazzini. To the west, it continued the grid and closed it at its encounter with the curvilinear Circonvallazione Clodio. The construction of that neighborhood—Quartiere Trionfale—was decided in 1911 and was to become, after Testaccio and San Saba, the main project of the ICP on the Vatican side of the river. The successive sections of construction designed by architect Innocenzo Sabbatini were the Trionfale II complex of 1919–1922, followed by the Trionfale III, built between 1923–1926 between Via Bernardino Telesio and Via Andrea Doria, the Trionfale IV built between 1925–1927 in Via Trionfale, and the economic house of Trionfale V in Via Premuda in 1927. Sabbatini took the block structure for granted and focused on the subtle differences that could be achieved regarding the relationship between courtyard, building, and the public realm. He applied a series of hygienic principles that were affirming themselves in European urban projects of those years (let us mention Berlage's Amsterdam, from 1915, and Red Vienna, from 1919), and in the manuals of Josef Stübben (*Der Städtebau*, 1907) and Camillo Sitte (*Der Städte-Bau nach seinen künstlerischen Grundsätzen*, 1889).

Aerial view of the Quartiere Trionfale in connection with Prati.

Innocenzo Sabbatini, ICP building, elevation along Via Ruggero di Lauria, 1919–1921.

Innocenzo Sabbatini, ICP building, section across courtyard (Via Pomponazzi to the left), 1926–1927.

Sabbatini's organization of the reform blocks with semi-public internal gardens, often interconnecting, ensured transverse ventilation and appropriate lighting of the buildings on both sides as well as an efficient typological distribution of the apartments. Control of children's play and security were achieved by a limited number of entrances from the streets and the opening of all vertical circulation from the inner gardens and courts. Therefore, the closed and open courtyard became a model on which to set urban development to ensure hygiene, security, and high density. In the ICP projects, the size of the courtyard gardens varied with the deployment of various interior volumes subdividing the open space into multiple interconnected courts. The collective spaces of the Trionfale projects create pedestrian passages between the lots and were designed to ensure the continuity of the paths, as if they were genuine pedestrian counter-ways to the streets, furnished with vegetation and trees. The views of St. Peter's from Via Pietro Pomponazzi, the only connection to the dome from anywhere in Prati and Trionfale, heightened the impression of belonging and were made more remarkable by the closure of the street to traffic and the addition of decorative gates.

In Sabbatini's projects for the Trionfale, some architectural elements recurred—above all the presence of thermal windows and the use of the brick texture with a decorative effect as deployed by Pirani in San Saba and Testaccio—and aimed at creating a hierarchical design of the facade that in many solutions also featured colored plaster. Typical elements of the Roman *Cinquecentismo* also recurred in the projects by Sabbatini and De Renzi—such as aedicules and roof terraces, gables on the windows, and decorative hierarchy between the floors, etc.

On the eastern edge of the Trionfale, Mario De Renzi, in association with Luigi Ciarrocchi, built one of the most typologically innovative structures of the period. The first version of the Casa per impiegati del Governatorato (apartment building for employees of the Governorate), occupying a half-block at the intersection of Via Andrea Doria and Via Leone IV, was structured around a traditional courtyard. The final version, eventually built in 1931, inverted the strategy. The building has a comb-like plan, with three courtyards located on the first floor above shops that allow all the apartments to enjoy full illumination. Epitomizing Sabbatini's masterful deployment of abstracted classical ornament in combination with careful massing and judicious surface modulation was the Casa Economica Trionfale V (Sabbatini, Circonvallazione Clodia, 1927). Its elevations achieved a grandeur that appears anything but economic or austere, and which are

Innocenzo Sabbatini, Casa Economica Trionfale, at Circonvallazione Clodia, 1927.

sadly now pretty much hidden by other large apartment buildings.

Regarding the program and in particular the relation between buildings and sidewalks, Trionfale offered a surprising variety of uses, from small-scale retail and communal rooms, to the presence of cafés, and even repair garages at important corners, to a day-care center and the singularity of the full-size Cinema Doria expertly inserted between two housing blocks on the Via Andrea Doria. This quest for functional mixture was on the social level complemented by a policy that avoided, as had happened for other developments, the clustering of tenants according to equal professional backgrounds. As a major European example of state-sponsored public housing the district might therefore have been homogenous in terms of social mixture, but it avoided the trap of ghettoization. This was also facilitated by the proximity of the historic center and the application of a similar spatial paradigm in the Prati neighborhood. As a result, Trionfale can be perceived as part of a wider urban continuum.

Innocenzo Sabbatini, ICP building along Via Ruggero di Lauria, 1919–1921.

Mario De Renzi (with Luigi Ciarrocchi), apartment building for employees of the Governorate, at Via Andrea Doria, 1927–1931. Third and built solution for the half block.

Mario De Renzi (with Luigi Ciarrocchi), apartment building for employees of the Governorate. View of the attic portico, formerly adorned with decorative spheres in a Renaissance manner.

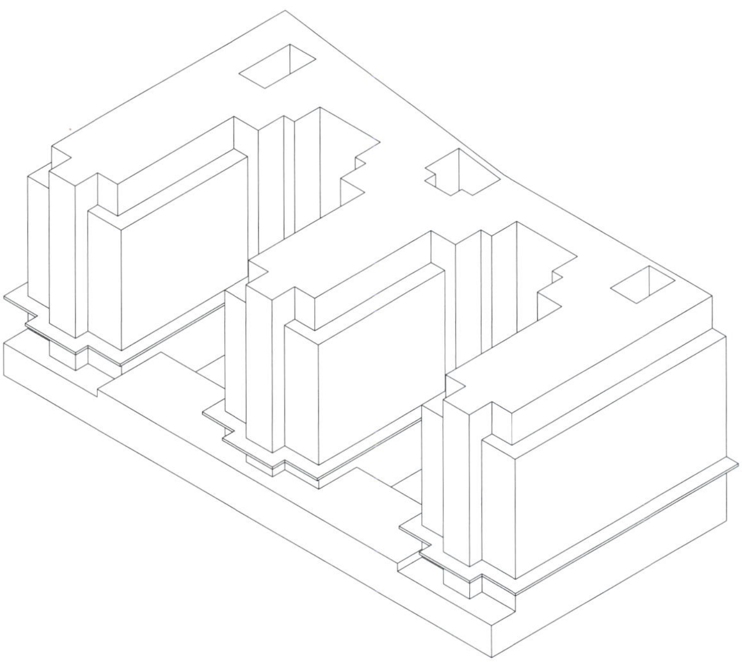

Mario De Renzi (with Luigi Ciarrocchi), apartment building for employees of the Governorate. Axonometric.

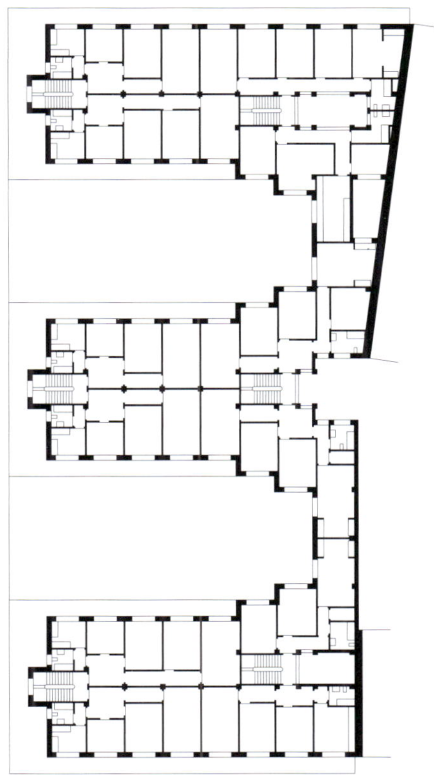

Mario De Renzi (with Luigi Ciarrocchi), apartment building for employees of the Governorate. Typical floor plan.

Interior garden in Trionfale (ICP), view from entry gate on Via Caracciolo (southside).

Interior garden in Trionfale (ICP), view from entry gate on Via Andrea Doria (southside).

Interior garden in Prati, view in direction of main gate on Via Leone IV (Prati). The garden occupies the core of a large and single apartment block known as the Palazzone (formerly Palazzo Allegretti), c. 1900. The block is contained between Via Leone IV, Via Candia, Via Tolemaide, Via Ostia.

Innocenzo Sabbatini, ICP housing block (Piazza d'Armi II), 1925–1926. Detail of the entrance portico, Via Fulcieri Paulucci de Calboli. The inscription reads "Domus Amica Domus Optima" (Friendly house best house).

Piazza Mazzini—Quartiere della Vittoria 1909–1940

In 1911, Gustavo Giovannoni invited Josef Stübben to Rome to discuss the plan for the Piazza Mazzini district, an enormous tract of publicly owned land adjacent to Prati and soon to become one of the most important 20th-century neighborhoods. With the German planner he shared two apparently contradictory enthusiasms: first for Camillo Sitte and second for Georges Eugène Haussmann and his grandiose transformations of Paris. This unending tension between modernity (Haussmann) and memory (Sitte) was to play itself out for the next 50 years in Rome, for the most part, to the eternal benefit of the city. Nothing came out of Stübben's involvement and it is with Marcello Piacentini that Giovannoni arrived at the final version of a Haussmann-inspired plan. This "French" center of the Mazzini quarter—a large green square at the intersection of radial tree-lined boulevards—is nice but executed much better all over Paris. Yet, the truly Roman parts of Mazzini are splendid. Fake Paris ends and real Rome begins, a short block away from the Piazza itself. Parts of the plan are circumferential streets that intersect with the radial avenues. These streets are beautiful, create closed vistas, and are bordered with six- or seven-story housing blocks, some of them built as social housing. The curving streets, the big buildings, the rich over-scaled detail, and the Roman colors result in a continuously unfolding panorama of pictures. Camillo Sitte's concepts have come to life on a grand metropolitan scale and in a truly inventive Roman way. (D. S.)

Architects

Alberto Calza Bini
Luigi Ciarrocchi
Vincenzo Fasolo
Marcello Piacentini
Quadrio Pirani
Mario De Renzi
Innocenzo Sabbatini
Antonio Titta

After the Universal Exposition of 1911

As planned in Teulada's 1909 *Piano regolatore*, the future Mazzini district north of the Viale delle Milizie and the line of military barracks, reflected strong influences from French urban design. The grid that had dominated Roman planning since 1871 made space for a French-inspired Beaux-Arts vision of urbanism, consisting of a series of radial streets converging toward a large green square; the wide boulevard Viale Mazzini assured the connection from the Ponte del Risorgimento to the east, and the Circonvallazione Clodio to the western edge of the neighborhood.
On the 50th anniversary of the unification, Italy presented itself to the European nations with the *Esposizione Universale di Roma* (1911) convinced of the strength of its national culture and the various regions of the country. Urbanistically, the exposition was planned on the principles defined by Sanjust and occupied two large sites on both sides of the Tiber, Valle Giulia and the flood-prone Piazza d'Armi on the Castel Sant'Angelo shores.
In the years immediately following the exposition, the debate on the shape of the new district—which had been occupied by the regional and ethnographic pavilions—intensified and made of the Quartiere Mazzini, to be built entirely on public land, the first experimental project of urban design in modern Rome. Eventually, the stellar layout provided by the Sanjust plan remained the dominant theme, in part because of the French influence already mentioned and the infrastructural leftovers of the 1911 exhibition. German urbanist Josef Stübben's alternative proposal of 1911—inspired by Camillo Sitte and rich in public buildings and new public spaces—had no real follow up. Then, two distinct and contemporary proposals were elaborated: one by Gustavo Giovannoni (on behalf of the Associazione Artistica tra i Cultori di Architettura, AACAR) and one by Marcello Piacentini, both radiocentric but more spacious and with better-defined public spaces. The proposals merged into a single project (1915) signed by Giovannoni and Piacentini. In 1919, a variant was adopted which served as the final design for the construction of the district. The central axis—Via Giuseppe Ferrari and Via Oslavia—prolonged the grid of the Prati district, linking Piazza Cavour and the Palace of Justice, first to the line of barracks, then to Piazza Mazzini and to Monte Mario to the north. Structuring the entire plan and giving it its unique urban form is the boulevard starting from the new Ponte del Risorgimento, crossing Piazza Mazzini and then curving to join the Piazzale Clodio to the west.

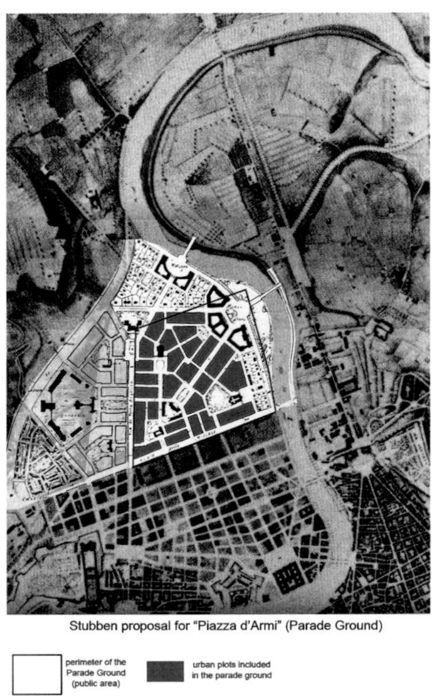

Josef Stübben, masterplan for the Mazzini district, 1911-1914.

Gustavo Giovannoni and AACAR, first proposal for the Mazzini district, 1915.

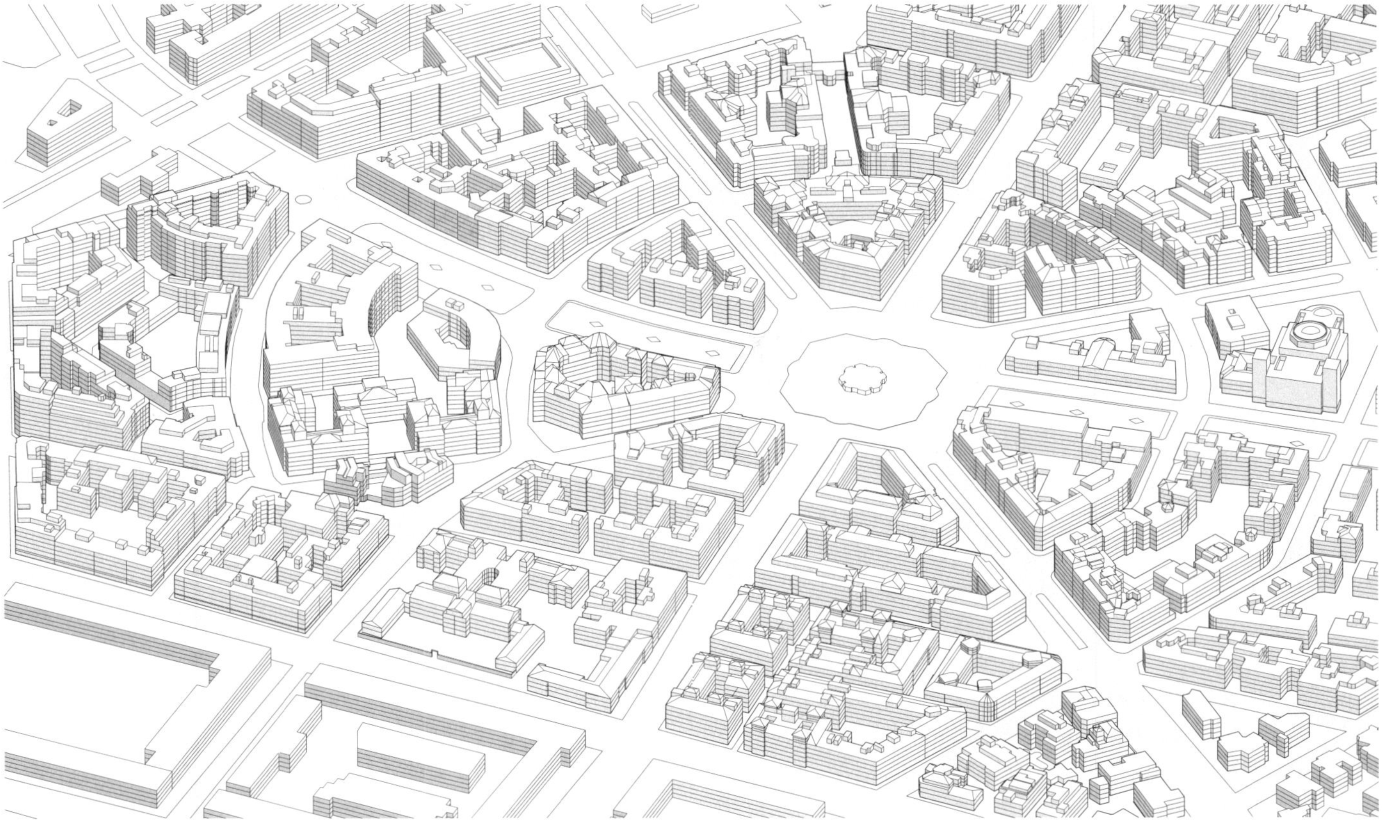

Partial axonometric view of the Mazzini district with Piazza Mazzini at the center.

Marcello Piacentini, first proposal for the Mazzini district, 1915.

Marcello Piacentini, second proposal for the Mazzini district, 1915.

Gustavo Giovannoni and Marcello Piacentini, joint proposal for the Mazzini district, 1915.

The original name of the "Quartiere della Vittoria" changed under Fascism to delle "Vittorie" (i.e. the plural, "of victories") although it is commonly called the "Mazzini district" from the name of its central square. The whole area was under municipal ownership, which allowed Mayor Nathan and the city council to envision the future district as a radical new opportunity for the extension of the Third Rome. The involvement of the State in the construction of the neighborhood was not only significant but also very well integrated within the blocks developed by the private sector. Between 1920 and 1923, Quadrio Pirani was responsible for the first interventions. Working for the IRCIS, he designed the two blocks between Piazza Mazzini, Via Luigi Settembrini, and Via Guiseppe Ferrari, around beautifully landscaped interior gardens which allowed for well-ventilated apartments opening on to both the streets and the gardens. In the manner of his works in the San Saba district, Pirani deployed his multi-material language—exposed brick, smooth and grainy stucco, pilaster-like articulations, and stone and metal balconies—which here seems to merge both the popular and the bourgeois image. Worthy of note is the combination of projecting balconies with recessed terraces along the side streets and the floral panels that he introduced between the last floor windows and which wrap around the entire blocks under a potential influence by Otto Wagner in Vienna. Another early structure of great interest was designed by Alberto Calza Bini in 1921 as a mid-block social housing project between Via Ruffini and Via Giuseppe Avezzana. In contrast with Sabbatini, who chose to match his buildings with the curved line of the street, Calza Bini articulated the buildings as a picturesque composition centered on a recessed entrance and made up of curved corners, towers, a bridge functioning as a gate, and a very elegant garden.

Figure-ground plan: Innocenzo Sabbatini, ICP housing blocks (Piazza d'Armi II), 1925–1926 (1.1, 1.2); Quadrio Pirani, INCIS housing blocks, 1924 (2.1, 2.2).

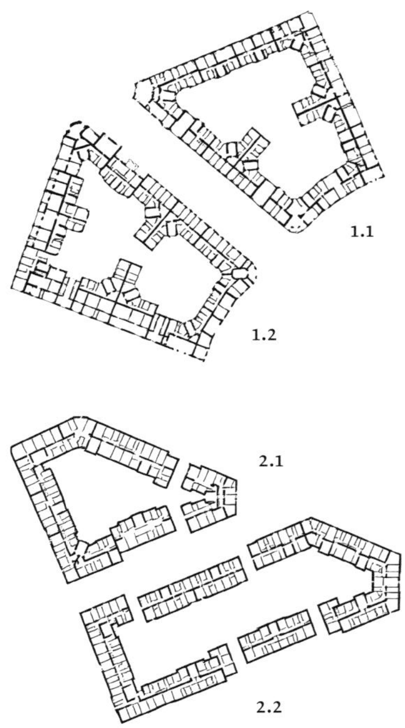

Ground floor plans. The two ICP blocks by Innocenzo Sabbatini (Piazza d'Armi II, 1925–1926) are marked 1.1 and 1.2. The INCIS housing blocks by Quadrio Pirani (1924) are marked 2.1. and 2.2.

Marcello Piacentini, Basilica of the Sacro Cuore del Cristo Re, 1936.

In the center, view of the two ICP housing blocks by Innocenzo Sabbatini and Quadrio Pirani (Piazza d'Armi II) along Via Fulcieri Paulucci de Calboli.

Designed by Innocenzo Sabbatini for the Istituto delle Case Popolari (ICP), the two trapezoidal blocks facing the ring street (Via Fulcieri Paulucci de Calboli) between Via Sabotino and Via Oslavia—an operation known as Piazza d'Armi II (1925–1926) formed a remarkable ensemble organized around two large interior gardens and separated by a private street. Here again, Sabbatini deployed his virtuosity in combining different buildings into a seamless whole and making use of the street geometry—curvilinear—to create remarkable urban moments: among these, the church-like pedimented roof in the perspective of the curving street and the two polygonal towers framing the pedestrian street. Built from 1925 to 1929 for the Istituto autonomo per le famiglie degli Impiegati del Governatorato, the triangular, plug-like block designed by Mario De Renzi and Luigi Ciarrocchi between Via Angelo Brofferio and Viale Giuseppe Mazzini (1925–1929), acts as a subtle articulation between two avenues, the square, and the circular ring of streets around the square. The architectural language combines classical and *barocchetto* compositions, but De Renzi introduced subtle allusions to Futurism in the treatment of the volumes and towers that scansion the roofscape.

View of Via Giuseppe Ferrari. The INCIS complex by Quadrio Pirani (2.1/2.2) appears to the very left of the view.

Apartment block on the half-circular Piazza dei Prati degli Strozzi.

Mario De Renzi (with Luigi Ciarrocchi), apartment block for the Istituto autonomo per le famiglie degli Impiegati del Governatorato, between Via Angelo Brofferio and Viale Giuseppe Mazzini, 1925–1929.

Innocenzo Sabbatini. Baroque-influenced window sills in the courtyard of the ICP apartment block, 1925–1926 (1.2).

Alberto Calza Bini, entry gate to the ICP housing complex, 1921. Organized around a large garden, the apartments face Via Ruffini and Via Giuseppe Avezzana.

Quadrio Pirani, INCIS housing blocks, Via Luigi Settembrini, 1924. Entrance gallery.

Rationalist apartment building (streamline Moderne/Art Deco), Via Timavo, 1930s.

Rationalist apartment building, Via Augusto Riboty, 1930s.

Innocenzo Sabbatini, ICP housing blocks (Piazza d'Armi II), 1925–1926. Entrance gallery (1.1 in plan).

Cesare Valle, apartment block with three U-shaped courtyards between Via Carlo Poma, Via Antonio Baiamonti, and Via Giuseppe Andreoli. Detail of facade on Baiamonti.

Overall, the architectural quality of the district was very high, thanks to the quality of and the seamless integration between the blocks built by the public sector and those by private developers and cooperatives. Many of the blocks in the Mazzini district, particularly those at the center, have open pedestrian passages, like in the Trionfale neighborhood, but lack the quality of an interconnected system; most have generous internal courtyards, beautifully designed and planted. Within this framework, the public gardens, which adorned the main avenues and the center of the district, Piazza Mazzini, were designed by Raffaele De Vico (1881–1969), the most important landscape architect of the interwar period and author of many Roman parks including the Colle Oppio Park and the green belt surrounding the EUR district. His "fountain-garden" at the center of the piazza was completed in 1927–1930 in collaboration with the sculptor Ermenegildo Luppi (1877–1937). Among the most significant public buildings of the district are the Basilica del Sacro Cuore di Cristo Re by Marcello Piacentini (1929–1936), Vincenzo Fasolo's state high-school Liceo Terenzio Mamiani (1924), and Antonio Titta's Palazzo delle Poste (1935).

Raffaele De Vico, landscape architect. View of the gardens at Piazza Mazzini, 1937

Quadrio Pirani, INCIS housing blocks, 1924. Detail of the facade inspired by the works of Otto Wagner in Vienna.

Alessandro Limongelli, Giuseppe Wittinch, Mario De Renzi, ICP apartment houses, 1926. Detail of the *barocchetto* facade on Piazza Perin del Vaga, with one of the two fountains of the Dolphins (Fontana dei Delfini). Their author is unknown, but the fountains recalled other works by Pietro Lombardi. The gates were designed by Duilio Cambellotti.

Quartiere Flaminio
1909–1940

The *Piano regolatore* of 1909, designed by Edmondo Sanjust di Teulada under the administration of Mayor Ernesto Nathan, established the structure of what would become known as Quartiere Flaminio. The neighborhood was planned as a large trident to be built in the bend of the Tiber, across from the slopes of Monte Mario and the future Foro Italico. The three streets radiating from Piazza Gentile da Fabriano were zoned, as was the piazza, for intensive residential use. They connected with the Passeggiata Flaminia, a linear green park linking the Piazza Flaminio to the Ponte Milvio, and now almost entirely built and given over to *palazzine*. The Risorgimento Bridge was built in 1911 to connect the Piazza d'Armi area with the International Exhibition at Valle Giulia, thus opening the neighborhood to development. The start of the First World War changed the fate of the small industrial area created in 1905 by Società Automobili Roma. The factory was transformed into the military Royal Arms Factory, housing mostly linear barracks and workshops. Over the years, various residential projects with innovative typology and morphology have occupied the spaces recuperated from the abandoned or underused industrial structures. With the Museo nazionale delle arti del XXI secolo (MAXXI, Zaha Hadid, 2010), the Auditorium Parco della Musica (Renzo Piano, 2002, on the other side of Via Flaminia), and other projects in planning such as the Museo della Scienza di Roma, the formerly mixed-use industrial district is being converted into a metropolitan center of primary importance for the performing and visual arts.

Architects
Tito Bruner
Giulio Gra
Alessandro Limongelli
Ernesto Negri
Quadrio Pirani
Mario De Renzi
Giuseppe Wittinch

Villa Ricio Superblock

Between Via Flaminia and the head of the Trident along the Lungotevere Flaminio, a series of innovative housing blocks were built in successive phases, from the garden city typology of Villa Riccio to the metropolitan image of the blocks facing Piazza Gentile da Fabriano and the Ponte della Musica (Armando Trovajoli, 2008–2011). From 1919, under the direction of Vincenzo Riccio, Minister of Economy and Railways, a large complex of middle-class apartments for post and telegraph workers, known as Villa Riccio, was established in a quadrant consisting of Via Donatello, Via Raffaele Stern, Viale del Vignola, and Lungotevere Flaminio. Designed by Ernesto Negri, it was an early prototype for the garden superblock that would be prevalent later, particularly at La Garbatella. The generous gardens, accessible by gates from the streets, connect the apartment rows and create a series of tranquil alleys deep within the block. A series of U-shaped buildings open to the green establish the edge of the superblock, while simple rectangular structures seemingly float amid the overall garden atmosphere. Another experimental project, known as Piccola Londra, can be found on the northern side of Via Vignola. Conceived by Quadrio Pirani (1909), it appears like an intimate street of rowhouses preceded by small gardens, like the British model.

Aerial view of the Flaminio district. Starting at the top left and following the bend of the river: the Villa Riccio superblock; the ICP district and its two squares; the 1930s apartment buildings forming the trident across from the Ponte della Musica (2008–2011). The Gra Condominio is the last building in the bottom right.

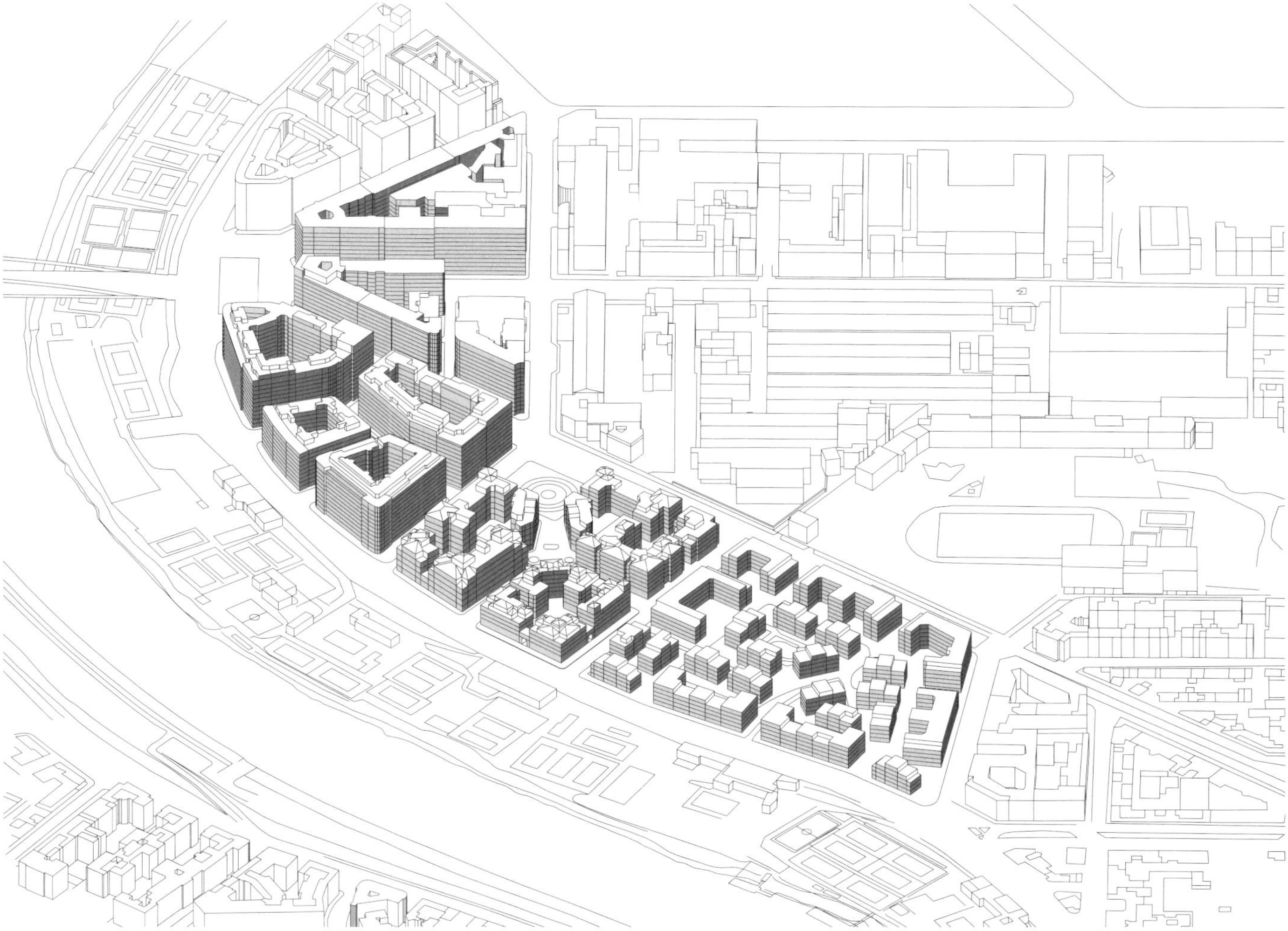

Axonometric view of the Flaminio neighborhood. See the aerial view for details.

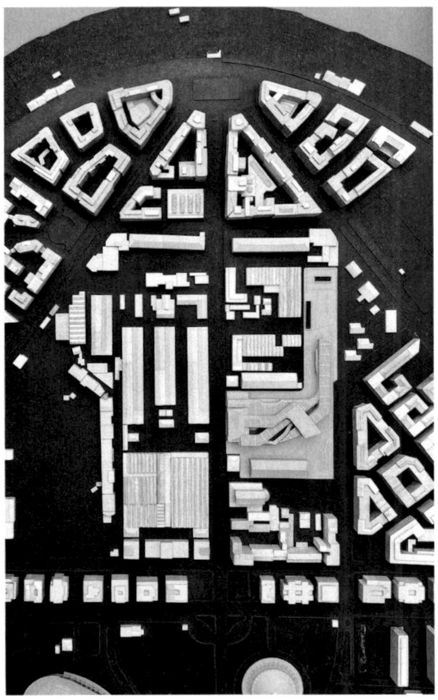

Model of the Flaminio district along Via Reni, with the MAXXI in the center. On the bottom edge, Via Flaminia and the Palazzetto dello Sport (Pier Luigi Nervi, 1960).

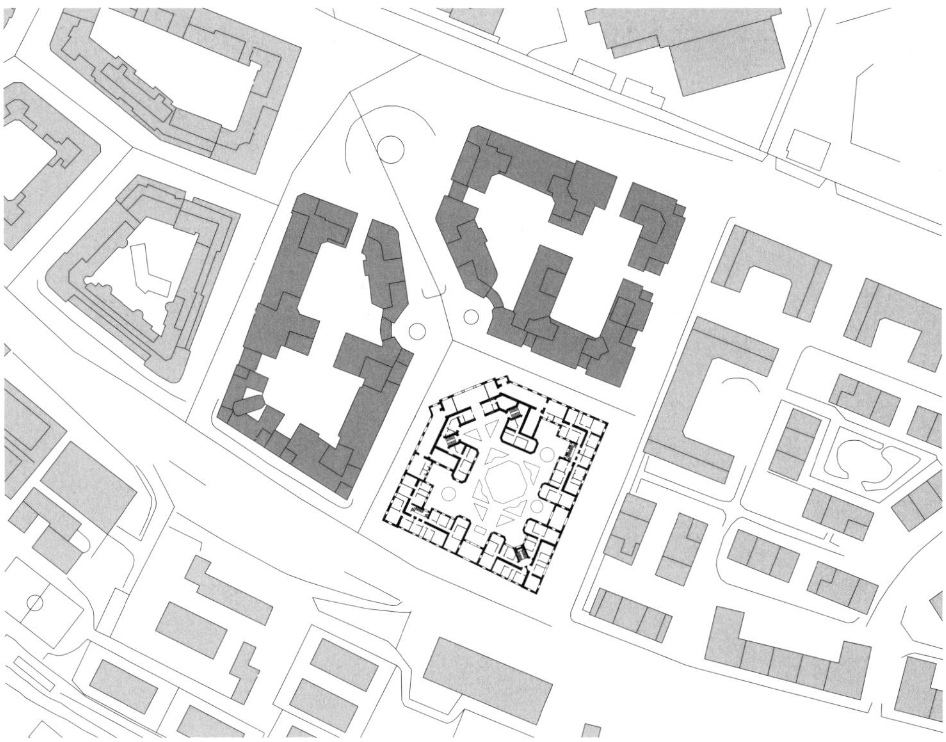

Detailed figure-ground plan of the ICP complex.

Between Rome and New York

The three residential blocks that make up the Flaminio II complex were structured around two residential squares, a large one opening on Viale del Vignola, Piazza Melozzo da Forlì, and a smaller square, the fully pedestrianized, Piazza Perin del Vaga. The project for 340 apartments was drawn up by Mario De Renzi (central block), Alessandro Limongelli (both trapezoidal blocks), Giuseppe Wittinch, and Tito Bruner (completion of the trapezoidal courts) between 1925 and 1927. The buildings of the Flaminio II project form a compact front along the Lungotevere between the Villa Riccio ensemble and a set of four streamline Moderne/Art Deco apartment buildings. Made up of three large courtyard blocks, the intervention has a unitary character, consisting of a pleasant sequence of courtyards, urban spaces, and passages in continuity between inside and outside. The three blocks are geometrically articulated to establish continuous street edges along the perimeter and to create a diagonal interior street that opens into an elliptical piazza. The latter reproposes the spatial conditions of a square in a Baroque town, for example Piazza San Ignazio in the center of Rome. It is one of the first attempts to experiment with new typological solutions and to break the rigidity and uniformity of the 19th-century block in favor of greater compositional freedom in the articulation of the interior spaces and the relationship between street and courtyard. The buildings are articulated with multiple height variations and setbacks to facilitate the access of light and air by the courtyards, as well as to generate expansive terraces.

Mario De Renzi, central building of the ICP complex, 1926. In the entablature above the three entry arches, "ISTITUTO PER LE CASE POPOLARI".

Mario De Renzi, facade of the ICP central building on Lungotevere Flaminio.

In the facade attributed to De Renzi, the one that terminates the diagonal from Piazza Melozzo to Piazza Perin del Vaga, there are references to the minor architecture of the late 16th century, recombined in a language of invention. The sophisticated spatial articulations and decorative elements—doors, balconies, sill bands, pilasters, cornices, roof terraces, dormers—create the episodes in which the lemmas of the *barocchetto* are declined; a language oriented toward the recovery of themes typical of minor architecture found in Rome from the 16th to the 18th century, often mixed with echoes of Northern European modernist lexicons. On both sides of the diagonal, the plan is symmetrical, yet the shape of the blocks delimits different internal courtyards. The concave walls perforated by loggias at all four levels lend access to the courts and some upper-floor apartments and give the square its unique elliptical shape. The design of the internal gardens and entrance spaces, with the positioning of the two symmetrical fountains—both displaying two dolphins with raised tails placed on two pillars—responds to that character of unity sought by the designers. The gates were designed by Duilio Cambellotti (1876–1960).

Piazza Melozzo da Forlì, serving as entrance to the ICP complex.

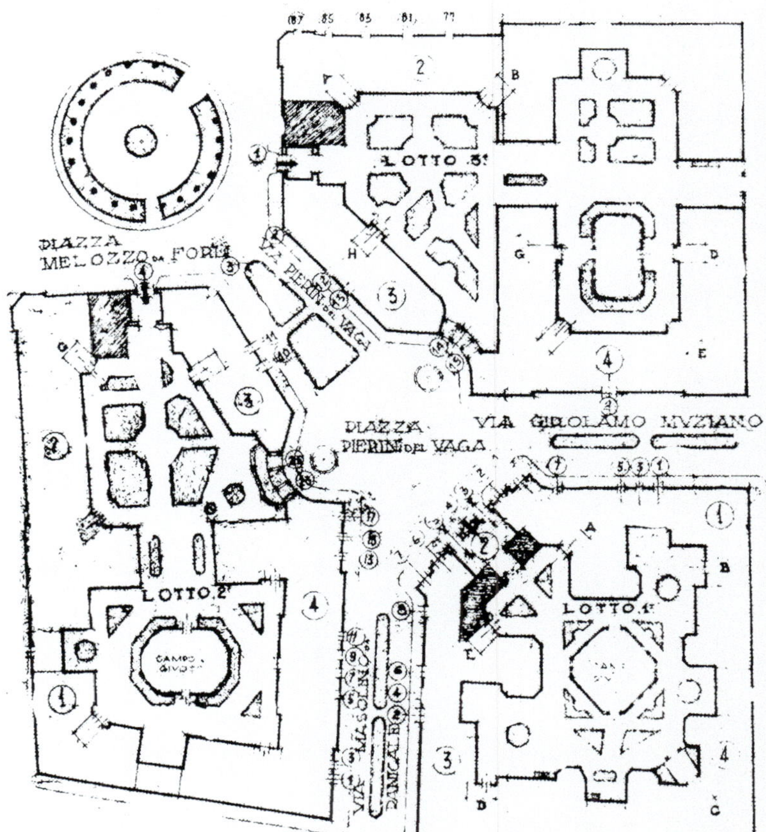

Alessandro Limongelli, Giuseppe Wittinch, Mario De Renzi. Detail plan of the ICP complex, 1924–1926.

View of apartment building Villa Riccio along Lungotevere Flaminio (E. Negri, 1919).

Rationalist (streamline Modern/Art Deco) apartment house on Lungotevere Flaminio, 1930s.

Mario De Renzi, courtyard of the ICP apartment building, 1926.

View of the ICP complex between Villa Riccio (right, not visible) and the 1930s Rationalist apartment building (left).

As for the eleven blocks of high-density apartment buildings—the two rationalist and symmetrical entry buildings to Via Guido Reni reach eleven floors—located along the Lungotevere Flaminio and the trident streets on both sides of Piazza Gentile da Fabriano, they constitute a 1930s privately built metropolitan ensemble of overall architectural relevance. Of value is the block containing the 1410-seat Teatro Olimpico, constructed on behalf of the Società generale immobiliara (SGI, 1935–1936) at the intersection of Piazza Gentile da Fabriano, Viale del Vignola, and the Lungotevere. The so-called Gra Condominio which stands at the other end of the Lungotevere near the Ponte Duca d'Aosta is the masterpiece of the company owned and designed by the two brothers Giulio and Enrico Gra. Its combination of classical, streamline Modern, and Rationalism makes it a unique synthesis between Rome and New York (1936).

Giulio Gra, Gra Condominio, Lungotevere Flaminio, 1936.

Giulio Gra, Gra Condominio. Staircase and entry portal.

Quadrio Pirani, wall and window detail of apartment building, Viale Giotto, 1906–1923.

San Saba
1906–1923

More than a century after its foundation, the San Saba district remains one of the most significant examples of public residential intervention, especially owing to the quality of the execution, the performance in the long term, and the reduced need for maintenance—mainly due to the use of brick scores, alternating with stone elements such as travertine, tuff, peperino, and plaster fields and to the appropriate choice of building types with respect to the topography and context. Another singular aspect of this district's quality is the measured compactness between pedestrian and vehicular paths, proposed in an exemplary and essential way. It is a theme that recurred in most public residential Roman interventions of these years (ICP, INCIS), designed according to different modalities, variants, and proportions between built and public space. In the case of San Saba, Quadrio Pirani and his colleague Giovanni Bellucci designed all the buildings to achieve a unique and original urban dimension, fully effective, and on a human scale.

Architects

Giovanni Bellucci

Quadrio Pirani

Built between the 7th and 9th century, the church of San Saba and the attached monastery were the only populated settlement on the small hill between the Aventine and the Baths of Caracalla. The monastery soon became a powerful institution, with many properties and an advanced diplomatic activity that made it influential in Constantinople and among the so-called Barbarian worlds. At the beginning of the 20th century the church and the monastery were still surrounded by the countryside. The Viviani masterplan of 1883 reserved the area for a public green near the Aurelian walls, between the Baths of Caracalla and the Pyramid of Cestius in close reach to the Passeggiata archeologica (Archaeological Promenade, 1908–1914). However, the subsequent *Piano regolatore* of 1909 (Sanjust di Teulada) substituted the public green with a workers' housing quarter. In 1906, in parallel with its intervention in Testaccio, the Istituto per le Case Popolari (ICP) initiated the first organic intervention intended to house the workers of the industrial area south of Rome. The new settlement at San Saba, which included 546 lodgings for about 2500 people, was located far from the city center but within the Aurelian walls and close to the industrial areas in development, among which the Mattatoio (slaughterhouse, Gioacchino Ersoch, 1891), the gasometers (1910 and 1937), the former electric power plant known today as Centrale Montemartini (1912, engineer Puccioni), and other facilities on both sides of Via Ostiense. Designed by architect Quadrio Pirani in collaboration with Giovanni Bellucci, the Quartiere San Saba was built from 1906 to 1923, with a considerable pause during the years of the First World War. During that period, the building types and density of the different phases evolved considerably. However, the intervention remained strongly unitary regarding the linguistic aspects of the architecture, the selected materials—mostly brick—and the inventive adaptation to the topography of the site.

View of the apse of the Basilica of San Saba.

Aerial view of the San Saba district.

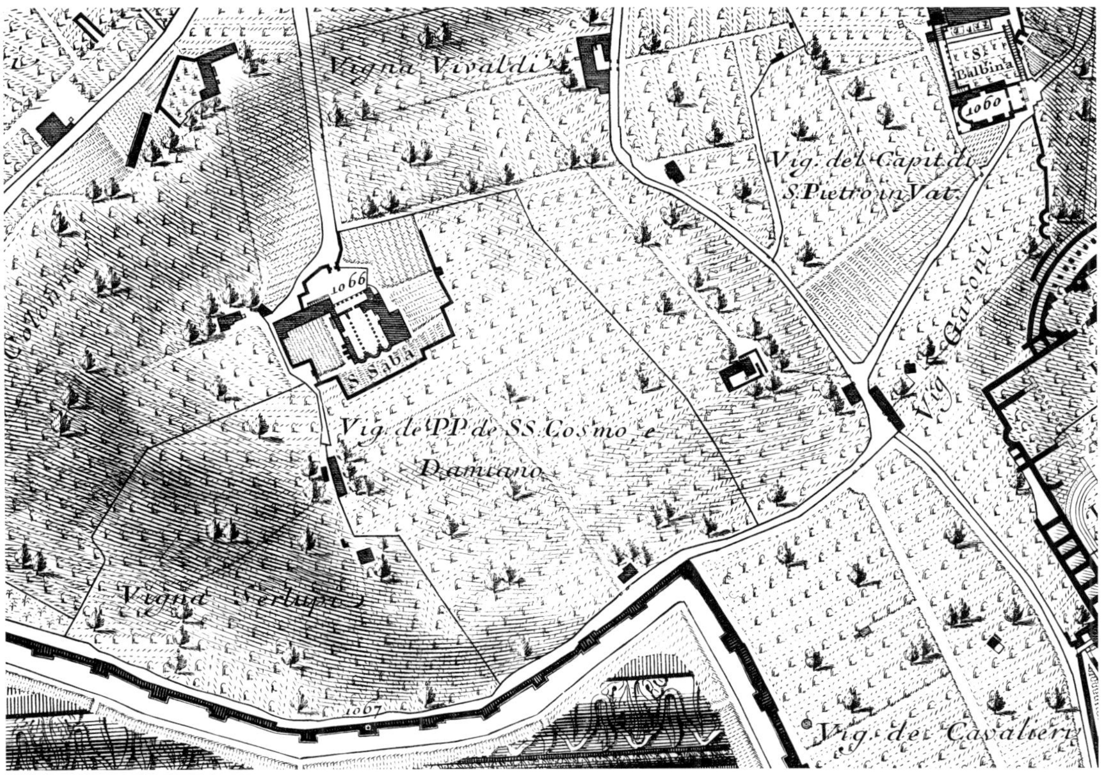

Detail of the Nolli Plan, 1748. Notice the Aurelian walls, the Basilica of San Saba, and to the very right, structures from the Baths of Caracalla.

Three Phases

The first nucleus (1906–1909, lots 1, 4, 5, and part of 6) was built on the flat and highest section of the site and faced the apse of the church across a landscaped rectangular square, now known as Piazza Bernini. It was laid out as a garden village, composed of single-family houses on two floors, plus a basement, isolated or aggregated in rows of two or four houses, all set back from the street and with independent entrances and gardens. Albeit beautifully designed, the wide, tree-lined roads and the square itself, named after prominent architects and artists, had greater connections to the Anglo-Saxon model of the garden suburb than to the Roman tradition.

Figure-ground plan with first floor plans.

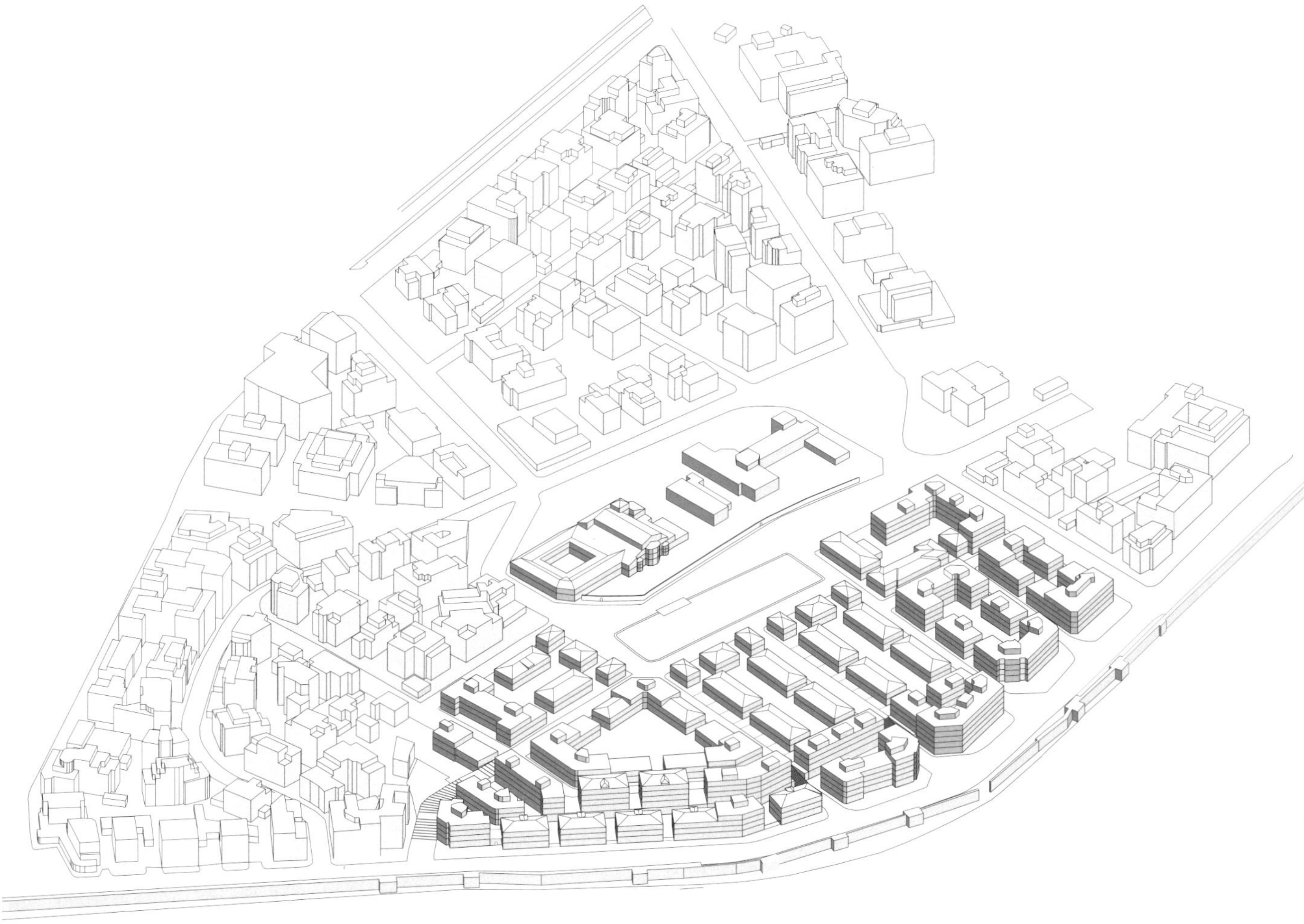

Axonometric view of the Quartiere San Saba.

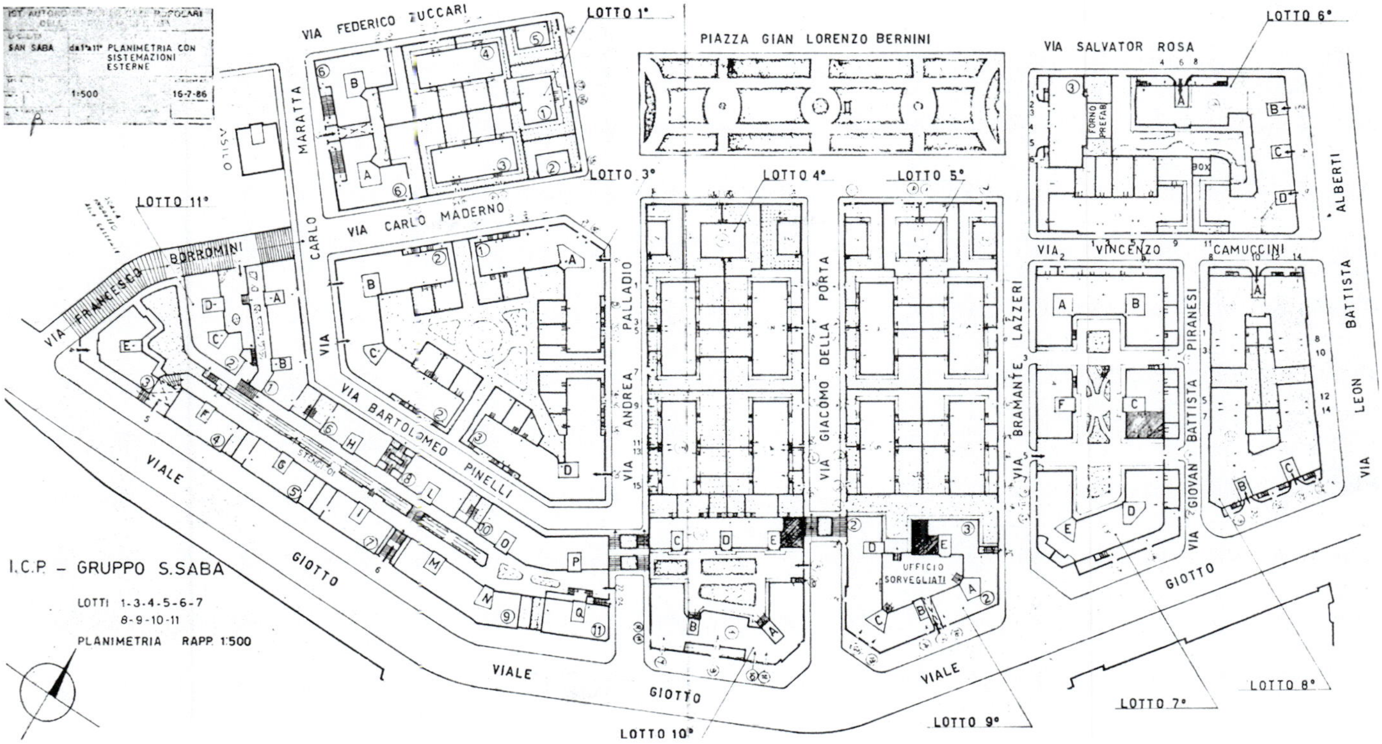

Quadrio Pirani, masterplan of the San Saba district.

Quadrio Pirani, townhouses with front gardens Via Giacomo della Porta.

Quadrio Pirani, townhouse, Via Andrea Palladio.

In the next phase (1909–1913)—the construction of lots 3, 7, 8, and the completion of lot 6—multi-family types were used, organized around a collective courtyard and with at least three floors above ground. The presence of numerous underground tunnels and quarries encountered at the start of this second phase made deep foundations necessary and therefore, higher costs had to be compensated for with increased density. In particular, the buildings on lots 7 and 8, facing the Viale Giotto and the Aurelian walls, consisted of three-story houses with three to four apartments per floor on the corners, combined with two-floor terraced houses in-between. Typologically, these blocks were more urban in character and were like those used by the ICP at Testaccio. Also on flat ground, the triangular block between Via Maderno and Via Palladio (lot 3) was organized around a semi-public courtyard. Three-story buildings stand on the corners and are connected to each other with two-floor terraced linear houses. In the courtyard, the terraced houses have their own private gardens. This logic of the terraced house alternating with taller and higher-density buildings, in the corner and edge conditions, was eventually adopted in all lots.

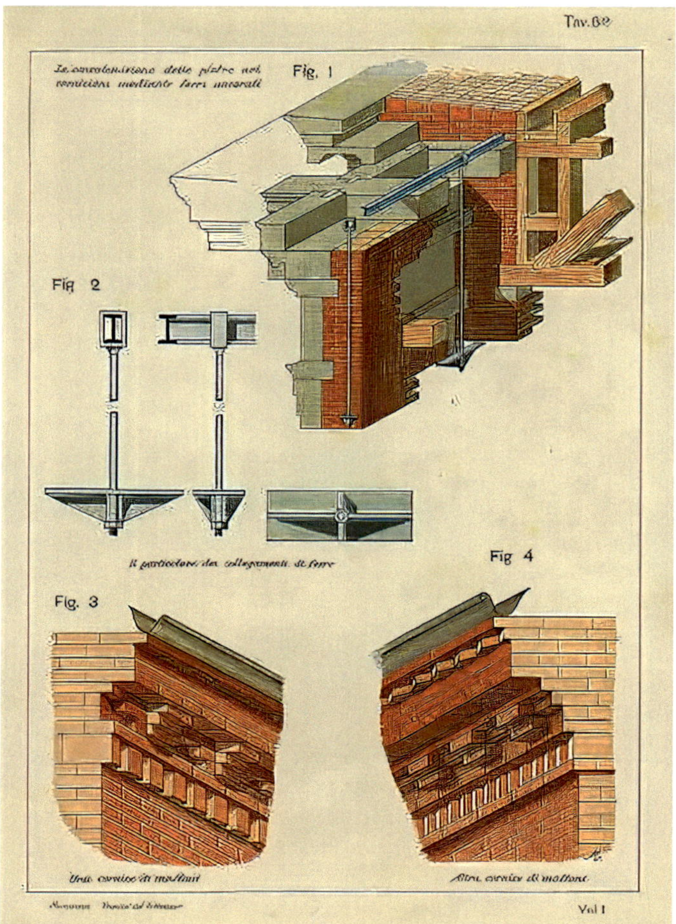

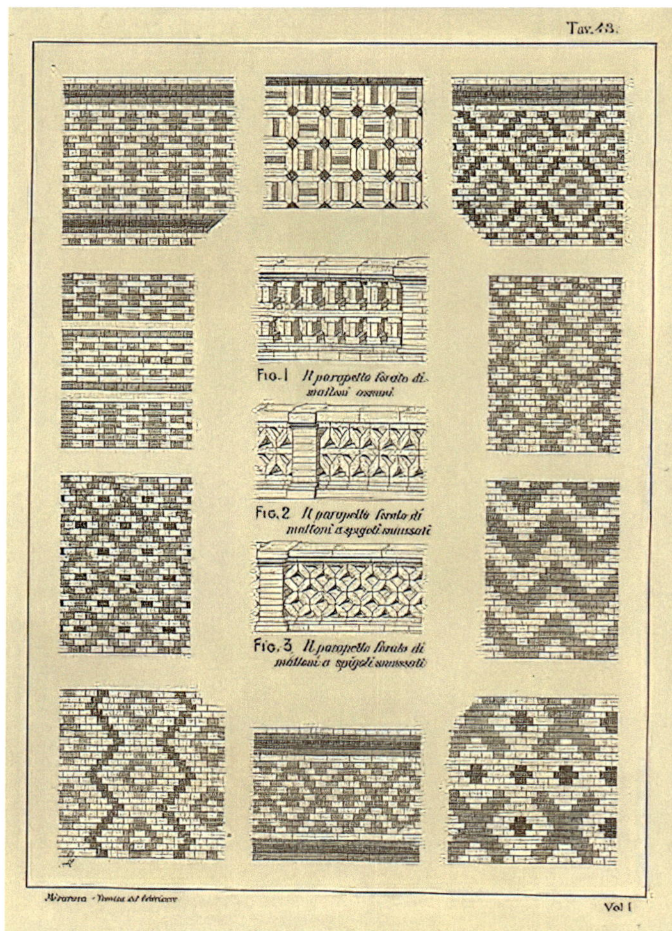

The use of brickwork in many San Saba residential buildings contributed to their durability. Typical brick construction details.

Street intersection of Viale Giotto and Via Bramante. A colossal brick corner characterizes the residential building by Quadrio Pirani.

Intersection of Viale Giotto and steps of Via Francesco Borromini.

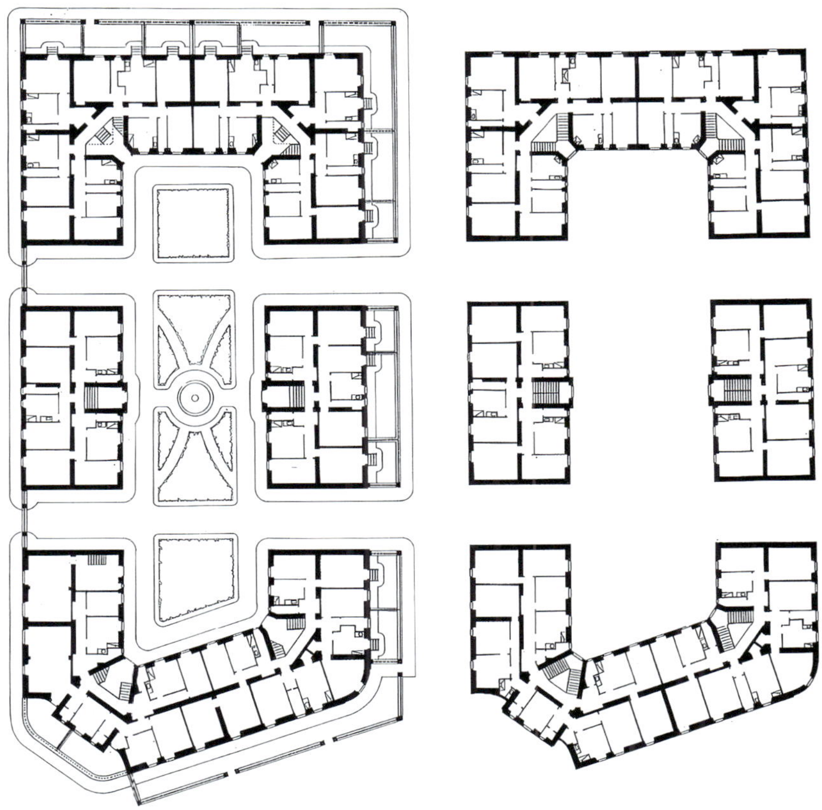

Quadrio Pirani, ground floor and second floor plan of ICP block between Viale Giotto, Via Bramante, Via Vincenzo Camuccini, and Via Giovanni Battista Piranesi.

Urban staircases, Viale Giotto and Via Giacomo della Porta.

The third phase began in 1919 and consisted of the final group of houses between Via Pinelli and Viale Giotto, designed to complete the urban facade along the Aurelian walls. The higher section of Viale Giotto—the old Via del Pomerio—reached the same level as the square of San Saba at the height of Via Bramante (lots 7, 8). However, the lower section (lots 9, 10, 11) faced a considerable denivelation between the lower section of the avenue and the flat top of the hill, of about 10 meters. These complex transversal connections were beautifully resolved with a series of scenographic urban staircases and pedestrian passages. At the same time, the architects designed the semi-buried ground floors for collective use such as bathrooms, storage, clinics, meeting rooms, etc. Separated from the townhouses of the pre-existing first phase by a pedestrian street, two open courtyard buildings (lots 9 and 10) make the transition to Viale Giotto with four-floor-high structures as in the adjacent lots 7 and 8. The architects reached an apex of urban effect in developing the long block XI as two parallel barres of apartments separated by a multi-level linear courtyard connected to the upper section with small staircases. A commanding corner building completes the project at its lowest point.

Multi-level pedestrian street between Via Bartolomeo Pinelli and Viale Giotto.

View of Piazza Sempione from the parvis of the church of Santi Angeli Custodi (Gustavo Giovannoni, 1922–1925). In the background from left to center, the mixed-use bloc containing a cinema and the Florentine-inspired Palazzo Pubblico with its curved arcade and body (Innocenzo Sabbatini, 1920–1927).

Aniene Garden City—Montesacro 1920–1940

The construction of the Città Giardino Aniene (Aniene Garden City) was part of the large-scale interventions promoted by the municipality of Rome and the national government to boost the building activity with the help of the Consolidated Law on economic and popular construction (1908). For Giovannoni, the urban plan of the Aniene Garden City—originally destined to house governmental employees as well as dependents of the Italian railroads—provided an exceptional opportunity to verify the theoretical principles that he had been defending as a member of the Associazione artistica tra i cultori di architettura (AACAr) and would develop in his treatise of 1931, "Vecchie città ed edilizia nuova" (Old Cities and New Buildings). About 5 kilometers from the historic center, the new town was planned next to the legendary area known as Monte Sacro—the Sacred Hill—located along the Via Nomentana to the north of the Aniene river, near the antique Ponte Nomentano and close to the tuff and pozzolana quarries of the area known as Tufello. In contrast with the geometric squares that have established the modern identity of the neighborhoods of Roma Capitale—the rectangles and circular forms that appeared in Esquiline, Prati, and Testaccio—Giovanni's design of Piazza Sempione, the civic heart of the garden city, reflected Camillo Sitte's lessons for a more organic approach to the open spaces.

Architects
Vincenzo Fasolo
Gustavo Giovannoni
Alessandro Limongelli
Gaetano Minnucci
Camillo Palmerini
Massimo Piacentini
Innocenzo Sabbatini

Camillo Sitte's Influence: Piazza Sempione

Considering the topography, Giovannoni resorted to a general plan that consisted of curvilinear streets, irregular squares, terminated views, and extensive landscapes—a combination that he saw as the only suitable means to give harmonious form to building groups when it is not possible to endow them with real architectural unity or when the topography does not allow for regular arrangements. The overall project was structured according to two main elements: first, the axis of entry to the garden city was dictated by the position of the new Tazio bridge over the Aniene and its prolongation along Corso Sempione to the Piazza Sempione, the heart of the new town. The second one was a large public park, now incorporated into the Aniene Nature Reserve. The overall street system incorporated a "ring road" that formed an irregular and curvilinear figure 8 pattern that followed the orography; a series of secondary streets branched from it. In plan and in three dimensions, Piazza Sempione emulates the concept of a medieval square. Two public buildings overlook the piazza and are visible from the two main entrances: the neo-Baroque church of Santi Angeli Custodi (1922–1925), designed by Giovannoni, terminates the axis from Corso Sempione, while the volume of the neo-medieval Palazzo Pubblico can be seen obliquely from Via Monte Subasio. Inspired by municipal buildings in Tuscany, Innocenzo Sabbatini conceived the Palazzo Pubblico as a curved volume symmetrically organized around a central tower capped by a cast-iron motif in the Borromini manner. A wide and curving arcade projects from the facade, thus providing space for a cinema and a civic terrace connecting the palazzo to the residential block on one side and to the church on the other. Except for the south side, occupied by the Energici block (named after its architect Alfredo Energici), all buildings around the square were designed by Sabbatini, who connected them by arcades or arcaded passages, thus creating a continuous front with various stylistic influences. The block he designed to link the Via Gargano to the Palazzo Pubblico is particularly remarkable, with its complex medieval skyline, the references to *architettura minore*, and the five arcaded windows on the first floor that face the square and indicate the presence of the Cinema Aniene and its large auditorium.

Giuseppe Vasi, *Ponte Nomentano*, engraving (1747–1761). The Ponte Nomentano, first erected around 100 A.C. and rebuilt several times, is a Roman bridge, which carried the Via Nomentana over the Aniene river. The bridge is noted for its two medieval towers (772–795) which served to protect this important northern approach to Rome.

Gustavo Giovannoni, Quadrio Pirani, Edmondo Del Bufalo, masterplan for the garden city of Monte Sacro, 1921. The curvilinear design adapts itself to the complex and hilly topography of the site.

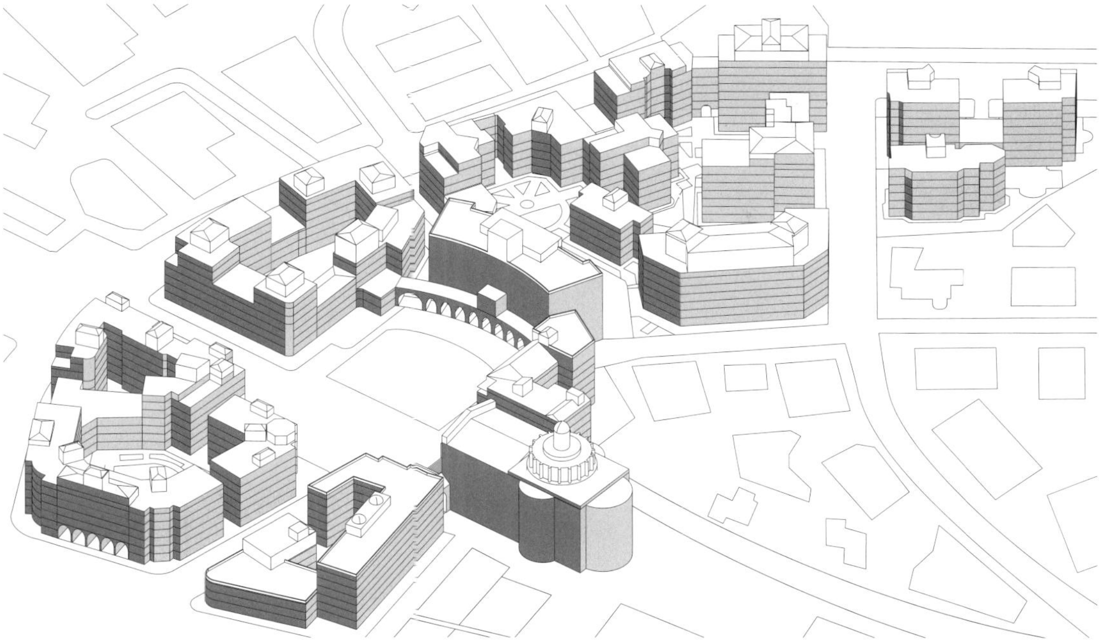

Axonometric of Piazza Sempione and surrouncing ICP housing blocks.

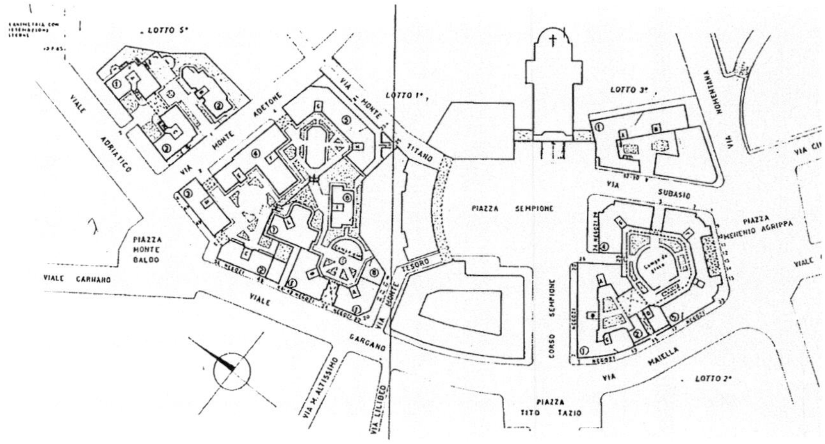

Innocenzo Sabbatini, et al. ICP apartment blocks around Piazza Sempione.

Piazza Sempione in construction, c. 1922. Piazza Sempione is taking shape at the heart of the original *villini* that made up the urban fabric until its transformation in the post-war era.

Typologically, Gustavo Giovannoni gave priority to the *villini* immersed in the greenery as the main building type, many of them designed by Camillo Palmerini. In this context, the vegetation along and between streets and buildings played a fundamental role. Designed by Raffaele De Vico, the Parco Caio Sicinio Belluto, Parco Simón Bolivar, and Parco Ponte Vecchio memorialize historic events such as the first workers strike recorded in history during the Republican era, the pledge of Simón Bolivar in 1825, and the antique Nomentana bridge. From 1924, the Istituto Case Popolari (ICP) initiated the construction of large housing groups organized around planted courtyards to accommodate a greater density of inhabitants. The management of the ICP entrusted the most qualified architects of the time with the apartment complexes. Among them were Innocenzo Sabbatini, Alessandro Limongelli, Massimo Piacentini, and Vincenzo Fasolo—a group which epitomizes the transition of Roman architecture from the Umbertine period inspired by Renaissance classicism to a stricter Rationalism, passing through the so-called *barocchetto*. As a result, the east side of the Via Gargano, beautifully landscaped in the French manner, is marked by a series of residential blocks, interconnected and organized around intimate gardens. Sabbatini and Palmerini were the principal designers. Along that organic axis, the modern elementary school known as Complesso Don Bosco (1931) projects its half-circular entrance loggia in triangle form by Viale Adriatico and Viale Carnaro. Further north along Viale Adriatico is the Casa della Gioventù Italiana del Littorio (Casa GIL), a significant Rationalist building of the 1930s Rome. Built by architect and engineer Gaetano Minnucci (1896–1980), it was originally dedicated to Fascist education and included a 650-seat theater, a gymnasium, and both open and covered swimming pools.

View of the church of Santi Angeli Custodi from the arcade of the Palazzo Pubblico.

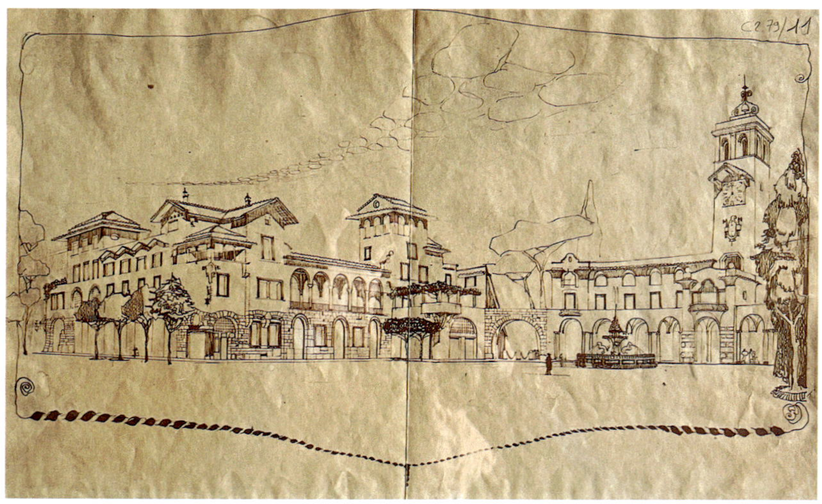

Gustavo Giovannoni, sketch for the design of Piazza Sempione, 1921.

Innocenzo Sabbatini, entrance gate for the ICP apartments at Piazza Monte Baldo.

Innocenzo Sabbatini, ICP apartments along Via Gargano (1921–1927). In the background, the modern elementary school Complesso Don Bosco (1931).

Contemporary aerial view of Piazza Sempione. Most of the original *villini* have been replaced by higher density *palazzine*.

Townscape of Piazza Sempione seen from the Parco Caio Sicinio Belluto. The park and the fountain were designed by Raffaele De Vico in the 1920s.

The 1950s residential boom that followed the Second World War radically changed the original low-density profile. Groupings of villas remain around Piazza Sempione and in the section north of Piazza Conca d'Oro, but overall, and particularly along the main streets, the high-density *palazzine* have replaced the *villini*. Piazza Sempione and the residential blocks that surround it have fortunately remained unchanged. However, Giovannoni did not plan nor anticipate how the heavy traffic of Via Nomentana would impact the square: the elegant steps that lead to the church entrance and to the terrace overlooking the piazza directly face the traffic. The elimination of the parking in front of the town hall and the widening of sidewalks was the first step, completed in 2023, toward making the piazza a more vital urban space.

Detail of an entrance gate within ICP complex, Via Gargano.

Gaetano Minnucci, Casa della Gioventù Monte Sacro, Viale Adriatico, 1934–1937. On the model of the Casa GIL in Trastevere, Minnucci's structure included a theater, a palestra with an open and covered swimming pool, a school of domestic economy, a library, and a daycare center.

Val Melaina, 1932–1943

In the early 1930s, under the impulse of Alberto Calza Bini, the Istituto per le Case Popolari succeeded in organizing large-scale building interventions in favor of the less affluent classes, in particular the excluded from the city center by the Fascist urban policies. Like at Donna Olimpia, the large innovative project of Val Melaina—on the small plateau north of Aniene Garden City known as Tufello—tackled the problem of hyper-economic housing by introducing it as a fundamental theme in the broader research on the form of the modern city. Built in the years 1932–1943, the ICP Val Melaina housing project was built as a super-block, (150 × 130 meters) consisting of a unitary complex of ten apartment buildings up to seven floors high arranged around four courtyards acting as gardens. With its continuous three-level base from which the housing floors emerge as rhythmically organized towers, the whole finds its direct inspiration in the projects known as Red Vienna, and particularly the 1927 Karl Marx Hof. In the vicinity, from 1940 and under the direction of architect Pietro Sforza, the ICP built the parallel rows of housing that Vittorio De Sica selected as a background to the emerging modern city in his *Bicycle Thieves* (1948).

Ufficio Tecnico ICP, housing group VI, Val Melaina, 1932–1943.

View of the ICP housing complex, Val Melaina.

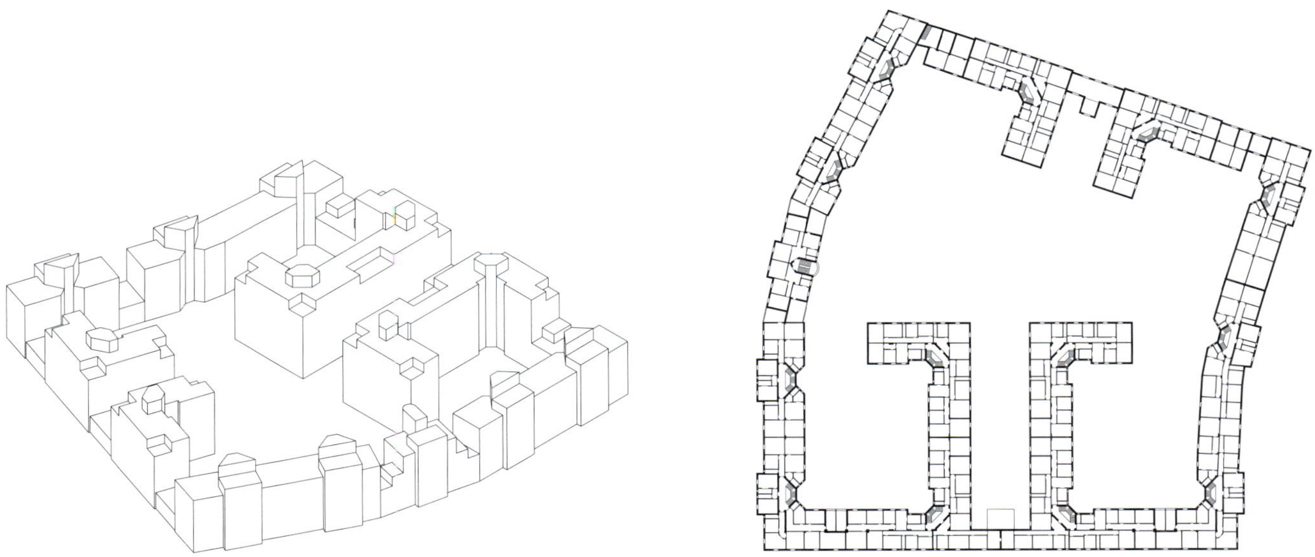

Ufficio Tecnico ICP, housing group VI. Axonometric massing and typical floor plan.

Giuseppe Battista Trotta. One of the two symmetrical arched buildings at Piazza Giuseppe Sapeto, 1925.

Garbatella Garden City 1920–1935

At Garbatella, Camillo Sitte-inspired sequences of urban spaces—streets winding up the hills with ever-changing vistas and blocks which are pierced by walkways, staircases, and terraces—are put to work with high social and political purposes, creating a familiar and welcoming place, originally for displaced Romans and rural immigrants. Streets and parks are packed with life, filled with children, family gatherings, growing vegetables, and places for commerce. It is a continuous spatial experience that every building, path, and garden contributes to. The basic unit of Garbatella is the semi-enclosed perimeter block, whose irregularity and typological organization was usually generated by topography. In its familiar references to the vernacular of the Lazio countryside, it is also continuous, both temporally and culturally. The ICP's favored architect was the incredibly versatile and talented Innocenzo Sabbatini. At Garbatella, he thoroughly mastered the rural vernacular and spiced it up with learned Roman references of all sorts—to Antiquity, the Renaissance, Borromini, even to Erich Mendelsohn and Futurism—rich and eclectic, but never pedantic. At the top of the hilly site, the picturesque meets Fascist *grandezza* in the great civic space of Piazza Damiano Sauli. The centerpiece is a wildly flamboyant middle school by Giovanni Brunetto, topped with a giant row of bronze eagles, and the monumental church by Alberto Calza Bini standing deferentially to the side. While older residents chat, sitting on the long benches, a monumental middle-school water fight is happening. People belong to Garbatella, and it belongs to them. (D.S.)

Architects
Alberto Calza Bini
Oriolo Casali
Costantino Costantini
Plinio Marconi
Giuseppe Nicolosi
Innocenzo Sabbatini
Giovan Battista Trotta

Innocenzo Sabbatini, entrance at La Garbatella from Piazza Benedetto Brin, 1921. The gate gives access to the first houses and the entire development of the garden city. An urban staircase connects it to the Ostiense area.

ICP plaque commemorating 90 years since the foundation of La Garbatella. It is located next to the staircase at Piazza Benedetto Brin.

The Città Giardino Garbatella was the largest residential project to be developed and managed by the ICP (Istituto delle Case Popolari, Roma) between 1920 and 1935. The first nucleus of the district, known as Borgata Garbatella, was designed by Gustavo Giovannoni and Massimo Piacentini (representative of the ICP and relative of Marcello Piacentini). Originally intended to service a new industrial zone and harbor on the southern section of the Tiber—later abandoned in the early 1920s—it was built between 1920 and 1922 on a hill overlooking the Tiber, Via Ostiense, and the railway line under construction between Rome and Ostia. Due to the topographic conditions, the urban layout offered a varied and picturesque ensemble according to different points of view. The heart of the project was Piazza Brin, a semi-enclosed urban space centered on a garden, a fountain, and connected to Ostiense and the river by a monumental staircase designed by Plinio Marconi. The U-shaped block serving as a gate to the piazza was the work of Innocenzo Sabbatini. Other buildings—half of the project was later demolished and replaced by an open park—were designed by Felice Nori and Camillo Palmerini.

The overall planning resulted from the intervention of many designers and the collaborative process was supervised by Gustavo Giovannoni. From 1923, a second nucleus developed east from Via della Garbatella (the limit of the first phase) toward Via Giovanni Ansaldo all the way to Piazza Randaccio and Piazza Masdea, both quite rural in appearance and architectural language. Typologically, these extensions, planned and in greater part designed by Plinio Marconi, were still characterized by low-rise and free-standing residential structures. In 1926, Marconi designed the first intensive block (lot VIII, 1923–1926, Via Luigi Fincati, Via Giovanni Ansaldo, Via Giuseppe Ferrari), made up of three attached and highly articulated apartment buildings with a large central garden and a characteristic curving facade across the future bathhouse. The Garbatella district further expanded to the east between 1925 and 1927, with the *quartieri per i baraccati* planned by Giovan Battista Trotta to house families evicted from Rome's city center or relocated from shacks at Ponte Milvio, Porta Metronia, and Ponte Lungo. The area formed a distorted lozenge bordered by two streets going down the hill, Via Roberto de Nobili and Viale Massaia. A bridge-like gate made up of two triangular blocks marked the scenographic entrance to the central street, Via Antonio Rubino, running down the *crinale* (ridge) to the spectacular and symmetrical belvedere of Piazza Giuseppe Sapeto. From there, a long pedestrian staircase led to the bottom of the hill and the *alberghi suburbani*.

Giovan Battista Trotta, intersection between Via Giovanni da Montecorvino (urban steps) and Via Roberto de Nobili.

Urban staircase, Via Scalabrini.

Giuseppe Nicolosi, Casa a scala, 1931. The apartment building, atypical in the panorama of Garbatella, resolves a strong difference in height by setting the facade back from the street to form a public space which gives access to the courtyard below. The symmetrical building surrounded by gardens is structured on two rotated axes and each stairwell serves four apartments per floor.

Sabbatini's Garbatella

Having created the initial entrance to Garbatella at Piazza Benedetto Brin in 1920, Innocenzo Sabbatini designed the first mixed-use public buildings at Piazza Bartolomeo Romano, and in doing so gave the new entrance to Garbatella (from the metro station built after World War II) a powerful identity, reflecting the history of the city from Antiquity to the modern. Although not really a square, the intersection of Via Enrico Cravero and Via Francesco Passino was exalted by the presence of the cinema-theater (1927–1929) whose half-circular convex theater literally projects into the urban space, as if emulating the form of the antique theater. To create an architectural and skyline-like background, Sabbatini stacked the six residential floors behind the theater, folding them in the form of a broken embrace, capped with a small temple on the roof. Elliptical in plan, the theater balconies and ceiling combine the Art Deco language of movement with an expressionist structure of intertwined concrete beams that outline a double-star figure. Closing the triangular block behind the theater, a series of elegant and at times idiosyncratic L- and U-shaped buildings by Camillo Palmerini (1929–1930) surround an inner circular garden.

On the other side of the street, Sabbatini's mixed-use bathhouse and apartment complex, built in the same years, marks an exceptional architectural response to a complex program and site situation. The basement and ground levels hosted the public baths, in use until the 1960s, with the shower block projecting at the back as a half-cylinder whose roof served as a water reservoir. The building's ground floor, covered entirely in exposed bricks, displays a curving cantilevering balcony, directly inspired by the Casa di Diana in Ostia Antica. Likewise, the three half-circular thermal windows prominently jutting out on the roof make an explicit reference to the Roman baths. Sabbatini completed the composition of the bathhouse's U-shaped structure with thin pedimented volumes seemingly embracing the bathhouse on each side; he also designed the five *palazzine* that wrap the block around a central garden.

Plinio Marconi, detail of a house on Piazza Masdea. The building makes a direct reference to rural house types in the Lazio.

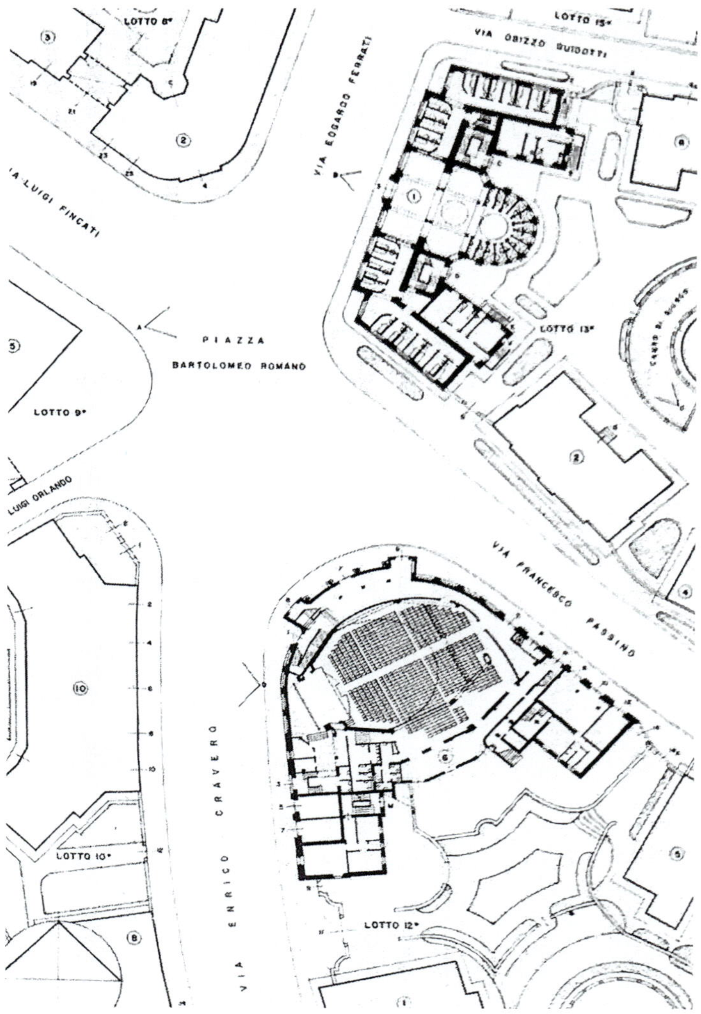

Plan of Piazza Bartolomeo Romano with ground floor plans of Sabbatini's bathhouse and cinema-theater.

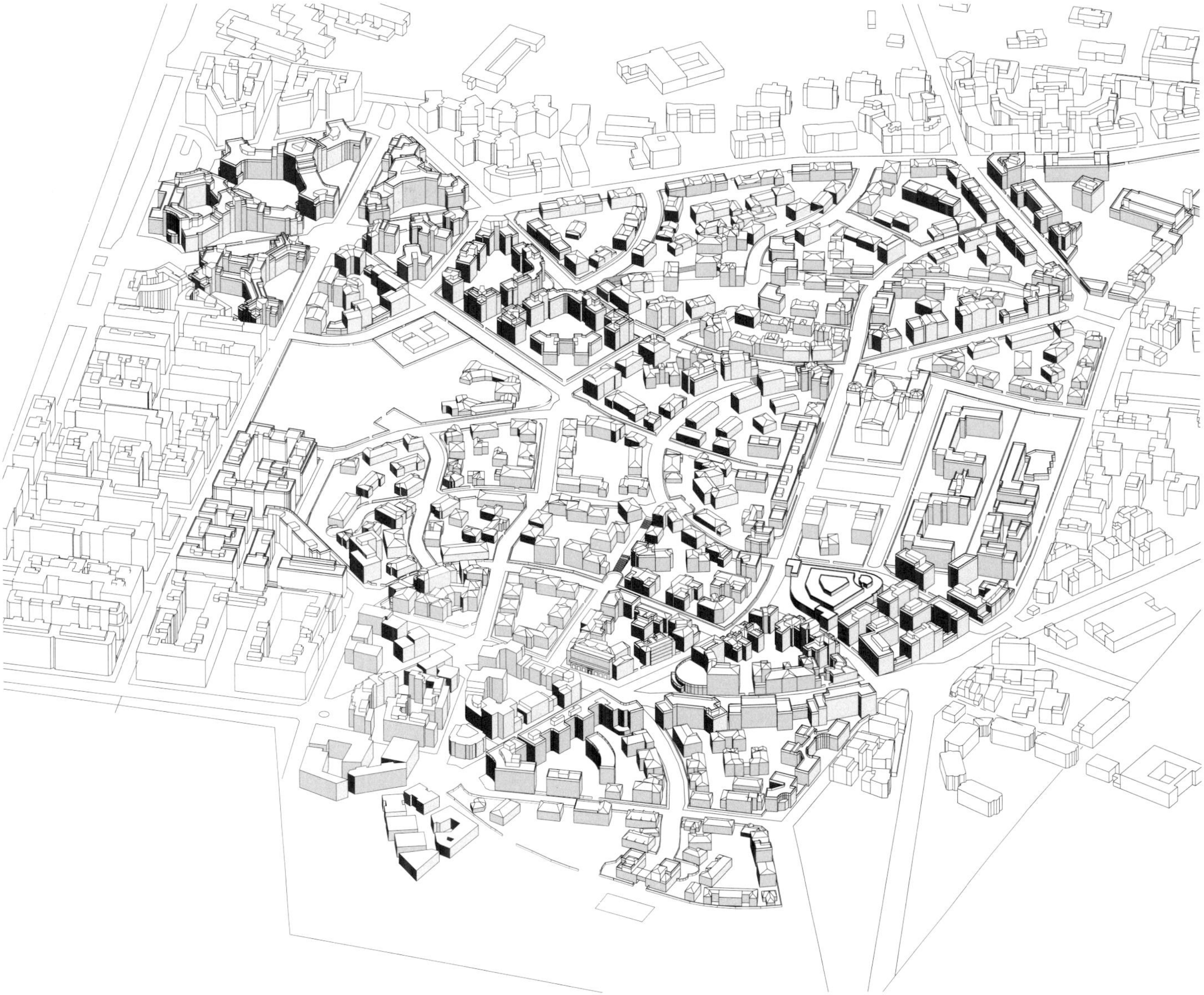

Axonometric view of La Garbatella. From the bottom center, in anticlockwise direction: the initial nucleus of the district generated from Piazza Benedetto Brin; the civic center with the baths and the theater; the covered market; the central plaza with the school, church, and shops; Piazza Sapero and the urban steps down to the *alberghi suburbani*.

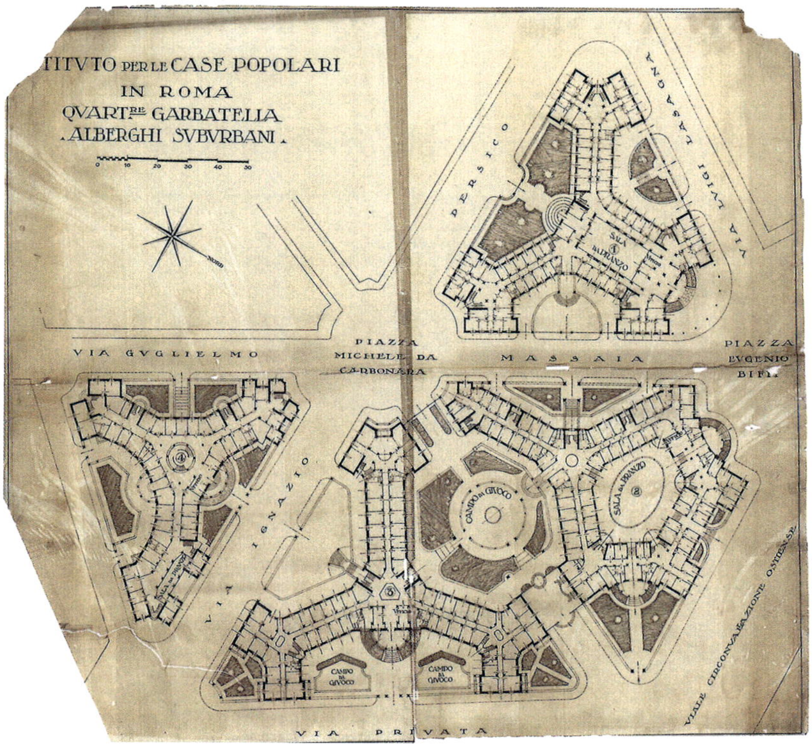

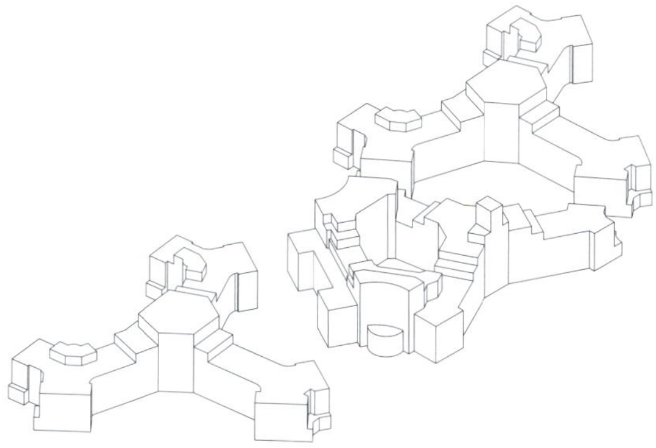

Alberghi suburbani, massing.

Innocenzo Sabbatini. Complex of *Alberghi suburbani,* plans of buildings, gardens, and public spaces, 1927.

Innocenzo Sabbatini, *Alberghi suburbani,* original elevation on Piazza Eugenio Biffi, 1927.

Innocenzo Sabbatini, Albergo Giallo, 1930. Facade on Via Francesco Orazio da Pennabilli.

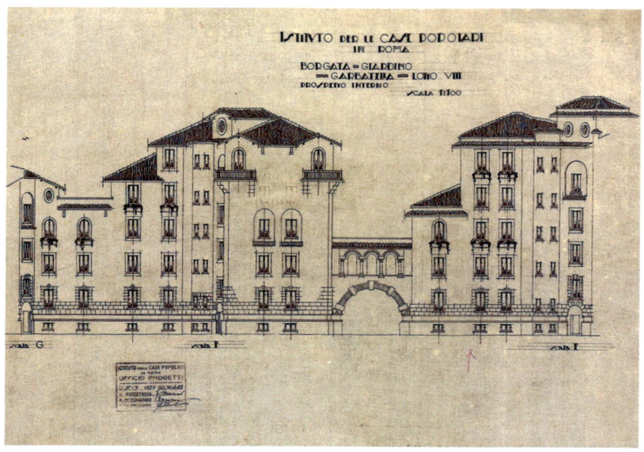

Plinio Marconi, facade of the first intensive block (lot VIII, defined by Via Luigi Fincati, Via Giovanni Ansaldo, Via Giuseppe Ferrari), 1926. The block is located opposite the former bathhouse by Innocenzo Sabbatini.

Innocenzo Sabbatini, Albergo suburbano, 1929. Angle: Via Ignazio Persico and Guglielmo Massala.

Innocenzo Sabbatini, Albergo Rosso, 1927–1930.

Between 1927 and 1929, Innocenzo Sabbatini was commissioned by the ICP to design the three *Alberghi suburbani* (red, white, yellow) located at the northern edge of the district and at the foot of the hill. The project consisted of three impressive Y-shaped apartment structures, articulated with each other and three new squares forming a triangle, Piazza Michele de Carbonara, Piazza Eugenio Biffi, and Piazza Giovanni de Lucca. The construction of these so-called *Alberghi suburbani* (suburban hotels) was requested to temporarily house more families displaced from the historic center following the demolitions in the 1920s. The complex experimented with a new building typology designed to deal with an emergency situation and differed considerably from the context due to its urban layout and peculiar architectural forms. The spectacular stairwells and terraces, located at the intersections between the different arms of the buildings, constitute hinges of the internal distribution routes that function as real corridor streets. The work formally refers to modern and Futurist precedents and contrasts with the picturesque and "rural" image of the previous phases of the garden city. These typologies were presented at the "First Exhibition of Rational Architecture" which was held in Rome in 1928. In 1929, the hotel houses underwent a very important transformation: the temporary accommodations of collective living—central dining hall, shared baths, shared kitchens—were modified and real single-family lodgings were created. First in Rome and in the ICP program, the *Alberghi suburbani* marked the passage from a traditional masonry construction to a new, mixed structure of reinforced concrete, perimeter walls in *tufo* stone, interior structures in reinforced concrete, and floors in wood.

The Third Phase

In response to the increasing population, the third phase of development focused on the public infrastructure, which was concentrated on the upper and flat section of the hill at Piazza Damiano Sauli. Here, the organic layout of the lower areas gave way to a geometric design, at the center of which stands the elementary school by Giovanni Brunetto, built in 1929–1930. The long, ribbon-like building was articulated in three sections, the central one recessed to mark the entrance, and capped by a tower and a wrought-iron cupola-like structure. To the left side of the square, the Church of San Francesco Saverio, dedicated in 1933, and designed by Alberto Calza Bini (President of the ICP until 1943) completed with clear classicist quotations the allusive dialogue between the new garden city and the historic city center. Its cupola is typically Roman and can be seen from any place in Garbatella. It certainly contributes, like all buildings on the plateau, to mend and complete the district, elevating the garden city to the status of a full-fledged urban environment, a city within the city. Facing the school on axis, the square is closed by the brick Rationalist building designed by Oriolo Casali, and completed in 1940. It forms a three-story-high backdrop and acts as a separation between the new social spaces and the lots occupied by the residential villas down the hill. A three-bay series of thick brick pillars and arches open in the direction of the daycare building, another graceful composition by Sabbatini located at Piazza dei Longobardi, whose double loggia—three Florentine arcades at ground level and the open gallery with six columns above—give it a delicate aura. Facing the square and noteworthy, the Rationalist two-house structure *casa a scala* by Giuseppe Nicolosi (lot 27, 1931) substantially added to the long experimental experience of the ICP, which began twenty years earlier with San Saba and Testaccio, causing the breakthrough of the modernist language in this pluri-typological and pluri-language experiment.

Giovanni Brunetto, Cesare Battisti primary school, Piazza Damiano Sauli, 1930–1933. Note that the two side wings were raised by one floor in 1937.

Alberto Calza Bini, Church of San Francesco Saverio, Piazza Damiano Sauli, 1931–1933.

Innocenzo Sabbatini. In the foreground, the *bagni pubblici* and apartments complex, 1927. In the background, the cinema-theater and apartments (now Palladium), 1927–1931.

Innocenzo Sabbatini, Cinema-theater with apartments, 1927–1929.

Oriolo Casali, mixed-use commercial and residential row building, closing Piazza Sauli. The arcades give access to the lower residential, 1938.

Identity and Density

The Sanjust di Teulada masterplan of 1909 provided for two main types of dwellings: apartment buildings (*fabricati*) and family villas (*villini*). In response to the lack of housing, the definition of building types was modified, and in 1920 a new law permitted the construction of detached multi-story buildings (*palazzine*) in place of the villas. These measures did not directly affect the settlement choices implemented in Garbatella, at least in the first phases of development. However, between 1926 and 1929, the *palazzine* started to appear, dramatically increasing the urban character of the neighborhood and largely contributing to the exceptional urban skyline of the district. The intention was to build a model modern district, capable of suggesting a modern city on a human scale. Therefore, although the general inspiration continued to be the English garden city, the evolution of the district between 1920 and the early 1930s aimed directly at increasing density. In effect, the combination of *villini*, full apartment blocks, *palazzine*, and inventively designed semi-public gardens and public spaces create a stylistically homogeneous combination of low and high density that makes Garbatella a unique example in the panorama of the international garden city. In addition to the aforementioned ICP, the Istituto Nazionale Case per gli Impiegati dello Stato (INCIS), Istituto Nazionale della Previdenza Sociale (INPS), Istituto Nazionale Assistenza Infortuni sul Lavoro (INAIL), Gestione INA-Casa, and Consorzio "Il Cantiere" were the main developers.

Typological analysis of La Garbatella.

View of Piazza Bologna.

Piazza Bologna 1920–1940

A few blocks north along the western edge of Viale XXI Aprile from Piazza Bologna rises a huge residential complex, known as Palazzo Federici (1931–1937). It reaches 11 stories, stepping down to five and six to match the neighboring *palazzine*. Faced with the constraints of a normal housing budget, Mario De Renzi chose to make the exterior a simple, lightly articulated, undecorated box in a tawny Roman ochre. The perimeter block is pierced by a series of large apertures, one of which bears the inscription "The 11th Year of Fascism," perhaps one of the reasons why Palazzo Federici is hard to find in history books or guidebooks. One passes through any of the apertures and arrives in a prodigious and staggering sequence of courtyards on two levels. The lower level is devoted to an automobile entrance and parking, neatly handled; the upper level is for pedestrians and communal open space. Around the courtyard is an elaboration of the normal *casa in linea* building type shared by most Roman neighborhoods. Around the perimeter of Palazzo Federici there is a beautifully detailed glass stair/elevator tower every other unit. All the apartments and the glazed stair landings face the court, making the high drama of the serial glass towers are a spectacular expression of the hopeful spirit of exhumed Futurism. One can practically hear the echoes of Filippo Marinetti's rants ringing in the courtyard and throughout this building. In addition to its architectural quality, the building is known for being the main location of Ettore Scola's film *A Special Day* (1977) starring Sophia Loren and Marcello Mastroianni. Uplifting. (D. S.)

Architects
Giorgio Guidi
Mario De Renzi
Innocenzo Sabbatini

Aerial view. From bottom left, clockwise: Casa del Sole and the ICP "green" district of Tiburtino II; Piazza Bologna; the German Academy in the park remaining from Villa Massimo, with the military structures across the street; top right, the Palazzo Federici.

The radial scheme of the Piazza Bologna neighborhood was first established in Edmondo Sanjust di Teulada's masterplan of 1909. The piazza was placed at the center of the district to be developed on both sides of the north–south axis Via Aprile XXI—Viale delle Province. The masterplan envisioned that the area between Via Nomentana and the remains of Villa Massimo—the Casino di Villa Ricotti and the new German Academy (1910–1914)—would be developed as a low-density area for the upper middle class. From a planning point of view, the objective was to preserve what was left of the large villas (Massimo, Torlonia, and Mirafiori) by creating a green buffer zone of luxury multi-story *villini*. For the other areas to be laid out around the piazza, Sanjust proposed a dense network of urban blocks (*fabbricati*, five to six floors high, like in the Mazzini, Flaminio, and Verbano neighborhoods), interspersed with a series of parks particularly along the railroad lines to the eastern edge. By the mid-1920s, early *palazzine* started to appear in the urban landscape, signaling the developers' and builders' demand for more density and profit, yet the piazza and the area to the east remained almost entirely unbuilt until the 1930s.

Innocenzo Sabbatini, Casa San Ippolito II or Casa del Sole, 1929–1930. (Plans and axonometric p. 90).

Innocenzo Sabbatini and Giorgio Guidi, gatehouses to Tiburtino II, Via Adalberto, 1926.

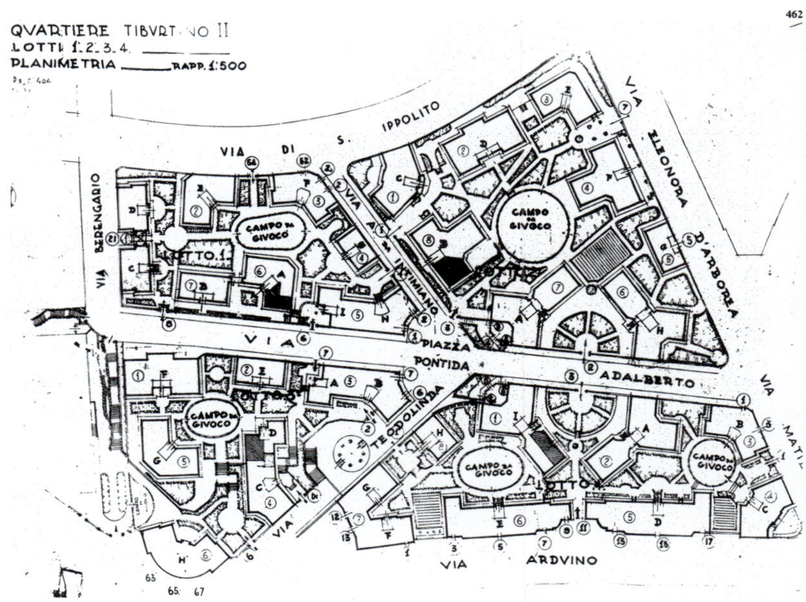

Innocenzo Sabbatini and Giorgio Guidi, masterplan of the ICP garden district Tiburtino II.

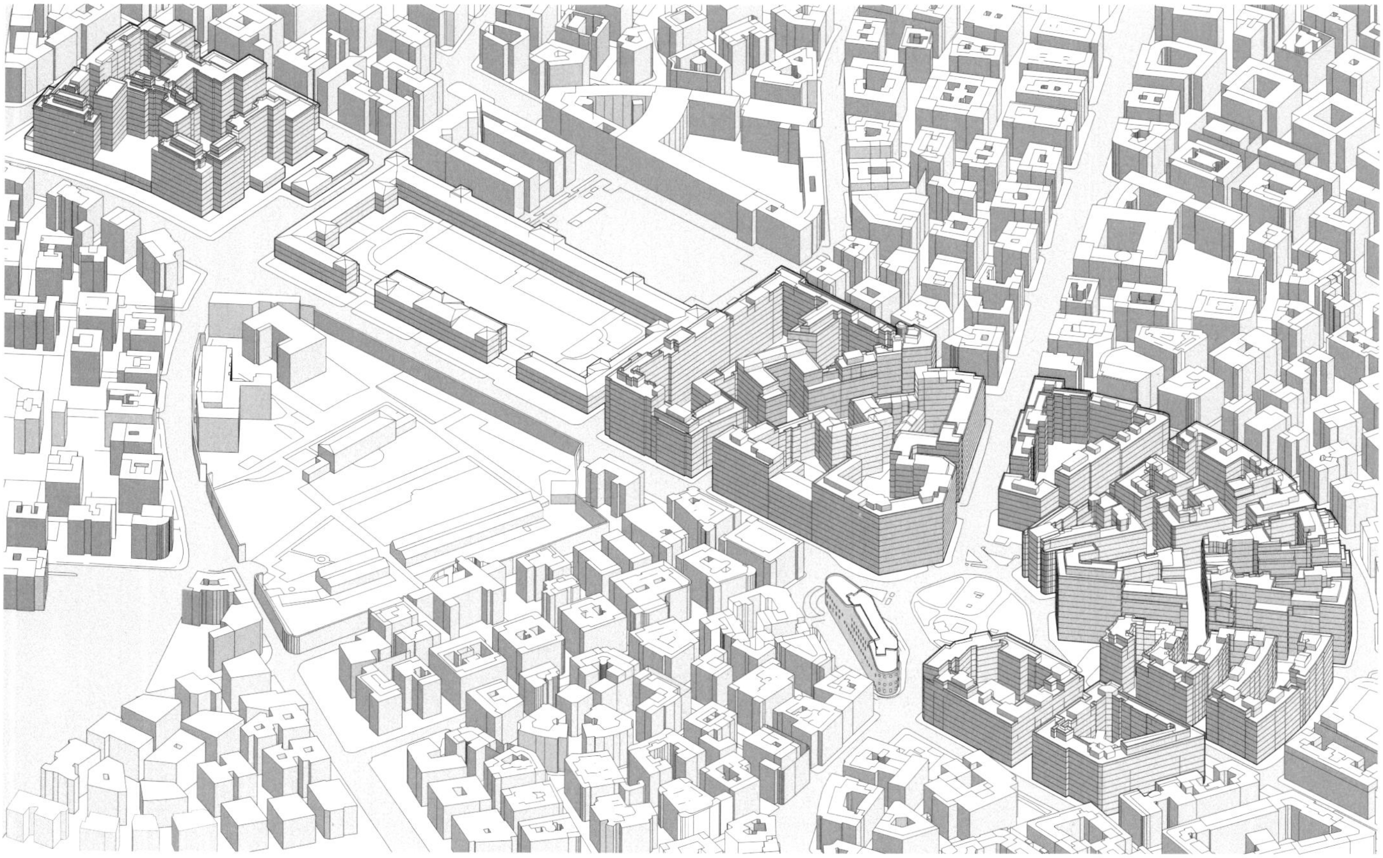

Axonometric view of the district. Piazza Bologna is to the right; Palazzo Federici to the top left.

ICP in the 1920s

At the same time, south of Piazza Bologna, at the intersection of Via Catania and Via della Lega Lombarda, the ICP embarked on a large-scale operation called Tiburtino II and designed by Innocenzo Sabbatini and Giorgio Guidi. Located in an area originally reserved for *villini* in the 1909 masterplan, but allocated to higher density in the revision of 1926, the complex consists of 28 buildings and 600 apartments. Completed in 1927, the largest of the two groups of small-scale *palazzine*, fully immersed in a green environment, were centered on the residential Piazza Pontida. The various apartment structures that face the square show a great degree of formal freedom and eventually create a memorable public space. The lowest and flattest section, along Via Arduino, is characterized by a series of strong and plastic facades, whose volumetry culminates with the semi-circular apartment house designed by Guidi.

Innocenzo Sabbatini built one of his most iconic housing projects along Via della Lega Lombarda (ICP San Ippolito II, 1929–1930). Exploiting the edges of the triangular block, he designed a symmetrical system that consists of a double structural body that runs on three sides around a central courtyard, also triangular. The terraced complex is known as the Casa del Sole, a name derived from the ingenious solution of decreasing the number of floors—from seven to two—toward the south to illuminate the small triangular courtyard. Containing 89 units, the Casa del Sole stands as a skillful meeting and mending point between two aesthetically opposite styles and typologies: on the eastern side, the small scale ICP complex; on the other side, the metropolitan image of intensive apartment structures that reach up to ten floors.

Figure-ground plan, with Piazza Bologna at the center.

Mario Ridolfi and Mario Fagiolo, post office, Piazza Bologna, 1933–1935.

View of the circular street around Piazza Bologna, Via Giacomo Boni.

Piacentini's Masterplan of 1931

In 1930 and to solve the dramatically increasing demand of housing for evicted families from the *centro storico*, the Governorate of Rome enacted a law which offered generous subsidies to private developers if they agreed on rent limitations and a public allocation process for tenants—the so-called *case convenzionate*. This trend accelerated the urbanization of large urban areas, as in the case of the Piazza Bologna district, where the INA (Istituto Nazionale Assicurazioni), the Società Generale Immobiliare (SGI), and the Federici company developed important real estate projects. This radical change in urban density coincided with the development of the new *Piano regolatore*, under the direction of Marcello Piacentini and approved in 1931. The plan did not deviate much from Sanjust's urban form but permitted a serious buildup in density by increasing the number of floors of the *fabbricati* (urban blocks) and replacing areas of *villini* with multi-family palazzine. Accordingly, the radial design of the neighborhood was maintained, with some changes in geometry such as the introduction of a semi-circular street around the piazza in the manner of Piazza Mazzini. Intensive buildings up to nine or ten floors were permitted around the Piazza Bologna and the major axes leading to the north and to the south. The implied change of scale was complemented by the introduction of a new architectural language, a streamline Moderne architecture characterized by projecting semi-circular or long horizontal balconies, terraces, and other architectural features. Those buildings contributed to establish a strong metropolitan image for the new axes and squares of the 1930s neighborhoods, around Piazza delle Provincie and the streets radiating from it such as Via Ravenna, Via Catania, and Via della Lega Lombarda.

Apartment structure from the 1930s at Largo S. Ipolito.

Apartment structure from the 1930s along Via della Lega Lombarda.

Courtyards of subsidized housing (*casa convenzionata*, architect unknown), Piazza Bologna, 1929.

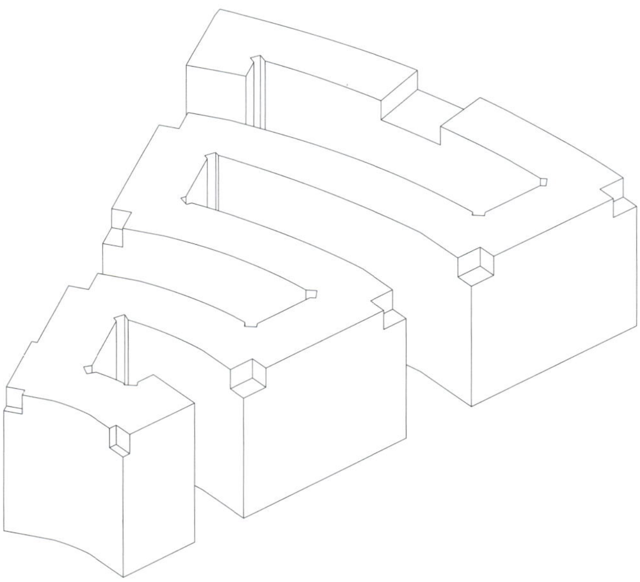

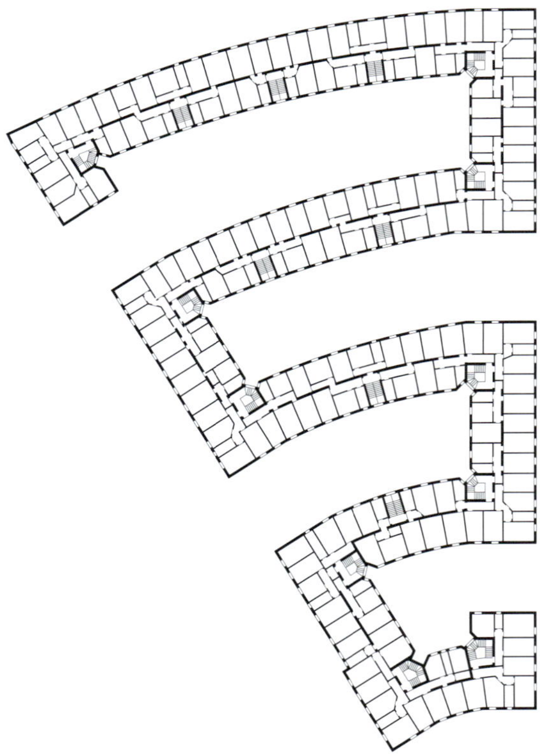

Typical plan and three-dimensional massing of subsidized housing (*casa convenzionata*, architect unknown), Piazza Bologna, 1929. The S-shaped structure is unique in the Roman urban landscape. Its length increases the number of units which are, mostly, cross-ventilated. The structure has 15 separate entrances, some from the streets—a primary and more formal entrance faces Piazza Bologna—and others from the open courtyards.

Superblocks

The first *casa convenzionata* was completed in 1929 (architect unknown) and has one main entrance facing Piazza Bologna. Occupying a trapezoidal block on a sloping terrain, the dense complex of apartments appears as a linear housing block, folded multiple times in a snake-like image to match the contours of the site. Four deep and slightly curved courtyards provide light to the apartments, which are for the most part cross-ventilated. However, the largest and most photogenic subsidized housing complex—the Palazzo Federici—was built 300 meters north of Piazza Bologna. Erected between 1931 and 1937 by Mario De Renzi, the superblock comprised 442 apartments, 70 shops, a garage, and a cinema for 1600 spectators, which was later transformed into a supermarket in 1968. De Renzi resolved the challenge of size, program, and circulation systems by choosing the path of the megastructure, evoking the Futurist designs of Antonio Sant'Elia by the way in which the various sections of the complex were connected by vertiginous towers clad in glass for staircases and elevators. With two apartments per floor, cross-ventilated and distributed from 28 vertical staircase towers, the Palazzo Federici was organized around two interconnected courtyards developed on two main levels. The facade treatment insists on verticality and, on the street, culminates in a sort of modern roof terrace, while the treatment of the surfaces is resolved in brick for the basement bands that contain shops and services, and plaster in the residential elevations. The original theater facing Via Aprile XXI was eventually converted into a supermarket.

By the mid-1930s, the neighborhood had started to take shape. Beyond the semicircular street, the dense fabric of three- to five-floor-high *palazzine* would eventually expand relentlessly down to the railroad lines without the park and green buffer reserved in both the masterplans of 1909 and 1931. In 1933, Mario Ridolfi won the competition for the Palazzo delle Poste at Piazza Bologna. Completed in 1935, the building deploys a continuous curtain wall of very thin marble slabs that skillfully hides the structure behind it and thus suggests a hybridization process of construction frame and masonry. In doing so, Ridolfi tries to combine tradition and modernity through the tension of the materials: the load-bearing skeleton and infill. In the context of the significant transformation that Rome underwent in the 1920s and 1930s, the Piazza Bologna district ranks between the wealthier area of Via Nomentana and a more popular area such as Via Tiburtina. It strongly identifies, starting from the synecdotic and aggregating presence of the homonymous square, as a large urban quarter, endowed with a very precise recognizability by Roman citizens.

Mario De Renzi, Palazzo Federici, 1936–1937, courtyard with double level for cars and pedestrians.

Mario De Renzi, Palazzo Federici, 1936–1937.

Mario De Renzi, Palazzo Federici, 1936–1937, courtyard view. Of particular interest are the Futurism-influenced vertical circulations.

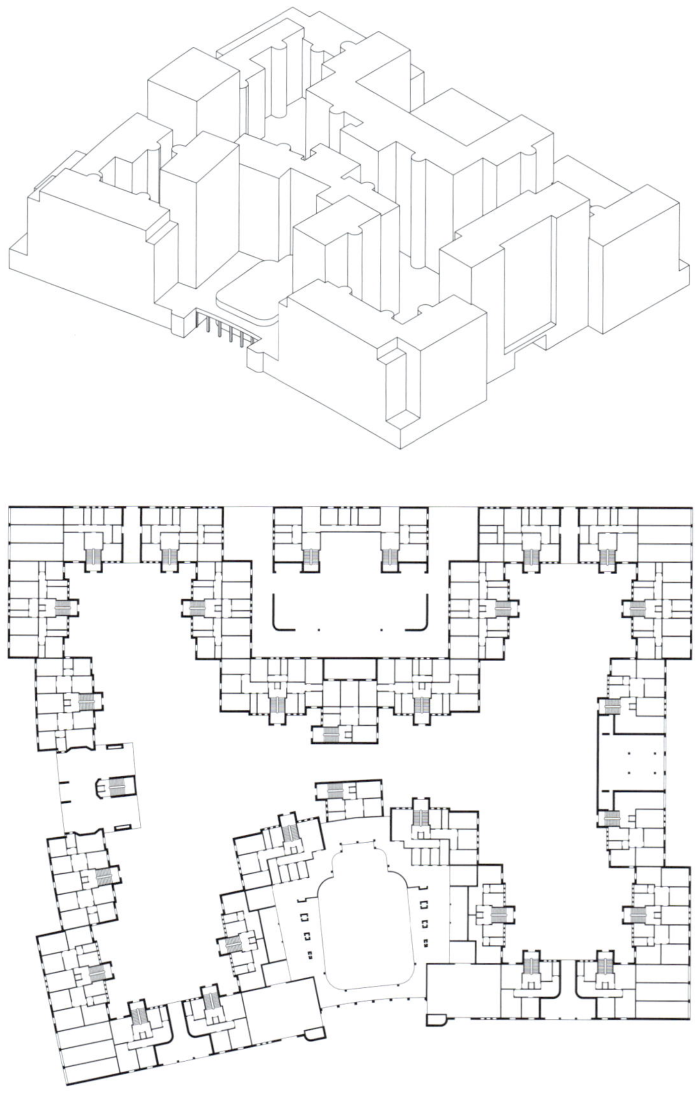

Mario De Renzi, Palazzo Federici. Typical floor plan and massing.

Mario De Renzi, Palazzo Federici, 1936–1937, view from a side street.

View of Piazza Mincio and Via Doria from the Fontana delle Rane (1924).

Piazza Mincio 1917–1927 Piazza Verbano 1924–1931

Two squares, two neighborhoods, two architects, a couple of blocks apart. Gino Coppedè at Piazza Mincio, Quadrio Pirani at Piazza Verbano. Both places are part of the larger Quartiere Trieste. Born in Florence, Gino Coppedè developed his love of decoration in the workshop of his father, who was a woodcarver. There and in Genova, Gino and his brothers learned to carve intricate figures to adorn the homes of the bourgeoisie. The rewards of this apprenticeship would be reaped in full in a small corner of Rome, where architecture, sculpture, painting, ceramics, ironwork merged into a genuine, most unexpected *Gesamtkunstwerk* (total work of art). Quadrio Ferruccio Pirani's father was a master builder in Jesi and from him the young man learns the secrets of craft, cultivating in daily practice the love for the uncontaminated strength of the artisanal tradition. Steeped in the Reformist Socialist party, he fused his ideological drive with technical rigor, bringing a new expressive richness to Roman architecture. In the districts of San Saba, Mazzini, and here around Piazza Verbano, the lessons of this underappreciated master constitute an irreplaceable point of reference in the evolution of Roman language architecture of the 20th century.

Architects

Dario Barbieri
Gino Coppedè
Quadrio Pirani

Quartiere Coppedè

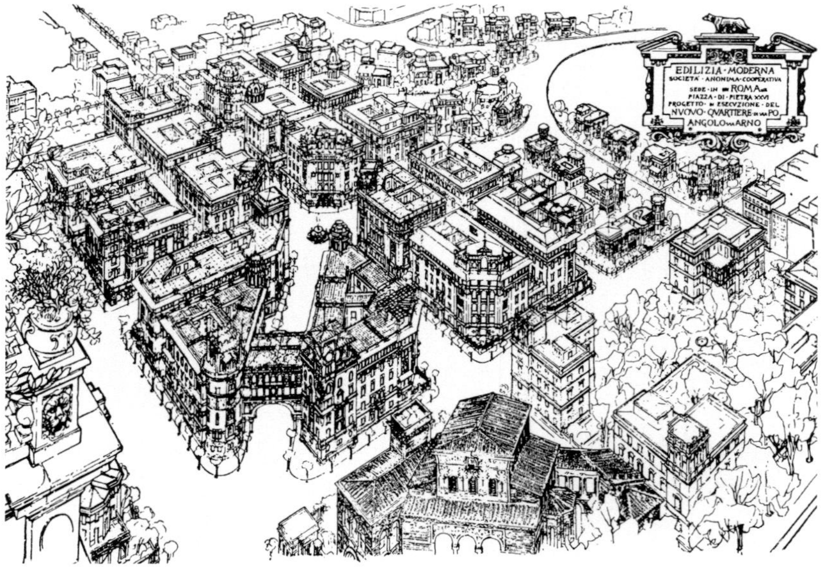

Gino Coppedè. Original residential project for the Quartiere, 1916. The blocks, called Palazzo degli Ambasciatori, were built along the diagonal and connected by a bridge while two blocks face the Piazza Mincio and its central Fontana delle Rane (Fountain of the Frogs).

The area known as Quartiere Dora (or Coppedè from the name of its architect) and the adjacent Quartiere Verbano were first outlined in Sanjust di Teulada's 1909 masterplan and consisted of a slightly bent grid of blocks (five blocks northwest-southeast by nine blocks northeast-southwest) with a circular square—the future Piazza Verbano—at its heart. The plan implied the demolition and subdivision of Villa Lancellotti adjacent to Via Salaria and Villa Ada (now a huge public park). In 1916, the Società Anonima Cooperativa Edilizia Moderna purchased a large section of the lower part of the site in proximity to Piazza Buenos Aires (formerly Piazza Trasimeno). Commissioned to the Florentine architect Gino Coppedè (1866–1927), the residential project consisted of 18 apartment structures and 27 *villini*. Interrupted by World War I and significantly reduced in scope, Coppedè's final project resulted in one of the most idiosyncratic urban and artistic-architectural experiments of the early *Novecento* (1917–1927). Urbanistically, Coppedè's decision to create a small diagonal street leading to a square, Piazza Mincio, defined by chamfrain corners and centered on a superb circular fountain—Fontana delle Rane (Fountain of the Frogs)—reflected the lessons of Camillo Sitte and Gustavo Giovannoni to emulate the medieval urban space adapted to contemporary dimensions. Architecturally, it marked the late triumph of eclecticism, mixing neo-Gothic, Art Nouveau, Stile Liberty, Baroque, and even modern elements. The entrance section is made up of two triangular buildings (called Palazzi degli Ambasciatori, 1915–1921) divided by the diagonal Via Dora and connected by a multi-story bridge supported by a dramatic arch. Towers, projecting eaves, Baroque pediments, giant cherubims and athletes create a vertiginous effect that renews itself at every step. Facing the square is the Palazzo del Ragno (Palace of the Spider) which takes its name from its giant door marked by a gilded spider on a black background. The image represents the work of mankind through the praise of the industrious spider and the work of the architect, as can be seen on the third level where a sgraffito-like painting depicts a knight between two griffins with the word "Labor." The facade of the building bears a declaration of intent by Coppedè: *Artis praecepta recentis/maiorum exempla extendo* (I represent the precepts of modern art through the examples of the ancients). The last palazzo on the square (unnamed) is equally chamfered and plastically the most developed, with a neo-Romanesque entrance arch and four idiosyncratic residential floors—the last one with two projecting half-circular balconies—corbelled over the two-story base. The structure is capped with a three-arch open loggia. The Florentine Villino delle Fate and its garden completes the square. Its facades and perimeter walls are accentuated by irregular arcades, arches and semi-arches, stairways, and canopies. The materials used include marble, travertine, brick, glazed terracotta, glass, and masterful wrought-iron works.

Piazza Mincio
Piazza Verbano

Gino Coppedè, detail of the facade of the Palazzo del Ragno (Palazzo of the Spider), 1926.

Gino Coppedè, Palazzo on Piazza Mincio, detail of the entrance, 1926.

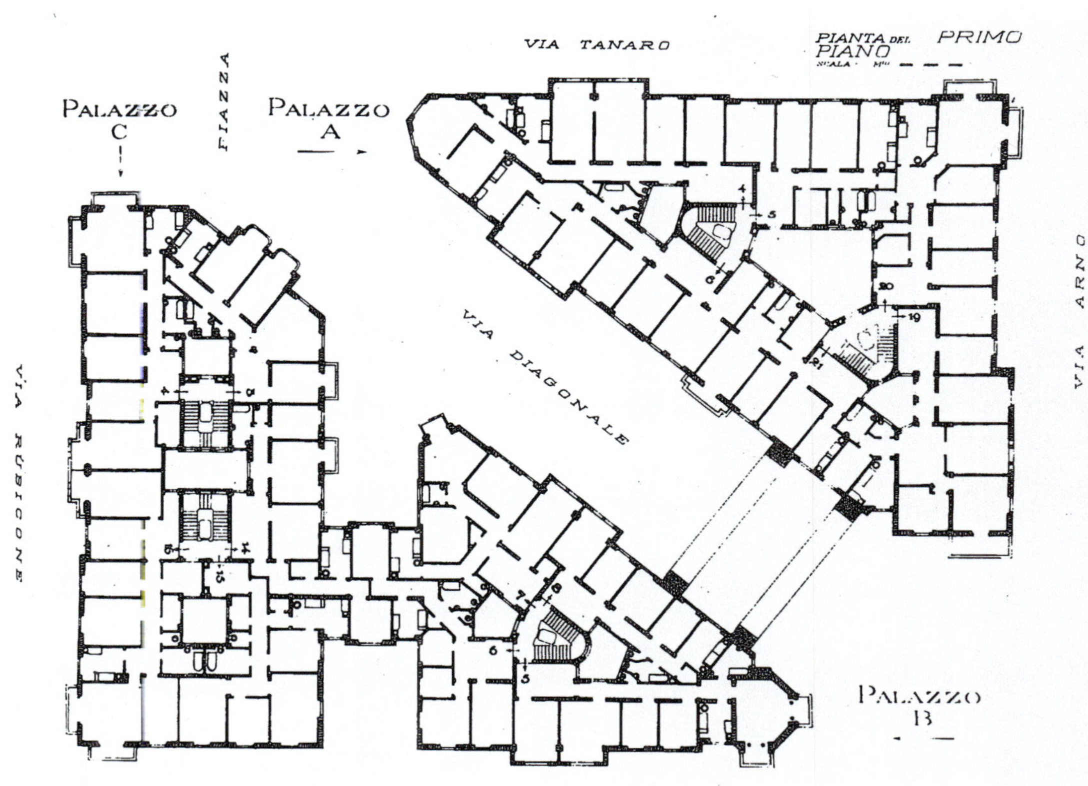

Gino Coppedè. Detailed plan of Palazzo degli Ambasciatori, Quartiere Dora. Missing on the plan are the three blocks completing Piazza Mincio.

Piazza Verbano: Masterwork of Dario Barbieri and Quadrio Pirani

At the opposite end of the neighborhood projected by Sanjust di Teulada, it was only in 1924 that the INCIS (National Institute for Employee Homes of the State) launched a vast program of 2000 apartments to house about 10,000 middle- and high-income state employees. Engineer Dario Barbieri oversaw the entire project according to the design and layout of the 1909 masterplan, albeit with slight modifications. The operation took place between 1924 and 1931 and led to the construction of a genuine and unitarian neighborhood consisting of three interconnected parts. The first section comprises a group of four identical buildings (in site plan but with different facades) whose arrangement outlines the octagon of Piazza Verbano with the circular garden in its center. Designed by Quadrio Pirani in collaboration with Barbieri in a conservative classical manner, they are five- or six-floors high with wavy facades, enriched with cornices, balconies, and built around richly planted triangular gardens. South of the square, a grid of nine blocks with large interior gardens is structured along the perpendicular axes of Via Tagliamento and Via Chiana. Quadrio Pirani was equally in charge and all apartment buildings are mostly five stories with most services and shops lined up along Via Tagliamento. Here, Pirani produced one of the most successful residential ensembles of modern Rome. His architecture is quite remarkable and displays with stunning invention, a combination of stone bases, brick and plaster sections, elegant ironwork, shifting planes accentuated with projecting and recessed balconies of all dimensions and styles, and a sophisticated system of interior passages across gardens. As in the Mazzini district, Pirani capped most structures with deep projecting eaves that protect floral decorative panels which are reminiscent of Otto Wagner's apartments in Vienna. The third part of the district is made up of open blocks with *palazzine* of various sizes and styles. Adjacent to Corso Trieste and particularly remarkable is the group of four U-shaped structures set up around a garden adjoining Corso Trieste and attributed to Dario Barbieri.

Quadrio Pirani, INCIS blocks around Piazza Verbano, 1924–1931.

Axonometric view of the Verbano area within Quartiere Trieste. The marked blocks indicate the extent of the INCIS housing program designed by Dario Barbieri and Quadrio Pirani, 1924–1931. Also visible to the right is the INCIS four-block complex on Corso Trieste by Dario Barbieri, 1929. Top left is the public park of Villa Ada.

Figure-ground plan. In the upper right, the octagon of Piazza Verbano; in the bottom right, next to the square Piazza Buenos Aires, Piazza Mincio.

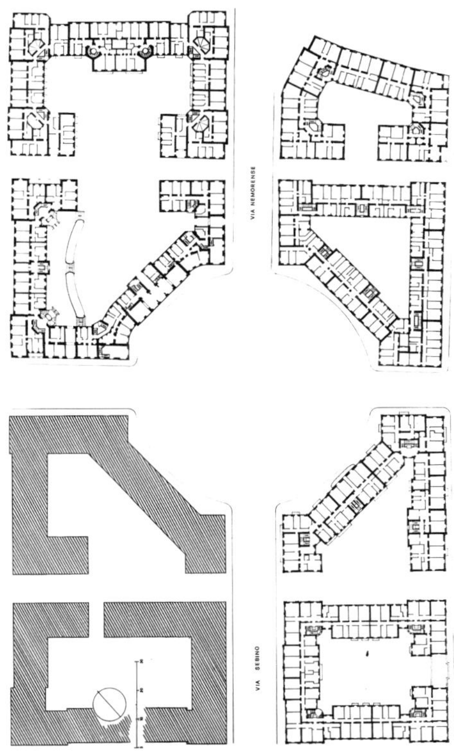

Quadrio Pirani, typical floor plans of the INCIS blocks around Piazza Verbano.

INCIS buildings along Via Tagliamento.

INCIS complex Corso Trieste and Piazza Ledro, inner garden.

INCIS complex Corso Trieste and Piazza Ledro, entrance passage.

The general layout of the project—while following a traditional but somewhat loose checkerboard system—managed to reconnect with the former natural state of the site: most streets are tree-lined; from Via Salaria to Corso Trieste, Via Chiana occupies the part of the avenue that, lined with dark holm oaks, formerly structured the garden of Villa Lancellotti; and finally, there is the extensive park of Villa Ada (Villa Savoia), the remainder of Villa Lancellotti, and the new Parco Nemorense inaugurated in 1930 and based on the design of Raffaele De Vico. The differentiation of the urban fabric along a single topographical axis—the route that starts Via Tagliamento in the Dora district, continues with Via Sebino, Piazza Verbano, Via Nemorense, and ends with the park—is the greatest value of the neighborhood.

Dario Barbieri, INCIS complex Corso Trieste and Piazza Ledro, 1929. Facade on Piazza Ledro. The complex is made up of four buildings, each facing the inner garden diagonally.

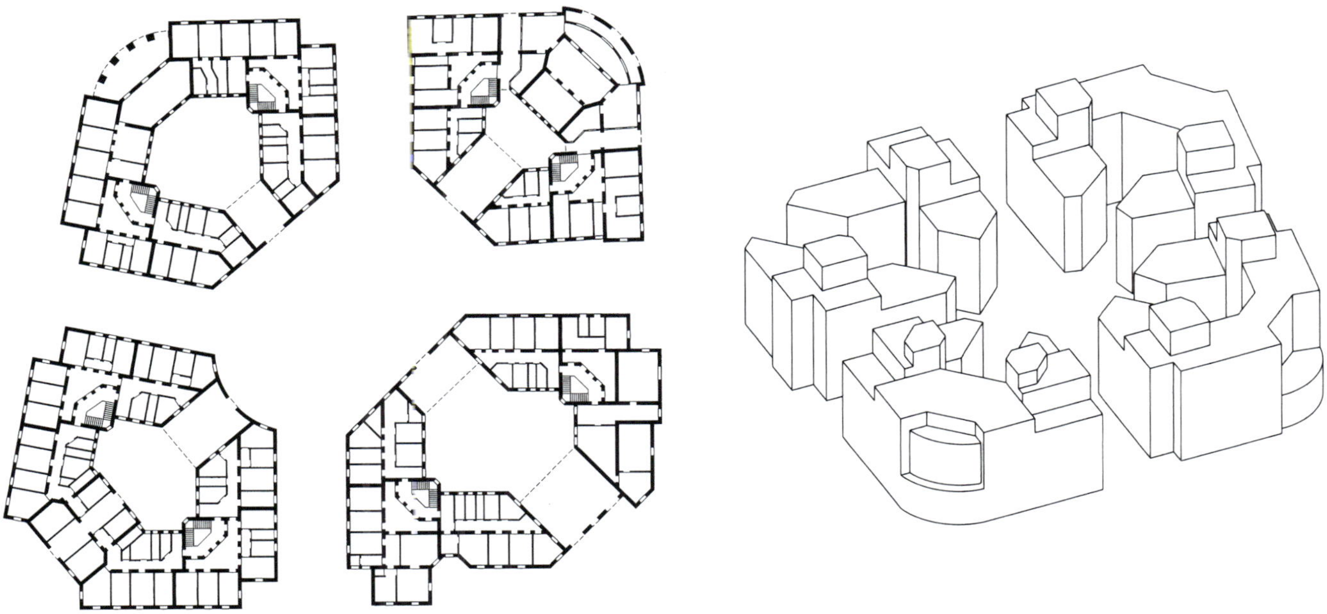

Dario Barbieri, INCIS complex, Corso Trieste. Typical plan and axonometric view.

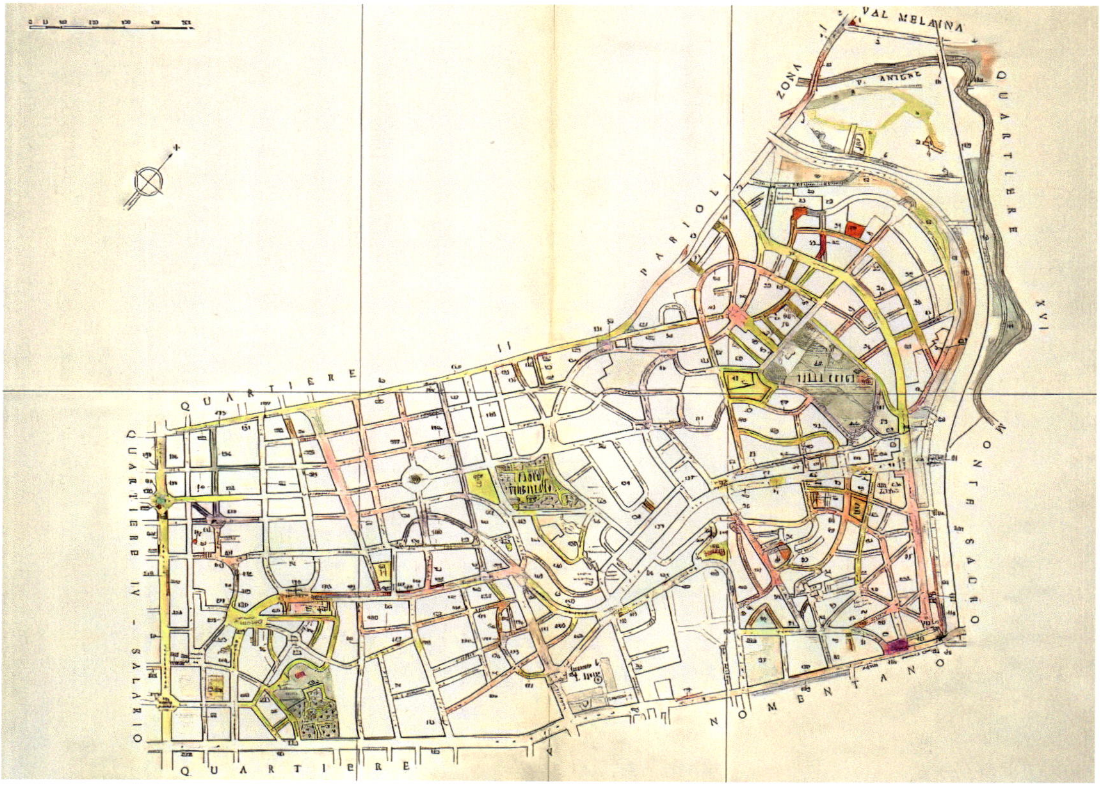

Overall plan of the Quartiere Trieste. The Piazza Mincio and Piazza Verbano can be seen in the upper left. The sinuous Corso Trieste structures the entire area in relation with its complex topography. The post-war quarters around Piazza Vescovo and Parco Villa Chigi were developed using the *palazzina* typology as a mediator between landscape, hilly topography, and modernity.

Corso Trieste, in the area of Piazza Verbano.

Quartiere Trieste

Following the completion of the Dora and Verbano projects, a new urban district was officially introduced in 1926 as Quartiere Savoia (from the former name of Villa Ada) and renamed Quartiere Trieste 20 years later. Up until the end of the war, construction continued in the district with an emphasis on Corso Trieste, the sinuous and central boulevard that runs from Via Nomentana to Piazza Annibaliano and the Aniene river to the north. The construction of the quarter employed various quality residential typologies, chiefly villas and elegant apartment blocks with interior gardens. After the Second World War, the quarters around Piazza Vescovio and Parco della Villa Chigi were rapidly developed, deploying the *palazzina* typology to mediate the complex and hilly topography with the rise of a new concept of modernity among the bourgeois classes. Thus arose the areas of Piazza Vescovio and the so-called Quartiere Africano—the names of its main streets and arteries were, from the 1920s, selected to celebrate the Italian colonies in Africa, like the Viali Eritrea, Libia, Etiopia, and Somalia.

Street intersection at Via Chiana and Via Volsinino. Quadrio Pirani, INCIS buildings, 1920s.

Placed diagonally from Pirani's INCIS building, a Rationalist Art Deco building from the 1930s provides a contrast.

View of Piazza di Donna Olimpia. At the center, the head part of the Pamphili II complex.

Monteverde Vecchio
Donna Olimpia
1926–1938

Most of the buildings in Monteverde Vecchio are *palazzine*—free-standing structures with four facades and limited to 19 meters in height—decently designed and generally well-built. Both neighborhoods contain important works by architects of distinction. They are not very different from what is around them—just better, with layers of subtle refinement their neighbors lack. The *palazzina* is a noteworthy invention that reconciles a fundamental conflict of the modern city: the urban street wall that defines the street as a public place and the modernist tenets of abundant daylight for everyone. Parioli, Monteverde, and other parts of Rome like Piazza Bologna make use of the *palazzina* type to accomplish this synthesis. But Monteverde Vecchio has other qualities that make it an urban design textbook. First, it is a good size neighborhood—about 20 minutes' walk north–south and a five- or ten-minute walk east–west. Further more, it is surrounded by great parks—the huge property of the Doria Pamphili, made a municipal park in 1965–1971 and to the east, the former Villa Sciarra, donated to Mussolini and the Italian state in 1932. Thanks to its loose grid, Monteverde Vecchio is studded throughout with small shops, bars, restaurants, churches, and schools. Street life is everywhere, it is a great place to live, even if the public transport is deficient at best. At the southern end of Monteverde Vecchio starts Monteverde Nuovo which adds to its post-World War II modern *palazzine* a fascinating layering of urban and social history: the Donna Olimpia ICP complex designed by Innocenzo Sabbatini, Innocenzo Costantini, and Pietro Sforza in the 1930s. Those blocks are decidedly modern and reveal the imprint of Italian Futurism and German Expressionism, particularly Erich Mendelsohn. Due to its height, the Futurist skyline, and the compactness of the groups of buildings, the development was soon nicknamed *grattacieli di Monteverde* ("skyscrapers" of Monteverde)—a popular district next to which Pier Paolo Pasolini lived for a couple of years and where he set his novel *Ragazzi di Vita* (1955). (D.S.)

Architects

Alberto Calza Bini
Innocenzo Costantini
Fernando Malgarini
Innocenzo Sabbatini
Pietro Sforza
Giovan Battista Trotta

The 1909 masterplan by Edmondo Sanjust di Teulada opened the way to a radical transformation of Monteverde, a scarcely populated landscape, and place of historical and naturalistic importance, which until the beginning of the century appeared as a green *tufo* hill crossed by old rural roads and marked by a series of small valleys or depressions that at times created insufficient connections within the area. Starting from 1910, the housing cooperatives and private developers provided quality accommodation for the working class, the civil servants, and the middle-class families—the latter in the many Art Nouveau- and Art Deco-style villas. Given the complex topography, the masterplan focused on a loose gridded *urban* figure with four diagonals converging to a rectangular square straddling the rectilinear axis of the Via Giacinto Carini. By the 1920s the areas intended for villas were rezoned to permit the higher density type of the *palazzina*, well adapted to the changing conditions of the terrain. The 1931 masterplan by Marcello Piacentini further extended the district by tracing a mostly curvilinear urban network that overall, respected the topographical lines and made the *palazzina* type the exclusive typology.

Between 1926 and 1929, the first public housing district (ICP) called San Pancrazio—for its proximity to the gate Porta San Pancrazio—was established along the northern section of Viale dei Quattro Venti at the edge of the Gianicolo. It consisted of three urban blocks on both sides of the avenue. The western one, lot II (Viale dei Quattro Venti, Via Alessandro Algardi, Via Basilio Bricci, Via Francesco Bolognesi) was designed for the ICP by Innocenzo Sabbatini in collaboration with Giovan Battista Trotta and Fernando Malgarini. It is a beautiful urban and architectural project, made up of eight *palazzine* organized symmetrically on both sides of a green axis joining the entry gates. The complex develops around a luxuriant terraced garden with tall trees and a pond at the center. On the other side of the avenue, the INCIS built two blocks of *palazzine* (Via dei Regnoli, Via dei Bolognesi, Via Guastalla) for the employees of the Ministry of Education and Justice. Here again, as in the block adjacent to the north side of Via dei Regnoli, all the buildings, designed by Alberto Calza Bini, were articulated with densely planted courtyards and gardens.

Alberto Calza Bini. INCIS block at the intersection of Viale dei Quattro Venti and Via Oreste Regnoli.

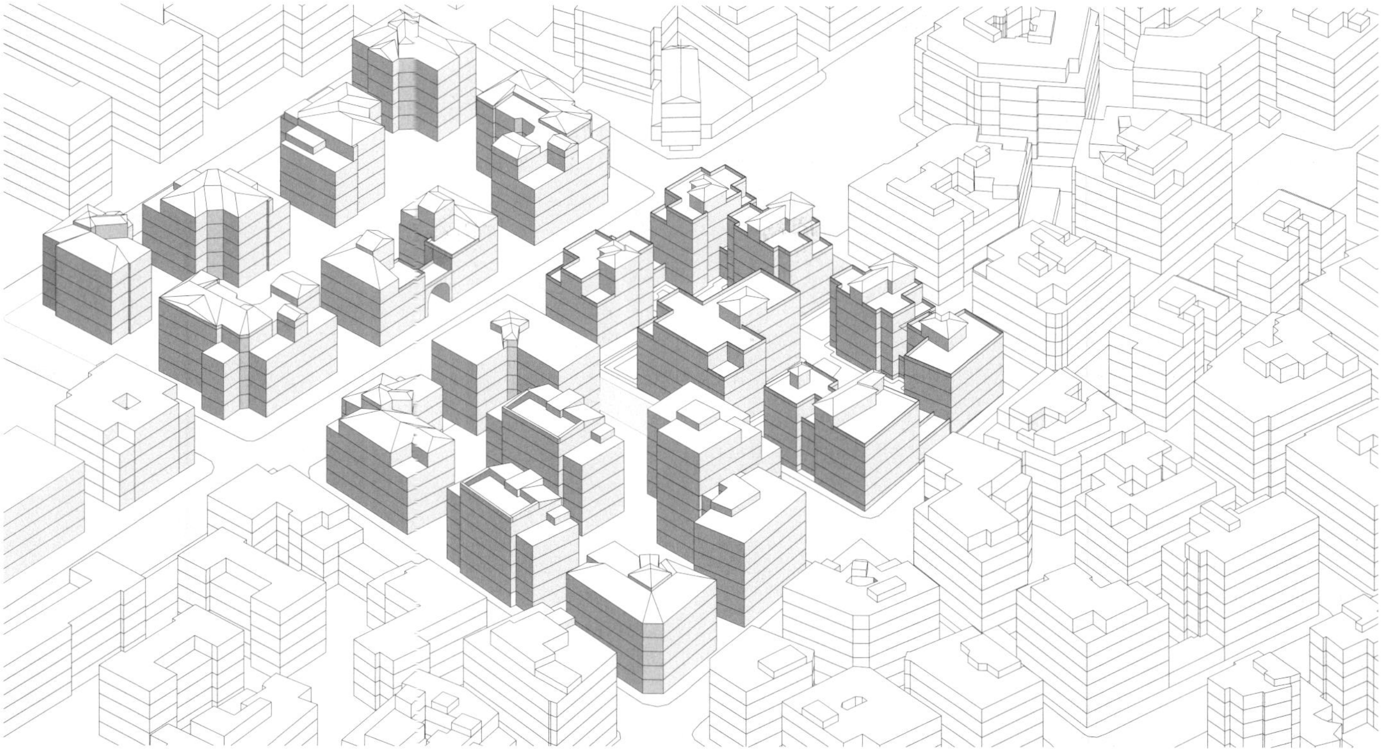

Axonometric view of the three ICP San Pancrazio blocks in Monteverde Vecchio on both sides of Viale dei Quattro Venti. Block at the top left: Innocenzo Sabbatini, Giovan Battista Trotta, and Fernando Malgarini (1926–1929). Opposite: Alberto Calza Bini. Two INCIS blocks at Viale dei Quattro Venti, Via Fratelli Bonnet, Via del Vascello and Via Oreste Regnoli, 1926–1929.

Aerial view of the three ICP San Pancrazio blocks on both sides of Viale dei Quattro Venti.

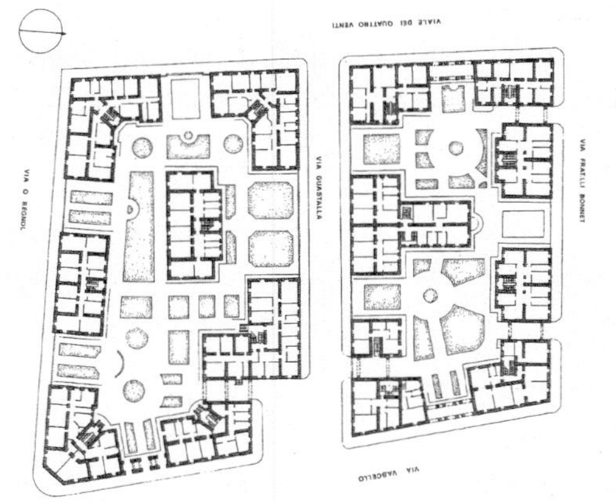

Alberto Calza Bini. Plans for the two INCIS blocks at Viale dei Quattro Venti, Via Fratelli Bonnet, Via del Vascello, and Via Oreste Regnoli, 1926–1929.

The *grattacieli di Monteverde*

During the 1930s, the Fascist regime accelerated its program of demolition in the historic center and many residents were forced to leave and relocate to low-density ICP *borgate* far from the city. At the same time, under the guidance of Alberto Calza Bini, the ICP built a series of high-density superblocks that quickly became genuine monuments to a Fascist vision of the working class that was paradoxically not fundamentally different from that of the socialist Vienna. It is within this context that the Donna Olimpia ICP campus rose in the early 1930s amid the and quasi-rural context. The entire compound was made up of three super-blocks, which are separated by two descending streets, Via Federico Ozanam and Via Paola Falconieri, that converge downhill to form the Piazza di Donna Olimpia. All together, they are classified under the names Pamphili I and Pamphili II. The Pamphili I complex is attributed to Innocenzo Sabbatini; the Pamphili II project to Innocenzo Costantini (son of Costantino Costantini and relative of Sabbatini) and Pietro Sforza.[1] The sections were built between 1932 and 1938, and the entire intervention was coordinated by the ICP Technical Office directed by Costantino Costantini. The first phase (Pamphili I) consists of a super-block symmetrically arranged along Via di Donna Olimpia. A central garden, opening onto the street is framed by two landscaped blocks rising from seven to nine stories. The overall volumetry of the blocks—deploying multiple setbacks and sections of various heights to create spectacular terraces and balconies—is part of Innocenzo Sabbatini's housing grammar as implemented earlier at Trionfale and Piazza Mazzini.

1 In the only monograph on Sabbatini—Bruno Regni, *Innocenzo Sabbatini. Architetture tra tradizione e rinnovamento* (Rome: Kappa, 1982)—there is no reference to the Donna Olimpia complex. However, a recent publication confirms the fact that Innocenzo Sabbattini was involved, at least during the first phase. See Anu Kaisa Koponen, "From Utopias to Roman Residential Realities: The Golden Era of Roman Social Housing 1919–1932," in *Planning Perspectives*, 16 November 2024. DOI: 10.1080/02665433.2024.2427165.

Entrance gate, ICP block, Viale dei Quattro Venti and Largo Luigi Miceli.

Figure-ground plan of Monteverde. At the top, the ICP/INCIS three-block development; lower to the left, the Pamphili I–II complex around Piazza Donna Olimpia.

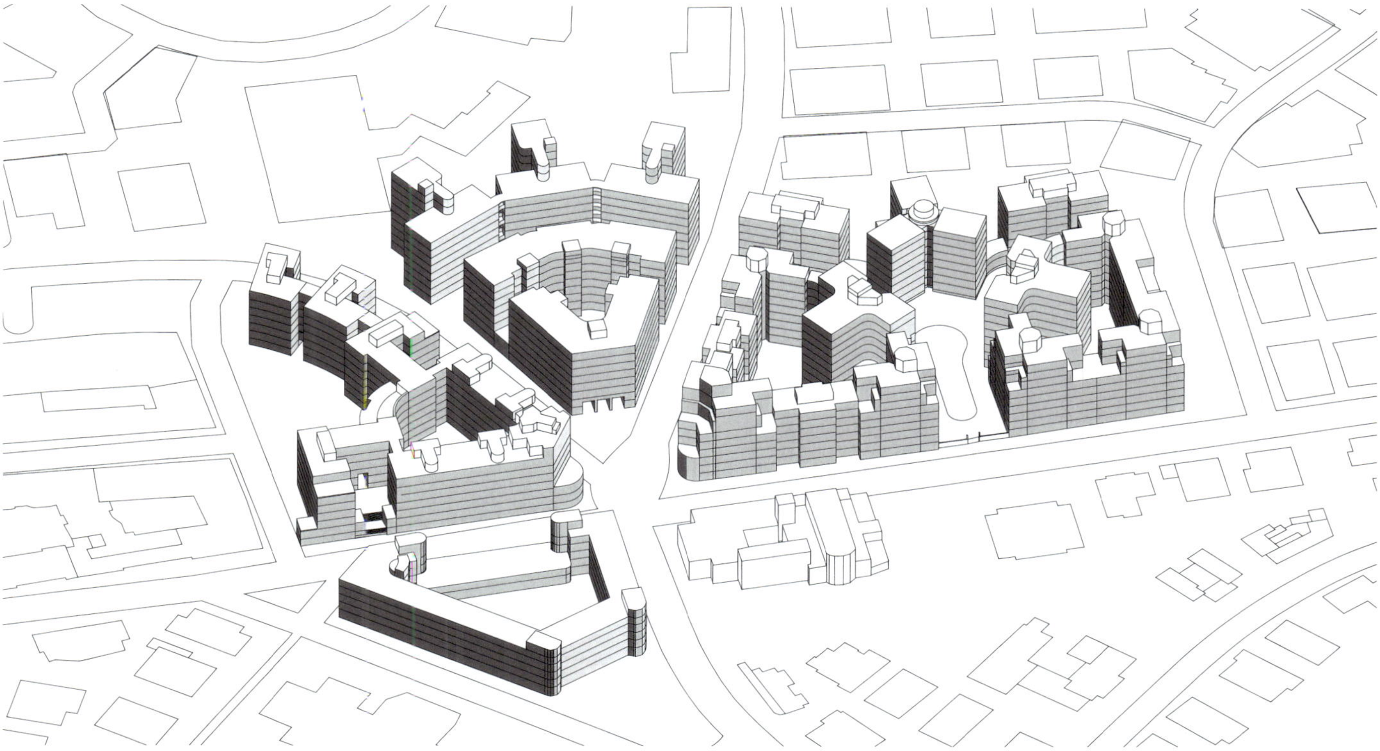

Axonometric view of the ICP Pamphili Donna Olimpia complex, 1932–1938.

Pietro Sforza (and Massimo Piacentini, engineer), view of Pamphili II along Via Paola Falconieri, 1932–1938.

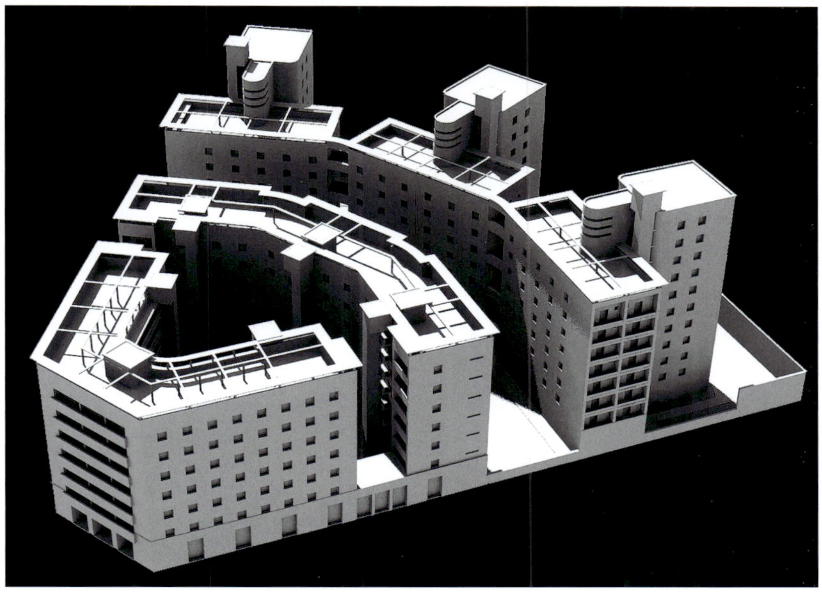

Innocenzo Costantini and Pietro Sforza. Digital model of Pamphili II.

The two symmetrical buildings that face each other on both sides of the central garden are markedly unique, with their two-story base in bricks and the open-air balconies that give access to the apartments in the three branches of the T-shaped plan. Completing the central garden is the free-standing clover-leaf tower, whose three arms are distributed from the central staircase made up of a cylindrical structure with open-air loggias accessing the apartments. Here again, Sabbatini demonstrates his affinity with Italian Futurism, which he had experimented with at the *alberghi suburbani* of La Garbatella.

View of Pamphili II across from Via Paola Falconieri.

View of Pamphili I tower.

Dedication to the ICP at the top of a Y-shaped tower in Pamphili I.

From the central garden of Pamphili I, a big staircase connects to Via Ozanam and across the street to a curvilinear garden that divides the V-shaped super-block of Pamphili II between the two downhill streets. The Pamphili II, completed later in 1938, features various other architectural elements that not only draw on the Futurist language, but also on the aesthetics of Italian Rationalism and the typology of the 1930s. On the hillside of the curved garden, Costantini located three T-shaped structures, separate but articulated by bent outdoor terraces, and a continuous concrete *pensilina* (a seemingly floating cantilevered roof) linking all three roofs. Three curvilinear volumes with horizontal openings surge on the roofs in a direct reference to Erich Mendelsohn's expressionist architecture in Germany, while some facades display an unusual pattern of small circular windows. On the other side of the garden, a curved concrete loggia gives access across a housing block to a masterful triangular garden. Here, above a two-story base, six levels of linear internal balconies with continuous curved balustrades, accentuate the Futurist, streamline Moderne architectural language. A three-bay entrance loggia opens onto Piazza di Donna Olimpia. Six continuous horizontal balustrades frame the balconies and give the block its Rationalist facade on the square, a composition which is reinforced by the *pensilina* that outline all the buildings.

As for the last super-block, also part of Pamphili II and the work of Costantini and Sforza, it is another variation on the increasingly Rationalist language of the last phase. To match the context, the architects created another triangular courtyard, surrounded by seven stories and connected by a loggia to a public garden that makes the transition with the neighborhood—the same Futurist curvilinear balconies appear again. A series of open courtyards articulate the composition along Via Falconieri, with a sophisticated sequence of steps, courts, and passages to match the uphill topography. Particularly interesting is the courtyard that opens on Via di Donna Olimpia with large steps and an architecture that could have been designed 40 years later by Aldo Rossi. A small church and a school, both in a Rationalist language, complete the mixed-use district. Throughout the entire Donna Olimpia complex, all the apartments were rather compact and small, one or two bedrooms plus kitchen and bathroom, and in some cases, not cross-ventilated. They were thus somewhat constricted on the inside, and yet had ample communal space in the courts and gardens. The intended monumentality of these structures perseveres as a factor in their role as Donna Olimpia's social epicenter. The buildings remain imposing, projecting an image of metropolitan modernity, which might suggest New York and Vienna.

Courtyard at the heart of Pamphili II.

Pamphili II, inner loggia.

Ufficio tecnico and Innocenzo Sabbatini, elevations of the group of three towers at the back of Pamphili I, 1930. The Y-shaped tower with its cylindrical staircase is at the center.

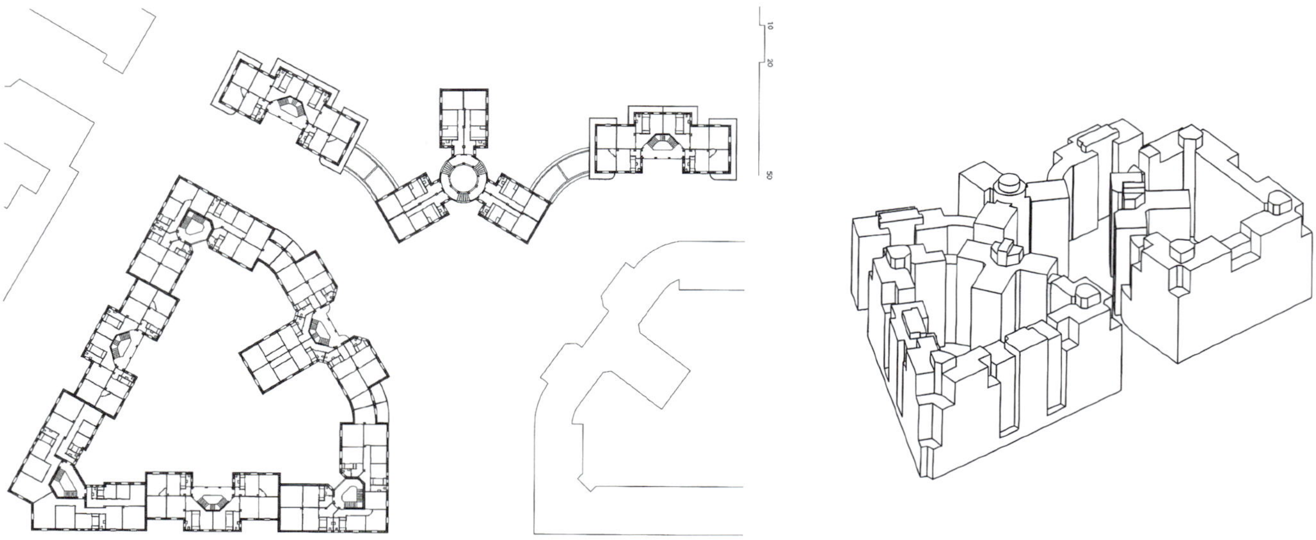

Pamphili I tower, floor plan and axonometric.

View of Y-shaped Pamphili I tower from Viale dei Quattro Venti on an axis with the interior garden.

Courtyard at the heart of Pamphili II.

Giulio Gra, central alley of the housing complex for the Cooperative Association for the Railroad Workers, 1932–1938.

Appio Latino
1924–1938

In addition to the quarters built around Piazza Mazzini, Piazza Verbano, Piazza Bologna, and the Flaminio district, the *Piano regolatore* of 1909 by Edmondo Sanjust di Teulada included a large district—known as Appio Latino—to be developed on both sides of Via Appia Nuova, a new boulevard running southeast from Porta San Giovanni and parallel to Via Appia Antica. From an urban design point of view, Sanjust's vision for the Appio neighborhoods was the most sophisticated project in the masterplan, combining gridded and radial sections with a variety of figural spaces in the Roman tradition. At Porta San Giovanni, a trident served as an entrance to the neighborhood; a large and circular square, Piazza Re di Roma, was placed along the main axis as the very center of the area; a series of small squares and green parks were spread within the curving edge of the railroad tracks to Termini; a second circle, even larger and later to become Piazza Tuscolo, formed the transition between the regular urban blocks and a long park proposed as the southwestern border. From the 1920s until the Second World War, the Istituto per le Case Populari, the Istituto Nazionale di Assicurazioni, and other development companies built a series of innovative (many of them Rationalist) projects that have sadly been ignored by most historians of the pre-World War II Roman metropolis.

Architects

Gino Cipriani

Giulio Gra

Vittorio Ballio Morpurgo

Camillo Palmerini

Innocenzo Sabbatini

Piazza Tuscolo

By 1925 the development of the district remained sporadic. Of all the major public spaces planned by Sanjust, only Piazza Re di Roma had taken shape, but no building had been erected on its perimeter. Likewise, the future Piazza Tuscolo was still undeveloped, with only two blocks of railway workers' *villini* facing Via Gallia. Moreover, on the site of the former Villa Fiorelli near the walls, the cooperative Il Progresso built, in the early 1910s, a multi-block complex of low-cost apartments between Via Terni and Via Vaghero. The first project of significance was the ICP public housing block at Piazza Tuscolo (Appio I, 1926), built between 1924 and 1926 under the direction of Camillo Palmerini (1893–1967). The Appio I complex is quite remarkable and consists of seven linked structures, each four-floors high, which share a large interior garden. The two central buildings facing Piazza Tuscolo are symmetrical and connected by a large entrance arch, covered with ashlar and surmounted by a terrace. The facades are characterized by a rustic ashlar on the ground floor, which sometimes reaches to the first-floor level. All around the block, the plaster is, in some places, rustic and, in addition, there are architraves covered with tiles. Unlike other architectural solutions proposed by ICP architects, Palmerini's facades are distinguished by the material-based coloring and the diverse decorative apparatus (ashlar infills like Roman spoglie, coats of arms, cornices, projecting eaves, brackets and consoles, turrets, niches, pilasters, etc.). On the roof, he played a "gothic-medieval" game with prominent vertical chimneys, arranged in a jagged way, and among which he inserted private and common terraces and balconies. Overall, the decorative apparatus was aimed at making the houses of the middle-class employees relevant according to a conscious strategy of building consensus during the Fascist period. On the contrary, the facades facing the courtyard were conceived with a simpler language emphasizing functional fenestration and balconies. In the large interior garden, planted with tall trees, there is a copy of the fountain of Piano Scarano in Viterbo, in peperino, created for the Ethnographic Exhibition of Rome in 1911, and reassembled here by Palmerini.

Figure-ground plan of the district.

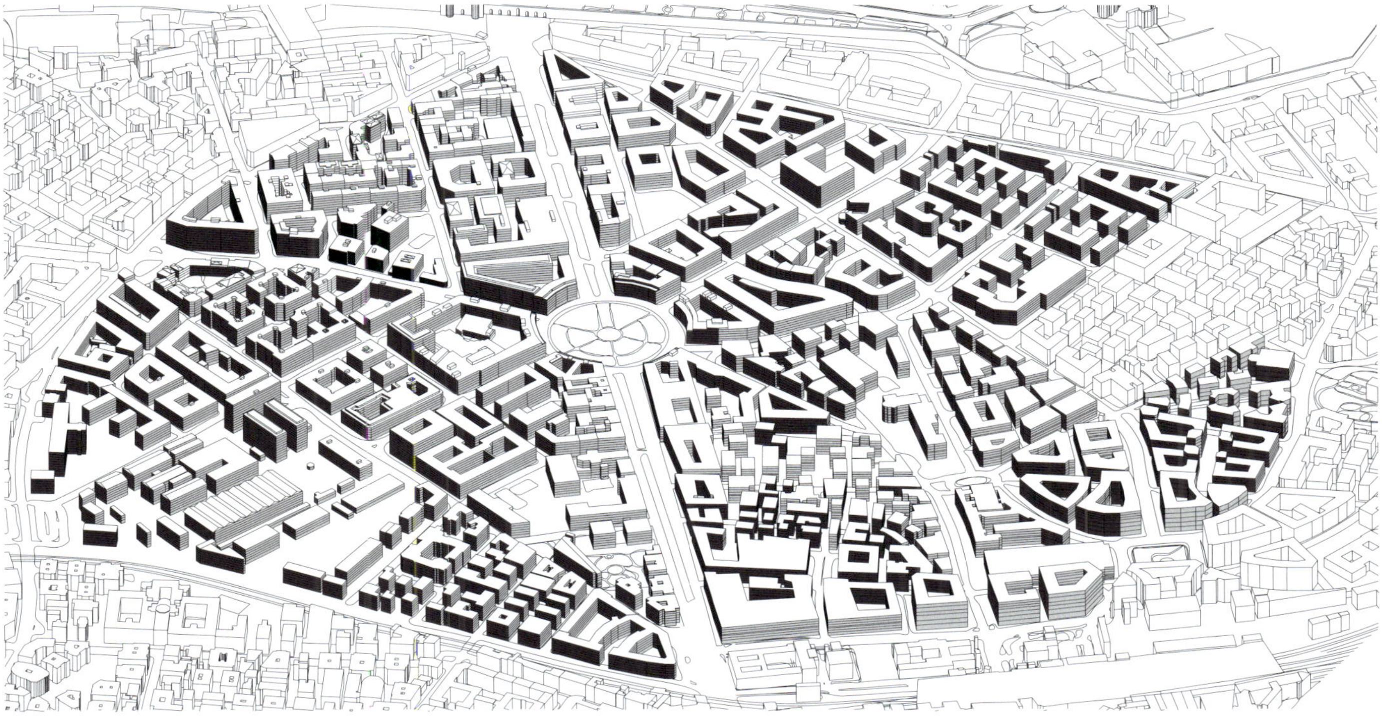

Axonometric view of the Appio Latino district. At the center, Via Appia Nuova starting at the Aurelian walls and Porta San Giovanni, and the circular square of Piazza Re di Roma. Center left edge: Piazza Tuscolo and the four blocks of the Cooperative Association for the Railroad Workers. Center right edge: Villa Fiorelli and the six-blocks INA complex at Via Taranto.

Innocenzo Sabbatini, *palazzine* and interior gardens, Villa Fiorelli.

Camillo Palmerini, facade of the Appio I block on Piazza Tuscolo, ICP, 1926.

The last remarkable ensemble built by the ICP next to the park of Villa Fiorelli (designed by Raffaele De Vico) was the work of Innocenzo Sabbatini (1926). Slightly set back from Via Taranto at Piazza Lugo, it consists of two triangular blocks mirroring each other along a semi-pedestrian street, Via S.S. Fabiano e Venanzio. Once again adopting the trident motif to compose the headpieces of the blocks, he signed here a masterwork of architectural wit, invention, and composition. Each block is made up of a series of *palazzine*, from small to large, that Sabbatini designed in languages ranging from classical to the most inspired *barocchetto*. The two structures that conclude the upper section of the interior gardens facing Villa Fiorelli negotiate the geometry of the site in an exceptional manner.

Camillo Palmerini, interior courtyard of the Appio I, ICP. The fountain, a copy of the Piazza Scarano fountain in Viterbo, was created for the Exposition of 1911 and reassembled here.

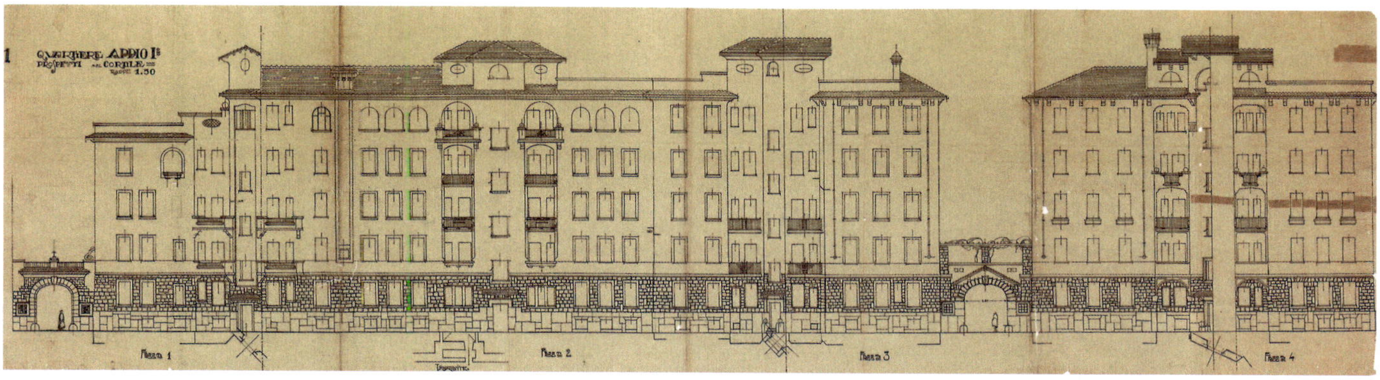

Camillo Palmerini, ICP complex Appio I. Facade on the courtyard.

Camillo Palmerini, ICP complex Appio II, Via La Spezia. Detail of a lateral facade.

Vittorio Ballio Morpurgo, mixed-use structure for apartments and former offices of the TETI (Società Telefonica Tirrena) in Rome, Via Sannio and Via Corfinio, 1926–1928. Morpurgo's structure recalls the plan and volume of the *insulae* of Ostia Antica with their superimposed balconies and loggias. The ground floor openings echo the shape and character of the ancient Roman workshops, using brick textures inspired by the *opus mixtum* and *opus spicatum*.

Innocenzo Sabbatini, social housing complex Villa Fiorelli, 1926. One of the two structures, immersed in a garden, that face each other at the eastern end (top) of the site; note Sabbatini's elegant use of *barochetto* language.

Innocenzo Sabbatini, Villa Fiorelli. Axonometric view.

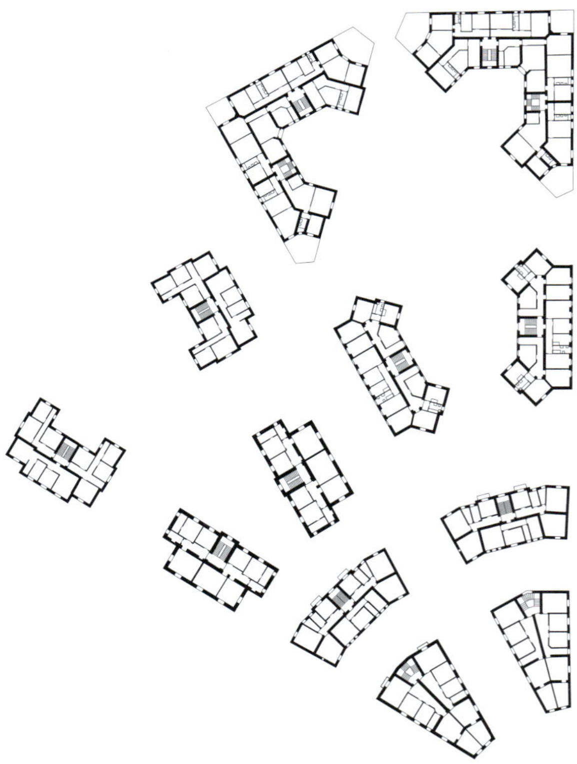

Innocenzo Sabbatini, Villa Fiorelli. Main floor plans.

Rationalism in the 1930s

In the 1920s and 1930s, the National Insurance Institute (INA) was a major actor for the construction of the new quarters of Rome. The INA had more funds than the ICP and was aimed at a much wider social range. The projects that can be found in many areas of the city were usually in charge of the technical office of the institute in collaboration with municipal architects. The most spectacular complex, organized in a manner relatively similar to the ICP projects, can be found facing Via Taranto and directly adjacent to Sabbatini's Villa Fiorelli. Coordinated by Gino Cipriani, it consists of a super-block, divided in four quasi-identical groups of buildings, on average six-floors high and with a garden at its heart. The whole ensemble is organized in a cruciform pattern (drawing on the ancient Roman *cardo decumanus* concept with two main streets crossing at right angles) along two perpendicular pedestrian *allées*, whose intersection is marked by four eight-floor tower-like structures. This volumetric solution is an obvious reference to Futurism, particularly visible in the vertiginous treatment of the vertical staircase glazing in the courtyards. In the following years, the northwest–southeast green *allée* was extended across the street to form the backbone of another super-block, itself mirrored in quasi-symmetrical manner on the opposite side of Via Taranto. Both blocks form a tower-like modern gate to the geometric Piazza Ragusa. Typologically quite similar, they are designed in a Rationalist manner that recalls late Art Deco and streamline Moderne language across Europe and the United States. The volumetric treatment of the upper floors and roofs became more plastic in the manner of Red Vienna, while the horizontality of the overall composition was emphasized by the projecting long balconies in front of the traditional vertical windows.

Innocenzo Sabbatini, Villa Fiorelli. Adjacent facades on Via Crema.

Aerial view of the four blocks for the Cooperative Association for the Railroad Workers (Giulio Gra, 1932–1938) on the left. On the right, the ICP I block facing Piazza Tuscolo (Camillo Palmerini, 1926).

Aerial view of the four-block INA complex at Via Taranto (Gino Cipriani, 1930), visible on the left. To the right is the Villa Fiorelli complex (Innocenzo Sabbatini, 1926).

Side view of the complex for the Cooperative Association for the Railroad Workers, along Via Etruria.

The towers marking the central space of the four-block INA complex at Via Taranto, 1930.

Located right behind the ICP's project of Piazza Tuscolo, the Società cooperativa ferrovieri per case economiche (Cooperative Association for the Railroad Workers) financed and built a super-block of housing between Via Etruria, Astura, Ceneda, and Pomezia. Designed by Giulio Gra (1932–1938), it consists of three separate sections, each arranged around planted courtyards. Like in the Via Taranto complex, two pedestrian semi-private *allées* structure the whole ensemble and intersect around an elegant fountain, placed at the center of a piazza created by chamfering the corners of the four adjacent apartment buildings. The volumetry is here simpler, more economic, and the roofs are essentially flat and usable as common terraces. Architecturally, the language is fully Rationalist with no ornaments left. These residential structures provide a resolutely metropolitan image to the 1930s modern architecture in Rome.

Gino Cipriani, central street of the four-block INA complex at Via Taranto (Gino Cipriani, 1930). The complex is based upon the Roman *cardo decumanus* structural logic.

Luigi Moretti, Palazzina Il Girasole, Via Bruno Buozzi 64, 1947–1950. View of the open entrance atrium.

Parioli
1911–1957

The Parioli district is one of the most emblematic areas in the contemporary urban and social history of Rome. Its residential architecture and particularly its post-1920 *palazzina* typology embody the high symbolic value tied to the modernizing middle-class lifestyle and status. Moreover, the relationship with historical paths and parks, as well as the omnipresence of streetside greenery, remains highly significant and integral to the unique and complex structure of the topography-driven street system. The Royal Decree No. 1937 of 16 December 1920 recognized the legality of building *palazzine* on lots initially attributed to *villini*. It established that the facade extensions along the street cannot exceed 25 meters in length, with a 5.8-meter setback from the boundary. Buildings can have no more than three floors above the *rez-de-chaussée*, which itself cannot be more than 3 meters above ground for use as shops. The maximum height may reach 19 meters, except for partial elevations that make the building's profile harmonious and varied, subject to the municipal administration's judgment. As a result, Parioli transformed into one of the eminent international examples where urban planning aimed at real estate speculation was successfully balanced with well-calibrated typological parameters, building regulations, architectural quality, and experimentation at the highest level.

Architects

Armando Brasini
Mario De Renzi
Carlo Mongini
Luigi Moretti

Aerial view of Parioli. The northern and northwestern section was primarily built after the Second World War. Top left: the park of Villa Glori; Piazza Euclide and the Basilica of the Immaculate Heart of Mary (Armando Brasini); the embassy with the park of Villa Elia/Villa Luna, and the curvilinear Via Archimede. From Piazza Euclide, the triangle of Via Filippo Civinini (left) and Via Domenico Chelini (right) connected by the Via Bruno Buozzi. The sinuous Viale Parioli is visible at the top and connects to Piazza Cuba (see right page).

The Geography of Parioli

Situated in the northeastern part of Rome, the Parioli neighborhood—the name "Parioli" likely derives from Monti Parioli, a group of three hills, or from *peraioli*, referring to the local pear orchards. For centuries, the area beyond Porta del Popolo was mostly agricultural and sparsely populated. The physical boundary of the Parioli with the Flaminio area was marked by a tuffaceous cliff, dotted with caves and cavities (still visible), and atop of which lies the public garden of Villa Balestra. The urbanization of the Parioli neighborhood began at the end of the 19th century, following Rome's designation as the capital of Italy. By the late 1800s, several key streets were constructed, including Viale Maresciallo Pilsudski (branching off Viale Tiziano toward the east), its prolongation Viale dei Parioli, as well as Via Bruno Buozzi which all rise uphill from Valle Giulia and the Galleria d'Arte Moderna. These streets were designed as wide city promenades, complete with riding tracks along the sides and bordered with elegant villas. A network of winding secondary roads was designed following the paths of ancient lanes, alleys, and gardens, often marked by gates and high walls that once protected villas and vineyards belonging to noble families. In the early decades of the 1900s, the Parioli experienced a rise in housing demand, leading to significant building development. It became one of Rome's most prestigious areas, home to prominent figures such as members of the bourgeoisie, senior government officials, film stars, entrepreneurs, and politicians. The Tiber defines the northern boundary of the district, passing by Acqua Acetosa and the Great Mosque of Rome (Paolo Portoghesi, 1995). Eastward, Viale Parioli and its continuation Viale Liegi connect to Via Salaria and the park of Villa Ada, which constitute the eastern edge, while Villa Borghese marks the Parioli's southern boundary.

Aerial view of Parioli. The southeastern section includes pre-Second World War (toward the right) and post-war structures. From left to right: Viale Parioli, the church of San Roberto Bellarmino and Piazza Cuba; the huge footprint of the former Zecca (Mint, now restructured for housing) at Piazza Verdi; the IRCIS housing complex (1910s), Via Salaria leading north to the park of Villa Ada. To the bottom left: the 16th-century Villa Taverna and gardens (now residence of the American ambassador) and the *palazzine* of the Tre Madonne (mid-1920s).

Armando Brasini, Basilica of the Immaculate Heart of Mary (1923–1936). The church remained incomplete.

Franco Albini and Franca Herg, Department store La Rinascente, Piazza Fiume, 1957–1961. The iconic structure, designed by the Milanese architects, marks the entrance of Via Salaria and the older section of Parioli.

Figure-ground plan.

The Birth of the *Palazzina*

The basic structure of the neighborhood was incorporated in the 1909 masterplan. Between Villa Borghese and Villa Ada, and adjoined to Via Salaria and Viale Liegi, Sanjust di Teulada planned a small district of apartment blocks that would eventually be centered on the ex-Zecca (Mint) at Piazza Verdi (1914–1930). Built by engineer Carlo Mongini, an IRCIS four-block complex of about 900 apartments quickly rose from 1911 to 1914 along Via Salaria. North of Villa Borghese, the masterplan highlighted the former agricultural network of paths, gardens, and villas to serve as future infrastructure for family houses or *villini*. A sharp right turn from Viale Maresciallo Pilsudski led up to what would become Piazza Euclide, one of the mixed-use centers of Parioli and later marked by the unfinished church of the Sacro Cuore Immacolato di Maria (Basilica of the Immaculate Heart of Mary) designed by Armando Brasini (1923–1936).

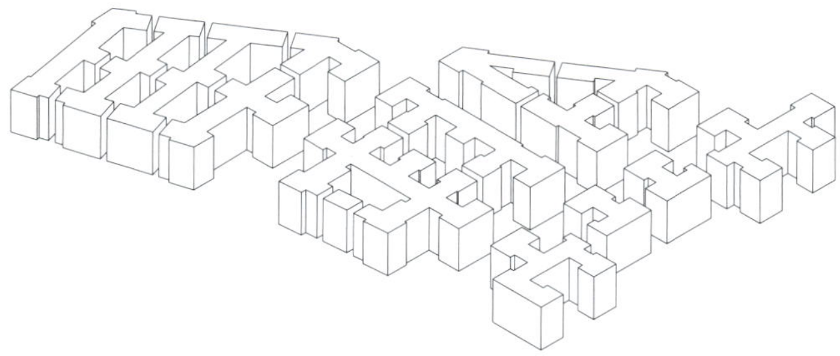

Mario De Renzi. Palazzina at Piazza Cuba and Via Panama, 1929.

Carlo Mongini, IRCIS complex between Via Salaria and Via Liegi, 1911–1914 (here intersection Via Gaetano Donizetti and Via Gaspare Spontini). A remarkably and typologically homogeneous housing development for employees of the Italian State, structured around a network of interior and exterior patios.

Mario Ridolfi and Wolfgang Frankl, Palazzina Colombo, Via San Valentino 21 (1935–1938).

Luigi Moretti, detail of the side facade of Il Girasole.

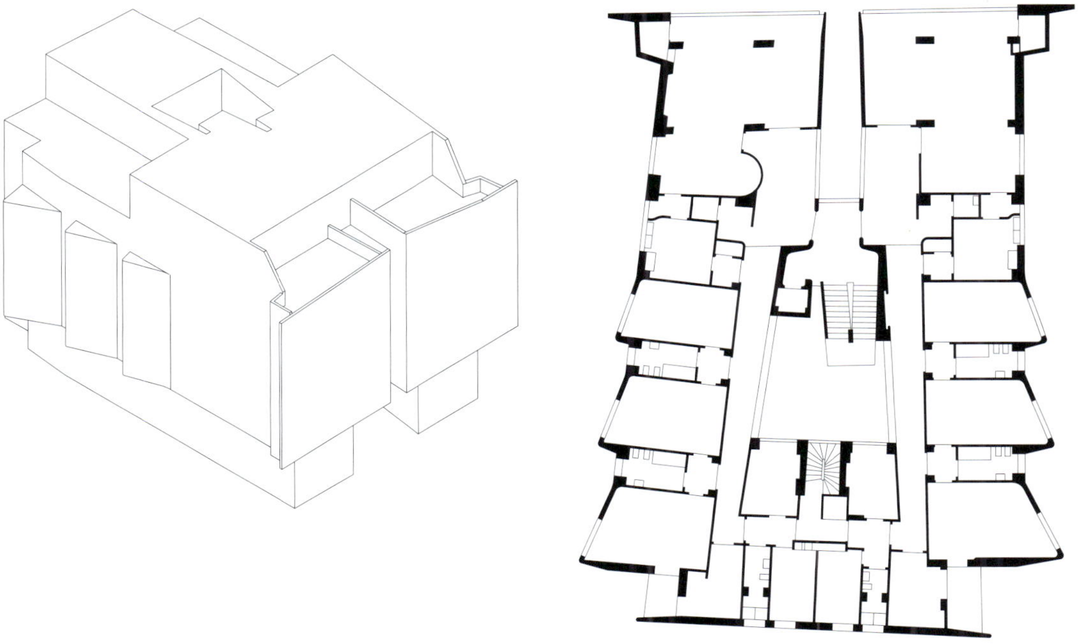

Luigi Moretti, Palazzina Il Girasole, 1947–1950. Typical floor plan and axonometric view.

Luigi Piccinato, Palazzina Via Archimede 148 (1939–1941).

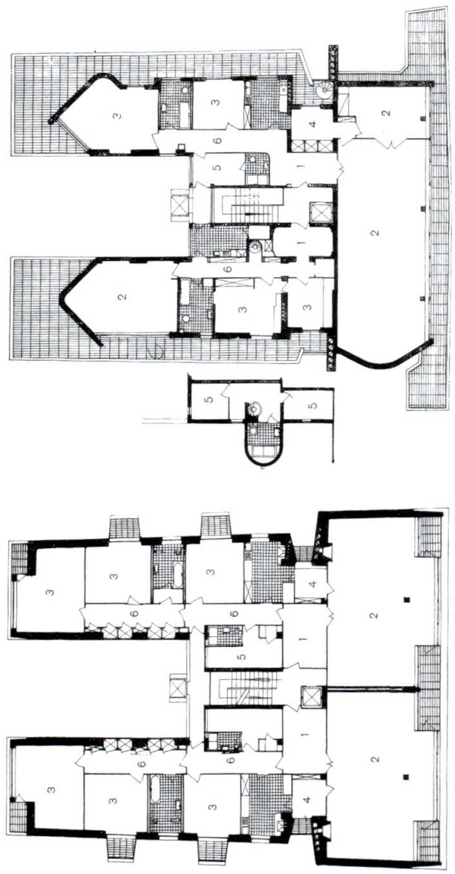

Amedeo Luccichenti and Vincenzo Monaco, Palazzina Via San Valentino 16 (1948–1950). View and floor plans.

Ugo Luccichenti, Palazzina Via Archimede 185 (1952–1953).

Vittorio Ballio Morpurgo, Palazzina Via Chelini (1934–1936). The building is the headpiece of a super-block containing five *palazzine*, all by Morpurgo.

Andrea Busiri Vici, Palazzina Via Bruxelles 47 (1934–1935).

Ugo Luccichenti, Palazzina Bornigia, Piazza delle Muse 6/7 (1938–1940).

Vincenzo Monaco and Amedeo Luccichenti, Palazzina Antares. On Via di San Valentino, the *palazzina* overlooks the Villaggio Olimpico and the Auditorium Parco della Musica.

In 1920, the Royal Decree No. 1937 of 16 December, legalized the construction of *palazzine* in areas planned for small houses. The new regulatory framework marked the beginning of the *palazzina*'s spread throughout Rome, mostly in the Parioli and Monteverde, reflecting a formal typological experimentation that had a significant impact on the city's urban fabric. The zones designated for villas in the 1909 Rome masterplan were transformed from small constructions in large green areas into multi-apartment structures, detached from each other and separated by small gardens. The *palazzina* became one of the two principal models of Roman urban architecture, embodying the upper middle-class city, while the so-called intensive type developed by the ICP and IRCIS was intended to represent the working class and lower middle-class city. In the Parioli, the Tre Madonne complex, constructed between 1927 and 1931 by Gino Cipriani's INA (Istituto Nazionale Assicurazioni) for Ministry of Foreign Affairs officials, and the Cooperative Tesoro development on the opposite side, pioneered and, in some way, masterminded the use of the *palazzina* at the block scale.

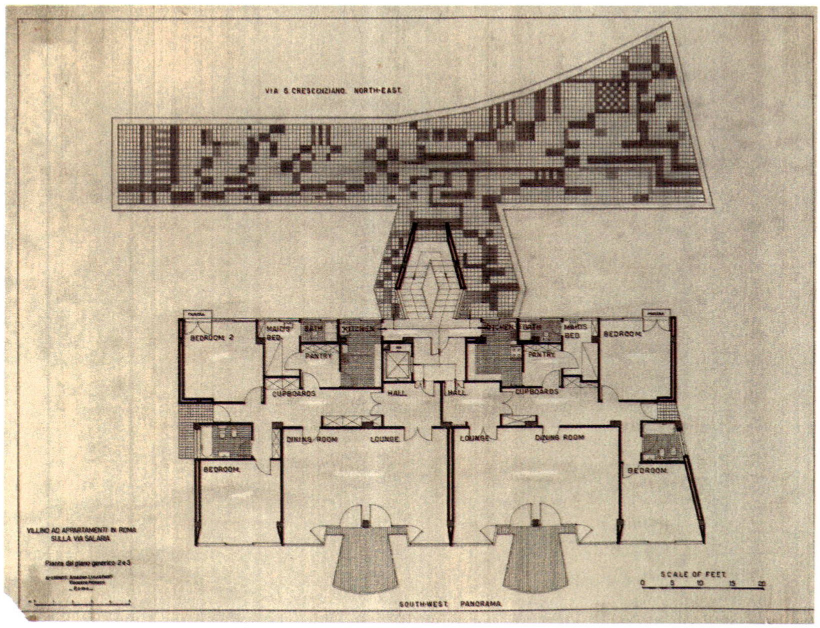

Ugo Luccichenti, Palazzina Via San Crescenziano 40 (1957). View and typical floor plan.

From an urban planning perspective, the *palazzina* was until relatively recently seen as a privately built speculative typology that represented a disintegrating element within Rome's urban fabric, introducing smaller, more fragmented structures with intermittent strips of greenery or access ramps to underground garages. However, from a formal architectural standpoint, the type marked a significant moment of experimentation in modern architectural history, offering examples that soon became prototypes for future generations of professionals. The tension between the preservation of Rome's historical cityscape and the demand for modern living spaces resulted in a dynamic architectural environment, where the *palazzina* stood out as a distinctive form. The long-standing negative interpretation—most formidably constructed by Italo Insolera—has finally given way to a more subtle interpretation of the role of the private sector in the construction of the modern city. In many ways, the *palazzina* continues to serve as a reference point for numerous recent residential developments, even though the size of the apartments has significantly decreased, and the architectural quality is far inferior. The Parioli district remains in the collective imagination as a place associated with social and economic prestige, adjacent to the historic center and some of the historical villas and gardens of the capital. It evokes a lifestyle reminiscent of the economic-boom era, one that perhaps does not entirely match the needs or urgencies of the contemporary world, given its relative isolation and the limited level of public transport.

Vincenzo Monaco and Amedeo Luccichenti, Palazzina Giammarusti, 1953–1954. Facade on Largo Messico.

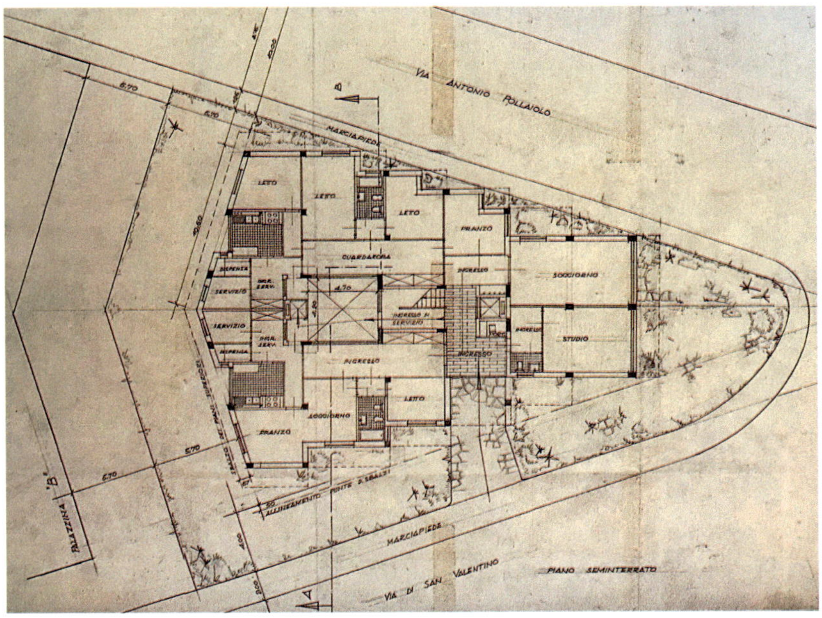

Vincenzo Monaco and Amedeo Luccichenti, Palazzina Antares, 1948–1951. Plan of the entry level. See view on opposite page.

Federico Gorio and Giorgio Rinaldi, linear apartment house type (*casa in linea*), backside of Via Cesena, 1950–1954.

Tiburtino
1950–1954

The Tiburtino district (INA-Casa) is a public housing project built after the Second World War, contemporary with the great post-war period of Italian cinema known as Neorealism. For me, as an architect who has struggled with the budgets of low-income housing for decades, I was immediately aware walking around Tiburtino of the pragmatism and extraordinary skill of these designers. They accomplished everything they aspired to with the simplest of means and a few strategic manipulations of the most conventional of Roman housing types, *the casa a schiera* or townhouse. The Garbatella, Prati, and Testaccio districts all make use of clever manipulations of the townhouse to create beautiful urban blocks, but those at Tiburtino are different. By introducing a diagonal wall to occasional stacks of units, the townhouse can bend with the street network that follows the topography, creating Sitte-like sequences of views. Every now and then, usually at street corners, the staircase emerges from the mass of the building and serves the second floor before disappearing inside. This is more costly, but it evokes the vernacular buildings that the painter Ettore Roesler Franz (1845–1907) recorded in Trastevere and other medieval parts of Rome. A particularly clever group of apartments by Ridolfi and his devoted protégé Wolfgang Frankl consists of two stories of townhouses stepping up a hill, over a tall story of ground floor workshops. The upper units are served by a grand stair that becomes a bridge. Between the bridge and the upper units are little private gardens. As they are discontinuous, the lower flats get charming little entry courts, full of sunlight. These are complex and sophisticated manipulations that are smart, and all over Tiburtino there are shifts of color in a beautiful Roman palette. (D.S.)

Architects
Ludovico Quaroni
Mario Ridolfi

Debate and Structure

Tiburtino—built on an area of 8.8 hectares along Via Tiburtina at the 7-kilometer mark—was one of the major interventions carried out in the first seven years of the INA-Casa scheme. This "Plan for the increase of workers' employment" was an organic program launched in 1949 for the construction of low-cost housing and for the development of employment in the field of construction, understood as a driving force for a more general economic recovery. Compared to the neighborhoods built in Rome by the INCIS and the ICP in the previous decades, the Tiburtino presents for the first time a planimetric system composed of mixed typologies and arranged on sloping and non-regular terrain, according to a concept that is an effective compromise between the courtyard-based projects carried out before the Second World War, and a rural settlement. The average height of the buildings attempts to restore the volumetric effects of a medieval town, albeit with a much lower settlement density. Designed by Ludovico Quaroni and Mario Ridolfi at the head of a large group of architects—Carlo Aymonino, Carlo Chiarini, Mario Fiorentino, Federico Gorio, Marta Lanza, Sergio Lenci, Piero Maria Lugli, Carlo Melograni, Gian Carlo Menichetti, Giorgio Rinaldi, Michele Valori—the neighborhood was built between 1949 and 1954 and included 771 dwellings for about 4000 residents.

It is mainly residential and was conceived according to three defined typologies. The basic typology is the linear agglomeration of townhouses (mainly four floors), some of which can be reached by stairs external to the building or arranged along the balcony. Also organized in a linear way are the terraced houses (two to three floors, Via Luigi Cesana) with outdoor staircases and ground-level workshops. Finally, a series of tower houses (seven floors with three to four apartments per floor) mark the edges of the neighborhood and create its singular skyline. Any concept of planimetric geometry was abandoned in the design of the system: it is the street that unites the irregular geometries of the buildings, for which the north–south and east–west orientation was taken into maximum consideration. The overall morphology uses broken lines—articulated by slips and rotations of the buildings of which the volumes of the stairs represent the fulcrums—to create loose blocks with open interior courtyards. The largest court, along Via Eduardo Arbid, contains a market-like structure providing small commercial spaces. The overall intention was to create a central public space square, but the design was unsuccessful.

General plan of the Tiburtino district, 1950–1954.

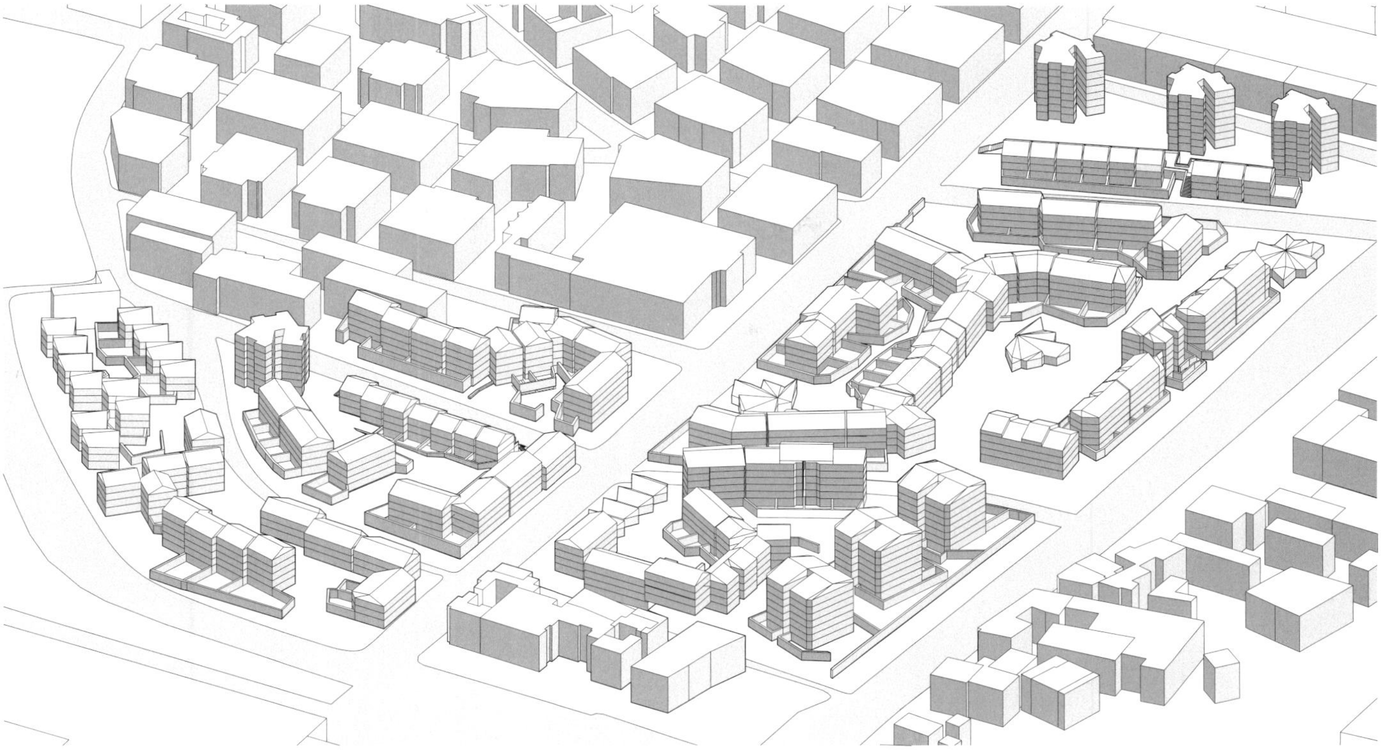

Axonometric view of the Tiburtino district. The contrast with the *palazzine* built in the following years is striking.

Aerial view of the Tiburtino district, now surrounded by *palazzine*.

Mario Ridolfi, Terrace houses, Via Luigi Cesena, 1950–1954. Street view.

Mario Ridolfi, Terrace houses, Via Luigi Cesena, plan and elevation.

To reread the Tiburtino district today, it is necessary to take into account the fact that for a long time it was mainly associated with the Neorealist movement and interpreted with respect to the "self-critical" affirmation that the leading architect, Ludovico Quaroni, made when he published an essay titled "Il Paese dei Barocchi" (The Village of the Baroques) in issue 215 of *Casabella Continuità* in 1957—thus immediately after the construction of the neighborhood. Quaroni made his thesis explicit when he wrote, a few years later:

> In the push towards the city we stopped at the town. That is to say, we fell into the picturesque and perhaps also into the error of proposing an overall design in which the very scenographic intentions that we intended to fight reappeared, albeit with a diametrically opposite architectural image. The Tiburtino however represents the generous attempt to decline the aspirations of those social strata in architectural and urban terms which, thanks to the democratic dialectic, reappeared with a new dignity in the life of the country.[1]

1 See Manfredo Tafuri, *Ludovico Quaroni e la cultura architettonica italiana del dopoguerra* (Milan: Edizioni Comunità, 1964), 91.

Almost all the houses up to five floors were built with the century-old technology of load-bearing masonry and walls. The structural system is made up of a continuous wall which conditions the distribution of the accommodation—a sequence of closed rooms with small hallways is thus obtained. Some homes have the living room and kitchen on the same front while others have them on opposite fronts. Variations in the typology are given by the possibility of having windows on three sides thanks to the rotations of the stairwells, or to the change in thickness of the buildings. The eight six- to seven-story-high houses designed by Ridolfi and Lugli were the only buildings to use the reinforced concrete skeleton for economic reasons and to make it easier to include roof terraces, balconies, and loggias, etc. Recent investigations have focused on the efficiency and cost of the traditional construction system in contrast with the increased use of reinforced concrete that will follow. The research led in the archives of the ICP by Ettore Maria Mazzola has shown that "traditional" buildings (including Tiburtino) can cost from 16 up to 40 percent less than current construction (brick-concrete frames), especially taking into account that the properties analyzed, in particular the San Saba, Garbatella, and Flaminio districts, now have 100 years of life.[2]

2 Ettore Mazzola, *The Sustainable City is Possible* (Roma: Gangemi, 2010).

Ludovico Quaroni, townhouse types with tower, 1950–1954, Via Eduardo Arbid. Street view.

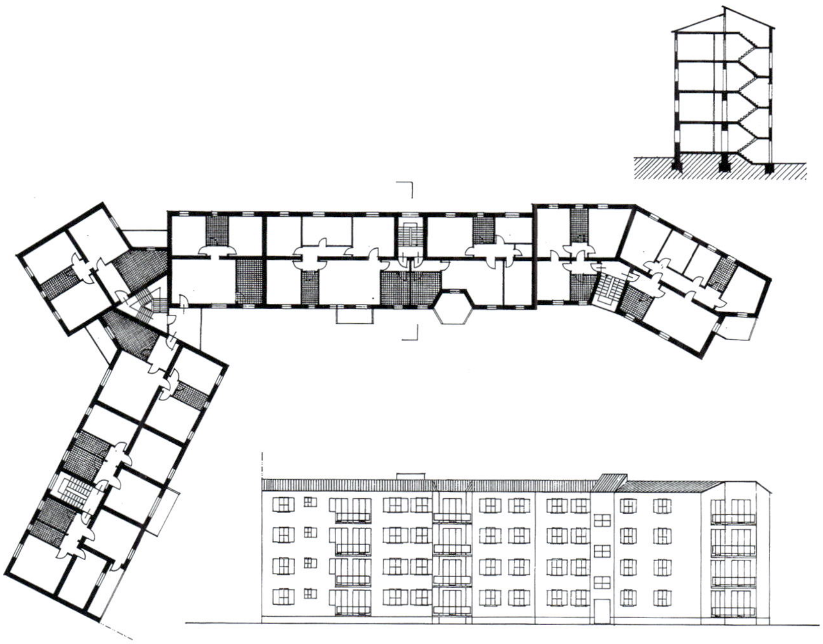

Ludovico Quaroni, townhouse types with tower, Via Eduardo Arbid. Plan and elevation.

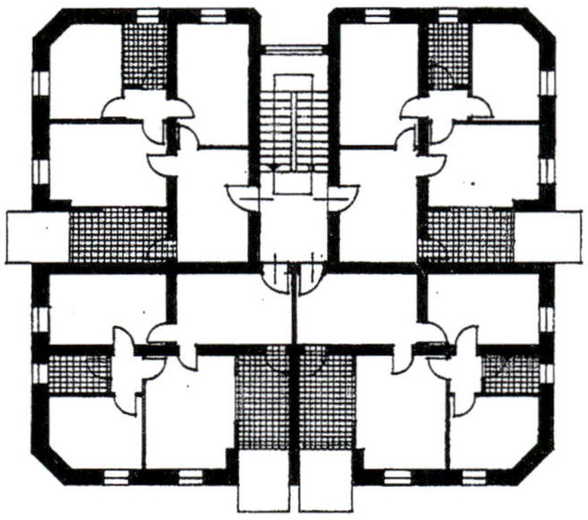

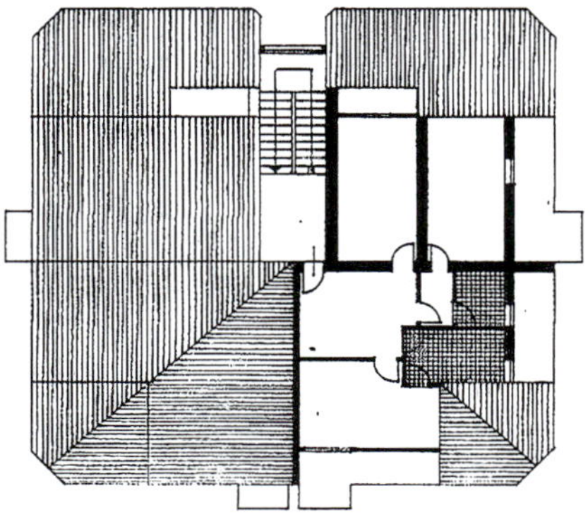

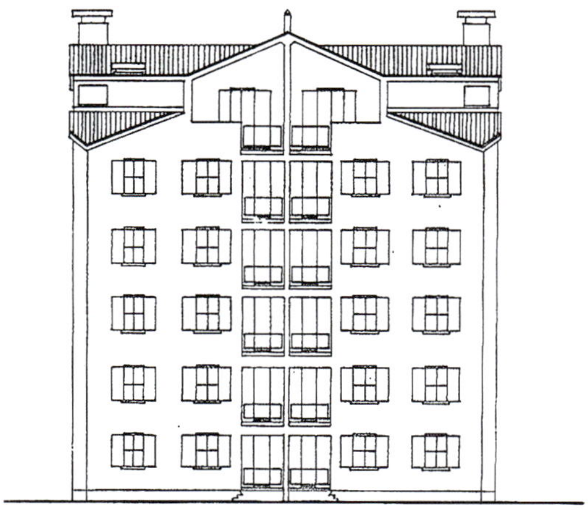

Mario Ridolfi. Tower type, 1950–1954. View from elevated walkway on backside of Via Diego Angeli.

Skyline from Via Luigi Cesena.

Mario Ridolfi. Tower type. Plan and elevation.

Mario Ridolfi, bridge and elevated walkway between townhouses (*casa a schiera*), Via Diego Angeli, 1950–1954.

Saverio Muratori and Mario De Renzi, V-shaped and mixed-use apartment building on Largo Spartaco at the entrance of Tuscolano II district, 1950–1954.

Tuscolano
1950–1964

Built on a flat area of 35 hectares, the Tuscolano district is the largest of the neighborhoods built in Rome by the INA-Casa. Designed for 18,000 inhabitants in 3150 dwellings, it consists of three sectors built between the Via Tuscolana (under which runs the Metro Line A) and the Parco degli Acquedotti. Tuscolano I (1950–1951) remained quite undistinguished in its attempt to both adapt to the *Piano regolatore* of 1931 and reject the conventional urban alignments. The masterplan of the second sector (1950–1957), drawn up by Mario De Renzi and Saverio Muratori—in collaboration with Lucio Cambellotti, Francesco Fariello, Giuseppe Perugini, Giulio Roisecco, Dante Tassotti, Luigi Vagnetti—distanced itself deliberately from the traditional urban grid and the understanding of the city as a compact and continuous organism. As a result, Tuscolano II appeared, both in plan and in three dimensions, as an autonomous design and urban figure. The last sector, Tuscolano III, designed by Adalberto Libera, is the Unità abitazione horizontale. Its network of one-story patio houses has its roots in Libera's interest in the oldest and most typical Mediterranean architecture, the Antique Greek and Arab-Islamic. Symmetrically located from the INA-Casa development on the northern side of Via Tuscolana, the privately built high-density Don Bosco district rose in the 1950s in connection with the construction of the Basilica of San Giovanni Bosco (1952–1959), the expansion of the pre-war Cinecittà film studios, and the establishment of the Istituto Luce—the oldest public institution dedicated to the diffusion of Italian cinema (1938). It is an alternative urban model to the multi-articulated morphologies of the Tiburtino and the Tuscolano, a neo-monumental antidote to the organicism of the period.

Architects
Adalberto Libera
Saverio Muratori
Gaetano Rapisardi
Mario De Renzi

The Urban Figure as Work of Art

The structure of the plan is graphically abstract and instantly identifiable. It consists of two long V-shaped housing bars—*case in linea*—articulated at 90 degrees, but quite diverse typologically. Muratori and De Renzi conceived the first one as the monumental entrance of the district from Via Tuscolana, facing a large open space, the Largo Spartaco. The five-story building, about 160 meters long, bends at the center in a V-shaped figure—it was immediately referred to as the "boomerang"—where the authors located a large-scale pedestrian passage leading to the heart of the neighborhood. Attributed mostly to Saverio Muratori, the 80-unit apartment building exposes its gridded concrete structure, modulated on the Roman traditional measure, here precisely 5.25 meters, and infilled according to the city's revisited constructive tradition, a masonry brick wall, 38 centimeters thick. In the original project, the mixed-use building—ground floor and mezzanine are commercial—was supposed to face a public square, with the social center, additional residences and shops, and a porticoed church. Only the latter, designed by Muratori, was partially realized in the 1960s: its hypogeal section barely surfaces and is unable to provide spatial substance to what is essentially a parking lot. The second structuring element of the plan consists of another linear building, 250 meters long along Via Sagunto, five stories high, and similarly V-shaped according to a slightly obtuse angle. Also designed by Muratori and De Renzi, it divides the housing district into two areas reconnected by a pedestrian underpass.
A series of terraced buildings with three floors above ground—designed by Dante Tassotti, Luigi Vagnetti, Giuseppe Perugini and Lucio Cambellotti—form a comb-like structure on both sides of the central spine. The long urban space formed between the continuous housing slab and the syncopated structure of the opposite side gives, from the air, the illusion of being a fascinating public space, akin to the linear squares of many German towns. However, the presence of the fenced gardens makes it a disappointing and unusable public space. Finally, the district's structure required that the limits and edges of the development be strongly marked, using recognizable morphological and typological elements. Tuscolano II is thus completed in the peripheral sections by star-shaped housing towers, nine floors high, and with two or four apartments per floor—a typology inspired by similar Scandinavian building types. The towers on the southeastern side, on Via del Quadraro (with four lobes) show the hand of De Renzi, whereas those on the western side on Via Cartagine were designed alternately by De Renzi and Muratori. Some compositional details, especially the movement of the angled balconies, are by De Renzi and reoccur in the different typologies that the neighborhood experimented with, giving it a strong unity of language.

Aerial view. From bottom to top: Tuscolano II with Largo Spartaco, the 160-meter V-shaped linear building, and the incomplete church; the 250-meter internal V-shaped structure and the fishbone network of townhouse types. In the background, the grid of patio houses of Tuscolano III and the Park of the Aqueducts.

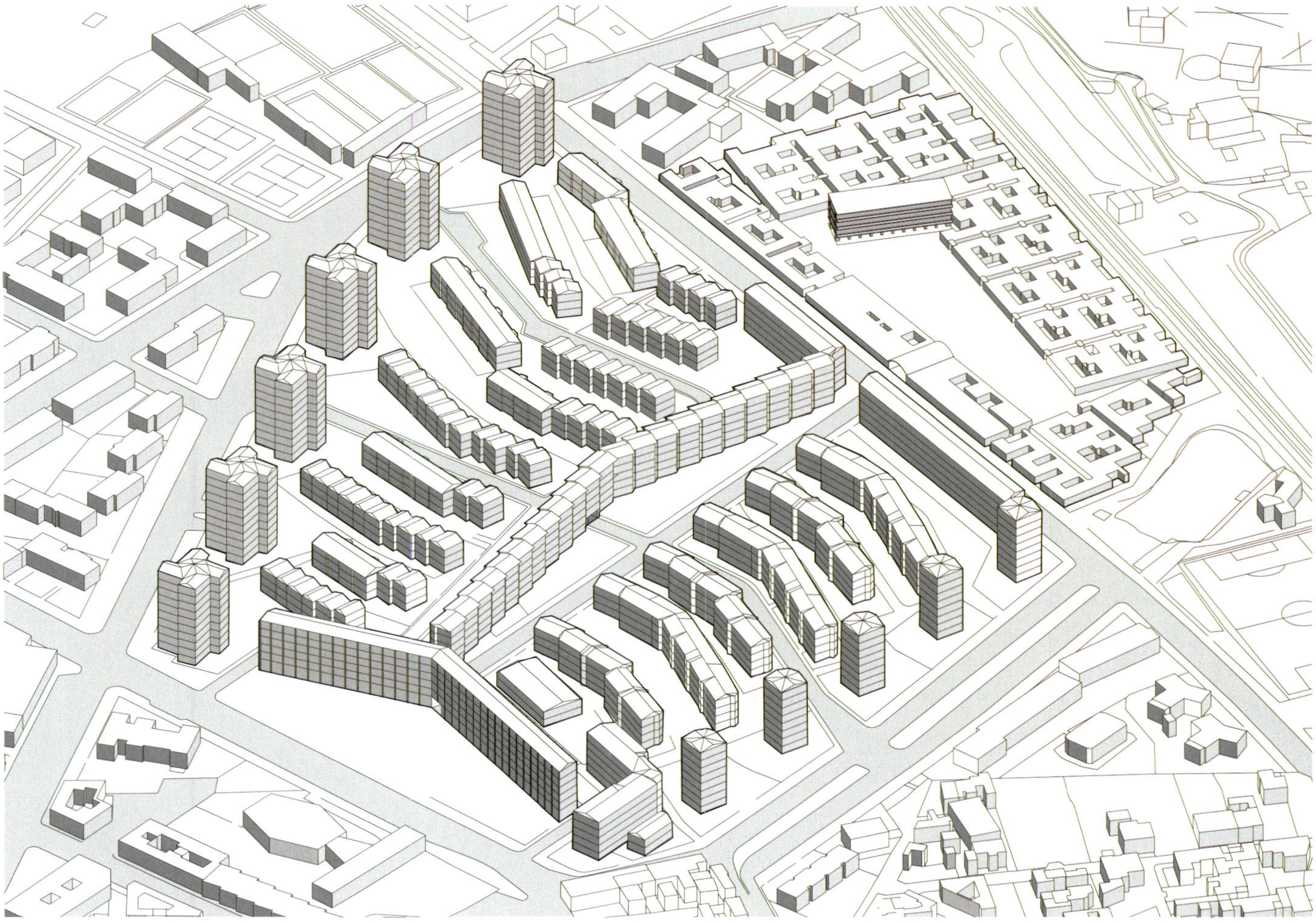

Axonometric view of Tuscolano II and III.

View of the perimeter wall around the Unità abitazione horizontale (Adalberto Libera, 1950–1954).

The Rational City According to Libera

The UIA Congress in Rabat, Morocco (1951), directed by Michel Écochard and in which Libera participated was an opportunity to visit Casablanca and its medina. In this context, Libera's project (1950–1954) was more inspired by the ancient urban architecture of Olynthus in Greece than by the modernist visions of Ludwig Hilberseimer or the Milano Verde project of Giuseppe Pagano, Irenio Diotallevi, and Francesco Marescotti (1940). The horizontal unit at Tuscolano was designed for 200 families (about 1000 people). Built on the edge of Tuscolano II and near the archaeological area of the aqueducts, Libera's complex is fully enclosed with shops on the outside and accessed by a reinforced concrete vaulted gate. Aligned with the portal of the Largo Spartaco building, it serves as a sort of vestibule into the inner triangular garden, originally overlooked by a café and a social center. The horizontal patio-based fabric is organized along a network of narrow pedestrian streets (2.7 meters wide), opening on to the garden. Each block consists of four L-shaped accommodations of different sizes (from two to four rooms) that include a living room located at the intersection of the arms of the L with the kitchen equipment in a niche. The entire composition of the patio-based fabric is interrupted in its geometry by the rotation of the three-story gallery building on pilotis, which contains 32 apartments and introduces an element of dissonance in the planimetric deployment, organized and measured by the golden rectangles of the patio grid.

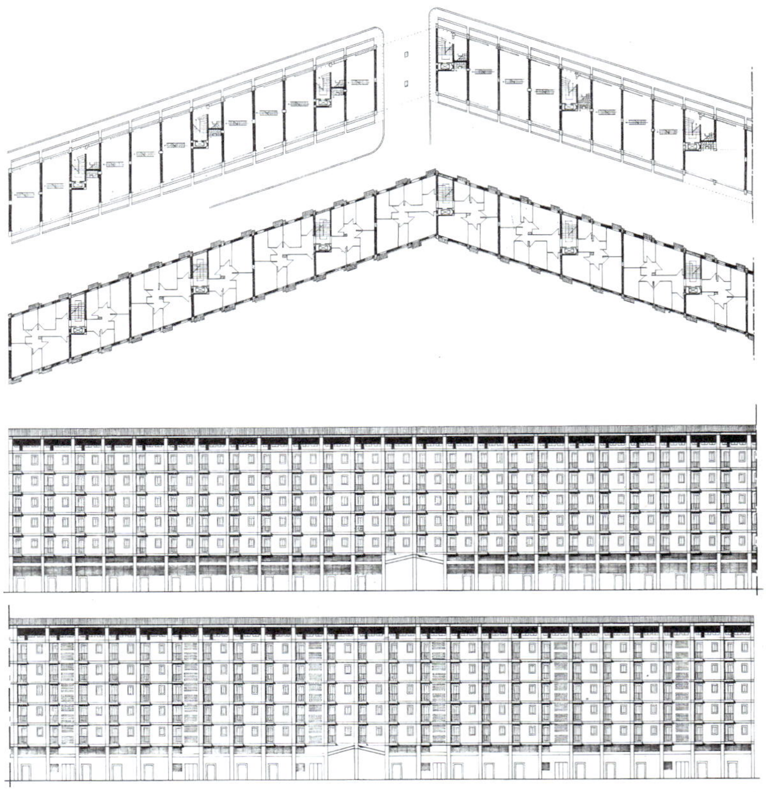

Saverio Muratori and Mario De Renzi, V-shaped apartment building and entry gate, detail of the back facade, plans, and elevation. Each housing unit occupies two structural bays, each punctuated by the same window-balcony alternation. Each cell of the structural grid, clearly delineated on the front and back facades, consists of a curtain of bricks with different textures, a window, and a projecting balcony.

Saverio Muratori and Mario De Renzi, townhouse type, 1950–1954.

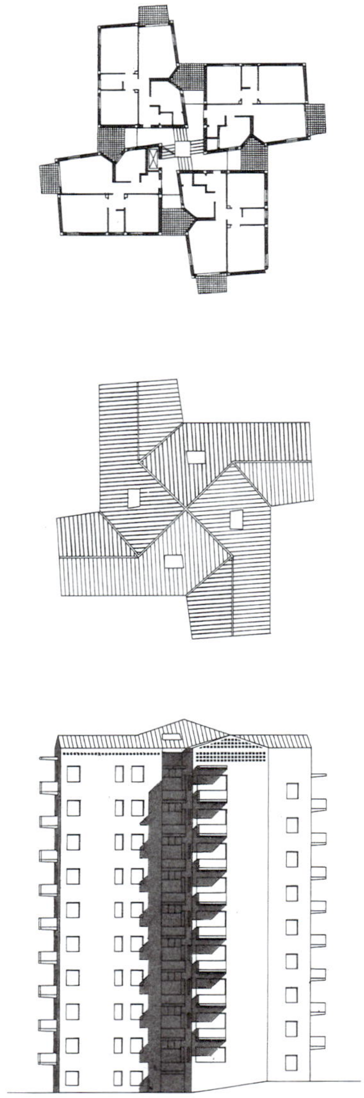

Saverio Muratori and Mario De Renzi, tower type along the northwestern edge, 1950–1954.

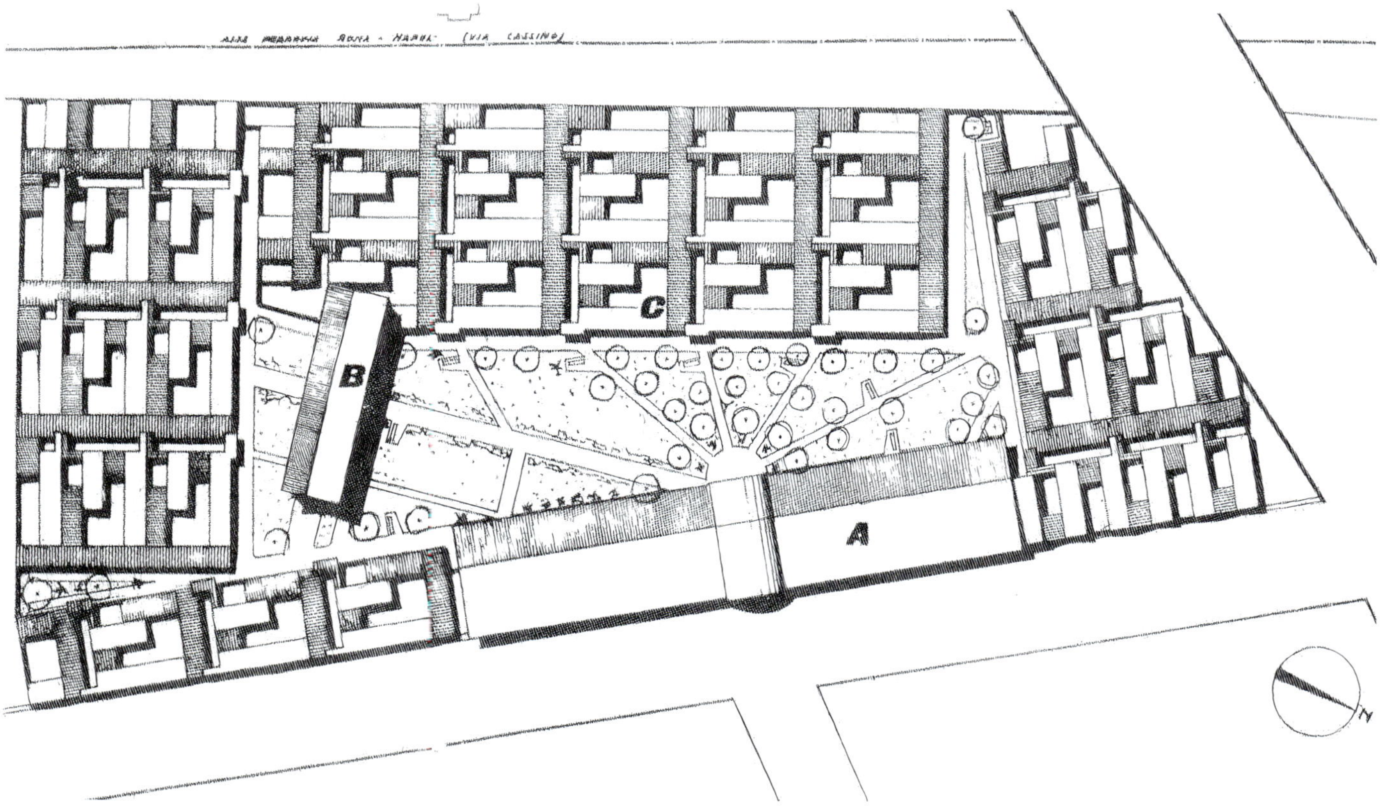

Adalberto Libera, Tuscolano III, 1950–1954. Plan, with shop row and entry gate (A), apartment block on pilotis (B), and grid of one-story patio house.

View of the entrance canopy to Tuscolano III from the inner garden.

Adalberto Libera, Tuscolano III, 1950–1954. Front (north) and back (south) views of the apartments on pilotis.

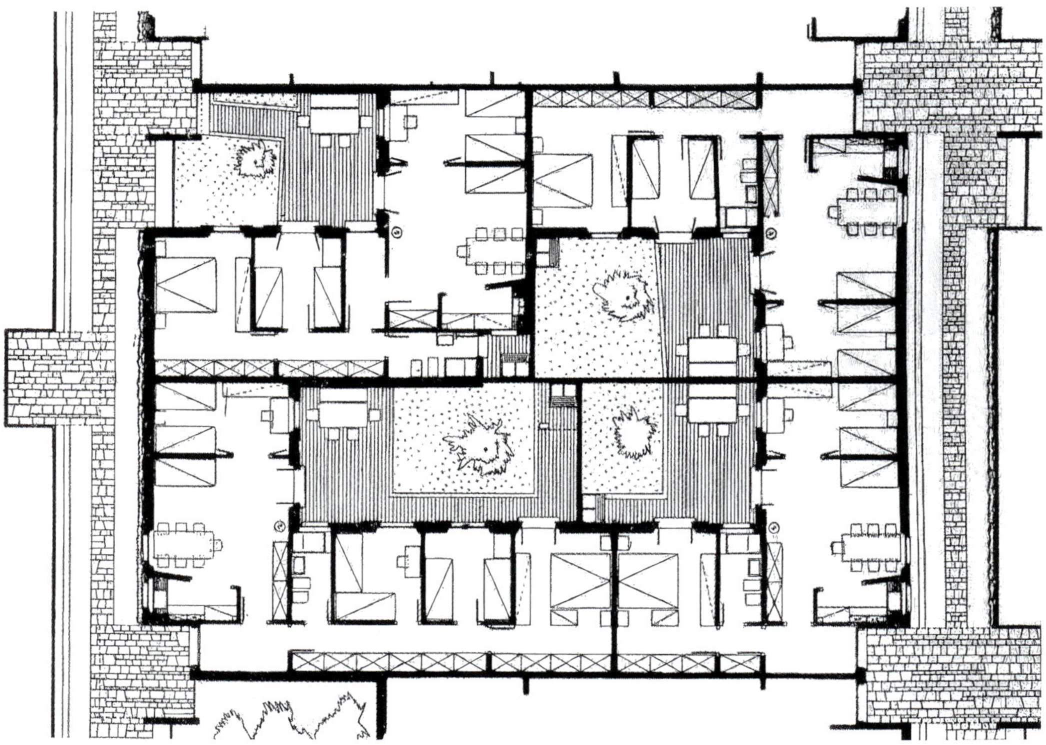

Adalberto Libera, Tuscolano III. Plan of assemblage of four patio units.

Adalberto Libera, Tuscolano III. View of a pedestrian alley between patio houses toward the central park.

Gaetano Rapisardi, perspective view of the Piazza Don Bosco, 1952–1964.

Quartiere Don Bosco

The Basilica of San Giovanni Bosco is in the square of the same name within the Tuscolano district. From the moment of its foundation, the church and its imposing metallic dome (47 meters high), smaller only than the Pantheon and St. Peter's, became an unmistakable presence in the desert-like southeastern landscape of Rome, an area mostly inhabited by indigent families living in shacks—a presence well documented by films such as *Il Tetto* and *Mamma Roma*. Based on the *Piano regolatore* of 1931—which already destined the area for intensive privately funded urbanization—the architect Gaetano Rapisardi designed the church and the 130-meter square piazza together to give the entire system a unitary character (1952–1964). From a typological and compositional point of view, this sense of unity is achieved through the two-floor-high giant order of porticoes and horizontal rows of apartment facades. However, the Rational style, together with the use of travertine for the facades facing the square and covering the entire Basilica, took up themes from pre-Second World War Roman architecture. Rapisardi's choice was the subject of harsh criticism and continues to be mostly ignored, but at the same time the residential square and church became the backdrop for many scenes in Federico Fellini's film *La Dolce Vita*, imagining them as part of the EUR district, itself very distant from the Cinecittà film studios. Following years of intense private development, the square now appears at the end of a long and wide avenue bordered by very high-density typologies yet to be studied and assessed.

View of the Piazza Don Bosco. The apartment blocks surrounding the square are eight stories high with a two-story continuous arcade and six floors of housing units. The horizontal emphasis of the design, with the continuous bands separating groups of two floors is unique in the Roman housing context.

Aerial view of the Quartiere Don Bosco with the piazza and the Basilica Don Bosco. The boulevard extending from the church is 1800 meters long. Note the density and special typologies of the district's housing units.

View of Via Cecoslovacchia at the intersection with Via Finlandia. On both sides: four-story linear type (*edificio in linea*); in the background, two-story cross-type housing (*palazzina a croce*).

Villaggio Olimpico 1958–1960

After a generation of resisting CIAM and its Athens Charter, Rome suddenly embraced its dogmas, just as it imploded as an organization. Like Ludovico Quaroni, the five urbanists and architects of Villaggio Olimpico—Vittorio Cafiero, Adalberto Libera, Luigi Moretti, Vincenzo Monaco, Amedeo Luccichenti—were ideological acrobats of astonishing agility, swinging from political branch to branch. They had done their best and most famous work before the Second World War, but the urbanism of Villaggio Olimpico—an undivided parcel of public land—is about as anti-Roman as can be. It is a conventional northern European *Zeilenbau*, consisting of a system of linear and cross-shaped housing slabs, all hoisted up on pilotis, completely divorced from streets, and floating in a giant green super-block. A couple of the bars are rotated in a feeble half-hearted attempt at creating a piazza with a couple of shops, Piazza Grecia, but it is mostly the color of the brick that makes the—slight—reference to the 2500 years of Roman building. Overall, it is quite a unexpected place, neither a park nor a real neighborhood. The traditional city of blocks and streets ends abruptly at its eastern edge with the Viale Tiziano, developed in the 1950s as a continuous street of *palazzine* on their little lots, just like in Parioli district. In contrast, the Olympic village was treated as a flat horizontal landscape whose centerpiece, if one can use such a hierarchical term for undifferentiated space, is the elevated motorway of the Corso Francia, whose elaborately sculpted concrete substructure was the work of Italy's technological hero, Pier Luigi Nervi. Inaugurated in 2002, the three-theater complex known today as the Auditorium Parco della Musica Ennio Morricone—which also includes shops, restaurants, and an open air cavea based on an antique theater—has rendered the Olympic Village more central to the life of the metropolis. (D.S.)

Architects
Vittorio Cafiero
Adalberto Libera
Amedeo Luccichenti
Vincenzo Monaco
Luigi Moretti

Pier Luigi Nervi, Palazzetto dello Sport, 1959.

Armando Brasini, view of the Ponte Flaminio, 1938–1951. Pier Luigi Nervi designed the prolongation of the elevated bridge across the Villaggio Olimpico.

Figure-ground plan of Villaggio Olimpico.

The masterplan of 1931 designated the area between Villa Glori, the Via Flaminia, and the current Viale Maresciallo Pilsudski as a public park but, in 1950, the zoning was changed. A competition was launched for the construction of a housing district and a new fast-flowing automobile axis to connect the Cassia and the Flaminia roads with Viale Tiziano and Viale Parioli. The project by Claudio Longo was the winner, but only a couple of slab buildings were built along Viale Tiziano near Ponte Milvio. Meanwhile, the agglomeration of housing shacks which gradually extended to occupy the disused sports facilities of Campo Parioli (National stadium for horse racing, Hippodrome of Villa Glori, Parioli tennis courts, and Cinodromo della Rondinella) were removed to make space for the Olympic Games of 1960. The two sports facilities were built by Pier Luigi Nervi—Stadio Flaminio (1957–1958) and the Palazzetto dello Sport (1956–1957, with architect Annibale Vitellozzi). Nervi was also the author of the elegant automobile viaduct that continues the Corso Francia south from the Flaminio Bridge and connects it with the Parioli hills. The construction of the Olympic Village was entrusted to INCIS, the Institute for the Homes of State Employees, which transformed it after the Games into a residential area for 6500 inhabitants. The architects Vittorio Cafiero, Adalberto Libera, Luigi Moretti, Vincenzo Monaco, and Amedeo Luccichenti were chosen to conceive the urbanistic and architectural project. Of the total 35 hectares of surface area, 16 were reserved for green areas, 12 for roads, and only seven were occupied by buildings that did not exceed five floors in height (150 inhabitants/hectare).

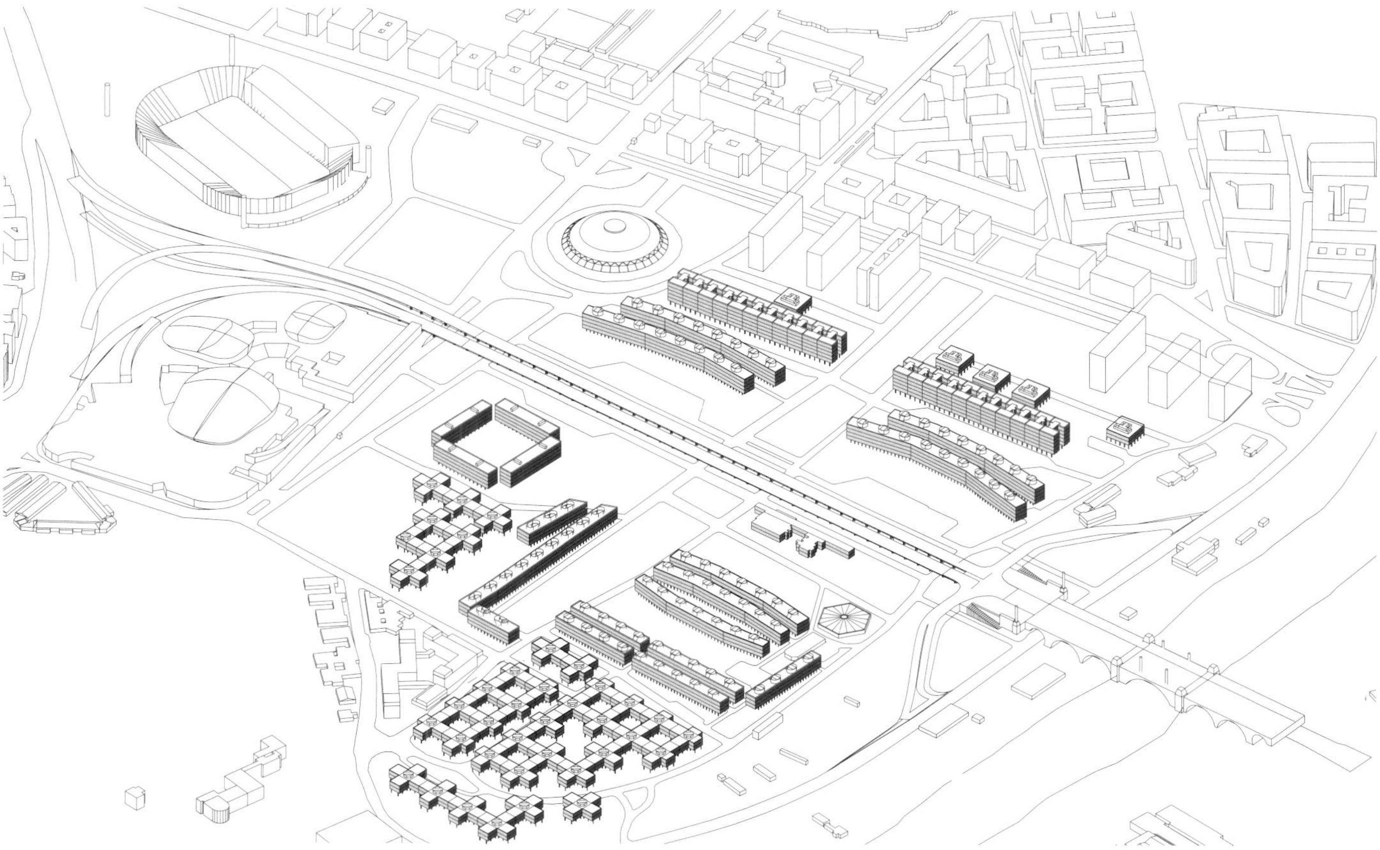

Axonometric view. At the center, the Olympic Village. Around from left to right: Renzo Piano's Auditorium Parco della Musica Ennio Morricone; Nervi's Flaminio Stadium; Nervi's Palazzetto dello Sport; Via Flaminia and Ponte Milvio; Ponte Flaminio.

Adalberto Libera, Vittorio Cafiero, Amedeo Luccichenti, Luigi Moretti, Vincenzo Monaco, view from the pilotis of the two-story cross-housing type.

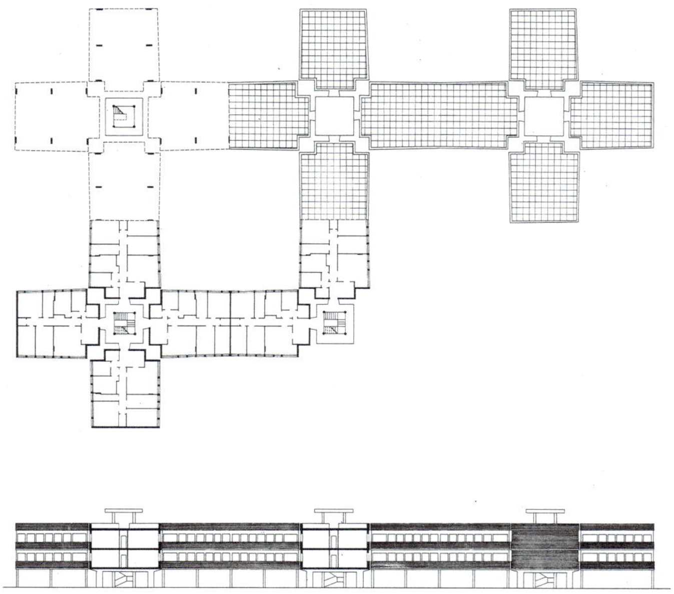

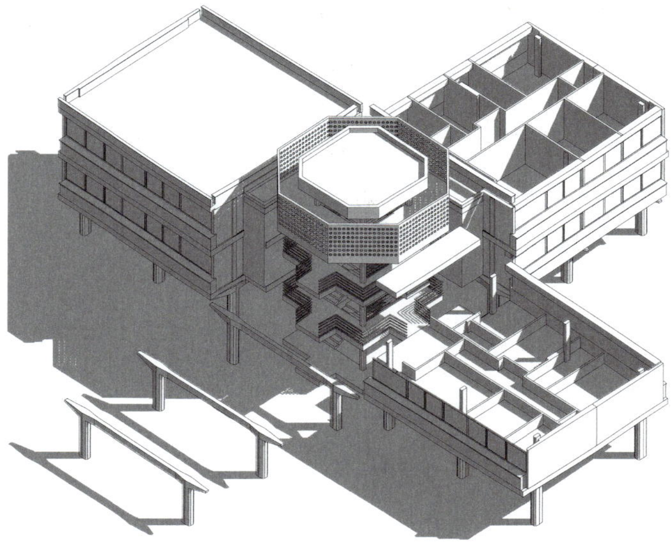

Adalberto Libera, Vittorio Cafiero, Amedeo Luccichenti, Luigi Moretti, Vincenzo Monaco, two-story cross-type housing (*palazzina a croce*). Plans.

View of the pedestrianized Piazza Grecia defined by linear housing types.

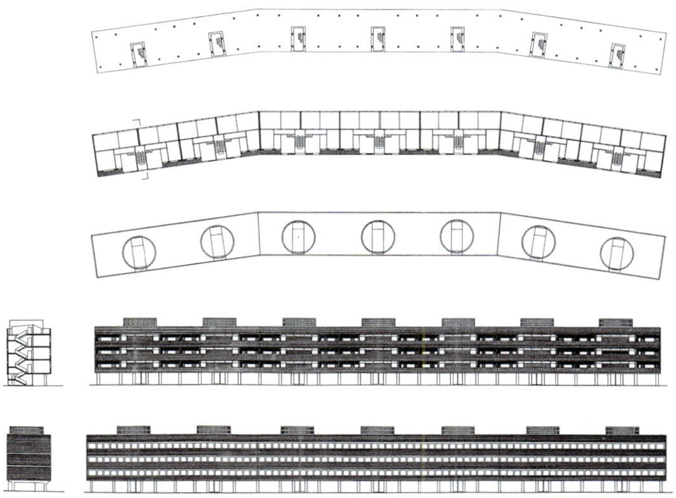

Adalberto Libera, Vittorio Cafiero, Amedeo Luccichenti, Luigi Moretti, Vincenzo Monaco, linear housing type.

For the first time in Rome, the Olympic Village was conceived according to the principles of the Modern Movement. The architects rejected the concept of urban continuity founded on a network of blocks, streets, and squares and chose instead to conceive of the district as the sum of a series of urban objects, not entirely isolated but subtly linked to each other by transparencies, typologies, and dimensions. The attempt to create a traditional urban space—the paved and pedestrianized Piazza Grecia—was well-intentioned but eventually failed due to the lack of appropriate enclosures and proportions. In choosing to elevate all structures on pilotis, the designers moved away from the millenary urban traditions of the city. Buildings are arranged to the right and left of the north-south Corso Francia viaduct, while the Viale XVII Olimpiade, perpendicular to the viaduct, constitutes the primary automobile entrance. From the point of view of morphology and typology, the overall project displays some unique elements. The most interesting typological case is certainly represented by the "carpet" of two-story houses on pilotis arranged to form a horizontal "cross" fabric with two different solutions for the staircase body, located at the intersection point of the meshes, which distributes four apartments per floor. The solution applied to the staircase system allows us to distinguish the Libera version (closer to the river) from the Moretti one (near the Auditorium, with the staircase placed at 45 degrees). Second, a group of four-story linear buildings are arranged to form a full and densely planted square courtyard (near the Auditorium). Moreover, there are four-story linear houses, sometimes folded and duplicated in pairs, sometimes as linear buildings. Two five-story linear buildings with a "triple body" (apartments arranged on two slats and a central cloister), the only ones with an elevator, mark the boundary of the neighborhood toward Viale Tiziano together with some smaller *palazzine*-like structures arranged on pilotis on a square plan. Overall, the typological variety was unified by the choice of architectural elements common to all the volumetric cases described: pilotis, concrete stringcourses, white-painted ribbon windows, ocher-colored brick curtain, crowning elements of the building and terraces. The church of San Valentino built by Francesco Barucci, a supermarket, and a pre-existing school are part of the neighborhood. Designed by Renzo Piano Building Workshop, the three-theater complex Auditorium Parco della Musica Ennio Morricone was completed in 2002. A small museum presents the archaeological discoveries and the models of three suburban villas and farmhouses which were excavated on the grounds.

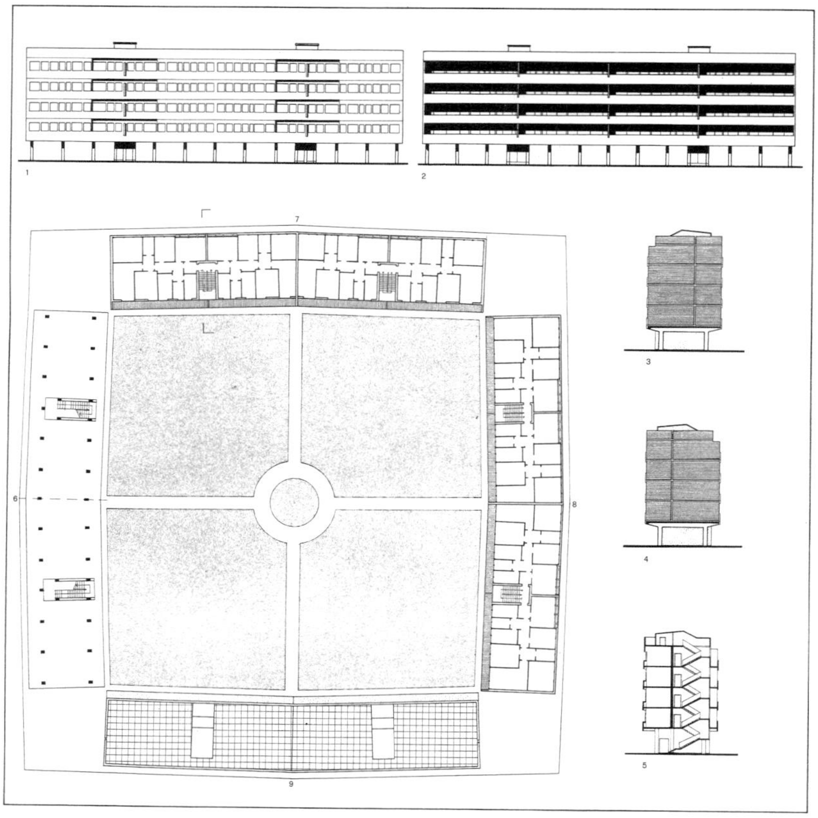

Adalberto Libera, Vittorio Cafiero, Amedeo Luccichenti, Luigi Moretti, Vincenzo Monaco. Courtyard housing type.

Francesco Berarducci, Church of San Valentino al Villaggio Olimpico, 1979. Detail of the perimeter wall.

View of an interior corner of the large courtyard housing type.

View of an exterior corner of the large courtyard housing type.

● The porticoes of Piazza Don Bosco, in a metaphysical moment in *La Dolce Vita* (Federico Fellini, 1960).

Modern Rome and the Cinematic Gaze

Salvatore Santuccio

In the brief period from 1958 to 1962, seven high-quality films—seven genuine works of art—lit up the cinema screens: *I soliti ignoti (Big Deal on Madonna Street)* by Mario Monicelli (1958), *La Dolce Vita* by Federico Fellini (1960), *Accattone* (1961) and *Mamma Roma* (1962) by Pier Paolo Pasolini, *L'eclisse* (The Eclipse) by Michelangelo Antonioni (1962), *Il Boom* by Vittorio De Sica (1962), and *Boccaccio '70* (1962), a film in episodes by four master directors (Monicelli, Visconti, Fellini, and De Sica). These movies were not only milestones in the history of Italian cinema, but they gave a live testimony of the tentacular urban development of the city of Rome, as well as the resounding transformation of its territory and population. In fact, between 1951 and 1961, the city's population grew by more than 500,000 inhabitants, from 1,651,700 to 2,188,160, leading to an enormous number of construction sites and new buildings that were also directly narrated in Italian cinema.[1] In step with this urban growth, Italian cinema was at the height of its splendor and Cinecittà was the driving force behind this great production. The association between Rome as a city under construction and Rome as a city of cinema was definitively enshrined—the starting point in tracing the role that cinema played in the narrative of modern Rome.[2]

The building on Viale XXI Aprile called Palazzo Federici by Mario De Renzi in the movie *A Special Day* (Ettore Scola, 1977).

Palazzo Federici by Mario De Renzi in the movie *A Special Day*. The residents are leaving to go to Via dei Fori Imperiali and attend the parade for Adolf Hitler.

Before the Boom

Before the great "economic miracle" and building boom of the 1960s, Rome was depicted in film first and foremost as a city characterized by a collective way of life that somehow reconstructed a town or village dimension within large building complexes. To do so, most movies relied on two modern types of buildings inherited from Fascist Rome: intensive housing blocks and working-class suburbs.

The best depiction of this reality of Roman life can be found in Ettore Scola's *Una giornata particolare* (*A Special Day*, 1977), whose story takes place in a subsidized housing unit on Viale XXI Aprile, a huge residential complex designed by Mario De Renzi and built between 1931 and 1937. The action narrated in the film occurred on 3 May 1938, when Hitler and Mussolini met in Rome on an official visit. Its architectural and tri-dimensional organization was spatially rich and complex, lending itself ideally to the development of an intense story between a disenchanted housewife (Sophia Loren) and a gay radio host (Marcello Mastroianni) on the road to professional and human failure. The plot not only required places to hide, spy, kiss, and flee—the kitchen, the apartments, the courtyard, the laundry roof terrace—but also large scenographic spaces for the Fascist crowds en route to the official pageant on Via dei Fori Imperiali. The complex where all the action takes place, also known as Palazzo Federici, was at the time a state-of-the-art residential project, which consisted of 442 residential units, 70 shops, a garage, two levels of public spaces, and a 1600-seat movie theater. The superblock of housing embodied a particular Fascist vision of the working masses, to which the character played by Sophia Loren—Antonietta, an uneducated and stereotypical mother of six children and the wife of a rough man, the "Duce" of the house—wholly belonged. It was equally the hiding place for Gabriele (Marcello Mastroianni), a more aware anti-Fascist than Antonietta, but a resigned homosexual, more willing to conceal himself than flaunt his public role on radio, and therefore well integrated with the living conditions of the social palazzo.[3]

Life in intensive high-density housing was displayed in many other films, precisely because it lent itself nicely to a communal dimension of living that was both frequent and organized. In *I soliti ignoti* (*Big Deal on Madonna Street*, 1958), Ferribotte (Michele Nicosia) and his very chaste and unreachable sister Carmelina (Claudia Cardinale) also live in a very interesting high-density complex, i.e., Palazzo Lamperini (1887–1900, Vincenzo Martinucci) on Via Tiburtina at San Lorenzo, a

The building with open circulation catwalks in *Big Deal on Madonna Street* (Mario Monicelli, 1958).

The Val Melaina complex in Montesacro in *Love in the City* (Alberto Lattuada, 1953).

building which is rich in outdoor catwalk-like balconies and remains a rare example of that typology in Rome. Another intensive housing complex, this time in Montesacro, served as the setting for *Tentato suicidio* (*Attempted Suicide*), the episode signed by Michelangelo Antonioni in *L'amore in città* (*Love in the City*, 1953). Located right next to the 1940s housing blocks featured in *I ladri di bicicletta* (*Bicycle Thiefs*) by Vittorio De Sica (1948), the social housing superblock built by the ICP in the early 1930s and organized around three large interior courtyards along Via del Valle Melaina was the powerful background for the dramatic relationship between Maria Nobili, her fiancé Giacomo, and her rival Marcella.[4]

Together with the most interesting projects of intensive housing, the life of the lower-middle classes in Rome was also set up within the working-class suburbs built by the Fascist regime to relocate families expelled by the demolitions enacted in the historic center to open the Via dei Fori imperiali and the Via della Conciliazione. Prominent among them was the Borgata Primavalle (Giorgio Guidi, 1938–1939), built between 1936 and 1939 to the west of the Vatican, whose life and modernist linear design were recounted by two great masters of Italian Neorealist cinema: Luchino Visconti and Roberto Rossellini. The former made a documentary about the violent death of Annarella Bracci in 1950 entitled *Appunti su un fatto di cronaca* (1951), in which the neighborhood was depicted as a positive and reassuring domestic landscape despite the tragedy of the girl's murder. In *Europe '51*, a movie from 1952, Rossellini focused on the poor segment of people in the suburb. Long fascinated by San Francesco di Assisi, he decided to create a film that placed a person of the saint's character in post-war Italy and showed what the consequences would be. A sumptuous Ingrid Bergman

The working-class suburb of Primavalle in *Europe '51* (Roberto Rossellini, 1951).

wanders around philanthropically and guilt-ridden in a desperate search for communication with her inner sensitivity. Additional film sets were designed by Virgilio Marchi (1895–1960), an important Futurist architect and set designer.[5]

Nanni Moretti's homage to the working-class garden city La Garbatella deserves a special mention in the "On My Vespa" episode of *Caro diario* (*Dear Diary*, 1993), where the idea of community stems from the very beginning of the construction and remains at the center of life in this extraordinary place. Moretti's Vespa crosses the squares and courtyards of the garden city—built by the ICP (Istituto Case Popolari) starting in early 1920s, a mix of *barocchetto*-style architecture typical of Rome in the 1920s with picturesque and vernacular accents. One stop on the Vespa tour is the quasi-futurist Albergo Rosso, designed by Innocenzo Sabbatini. This notable structure was built by the ICP in 1927–1929 to temporarily house evacuees as per Fascist plans for the demolition of the historic center, although it soon became their permanent residence. Another significant building in Garbatella includes the elementary school Cesare Battisti, built in 1930 and designed by the architect Brunetto. Facing the central Piazza Damiano Sauli, it was immortalized in many films as a sort of model school, a genuine emblematic building for these purposes.

The atrium of the Palazzo dei Congressi by Adalberto Libera at EUR, transformed into a Fascist government lobby, in *The Conformist* (Bernardo Bertolucci, 1970).

The roof of the Palazzo dei Congressi at EUR as a psychiatric hospital in *The Conformist*.

Anita Ekberg as a giant at EUR in *The Temptation of Doctor Antonio (Le tentazioni del dottor Antonio*, Federico Fellini, 1962).

The Metaphysical City

EUR is cinema: from 1945 with Rossellini's *Roma città aperta* (*Rome Open City*, 1945), more than 150 films have become an added value to the history and iconography of the district conceived and designed to celebrate the universal exposition of 1942, later known as EUR.[6] The films have transformed the historic place, desired by the Fascist regime and its architects and saved from abandonment after the war, in a location unique in the world, which film makers have turned into an abstract, absent, and metaphysical set. Over the years, the Italian *cinema d'auteur* has made extensive use of EUR's abstracted classicism, its arcades inspired by Giorgio de Chirico, its obelisk, its mushroom-like water tower, and the omnipresent white marble walls and surfaces used for its main buildings. Two the most stunning scenes can be found in Bernardo Bertolucci's *Il conformista* (*The Conformist*, 1970). The cubical atrium-like exhibition hall of Adalberto Libera's Palazzo dei Congressi (1938–1954) becomes a monumental entrance to Fascist headquarters; the white marble walls of the roof terrace metamorphosed into the theatrical setting of an asylum. Another example is the disturbing nightmare of Dr. Antonio (Peppino de Filippo) in Fellini's episode in *Boccaccio '70*: a gigantic Anita Ekberg wanders like an improbable Gulliver through a deserted and unassuming EUR between the Palazzo della Civiltà (Giovanni Guerrini, Ernesto Lapadula, and Mario Romano, 1938–1940, completed after the war) and the Palazzo dei Congressi. This scene recalls a similar shot of Anna Magnani arriving breathlessly on a motorbike at the Palazzo dei Congressi in Monicelli's *Risate di gioia* (*The Passionate Thief*, 1960), where the same metaphysical restlessness permeates the avenue leading to the Palazzo della Civiltà in the darkness of night.

The most profound metaphysical and realist depiction of EUR, however, is owed to Michelangelo Antonioni in *L'eclisse* (*The Eclipse*, 1962). Monica Vitti's wanderings through a deserted residential district, devoid of any vitality, sad and cold, has become one of the high points in Antonioni's narration regarding the restlessness of the society he described. As the maestro himself clearly stated, "The relationship between actor and environment is very important because I rely very precisely on the environment, whether natural or artificial, for particular psychological moments, so that each scene has the utmost effectiveness, its greatest suggestiveness," and this happens wonderfully in *The Eclipse*.[7] Antonioni does not show the EUR built in the 1930s but focuses on the other side of the district, constructed in the 1950s as a modern housing quarter. The urban void—not as a sparse landscape but as

Monica Vitti and Francisco Rabal in the empty landscape of EUR with the mushroom-like water tower in the background (Roberto Colosimo, A. Martinelli, Aldo Capozza, Sergio Varisco, 1960) in *The Eclipse* (Michelangelo Antonioni, 1962).

The 1950s urban landscape of *palazzine* in the residential section of EUR as shown in *The Eclipse*.

The Don Bosco neighborhood under construction in *La Dolce Vita*.

urban sprawl with no street life—becomes a fundamental element of the characters' unease, their incommunicable solipsism.[8] The buildings follow each other in a sort of series with no relative fabric of communication and the characters, amplifying this incommunicability, are often filtered in their participation within the surroundings, experiencing it through screens, windows, mirrors, glass: "The girl has dark, beautiful eyes, and a strange way of looking. Looks that are like rustles. ... Her world is behind the glass of the windows and every afternoon she goes out and goes around the world, which is the neighborhood where she lives."[9]

Interestingly, EUR is not the only metaphysical urban fabric borrowed by cinema. A second pole of interest is the Don Bosco district coordinated and designed by Gaetano Rapisardi (1893–1988) and whose construction started in 1952.[10] Don Bosco is narrated by Fellini in *La Dolce Vita* as an unusual place in modern Rome, portrayed in sunny daylight within a film that celebrates and recounts the Roman night. This is where the protagonist, played by Marcello Mastroianni, meets Steiner: "The encounters between Marcello and his intellectual friend take place entirely in this square: from the initial meeting in which Steiner calls to Marcello, busy with a photographer and model under the porticoes that lend themselves well to eccentric photos with a horse next to the café tables, to inside the church, a silent and mystical place contrasting the atmosphere of the journalist's work."[11] The Don Bosco district would reappear many times in various movies, perhaps also because of its relative proximity to Cinecittà. The porticoes and church are used as a backdrop to the night raid in *L'audace colpo dei soliti ignoti* (*Fiasco in Milan*, 1959) by Nanni Loy, in which the characters have to decide what to do with the suitcase full of money that no one wants to take home amid the accomplices' mistrust, and the nightmare of the approaching police. And in *The Eclipse* again, during the couple of seconds that the small plane flies over Rome, it is the Don Bosco district, perhaps the last major urban creation in the history of Rome, that Antonioni chose to show below the wings.

A third metaphysical place is Piazza Augusto Imperatore and the buildings designed by Vittorio Ballio Morpurgo (1890–1966). The famous comic actor Totò made a cameo appearance with these buildings in Rossellini's *Dov'è la libertà* (*Where is Freedom?*, 1954), when he gets out of prison and goes to look for the piazza but cannot find it amid the new architectural Fascist configuration of Ballio Morpurgo. He asks a passer-by where it is, only to declare, "How badly it has been reduced!" Piazza Augusto Imperatore also appears in the episode *Amore che si paga* (*Paid Love*) by Carlo Lizzani in the already mentioned *Love in the City* (1953). Here, Morpurgo's gigantic porticoes are a place of ill repute, where ill-concealed prostitution takes place amid dark shadows and sinful glances.[12]

Separate space is reserved for the interpretation of modern marble and the architecture of Termini train station, the setting for so many films and a constant presence in Roman cinematography. Indeed, the image of Rome's largest station is present in films ranging from *Love in the City* to *Un altra vita* (*Another Life*, 1992) by Carlo Mazzacurati, from *Fiasco in Milan* to *Il piccolo diavolo* (*The Little Devil*, 1988) by Roberto Benigni—all films describing arrivals and departures, first contacts with the Eternal City, and escapes from it. However, two films intertwine with Termini station in a particularly significant

The escape of thieves toward the portico of Don Bosco in *Fiasco in Milan* (Nanni Loy, 1959).

Piazza Augusto Imperatore by Vittorio Ballio Morpurgo, 1931–1937 as a place of prostitution in *Paid Love* (Carlo Lizzani, 1953).

Jennifer Jones at the ticket office of Termini train station in *Terminal Station* (Vittorio De Sica, 1953).

relationship: *Stazione Termini* (*Terminal Station*) by De Sica (1953) and Fellini's *Ginger & Fred* (1985). Three years after its post-war reopening, De Sica presented a very interesting and personal interpretation of the station, which becomes a sort of non-place where the love story between Mary (Jennifer Jones), an uncertain young American lady and mother, and Giovanni (Montgomery Clift), the restless young Italian boy, unfolds. The two live as if in a trance; the station, with its spaces, sounds, and chaotic dynamics, enhances the sense of their alienation. In a very different way, Fellini treats the station as a sort of gigantic postmodern caravanserai, truculent and monstrous, in which tiny Giulietta Masina wanders around, intimidated and awkward, with her expectations for the future. The space of Termini station even appears small, too intimate, to accommodate the great kermesse of humanity overflowing from it. From flying hams to the most absurd vendors of improbable trinkets, everything tends to define a truculent Babel *à la* Fellini that seems able to explode the architectural space of the Roman station.

Suburbs and Social Housing

One of the most complex and recurring themes in political Italian cinema has been the portrayal of social housing, that is, the relationship between the city and its suburbs, and between the underprivileged classes and their housing environment. From Luigi Zampa's *L'onorevole Angelina* (*Angelina*, 1947) to De Sica's *Il ladro di biciclette* (*The Bicycle Thief*, 1948), from Augusto Genina's *Tre storie proibite* (*Three Forbidden Stories*, 1952) to *Big Deal on Madonna Street*, the cinematography involves large Roman suburban settlements—Prenestino, Val Melaina, or Tiburtino—depicting not only their great size and problems, but also in some ways suspending judgment. If there is degradation, it is existential, sociological, rarely architectural and, despite the large number of users, the suburban settlement often seems to regain a state of community and solidarity among the inhabitants. In the face of everything, it remains a place of support and cohesion.

In this regard, some key episodes that took place in that crucial decade from 1950 to 1960 are interesting. The first is Luchino Visconti's *Bellissima* (1951). The film tells the story of Maddalena Cecconi (Anna Magnani), desperate to get her daughter hired for a movie, seeking in this her own affirmation, as if the redemption of her daughter's life could give meaning to the failure of her own. The large working-class settlement of Tor Pignattara, where Cecconi resides, becomes an essential narrative subject for the film's plot: "Through the chorus of women,

The popular Pietralata district in *Angelina* (Luigi Zampa, 1947).

Val Melaina district in *Bicycle Thieves* (Vittorio De Sica, 1948).

The Tufello district in *Big Deal on Madonna Street* (Mario Monicelli, 1958).

Visconti gives life to a lively kermesse atmosphere .... He views the block of flats where Maddalena lives as a sort of large theatre, in which private affairs immediately turn into public knowledge. The tenants in the building intervene in all family discussions, ready to back Maddalena against her husband."[13] The housing estate therefore becomes a living organism, a kind of Greek chorus, a literary place before an architectural one.

The second film containing a notable interpretation is Vittorio De Sica's film *Il tetto* (*The Roof*, 1956), realized in collaboration with Cesare Zavattini. Natale (Giorgio Listuzzi) and Luisa (Gabriella Pallotti) marry and move in with Natale's family on the periphery of Rome. The young couple are soon at each other's throats when they're unable to get any privacy. Lacking money, they decide to build a house for themselves on unclaimed land. The law states any building with a roof cannot be pulled down, so with the help of friends and family, the pair build a modest dwelling in one night before the police arrive. The epic story of the couple who views self-building as the only possible solution to their desire to live together, sends a message that is not exactly educational, but which represents a common situation of squatting that was dramatically relevant in post-war Rome. The whole affair takes place at the very foot of Ridolfi's and Frankl's towers of Viale Etiopia, shown in construction. Moreover, in the background of the shack, the modern dome of San Giovanni Bosco rises as a moment of order amid the city's building chaos.[14]

The third important contribution consists of the exceptional films by Pier Paolo Pasolini in the early 1960s. In his debut film *Accattone* (1961), and even more so in *Mamma Roma* (1962), he clearly illustrates the interweaving that takes place between the destitute conditions of the lower class and the places where they live. Closely tied to Pasolini's previous novels, *Ragazzi di vita* (1955) and *Una vita violenta* (*A Violent Life*, 1959), these two films mirror the reflections of a great intellectual "looking at what was going on inside the soul of a person from the urban lower class."[15] While the decay of the suburbs in *Accattone* simply serves as a backdrop to the vicissitudes of the hapless Vittorio Cataldi (Franco Citti), the place of dwelling is important in *Mamma Roma* because it marks the aspirations and disappointments of the protagonist's life. Roma Garofolo (Anna Magnani) works for her redemption and the protection of her son Ettore, first of all by removing him from the degraded places where she and the little boy lived, Casal Bertone and Guidonia. The "new life" of the perplexed and slouching Ettore and Mamma Roma begins in a public housing apartment block near Cinecittà, as if the aspiration of the lower

Apartment house in the popular working-class settlement Tor Pignattara in *Bellissima* (Luchino Visconti, 1951).

"This was a meadow," in *The Roof* (Vittorio De Sica, 1956).

Apartment towers under construction in *The Roof.*

Vittorio, known as Accattone, killed in a motorcycle accident with the 1920s social housing of Testaccio seen from Ponte Testaccio in *Accattone* (Pier Paolo Pasolini, 1961).

The INA-Casa Tuscolano district with a view of Saverio Muratori's gate building in *Mamma Roma* (Pier Paolo Pasolini, 1962).

The Tuscolano district, Via Lucio Sestio and Parco degli Acquedotti, in *Mamma Roma.*

class to conform—see the desperate search to resemble the middle class which Pasolini uses for his analysis—lay entirely in moving from the squatter suburb to an official apartment in social housing. This apparent social progress is played to perfection by the buildings that Pasolini used in the Quadraro district in the area of Tuscolano.[16]

This illusion is destined to collapse, of course, and the residential difference is only apparent; the social condition is the same. The illusion of social redemption does not depend on a change in neighborhood; in 1960s Rome, it simply cannot exist. The social conditions of the lower classes amount first and foremost to an inner drama and thus cannot interact with the planned environment, i.e., with the message that urban planners attempt to convey by promoting a middle-class ideology that determines choices and justifies economic hoarding.

Opening scene of the movie *The Easy Life* (Dino Risi, 1962), with a long sequence of *palazzine* in Balduina district.

Penthouse apartment of Alberto Sordi in the film *Il Boom* (Vittorio De Sica, 1963), with the large terrace overlooking the EUR.

Facade of Casa Papanice by Paolo Portoghesi, 1967, in *Jealousy, Italian Style* (Ettore Scola, 1970).

Interior of Casa Papanice in *Jealousy, Italian Style*.

Palazzina Dreaming

Running counter to the residential living conditions presented by the suburbs, the middle-class or upper middle-class condition was essentially rooted in the cinematographic spectacle of the *palazzina*, the unique Roman typology of detached and four-facades apartment buildings. These buildings represent an affluent and conformist city, rich and elegant, but also often empty and absent. It is a symbol of the Roman middle-class urban architecture of the 1940s and 1950s, its widespread social aspirations, and the economic, productive, and professional dimension of small capitalism. Their cinematic presence began to appear more systematically around 1950, with Luciano Emmer's *Domenica d'agosto* (*Sunday in August*, 1950), Rossellini's *Europe '51*, Luigi Zampa's episode "Isa Miranda" in *Siamo donne* (*We, the Women*, 1954), Antonioni's *La signora senza camelie* (*The Lady without Camelias*, 1953), and again, as an unattainable dream for the two gentle proletarians, in De Sica's *The Roof.*

Right from the opening credits, the beginning of *Il sorpasso* (*The Easy Life*, 1962) by Dino Risi offers us an aseptic black-and-white panorama of *palazzine* in a deserted city. We are in Balduina, one of the new emblematic places created when the "economic miracle" started to transform the country from a traditionally agricultural and family centered society into a more individualistic and consumerist one. The same applies, many years later, to Ettore Scola's *La terrazza* (*The Terrace*, 1980), which recounts the lives of the depressed and discontented upper-class, "sad intellectuals" as the director defined them, wonderfully played by Jean-Louis Trintignant, Marcello Mastroianni, Serge Reggiani, Ugo Tognazzi, and Vittorio Gassman, who are intertwined in the often-crowded rooms of large apartments with superb views over the city.

In the *palazzina* considered as a type, everything contributes to the aesthetic standards of the 1950s, from the architecture to the urban space, from the windows to the furniture, from the cars in the garage to the ladies' clothing and hairstyles. In fact, the 1950s were symbolized and celebrated through the Roman *palazzina*.[17] This is the case for the sumptuous penthouse where Giovanni (Alberto Sordi) lives in the film *Il Boom* (1963), with a wrap-around terrace with a view of the EUR and its glass high-rises and a funny mixture of modern furniture, implausibly inlaid fixtures, and gold candelabra. Giovanni mortgages the house and loses, leaving his wife in dismay as she returns to her father, having lost the symbol of her true, or rather, presumed wealth. Equally celebrated is the interior of Paolo Portoghesi's and Vittorio Gigliotti's modern Baroque Casa Papanice in Via Giuseppe Marchi across from the Palazzo Federici. It becomes the butcher's house in Ettore Scola's *Dramma della gelosia* (*Jealousy, Italian Style*, 1970), and then Mrs. Wardh's house the following year in Sergio Martino's sexy thriller, *Lo strano vizio della signora Wardh* (*The Strange Vice of Mrs. Wardh*, 1971).[18] Likewise in Antonioni's *L'eclisse*, the *palazzina*, built or in construction, plays a major role in creating a state of alienation and isolation. The most important scenes are all located in the residential districts of EUR: Sandro's apartment (appearing in the first scene) is in Via Antartide, from which Vittoria walks to get to her *palazzina* in Via dell'Umanesimo no. 317 (by Michele Valori, Leonardo Benevolo, Giampaolo Rotondi); her friend lives in Via dell'Umanesimo no. 307, in another *palazzina* from the late 1950s, also built by Michele Valori.

Eventually, the real celebration of the *palazzina* as an architectural type that dominates large sections of Roman urban space is found in the first episode of Nanni Moretti's *Caro diario* (*Dear Diary*) entitled "On My Vespa." Here, the director recounts his city from an unusual perspective: scooting around on a Vespa, traveling roads without traffic, peripheral districts, and further landscapes that are not particularly sought after or well known. Moretti presents a unified image of the city, which he is bound to by affection and daily presence. He successfully describes it through a skillful itinerary that avoids the universally recognized monuments and touristic places. The image of Rome that emerges from this not so casual Vespa trip by a curious resident is that of its "signature" modern architecture, the *palazzina*, that seems to spread throughout the city as a sort of uniform fabric. In fact, on this cruise through the streets of Rome, Moretti passes through residential neighborhoods and suburban quarters, established or not, and encounters important works of architecture from the 20th century without making judgments of either merit or sympathy about their temporal development. Moretti reviews the houses in his city, an empty city in August, to the background sound of "Didi" by Khaled, showing us a vast ensemble of *palazzine* from Parioli to Monteverde, Prati, Balduina, and Ostiense. In a heroic succession that depicts the quality of Rome through a few individual masterpieces, starting with the Girasole (1950), designed by Luigi Moretti on Viale Buozzi, and ending with the Belsito residential complex at Piazzale delle Medaglie d'Oro (1952–1953) by Monaco and Lucciched. The Girasole's famous entrance also appears in the episode "Italians Stare" by Alberto Lattuada in *L'amore in città* (*Love in the City*, 1953).

Viale Bruno Buozzi during the ride on a Vespa in the "On My Vespa" episode of *Dear Diary* (Nanni Moretti, 1993).

The entrance of Casa del Girasole by Luigi Moretti, 1950, in the episode "Italians Stare" of the film *Love in the City* (Alberto Lattuada, 1953).

The Growing City

The phenomenal growth of Rome in the 1960s, just after the Olympics, did not escape its celebration in film. The city was one huge building site, which invaded the filmic space and became the background where events often related to this growth took place. The *nouveaux riches* were given the face and the embarrassing arrogance of Alberto Sordi. Rome became full of such people who built or purchased apartments, taking symbolic refuge far from the historic center in the *palazzine* that certified their status as the wealthy middle class. Construction sites, cranes, and scaffolding became a constant cinematic presence from the mid-1950s, with *The Roof*, *Big Deal on Madonna Street*, and *Mamma Roma*, all the way to the late 1970s with Scola's *Brutti, sporchi e cattivi* (*Ugly, Dirty and Bad*, 1976).

Yet, the most significant examples of the city's enormous building growth in cinema were two aerial "flying scenes" and the already mentioned film *Il Boom* that more than any others embody this epic building craze. As Franco Pecori wrote, "Situated in the midst of the so-called

The rich lady who proposes to Alberto Sordi to sell an eye for her husband in exchange for richness and success, in the film *Il Boom*.

economic miracle, the film captures a moment in Italian society, poised between true and false, serious and ridiculous. The *nouveaux riches*, more or less small, are hanging by the thread of contingency and have to exploit the art of making do and everyday cynicism to the full, such that they wind up being unscrupulous monsters resolved in the miserable facade of smiling life-givers, with wives to show off and speculation to hide."[19] The story is that of a last-minute unscrupulous contractor played by Alberto Sordi, who is very attached to appearances but encumbered by debts and willing to defend his status at the cost of selling a cornea to a very rich builder whose unscrupulous wife suggests the exchange. The film revolves around this great ruckus of building activities and the social and personal story intertwines with that of the city, which is growing immoderately in the background.

As for the two aerial accounts of growing Rome, they are from 1960 and 1974 respectively. The first is found at the beginning of *La Dolce Vita*, in which a helicopter transports a statue of Christ with outstretched arms toward the Vatican. During the flight, the helicopter shows us the Parioli district under construction, the hill quivering under the builders' activity, while affluent bikini-clad ladies cavorting on the roof terraces greet the statue—and Jesus—with their handkerchiefs and fashionable sunglasses. The second appears, if possible, even more cogent in the film *C'eravamo tanto amati* (*We All Loved Each Other So Much*, 1974) by Ettore Scola. Here, on a construction site, the completion of the rough building structure is celebrated on the terrace, where a party has been set up. The builder, Aldo Fabrizi, dominates a large table with his daughter (Giovanna Ralli) and unscrupulous son-in-law (Vittorio Gassman) at his side. With them, workers, surveyors, engineers, and architects await a large steaming roast pig that arrives by crane from above, sanctioning the inelegant arrogance of a rustic but rich world and fully depicting the period in the capital.

The helicopter carrying a statue of Jesus over the Parco degli Acquedotti, in *La Dolce Vita*.

The helicopter transports a statue of Jesus over apartment towers under construction in the Parioli district in *La Dolce Vita*.

Marcello Mastroianni on a balcony in the EUR district with the Palazzo dello Sport by Marcello Piacentini and Pier Luigi Nervi, 1960 in the background in *La Dolce Vita*.

The party on the roof during the construction of a building in *We All Loved Each Other So Much* (Ettore Scola, 1974).

Small Homage, Great Masterpieces

Perhaps unconsciously but repeatedly, Italian cinema has paid homage to masterpieces of modern Roman architecture. A few years ago, in a public debate with Mario Monicelli, the author of this essay asked him about the fact that he had used some monuments of contemporary architecture in Rome as sets. He smugly replied that in cinema, architecture does not exist; only set design does! I then pointed out how he had used the Casa delle Armi (Fencing Academy, 1933–1937) designed by Luigi Moretti at the Foro Italico in two different movies and he laconically replied that in the case of *Big Deal on Madonna Street*, he needed a squalid building—which was the state of the building at the time—to portray a funeral home. For *The Passionate Thief*, it was a sad masquerade that the building was well suited to. Monicelli was a great joker—this was always his strength—but I have never understood whether, apart from a few enlightened auteurs such as Scola, Antonioni, and Pasolini, cinema was consciously involved in its homages to modern architecture, if it was only aesthetics, or perhaps it was just an accessible location to get filming permits.

Intriguingly, when Italian cinema needed to set up action in a post office, the choice often fell on two modern masterpieces: the Palazzo delle Poste in Piazza Bologna designed by Mario Ridolfi and Mario Fagiolo, and the Palazzo delle Poste in Via Marmorata by Adalberto Libera and Mario De Renzi. Both stem from the great competition announced in early 1932 for four post office buildings in Rome, and they are certainly the best among the four winners—the others were by Giuseppe Samonà in the Appio district and Antonio Titta on Viale Mazzini. Built between 1933 and 1935, they were immediately considered two masterpieces of contemporary Italian architecture, a judgment that has not only withstood the passage of time but has even been reinforced.

In Alessandro d'Alatri's film *Senza pelle* (*No Skin*, 1994) postmaster Anna Galiena works at Ridolfi's post office in Piazza Bologna. The building watches over the encounters and expectations through which the complicated psychological relationship between Anna and a young psychotic played by Kim Rossi Stuart unfolds, along with the awkward jealousy of her husband Massimo Ghini. The elusive perspectives of the curved complex create the backdrop to these tense rendezvous and the building supports the absence of a clear, open view, adding to the anxious condition underlying the story. When the situation changes and the young man decides to approach his beloved, the interior of Ridolfi's building opens up and

The covered walkway of a post office in Via Marmorata by Adalberto Libera and Mario De Renzi in the movie *Fantozzi Retires* (Neri Parenti, 1988).

shows itself and its vast space seems to add to the disquiet of the hapless Rossi Stuart.

Another film about a postmaster, this time played by Barbara de Rossi, involves the Via Marmorata post office by Libera and De Renzi: *Sono contento* (*I'm Happy*) by Maurizio Ponzi in 1983. Here as well, the archetypal role of the building is evident. The building interprets its type and the volumes are called into question in a climactic scene in which the postmaster, pressed by her boyfriend (Francesco Nuti), confesses to having an affair with a colleague. More effective in terms of the narrative use of the same building is Neri Parenti's *Fantozzi va in pensione* (*Fantozzi Retires*, 1988). The repeated gag of poor retiree Fantozzi (Paolo Villaggio) being mugged always takes place in the hall—where the endless queues and his pathetic attempts to avoid the inevitable mugging take place—and the front portico—with the rigged Vespas and teams who diligently wait their turn to perform the criminal act, depicted as a routine and absolutely normal job. Used as a set in other films as well, for example, *Io la conoscevo bene* (*I Knew Her Well*) by Antonio Pietrangeli (1965), or *Mollo tutto* (*I'll Leave It All Behind Me*) by José María Sánchez (1994), Libera and De Renzi's post office in Via Marmorata epitomized that happy combination between function and architectural language for which it is grasped easily outside architectural culture, finding a paradigmatic, clear, and conscious use and being read immediately.

As mentioned above, the Fencing Academy, Luigi Moretti's masterpiece at the Foro Italico, was also referenced by Monicelli in *Big Deal on Madonna Street* and *The Passionate Thief*, and by Dino Risi in a brief cameo in *The Easy Life*. Staying at the Foro Italico and overlooking the many sports films set in the Olympic stadium, the role of Moretti's Palestra del Duce in De Sica's *Miracolo a Milano* (*Miracle in Milan*, 1951) is interesting. This architectural jewel where Mussolini used to train, was transformed into a rich landowner's large office to which the poor slum dwellers are invited to express their demands.

One final building that is particularly celebrated in Italian cinema for its urban rather than architectural quality is the cylindrical Gasometro (Gasometer) built in the Ostiense district in the late 1930s. The image of an industrial and technological Rome contrasts with the reality of a city in which industrial equipment and uncultivated riverbanks offer a poetic idea of neglect. This interpretation happens in the celebrated walk along the river in *Bellissima* where, against the backdrop of the Gasometro, Annovazzi (Walter Chiari) speaks movingly of the hopes his mother has placed on him by renouncing men's embraces. It also occurs in the scene in *Europe '51* where Irene (Ingrid Bergman) wanders around the wasteland area near the river, reflecting on her own social marginalization. The Gasometro, as a simple aesthetic citation of a monument to the wonders of industrial heritage, is present in many other films, from the aforementioned *Sunday in August* and *I'm Happy* to *Troppo forte* by Carlo Verdone (1985), and the film that has consecrated it more than any other, *Le fate ignoranti* (*The Ignorant Fairies*) by Ferzan Özpetek (2001). Here, the terrace overlooking the industrial monument reflects the place's architectural contradiction—and Rome itself as a metaphor—with the structured, complex presence of the lives there: beautiful and decadent, rich and desperate.

The Gasometro in the Ostiense district, in a scene from *Sunday in August* (Luciano Emmer, 1950).

The Gasometro in *The Ignorant Fairies* (Ferzan Özpetek, 2001).

The Palestra del Duce by Luigi Moretti, 1936–1937, transformed into the office of a wealthy gentleman in *Miracle in Milan* (Vittorio De Sica, 1951).

1
According to official data, the number of constructed rooms rose from 31,300 in 1951 to 105,766 in 1955 to 159,134 in 1962. In 1963, there were still 257,895 planned rooms, but the number built had already dropped to 131,026. Throughout the 1950s and early 1960s, construction in Rome rose steadily: see Vittorio Vidotto, *Roma contemporanea* (Bari: Laterza, 2001), 280–281.

2
For a more complete study, see Massimo Casavola, Luisa Presicce, and Salvatore Santuccio, *L'attore di pietra: l'architettura moderna italiana nel cinema* (Turin: Testo e immagine, 2001); Gabriel Solomons, ed., *World Film Locations: Roma* (Bristol/Chicago: Intellect, 2014); Richard Wrigley, ed., *Cinematic Rome* (Leicester: Troubador, 2008).

3
Ettore Scola would eventually return to the same type of intensive housing structure years later for a new film, *Romanzo di un giovane povero* (*The Story of a Poor Young Man*) in 1995. For the Palazzo Federici, see Piazza Bologna in the neighborhood section of this volume.

4
There is no architect on record for Val Melaina: Ufficio tecnico, ICP, 1932–1943.

5
Alberto Farassino, ed., *Virgilio Marchi: il cinema* (Rome: Centro Sperimetale di Cinematografia, 1995).

6
See Laura Delli Colli, ed., *EUR è cinema* (Rome: Palombi Editori, 2008).

7
Michelangelo Antonioni, *Fare un film è per me vivere* (Venice: Marsilio, 1994), 51 (translation by Salvatore Santuccio).

8
See Jean-François Lejeune, "La metafisica del quotidiano: l'EUR di Antonioni e l'Eclisse dell'architettura," in Laura Delli Colli, ed., *EUR è cinema*, 43–55; Jacopo Benci, "Michelangelo Rome: Toward an Iconology of the Eclisse," in Richard Wrigley, ed., *Cinematic Rome*, 63–84.

9
Michelangelo Antonioni, *Quel bowling sul Tevere* (Turin: Einaudi, 1995), 135. (English translation by Salvatore Santuccio).

10
See Marco Falsetti, ed., *Gaetano Rapisardi architetto: 1893–1988* (Rome: Campisano Editore, 2022).

11
Luisa Presicce, "Le presenze ricorrenti," in M. Casavola, L. Presicce, and S. Santuccio, *L'Attore di Pietra*, 58–59. (English translation by Salvatore Santuccio).

12
See Spiro Kostof, *The Third Rome 1870–1950: Traffic and Glory* (Berkeley: University Art Museum, 1973).

13
Alessandro Bencivenni, *Luchino Visconti* (Milan: Il Castoro, 1995), 28. (English translation by Salvatore Santuccio).

14
See Karl Schoonover, *Brutal Vision: The Neorealist Body in Postwar Italian Cinema* (Minneapolis: University of Minnesota Press, 2012).

15
Lino Micciché, *Cinema italiano: gli anni '60 e oltre* (Venice: Marsilio, 1998), 184. (English translation by Salvatore Santuccio).

16
See Jacopo Benci, "'An Extraordinary Proliferation of Layers': Pasolini's Rome(s)," in Dorigen Caldwell, ed., *Rome: Continuing Encounters between Past and Present* (London: Routledge, 2011), 151–186; Serafino Murri, *Pier Paolo Pasolini* (Milan: Il Castoro, 1995), 31. (English translation by Salvatore Santuccio).

17
See Carlo Mezzetti and Fabio Lanfranchi, *Il disegno della palazzina romana* (Rome: Kappa, 2008) in particular.

18
About films and Casa Papanice, see "The Strange Case of Casa Papanice," https://hypnoticcrescendos.blogspot.com/2022/01/the-strange-case-of-casa-papanice.html.
According to Il Davinotti Location, https://www.davinotti.com/forum/location-verificate/il-boom/50000504, the apartment is in EUR, on Via dell'Arte, on the corner with Viale dell'Aeronautica.

19
Franco Pecori, *Vittorio De Sica* (Milan: L'Unità Il Castoro, 1995), 89.

Index of Names

Index of Places

The Authors

Lucio Valerio Barbera is Professor of Architecture and Urban Design at Sapienza University of Rome, where he holds the UNESCO Chair in "Sustainable Urban Quality and Urban Culture, notably in Africa" (2013). He was Coordinator of the Doctorate program in Architectural design and Theory from 1993 to 2007, and Dean of the Faculty of Architecture Ludovico Quaroni, Sapienza University of Rome from 2003 to 2009. He was the co-founder with Clementina Panella of the Master "Architecture for Archaeology-Archaeology for Architecture" and director from 2007 to 2009. He also practiced as architect, planner, and landscape designer internationally since the 1960s. He was Deputy Mayor of Rome for Cultural Politics and Historic Center from 1992 to 1993. He is director of the academic journal *L'architettura delle città – The journal of the Scientific Society Ludovico Quaroni* (from 2013) and recently published the book *La città radicale di Ludovico Quaroni* (Gangemi 2018).

Anna Irene Del Monaco is Associate Professor of Architecture and Urban Design at Sapienza University of Rome. She was a Junior Fellow at Scuola Superiore Studi Avanzati Sapienza SSAS (2016), visiting scholar at Tsinghua University of Beijing (2004), and at GSAPP Columbia University in the City of New York (2005–06). She is a member of the Teaching Board at Doctorate DRACO in Architecture and Constuction. Anna Irene Del Monaco graduated in Architecture from the Faculty of Architecture in Rome in 2000, and received her Doctorate in Architectural design and Theory in 2006 from the Sapienza University. She recently published with Editore Nuova Cultura, *Italian Architects in the Mediterranean. Institutions and Authors* (2021), *A southern Practice, The early work of a young Italian architect* (2019), *Vite Parallele, Colin Lucas – Pietro Barucci* (2018), and *Osservazioni sulle Corrispondenze fra la composizione in musica e in architettura* (2017).

Jean-François Lejeune is Professor Emeritus of architecture, urban design, and history at the University of Miami School of Architecture and Adjunct Professor at the University of Notre Dame in Rome. His books include *The Making of Miami Beach 1933–1942: The Architecture of Lawrence Murray Dixon* (Rizzoli, 2001), *Cruelty and Utopia: Cities and Landscapes of Latin America* (Princeton Architectural Press, 2005, CICA Award for Best Architecture Catalogue), *Sitte, Hegemann, and the Metropolis* (Routledge, 2009), and *Modern Architecture and the Mediterranean: Vernacular Dialogues and Contested Identities* (with Michelangelo Sabatino, Routledge, 2010). He is the secretary of DoCOMOMO-US/Florida. He was an Affiliated Fellow at the American Academy in Rome in 2007, and a Visiting Professor at the Doctorate Program in Architecture and Construction, Space and Society at La Sapienza, and at the Università di Pescara-Chieti. His most recent publications are *Rural Architecture and Water Urbanism: The Modern Village in Franco's Spain* (DOM, Berlin, 2021), and *Cuban Modernism: Mid-Century Architecture 1940–1970* (Birkhäuser, 2020, with Victor Deupi). He is currently at work on *Loos and Schinkel: The Metropolis between the Individual and the Collective* (Routledge, 2026). Lejeune holds a Ph.D. from TU Delft (2019).

Salvatore Santuccio is an architect and is professor in drawing and representation at the Scuola di Architettura e Design, Università di Camerino. He is a frequent visiting professor at the University of Miami School of Architecture in Rome, and has also taught at the Institut Universitaire de la Côte in Douala, Cameroon. He is the co-author of the book *Luigi Moretti. Le ville. Disegni e modelli* (Palombi, 2009) and has published essays in many other books and periodicals such as *La palazzina si fa palazzo: Moretti e il Girasole*. He is one of the authors of the book on cinema and architecture titled *L'attore di pietra. L'architettura moderna italiana nel cinema*. His most recent book is *La Cena picta: Osservazioni sul Ultima Cena prima di Leonardo* (Tab Edizioni, 2023).

Daniel Solomon, FAIA, is an architect and urban designer whose 50-plus year career combines achievements in professional practice with academic pursuits of teaching and writing. His projects have been published in architectural journals worldwide and have been recognized with more than 100 awards. Mr. Solomon's commitment to the construction and reconstruction of urban neighborhoods extends beyond his project work; he is a co-founder of the Congress for the New Urbanism (CNU), an organization whose principles have helped shape the contemporary practice of community design. He is author of four books: *Re-Building, Global City Blues, Bedside Essay for Lovers (of Cities)*, and most recently, *Housing and the City: Love versus Hope*. He is the 1998 recipient of the Seaside Prize for contributions to American Urbanism. In 2004, he received the Maybeck Award from California AIA for lifetime achievement in design, and in 2008 was named Housing Hero by the San Francisco Housing Action Coalition. Daniel Solomon received his Master of Architecture from UC Berkeley in 1966. He taught at Berkeley from 1966 to 2000 and is currently an active Professor Emeritus. He frequently serves as a visiting Professor at various institutions, including the University of Maryland, La Sapienza (Rome), and University of Notre Dame.

Acknowledgments

I started to teach for the University of Miami School of Architecture in Rome in 1990. The program was new, small, and housed in the wonderful rooms of Palazzo Pio whose daily life was under the spell of the University of Washington director in Rome, Astra Zarina. Like many young historians and design faculty, my knowledge of architecture and urbanism in Rome was mostly centered on the *centro storico* whose streets and *piazze* were still, in those years, real public spaces, with kids playing calcio on Piazza Farnese, Campo dei Fiori, Isola Tiberina, and many other places in the city. In 2008, our University of Miami School of Architecture Rome Center moved from Via della Gatta to Via del Falco at the edge of the Borgo and the gridded streets of Prati. Now living outside of the Aurelian walls, I started the discovery of what is called the Roma non *Interrotta* in this book, i.e., the many and richly built districts that were built outside of the walls when Rome became the new capital of Italy in 1871: Prati, Piazza Mazzini, Viale Doria, La Garbatella, the small hill of San Saba, the mythical Tiburtino, the EUR, and much later the *palazzine* of Parioli—a process of discovery strongly helped by my two-month fellowship at the American Academy in the fall of 2008.

The research entered a foundational phase following my Visiting Professorship at La Sapienza in the spring of 2014 at the invitation of Dr. Giuseppe Strappa, director of the "Ph.D. Program in Architecture and Construction: Space and Society"—a period which was marked by intense research and my first encounter with Professor Lucio Valerio Barbera. One year later, Dean Elizabeth Plater-Zyberk agreed to invite Daniel Solomon to lecture in Rome and we embarked together, along with Dr. Anna Irene Del Monaco, in a series of long discovery walks of the "Other Rome." How did we end up in September 2015, Daniel Solomon and me, in a small hamlet near Feltre on the edge of the Dolomites, in Lucio Barbera's country Villa Dal Corno-Lusa-Tonelli-Canella? I do not remember, but it is there through long conversations, interrupted by visits to Rovereto and Canova's temple in Possagno, that we started the planning of the book. In September 2018, we repeated the intense seminar in Calliol, agreed on the distribution of tasks, and drafted the table of contents for Lucio Barbera's ambitious essay. The same year, Daniel Solomon published his book *Housing and the City: Love Versus Hope*, which included many pages about Rome and served as a rehearsal for the book project.

Thanks to the year-long sabbatical generously awarded for 2022 by the University of Miami, the writing and editing work restarted in Rome, aided as well by Dean Stefanos Polyzoides's invitation to teach modern history (with a focus on that of Rome) at the Rome Gateway of Via Ostilia in the fall of 2022, 2023, and 2024. Likewise, on the initiative of Anna Irene Del Monaco, I received a three-month fellowship at La Sapienza Università di Rome between September and October 2023. Invited lectures at the La Sapienza, University of Miami, University of Notre Dame, Iowa State University, RISD in Rome, at the Congress for the New Urbanism in Buffalo, KTH Stockholm, Yale University, Pratt Institute in Rome, also helped to sharpen the direction of the book. On the practical side, all that time allowed me to take on the unexpected task of creating the photography for *The Other Rome*, district by district, one, twice, thrice, with the unparalleled help of Astrid Rotemberg who precisely recorded each image and location. Last, Alessandro Camiz, Professor at Università degli Studi "G. d'Annunzio" Chieti-Pescara set up a visiting position there for two months in 2025, the two months needed to verify the manuscript.

Having reached the completion of this book, I must first of all thank Dean Rodolphe el-Khoury for his strong academic and financial support; Veruska Vasconez for her precious help in organizing and following the work of the students who mapped the neighborhoods; Carmen Guerrero, director of the Miami Rome program who shared her insights on Modern Rome but also helped me to teach design studio and history for so many semesters; Gilda Santana, director of the Architecture Research Center at the Miami School of Architecture; the Interlibrary Loan Department at the University of Miami Libraries; visiting professors in Rome, Salvatore Santuccio, Luca Galofaro, Stefania Manna; and administrative assistant Ludovica Santuccio. Even more so to graduate student Arié Nathan Haddad who prepared and corrected all the drawings designed especially for this publication by University of Miami undergraduate and graduate students—including Konstantina Kritharidou, Michelle Wright, Jessica Abecassis, Rene Bello, Evan Bobo, Fuhong Wang, Jiayi Wang, Yibo Zhang, and Soran Rostami. Also in Rome, all my gratitude goes to Stefanos Polyzoides, Dean of the University of Notre Dame; Rev. Richard S. Bullene, Academic Director of the School of Architecture's Rome Studies Program; all faculty members and in particular Ettore Mazzola, Paolo Vitti; administrators Pamela Johnson, Giovanna Lenzi-Sandusky, and the whole staff. This work is dedicated to the late Jean-Louis Cohen in New York, colleague and friend for more than twenty years, and to Maurice Culot in Brussels and Paris: they were my primary mentors.

Finally, thanks to Lucio Valerio Barbera, Elena and Emanuela Calvini-Canella, and their entire family: they welcomed us three times in Calliol and hosted us for delicious Sunday outings and dinners at their apartment on Via Cassia. Lastly, I would like to thank my companion, partner, and wife, Astrid Rotemberg, for her constant encouragement, patience, and keen critical eye on text and images. The photography that structures this book would not have been possible without her.

AACAR, Centro Studi per la Storia dell'Architettura: 78, 79, 85, 158
Accasto, Gianni, Vanna Fraticelli, and Renato Nicolini, *L'architettura di Roma Capitale, 1870–1970* (Rome: Golem, 1971): 53, 85, 274
Angeletti, Paolo, Luca Ciancarelli, Marcello Ricci and Giuseppe Vallifuoco, *Case romane* (Rome: Prospettive Edizioni, 2009): 237 (bottom), 285 (bottom right), 316, 317, 318, 324, 326, 336, 337 (bottom left), 338
Antognozzi, Maria and Maria Chiara Carassati, *La Garbatella 1920–1940 – studio tipologico e morfologico* (tesi di laurea magistrale, Università degli Studi Roma 2018–2019 under the direction of Francesca Romana Stabile and Paola Porretta): 258, 259
Archidiap: 35 (top),102 (top), 135, 207
Architettura (December 1938, Esposizione Universale di Roma): 29, 113
Architettura (November 1935, Città Universitaria): 108 (top, bottom left)
Architettura e Arti Decorative (September 1923): 92
Archivio Centrale dello Stato, Fondo EUR: 111
Archivio Centrale dello Stato, Fondo Luigi Moretti: 97 (bottom left), 142
Archivio Del Debbio, MAXXI Museo nazionale delle arti del XXI secolo: 141
Archivio Storico Capitolino di Roma Capitale: 71, 72, 73, 74
Archivio Progetti Roma Capitale: 330
Archivio Studio Lucciche nti & Monaco Architetti, MAXXI Museo nazionale delle arti del XXI secolo: 136, 310 (top left), 311 (bottom)
Archivio Storico di ATER di Roma (previously ICP): 88, 136, 171 (bottom), 201 (bottom), 203 (top), 204 (bottom), 227 (bottom), 243 (middle), 244 (bottom), 246 (top), 252 (bottom), 254 (top, middle), 257 (bottom right), 263 (top), 263 (bottom right), 287 (middle), 290 (top), 297 (top and bottom left)
Barbera, Lucio: 30, 39, 45, 48, 49, 55, 58. 60 (top right), 64 (middle and bottom), 66, 68 (left), 98, 108 (bottom right), 129, 138, 139, 143, 147, 197, 212, 213 (bottom), 287
Bartolini, Francesco, *Roma Borghese: la casa e I ceti medi tra le due guerre* (Laterza, 2001): 101 (bottom)
Casabella Continuità, no. 199 (December 1953–January 1954): 132 (top left), 133 (bottom)
Casabella Continuità, no. 207 (September –October 1955): 131, 327 (top), 328 (bottom)
Casabella Continuità, no. 215 (April–May 1957): 127 (top), 314
Centro Archivi di Architettura, MAXXI Museo nazionale delle arti del XXI secolo: 229
Christ, Emanuel, Christoph Gantenbein and Victoria Easton (with ETHZürich),Typology: Hong Kong–Rome–New York–Buenos Aires (Zürich: Park Books, 2012): 90 (bottom), 96, 102 (bottom), 132, 185, 187, 200, 207, 246, 268 (bottom), 270 (middle and bottom), 279 (bottom), 290 (middle), 298, 306, 307
Cocchioni, Cristina and Mario De Grassi, *La casa popolare a Roma* (Roma: Kappa, 1984): 227
Controspazio, no. 2, July–August 1973): 31
D'Afflito, Sergio (Wikipedia): 159
Del Monaco, Anna Irene: 194
Esposizione Internazionale di Roma 1911: 82, 83
Esposizione italiana di architettura razionale: Roma: anno VI (Roma: De Alberti, 1928): 93
Fondo Mario De Renzi, Accademia Nazionale di San Luca: 102
Fondo Mario Ridolfi, Accademia Nazionale di San Luca: 127 (bottom), 133 (top), 307 (top left)
Fondo Ugo Lucciche nti, Accademia Nazionale di San Luca: 310
Fraticelli, Vanna, *Roma, 1914–1929: la città e gli architetti tra la Guerra e il fascismo* (Rome: Officina Edizioni, 1982): 203
Gaetano Minnucci, 1896–1980 (Accademia Nazionale di San Luca, 1984): 247 (bottom)
Galleria del Laocoonte, Roma (https://www.laocoontegalleria.it/giovanni-guerrini/): 119
Galleria Farnese, Palazzo Farnese: 33
gallerie.info.roma.it: 87
Getty Images: 42 (bottom)
Giovannoni, Gustavo, *Vecchie città ed edilizia nuova* (Torino, 1933): 242
Google Earth: 40, 60, 101 (top left), 106 (top), 169, 180, 196, 204, 205, 224, 233, 245 (bottom), 262, 285 (bottom left), 300 (top), 304, 305, 315, 322, 331 (bottom)
Gropius, Walter, *Das neue Berlin*, no. 4, 1929: 154
https://www.roma2pass.it/quartiere-trieste/storia/: 280
INCIS, *Villaggio Olimpico quartiere di Roma* (undated): 35
Info.roma.it: 173, 206, 270
Istituto Centrale per la Grafica, Roma, Calcografia, Fondo Piranesi: 42 (top), 140, 148, 151, 242 (top)
Krier, Léon, 11
Lanciani, Rodolfo, *Forma Urbis Romae* (1901): 80, 81, 179
Lejeune, Jean François (photography): 17, 22, 23, 26, 28, 30, 35 (bottom), 36, 51, 52, 53 (bottom), 57 (top), 59, 62, 63, 64 (top left and right), 65, 67, 68 (right), 76, 84, 89, 90, 91, 94, 97, 99 (bottom right), 101 (top right), 104, 105, 106, 107, 108, 109, 116, 117, 118, 119 (bottom), 120, 121, 122, 130, 134, 144, 146, 157 (postcards), 166, 169 (bottom left), 170, 171 (top left and right), 172, 173 (top), 174, 175, 176, 178, 180 (top), 185, 186 (top), 187 (top), 188, 189, 190, 191 (top), 192, 193, 198, 199, 200 (top), 206 (top right), 207 (top left), 208, 209, 210, 215, 216, 217, 218, 219, 220, 221, 222, 225 (bottom left), 228, 230, 232, 235 (bottom), 237, 238, 239, 240, 244 (top), 245 (top and bottom right), 246 (middle), 247 (top), 248, 250, 251, 252, 254 (bottom), 255, 256, 257, 260, 262, 265, 266, 267, 268 (top), 270, 271, 272, 275, 276, 278, 279 (top), 280, 281, 282, 284, 286, 288, 289, 290, 291, 292, 296, 297 (bottom), 298, 299, 300 (bottom), 301, 302, 305 (bottom right), 306, 307, 308 (top), 309 (top), 309 (bottom left), 311 (top), 312, 316, 317, 318 (right), 319, 320, 323, 324 (top), 325, 326, 327 (bottom), 328, 329, 330 (top), 332, 334, 336, 337, 339

Mariani, Riccardo, *Razionalismo e architettura moderna* (Roma,1989): 95
Mart Rovereto, Fondo Adalberto Libera: 99
Mazzola, Ettore, in Marcello Fagiolo and Alessandro Mazza, eds., *I Monti Parioli e il "Nuovo Campo Marzio" della cultura internazionale* (Rome: Artemide, 2022): 101 (middle)
Misuraca, Giacomo and Marco Aurelio Boldi, L'arte Moderna del Fabbricare. La tecnica del fabbricare (Milano: Vallardi, 1900): 88, 236
Muratori, Saverio, *Studi per una operante storia urbana di Roma* (Rome: Consiglio nazionale delle ricerche, 1963): 153
Nolli Map Website, University of Oregon: 4, 27, 233
Pagano, Giuseppe and Guarniero Daniel, *Architettura rurale italiana* (Hoepli, 1936): 125
Private Collection Mondadori Portfolio/Electa/Bridgeman Images. Artists Rights Society (ARS), New York/SIAE, Rome © 2025: 7
Puccini, Enrico and Giovanni Duranti, *Testaccio: Il quartiere operaio di Roma Capitale, 1870–1930* (Roma: Palombi Editori, 2009): 181, 186, 191 (bottom)
Ragazzi di vita (Garzanti, 1955): 21
Rerum Romanarum: 137, 143, 159 (top), 243 (bottom)
Roma Interrotta (Roma: Officina Edizioni, 1978): 8, 9, 11
Roma Sparita, Foto storiche: 57, 245 (bottom left), 270
romaierioggi.it: 82
Rowe, Colin and Fred Koetter, *Collage City* (Cambridge, MA: The MIT Press, 1979: 24
Sovrintendenza per i beni ambientali e architettonici del Lazio, Il quartiere Coppedè a Toma: Conoscenza e tutela: 275
Spazio, no. 3 (October 1950: 308 (bottom right)
Stabile, Francesca Romana, *Il quartiere San Saba e la casa popolare a Roma*, 1906–1923 (Roma: Edizioni Quasar, 2024): 87, 88, 235, 236
Städelsches Kunstinstitut, Frankfurt am Main: 47
Strappa, Giuseppe: 155
The Criterion Channel: 14, 34, 340
Tusczynski, Benon (Wikipedia): 123
University of Miami School of Architecture: 75, 97 (top left), 97 (top right), 160, 164, 182, 183, 184, 197 (top), 202, 213, 214, 225 (top, bottom right), 226, 227 (top), 234, 243 (top), 253, 264, 265 (top), 277, 285 (top), 286 (bottom), 287 (top), 294, 295 (bottom), 305 (bottom left), 315 (top), 323 (top), 334 (top right), 335
Urbanistica, no. 62 (April 1974): 138
Verso la casa esatta no. 1: 124
Web Gallery of Art (Gaspar von Wittel): 55
Wikimedia Commons: front cover, 169 (bottom), 175 (top), 201 (top), 334 (top)

All other images are from the archive of the editor and the contributors.

The editor and the publisher would like to thank Rodolphe El-Khoury (University of Miami School of Architecture), Elizabeth Plater-Zyberk (Center for Applied Transect Studies), Daniel Solomon and Shirley Sun, Lucio Valerio Barbera, Anna Irene Del Monaco, and Astrid Rotemberg for their support of this publication.

UNIVERSITY OF MIAMI
SCHOOL of
ARCHITECTURE

Acquisitions editor: Ria Stein
Copy editing: Ria Stein
Production editor: Amelie Solbrig

Layout, cover design and typesetting:
Bureau Sandra Doeller
(Sandra Doeller, Merle Petsch)

Paper: Magno Volume, 135 g/m²
Printing: DZA Druckerei zu Altenburg GmbH
Image editing: prints professional

Library of Congress Control Number:
2025909187

Bibliographic information published by
the German National Library
The German National Library lists this publication in the Deutsche Nationalbibliografie; detailed bibliographic data are available on the Internet at http://dnb.dnb.de.

ISBN 978-3-0356-2536-3
e-ISBN (PDF) 978-3-0356-2544-8

Im Westfeld 8, 4055 Basel, Switzerland
Part of Walter de Gruyter GmbH, Berlin/Boston

www.birkhauser.com
Questions about General Product Safety Regulation
productsafety@degruyterbrill.com

9 8 7 6 5 4 3 2 1

MIX
Paper | Supporting responsible forestry
FSC www.fsc.org FSC® C100411